NEVADA CONSTRUCTION LAW

2016 Edition

Leon F. Mead II

Nevada Construction Law – 2016 Edition

Nevada Construction Law – *2016 Edition*
Print ISBN: 978-0-9891930-1-6
eBook ISBN: 978-0-9891930-2-3

Published By DHG Publishing, a division of Mead Enterprises, Inc.
Previous editions published by Thompson Reuters / West

NEVADA CONSTRUCTION LAW

2016 Edition

ACKNOWLEDGEMENTS

The Author wishes to acknowledge the efforts, research, input, and assistance of the following attorneys and staff at Snell & Wilmer, without whom this 2016 Edition could not have been accomplished:

Alex Avalos
Marek P. Bute, Esq.
Bryan M. Gragg, Esq.
Lauren Kidd
Sarah A. C. Mead, Esq.
Robin E. Perkins, Esq.

The Author would also like to acknowledge the support and friendship of the following persons, who have in many tangible and intangible ways contributed to the contents of this book, in all of its editions, and their respective completion:

Madeline Albarran
Steve Brooke
Laura Ellen Browning, Esq.
John J. Bouma, Esq.
Patrick G. Byrne, Esq.
Jason Ebe, Esq.
Matthew P. Feeney, Esq.
Daniel Frost, Esq.
Kenneth C. Gibbs, Esq.
Margi Grien
Linda Harris
Steve Holloway
Jack Juan, Esq.
Greg Korte
William D. Locher, Esq.
Mark O. Morris, Esq.
Georlyn Spangler, Esq.
William P. Striegel
Terry Towle
Glenn E. Turner III, Esq.
"The Venerable" Dan Waite, Esq.
Donald "Butch" Williams, Esq.
Mandi L. Wilkins

Dedication

This book, and all its editions, are dedicated to my children for their love, support, and devotion to their as ever stubborn father:

Sarah A. C. Mead, Esq.
Michael P. Mead

Special Dedication

In memory of my friends and Nevada construction industry stalwarts who were taken from us before their time, and are truly missed:

Floyd Brooks Williams III
James Donofrio, Sr.

Special Thanks

A very special thank you goes out to Sarah A. C. Mead, Esq., for her dedication, hard work, excellent research, writing and "blue booking" skills.

TABLE OF CONTENTS

CHAPTER 1 INTRODUCTION TO NEVADA CONSTRUCTION LAW AND PRELIMINARY MATTERS

1:1 INTRODUCTION TO NEVADA CONSTRUCTION LAW

In 2016, construction in Nevada, as an industry, is finally showing steady signs of leaving the Great Recession behind. Before that calamity, construction was the third largest employer in the State of Nevada, behind only governmental agencies (state and federal) and the leisure and hospitality industries. At that time, most of this construction employment resulted from the economic boom happening to southern Nevada and more specifically to the City of Las Vegas and its surrounding communities of Henderson, North Las Vegas and Summerlin, and even stretching to Mesquite and Pahrump. Las Vegas had grown over the 1990 to 2007 period from under 1 million in population to over 2 million. Such significant population growth resulted in a boom of construction throughout the Southern Nevada region: residential, commercial and industrial properties flooded the market, while public works construction struggled to keep up. According to its website,[1] the Clark County School District has grown from 89,000 students in 1985 to over 219,000 in 2006, and built, 10 new schools each year. Highways, parks, recreation facilities, water resources, and a multitude of public agencies have had their own construction booms to keep up with the pace.

Since 2008, however, population rates and construction activity began to diminish rapidly and significantly. While the private commercial and industrial construction environment continues to be sluggish (resulting from an excessively overbuilt condition reached in 2008), the focus of construction has shifted to public works construction activities on both a state and federal level. Still, for Nevada, federal stimulus programs initiated in 2009 have had little on the ground effect. According to the Associated General Contractors' Southern Nevada Construction Industry Quarterly Market Briefing for the second quarter of 2011, construction accounts for only 7.5% of southern Nevada jobs, whereas in 2007 it accounted for 12.1%, losing 72,600 positions since June 2008.[2] Federal stimulus money has been a nonstarter for construction. The Associated General Contractors reported in the Southern Nevada Construction Industry Quarterly Market Briefing for the second quarter of 2011 that as the stimulus runs out conditions are likely to worsen. In 2013, construction employment again began to increase, although levels have not approached those in 2007 and may never again. As of this writing, there is a reported shortage of experienced construction workers capable of performing the available work.

---

[1] www.ccsd.net

[2] Associated General Contractors (Las Vegas Chapter), Southern Nevada Construction Industry, Quarterly Market Briefing for the Third Quarter of 2010, available online at http://www.agclv.org/Documents/Marketing% Briefs/%AGC_MB_Q2_2011.pdf (last visited October 19, 2011).

Efforts of the state government to bring diversity to the economy of the state, in conjunction with one of the largest tax increases in state history, continue the expansion of construction in 2015. Projects such as the Tesla Motors lithium battery "Gigafactory" outside of Reno have spurred new interest in Northern Nevada as a residential community, bringing with it the need for increased education and related infrastructure.

The construction-related cases and decisions issued by the Nevada Supreme Court continue to increase; however, the level of reviewed and analyzed construction law issues still remains meager. Until 2015, Nevada had only one appellate level court--the Nevada Supreme Court. As a result, since its establishment as a State in 1865, Nevada has produced only 130 volumes of reported cases. Of these scarce volumes, only a handful of their contents have related to construction issues. At the same time, legislation related to construction has morphed many times over and often the legislature reacts to trial court level decisions, rather than waiting for judicial review of those decisions. As a result, many times the Supreme Court will be ruling on a matter interpreting legislative enactments after those enactments have already been changed. Therefore, it is critical for the practitioner to review current legislative research on a particular construction law issue before reviewing case law history. As of this update, the newly established Nevada Court of Appeals has been assigned cases arising out of Nevada Revised Statutes Chapter 108, which governs mechanics liens on private works construction projects. Additionally, the Nevada Supreme Court is considering a rule change to allow unpublished Supreme Court opinions to be citable as precedent. If adopted, the significant number of unpublished opinions will clarify numerous construction issues.

More importantly, significant impacts to Nevada's construction industry have occurred with the economic collapse of 2008-2011. Nevada's construction practitioners are continuing to face new issues and challenges rarely seen previously: From bankruptcy of multi-use resort properties and lenders pulling construction financing mid-project, to massive residential foreclosures. Property values have made traditional mechanics lien remedies ineffectual, which has caused title companies to walk away from insurance obligations. The complexities of Nevada construction law are all the more important to understand.

1:2 Understanding Nevada courts and legal environment for out of state practitioners

Nevada is a small state. The Nevada construction industry is even smaller. Smaller even yet is the construction law practice within the State. The closeness of the construction bar means that the wise practitioner will enlist local counsel to assist the client with the various complexities of the Nevada construction law, and to avoid ethical complications involving the unlicensed practice of law in the State. The State Bar of Nevada takes a restrictive view of out of jurisdiction attorneys conducting even the most rudimentary acts.[3] For instance, even writing letters can be sufficient to run afoul of the State Bar's dictates. As they state:

> *Out-Of-State Licensed Counsel.*
> *Attorneys licensed in other states run afoul of SCR 189 in pre-litigation cases. Typically, Bar Counsel will approach these matters as discipline cases. Under SCR 99, the Nevada Supreme Court has exclusive jurisdiction to discipline attorneys admitted to practice law in Nevada, specially admitted for a particular proceeding, or "practicing law here, whether specially admitted or not." Nevada, like many jurisdictions, does not define "the practice of law," and each incident is considered on a case-by-case basis.[4] Generally speaking, when another relies upon your judgment or opinion as to his legal rights, you are practicing law.[5] ...*
> ...
> *A growing area where the Bar receives complaints of UPL is in construction defect cases. The Bar has received complaints of out-of-state counsel participating in the pre-litigation mediation procedures. Writing notification letters, engaging in discovery, and appearing at pre-litigation mediations in a representative capacity is generally the practice of law. In Nevada, there is no mechanism to obtain authority from the Supreme Court to appear in pre-litigation cases. Therefore, engaging in legal activities involving Nevada disputes and Nevada parties normally requires a licensed Nevada attorney.*
> *In addition, the Bar has received inquiries and complaints of out-of-counsel participating in private arbitration hearings in Nevada. Acting as a mediator or arbitrator is permissible. Parties to private arbitration can choose anyone as the Trier of fact. However, representing a Nevada client here or representing a client in a Nevada based dispute is practicing law, and requires a Nevada-licensed attorney.*
>
> *Finally, merely holding yourself out as an attorney can constitutes the practice of law. This issue most often arises in correspondence from an attorney licensed in another state but not in Nevada. A licensed attorney who is not admitted to practice in Nevada must clearly designate that fact on letterhead. Further, an attorney licensed only in a foreign jurisdiction must indicate any jurisdictional limitations following his signature on firm stationery.[6]*
>
> *Ultimately, the test is whether or not under the circumstances the public would believe that the person is a licensed attorney. This can differ from state to state. For example, in Nevada attorneys almost always use "esquire" following their name and the community and the local bar deem it interchangeable with "attorney." As a general proposition,*

---

[3] Nevada Standing Committee on Ethics and Professional Responsibility, Formal Opinion No. 20 (February 24, 1995).

[4] In Re Discipline of Lerner, 197 P.3d 1067 (Nev. 2008).

[5] See Pioneer Title Ins. & Trust Co. v. State Bar of Nev., 74 Nev. 186, 326 P.2d 408 (1958); Greenwell v. State Bar of Nevada, 108 Nev. 602, 836 P.2d 70 (1992).

[6] See, i.e., New York City. Lawyer s Assn. Comm. On Prof. Ethics, Op. 682 (1990).

persons not admitted in any jurisdiction (i.e. law clerks or law school graduates) may not use "esquire" because it can be misleading to the public.[7]

More important than simply the ethical prohibition on issues, obtaining local counsel early in a Nevada construction dispute can assist in understanding unique aspects of Nevada statutory and administrative law, and their effects on a construction project. It can also be vital to have "feet on the ground" in the local Nevada market. The size of the legal community means that judicial officers and arbitrators are drawn from the local bar, and have significant and ongoing local connections. While there is no overt bias, having local counsel who is likely to have been before the arbitrator or judge on numerous matters certainly bears more credibly on interpretations of Nevada law than someone who attempts a new interpretation of the law the first time he appears before the judge.

Nevada's construction laws usually end up with modifications about every two years, which correspond with the Legislative biennium session. As such, failure to maintain familiarity with the legal alterations can substantially affect your client's position and expectations.

1:3 Nevada Legislation and the Biennium session

Nevada's laws change about every two years, and the new or altered laws in most cases go into effect October 1 of that same year. In some rare cases, new laws may be effective on an earlier date or even immediately upon execution by the Governor. Each new bill needs to be reviewed for any early application dates.

But the most important thing to understand about Nevada's legislative process is the fact that it only happens once every two years and then the Legislature only meets for 120 consecutive days.[8] There is little time for new legislation to be reviewed and discussed, or even thoroughly vetted for all potential issues that could arise. As a result, new legislation brings with it a period of information and explanation by local attorneys and other entities.

All new bills must be sponsored. Only legislators, the Governor, the Supreme Court and select public entities or government departments are allowed to sponsor bills and request Bill Draft Request numbers, known by the acronym "BDR."[9] The BDR will be assigned a number and a short, usually one sentence, description of the legislation will

---

[7] Clark, Unauthorized Practice of Law, State Bar of Nevada, September 20, 2001. See also, In Re Discipline of Lerner, 197 P.3d 1067 (Nev. 2008); Bar Counsel Report, Letters of Reprimand, Nevada Lawyer, State Bar of Nevada, pub., July 2011 ed. (wherein two non-Nevada licensed attorneys were reported as reprimanded for the unauthorized practice of law for sending a demand letter and attempting to negotiation a settlement with Nevada based parties).

[8] Nevada Constitution, Article 4, §2(2).

[9] *See generally* NRS 218.240 to NRS 218.255.

be listed.[10] These descriptions do not contain much to reveal the intent of the legislation as a rule. The bill's sponsor will then provide to the Legislative Counsel Bureau ("LCB") draft language of the actual bill, or a summary of the concept, which is used by the LCB to actually draft the bill language. While the LCB drafts-people are hardworking, dedicated and very good at their work, there are moments when mistakes are made or the legislation's intent is not effectively or clearly communicated by the BDR language. If the language is not carefully vetted by the BDR sponsor after it comes out of the LCB offices, the enacted bill may have some unintended consequences or mistakes which can lead to absurd results. The biennium structure itself does not allow for simple correction of errors,[11] and so mistakes can and do occur to the detriment of those bound by the law.

The short period for actual enactment of new legislation necessarily means that much of the ground work for successful passage of a bill must occur before the legislative session begins. Those who seek to get new legislation passed are wise to begin gathering support and comment well before the first day of the Legislative session, and then make the necessary compromises on language to achieve a consensus bill approval from the various industry groups that the legislation will affect. This will often lead to unanimous passage from the Committee through both legislative houses and execution by the Governor. In this event, there will be little in the way of legislative history to reveal the intention of the legislative sponsor when the bill was enacted, which can occasionally leave the Nevada Courts as the final arbiter of what legislation means or actually does, when ambiguities are found in the legislative language. While some legislative history on any bill may be available, it is not necessarily always enlightening about every change in a statutory scheme. As a result, some significant changes may occur without any legislative explanation at all, leaving their effects entirely up to the court interpreting the resulting statute.

1:4 History of Nevada Construction Litigation and Legislative Reaction

As indicated in Section 1:2, Understanding Nevada Courts and Legal Environment for Out of State Practitioners, above, much of Nevada's construction law history can be traced to specific events in the construction and the legislative reaction to them. This is most evident after 1999, when the most important case in Nevada construction law was instituted: *In re Venetian Casino Resorts.*[12] While the legal principals arising from this

---

[10] *See generally* NRS 218.240 to NRS 218.255.

[11] *See* NRS 218.445

[12] While this label became the moniker for a large number of consolidated matters, the matters were consolidated under this name and remained consolidated for the largest part of the case history. Eventually, the case was settled without the Nevada Supreme Court ruling on most disputed issues. See In re Venetian Casino Resorts, 121 Nev. 1136 (2005), noting case appeal dismissed. But the implications of this case on the legislative history regarding many aspects of construction cannot be discounted. This case was the corner stone of significant changes to the Nevada mechanics lien law in 2003 and thereafter. See Nevada Legislative History, Minutes of the Senate Committee on Judiciary, SB206, 72nd Legislative Session, March 11, 2003.

complex matter will be discussed at various points throughout this text as they related to various issues, the place of the *Venetian* case in the history of Nevada construction law cannot be discounted. It is safe to say that no other single case has had as much impact on Nevada construction related legislation than *Venetian*.

As a result of these and other related matters, many of the laws impacting Nevada mechanics liens[13] and portions of the Nevada Contractors Licensing Law known as the "Prompt Payment Act"[14] have taken construction payment issues to levels not seen in any other state. While these laws will be discussed in detail in later chapters of this book, the fact remains that no practitioner of construction law should assume that Nevada construction law is uniform or follows the holdings of sister states or other locations where "standard industry practice" might be founded on legal principals. Indeed, the Nevada Supreme Court has recognized (citing the 2010 edition of this treatise) that the Nevada mechanics lien law is "unique" in the United States, and on that basis finding that sister state court interpretations of mechanics lien statutes are not binding.[15] This precisely demonstrates that Nevada's construction law is independent and must be viewed within its own historical context as a direct and critical factor in a construction project's administration and delivery.

1:5 ABOUT THIS BOOK

The purpose of this book is to provide information unique to Nevada construction law to the legal practitioner or industry participant. This book is *not* meant to be a complete examination of all aspects of construction law in general,[16] nor as the final analysis of how Nevada law will be applied in a given factual context. As such, this treatise does not attempt to thoroughly examine all elements of a given topic, except as they are affected by relevant Nevada laws and how those elements may be treated in the Silver State. The more general aspects of construction scheduling, claims analysis, contract provisions, etc., are only discussed sufficiently to provide a background to understand the Nevada treatment of the subject. It must always be kept in mind, however, that given the limited number of published (and therefore citable) cases interpreting Nevada's construction law statutes, the analysis contained in this treatise must be considered as a practice guide. A lawyer experienced in Nevada construction law and practice must always be consulted for specific analysis of each independent factual circumstance before any reader should rely on the information contained in this work.

When Nevada law subjects are discussed in detail, forms relevant to the information are provided in Appendix A. The forms are for the most part placed in order of discussion in

---

[13] *See* NRS 108.221 to NRS 108.246, inclusive.

[14] *See* NRS 624.606 to NRS 624.630, inclusive.

[15] *See In re: Fontainebleau Las Vegas Holdings LLC*, 128 Nev.Adv.Op 53, 289 P.3d 1199, 1211 (2012).

[16] For a complete and in depth examination of construction concepts discussed more generally in this book, the Author recommends a review of Bruner & O'Connor on Construction Law.

this book. We have tried to use actual forms from the various agencies or those which have been and are regularly used in practice by Nevada practitioners. It should be noted, however, that the forms are not necessarily in the proper size or with the appropriate margins for recording with any particular state agency. Pre-printed forms should be obtained from the particular state agency providing the forms before filing, and other forms should be duplicated after verification against the particular Nevada statutes which are the basis of the forms, in order to ensure compliance with any statutory changes that may have occurred between updates.

Chapter 2 Contractor Licensing and Related Issues

2:1 Contracting in Nevada

Contracting in Nevada is not as simple as grabbing a hammer and getting to work. In fact, such an action might land you in jail. Nevada's history and powerful construction lobby has required its legislature to mandate strict contracting rules and regulations to govern the profession of construction in the State. As a result, a construction lawyer needs to be familiar with the requirements and duties of a contractor found in the contractor's licensing law--NRS Chapter 624--to understand how best to advise his or her clients looking to become contractors or to operate their ongoing contracting businesses.

Many ordinary transactions to most people may be direct violations of Nevada's contracting laws, and may result in disciplinary action being taken against the licensee, or even criminal prosecution. Although most criminal prosecutions for illegal contracting are relatively minor violations, the extensive and continued violation of the law can result in significant charges of criminal activity. It is therefore of utmost importance that any person engaging the act of being a contractor should have a contractor's license.

Also, it cannot be stressed strongly enough that having a contractor's license in Nevada does not allow a person to just do anything with it--for instance, allowing another person to use your contractor's license (known as a license loan) is cause for immediate and summary revocation of your contractor's license. Performing work where the contractor has a correct license, but a license amount limitation that is too low for the contract is a cause for discipline for unlicensed contracting. Using money received from one construction project to pay for materials on another construction project is not only a cause for discipline to the licensee, but can also be a felonious act, punishable by time in prison. It is therefore critical that a person know what they can and cannot do without a contractor's license, and for a contractor to understand what s/he can and cannot do with the license once it is issued.

2:2 Definition of "Builder" and "Contractor"

Initially, it is important to understand the broad definition of "contractor," as that term is used to define the scope of the contractor's license law. The definition of "contractor" is found in NRS 624.020, which provides:

> *1. "Contractor" is synonymous with "builder".*
> *2. A contractor is any person, except a registered architect or a licensed professional engineer, acting solely in a professional capacity, who in any capacity other than as the employee of another with wages as the sole compensation, undertakes to, offers to undertake to, purports to have the capacity to undertake to, or submits a bid to, or does himself or herself or by or through others, construct, alter, repair, add to, subtract from, improve, move, wreck or demolish any building, highway, road, railroad, excavation or*

other structure, project, development or improvement, or to do any part thereof, including the erection of scaffolding or other structures or works in connection therewith. Evidence of the securing of any permit from a governmental agency or the employment of any person on a construction project must be accepted by the Board or any court of this State as prima facie evidence that the person securing that permit or employing any person on a construction project is acting in the capacity of a contractor pursuant to the provisions of this chapter.
3. A contractor includes a subcontractor or specialty contractor, but does not include anyone who merely furnishes materials or supplies without fabricating them into, or consuming them in the performance of, the work of a contractor.
4. A contractor includes a construction manager who performs management and counseling services on a construction project for a professional fee.
5. A contractor does not include an owner of a planned unit development who enters into one or more oral or written agreements with one or more general building contractors or general engineering contractors to construct a work of improvement in the planned unit development if the general building contractors or general engineering contractors are licensed pursuant to this chapter and contract with the owner of the planned unit development to construct the entire work of improvement.

As can be seen from this section, a person who "acts in the capacity" of a contractor is a contractor for purposes of the contractor's license law; that is, the provisions of NRS Chapter 624 will apply to them and compliance will be required. A number of specific exceptions arise here, as well as a number of exceptions to the applicability of Chapter 624 in general, and these will be discussed in ensuing sections. What is vital to understand from this definition is that the act of contracting begins with the assertion by a person that he "has the capacity to" act as a contractor and continues all the way through the contracting process. As such, the mere advertisement of a person to perform handyman work calls into play the provisions of the contractor's license law.[17]

Likewise, a construction manager is acting within the capacity of a contractor under the provisions of NRS 624.020(4) while performing tasks that fall within the concept of construction management. This is critical, because there are many organizations that purport to offer certifications for people to act as "construction managers." These certifications do not allow a holder to represent himself in Nevada as a "construction manager" seeking to perform such work. In fact doing so without a contractor's license will subject the person to a charge of unlicensed contracting, as performing "construction management" without the applicable general contracting license is illegal in Nevada.[18] As such, it is simply not proper for an out of state contractor, who does not

---

[17] NRS 624.341(1)(a) requires that the Board cite any person who has "acted as a contractor without an active license of the proper classification". Failure to comply the citation or order is classified as a misdemeanor. NRS 624.341(5).

[18] NRS 624.700(1) provides:

> *1. It is unlawful for any person or combination of persons to: (a) Engage in the business or act in the capacity of a contractor within this State; or (b) Submit a bid on a job situated within this State, without having an active license therefor as provided in this chapter, unless that person or combination of persons is exempted from licensure pursuant to NRS 624.031.*

hold a valid and active Nevada state contractor's license, to submit or solicit any bid on or otherwise negotiate any contract for the performance of work as a contractor or a construction manager.[19] Doing so can and will result in administrative and/or criminal investigation and prosecution.[20] Similarly, a "certified" construction manager may not manage any part of construction project without a Nevada contractor's license.

It should also be understood at this time that a licensed contractor in Nevada may also be found in violation of the law if he bids outside the scope of his license classification or the NSCB assigned maximum license financial limit.[21] This scope limitation will apply both to the trade work and to the amount of the contract, if the contract, including change orders, is beyond the financial limitation of the contractor's license.

2:3 Exemptions to Licensing Requirement

As discussed above, there are a number of reasonable exceptions to the contractor's license requirement. In general, these fall into two categories: 1) activities that are outside the scope of the definition of "contractor" in NRS 624.020(2), and 2) excepted activities found in NRS 624.031. These are discussed in turn.

In general, any activity that is not encompassed within the "contractor" definition under NRS 624.020 is arguably exempt from the licensing obligations of Chapter 624. For instance, acting as a licensed engineer or registered architect does not require a contractor's license to be issued under NRS Chapter 624, even though some of the activities of licensed engineers and registered architects do fall within the scope of the work of a contractor.[22] However, those activities are specifically authorized within the licensing requirements of those professions.[23] If a licensed engineer or a registered architect acts beyond the scope of his license or registration and ventures into the realm of a construction manager's duties, a contractor's license may be required for such activity.[24] Similarly, a person who works as a laborer, foreman, superintendent or other capacity for a licensed contractor, earning only his wages for that work, does not need his own contractor's license to hold that job. Once the laborer acts beyond his

---

[19] NRS 624.341(1)(a)

[20] NRS 624.341(1)(a)

[21] *See* Discussion at Section 2:4 Unlicensed contracting and penalties.

[22] *See* footnote 24, infra.

[23] *See* NRS 625.050 for professional engineers and NRS 623.023 for registered architects.

[24] *See Kourafas v. Basic Food Flavors, Inc.*, 120 Nev. 195, 88 P.3d 822 (2004) (abrogated on other grounds by, Buzz Stew, LLC v. City of North Las Vegas, 181 P.3d 670 (Nev. 2008)), holding that because of the conflicting nature of NRS 624.020(2) exempting registered architects from the definition of contractor and the inclusion of a construction manager under the definition of contractor in NRS 624.020(4), coupled with the fact that a registered architect is licensed to perform some construction management activities under NRS 623.023, it is a question of fact whether the architect was in violation of NRS 624.020 and can only be determined by determining what activities the architect actually performed.

employment, however, he does begin acting as a "contractor" and must possess his own license to do so. The dividing line here is the extent of the project manager's authority over the work being performed on his neighbor's house. Hence, the construction project manager who agrees to supervise and direct the construction of his neighbor's owner-builder custom home project is violating the contractor's license law by doing so. Not only is he subject to prosecution for contracting without a license, the subcontractors and even the homeowner entering into the agreement may be violating the law as well. If that construction project manager simply provides his neighbor with advice and leaves the direction to the exempt owner-builder, however, no violation occurs.

Additional exemptions from the provisions of Chapter 624 are found in NRS 624.031.[25] A couple of these issues are of important note. First, a Nevada state-issued contractor's

---

[25] NRS 624.031 provides:

> *The provisions of this chapter do not apply to:*
>
> *1. Work performed exclusively by an authorized representative of the United States Government, the State of Nevada, or an incorporated city, county, irrigation district, reclamation district, or other municipal or political corporation or subdivision of this State.*
>
> *2. An officer of a court when acting within the scope of his or her office.*
>
> *3. Work performed exclusively by a public utility operating pursuant to the regulations of the Public Utilities Commission of Nevada on construction, maintenance and development work incidental to its business.*
>
> *4. An owner of property who is building or improving a residential structure on the property for his or her own occupancy and not intended for sale or lease. The sale or lease, or the offering for sale or lease, of the newly built structure within 1 year after its completion creates a rebuttable presumption for the purposes of this section that the building of the structure was performed with the intent to sell or lease that structure. An owner of property who requests an exemption pursuant to this subsection must apply to the Board for the exemption. The Board shall adopt regulations setting forth the requirements for granting the exemption.*
>
> *5. Any work to repair or maintain property the value of which is less than $1,000, including labor and materials, unless:*
>
> *(a) A building permit is required to perform the work;*
>
> *(b) The work is of a type performed by a plumbing, electrical, refrigeration, heating or air-conditioning contractor;*
>
> *(c) The work is of a type performed by a contractor licensed in a classification prescribed by the Board that significantly affects the health, safety and welfare of members of the general public;*
>
> *(d) The work is performed as a part of a larger project:*
>
> *(1) The value of which is $500 or more; or*
>
> *(2) For which contracts of less than $500 have been awarded to evade the provisions of this chapter; or*
>
> *(e) The work is performed by a person who is licensed pursuant to this chapter or by an employee of that person.*
>
> *6. The sale or installation of any finished product, material or article of merchandise which is not fabricated into and does not become a permanent fixed part of the structure.*
>
> *7. The construction, alteration, improvement or repair of personal property.*
>
> *8. The construction, alteration, improvement or repair financed in whole or in part by the Federal Government and conducted within the limits and boundaries of a site or reservation, the title of which rests in the Federal Government.*

license is not required for any work of improvement performed on federal land or by a state agency with its own employees.[26] That is, neither a contractor retained by the

---

9. An owner of property, the primary use of which is as an agricultural or farming enterprise, building or improving a structure on the property for his or her use or occupancy and not intended for sale or lease.

10. Construction oversight services provided to a long-term recovery group by a qualified person within a particular geographic area that is described in a proclamation of a state of emergency or declaration of disaster by the State or Federal Government, including, without limitation, pursuant to NRS 414.070. A long-term recovery group may reimburse such reasonable expenses as the qualified person incurs in providing construction oversight services to that group. Except as otherwise provided in this subsection, nothing in this subsection authorizes a person who is not a licensed contractor to perform the acts described in paragraphs (a) and (b) of subsection 1 of NRS 624.700. As used in this subsection:

(a) "Construction oversight services" means the coordination and oversight of labor by volunteers.

(b) "Long-term recovery group" means a formal group of volunteers coordinating response and recovery efforts related to a state of emergency or disaster that is proclaimed or declared by the State or Federal Government.

(c) "Qualified person" means a person who possesses the abilities, education, experience, knowledge, skills and training that a long-term recovery group has identified as being necessary to provide construction oversight services for a project to be performed by that group.

11. A person licensed as a real estate broker, real estate broker-salesperson or real estate salesperson pursuant to chapter 645 of NRS who, acting within the scope of the license or a permit to engage in property management issued pursuant to NRS 645.6052, assists a client in scheduling work to repair or maintain residential property pursuant to a written brokerage agreement or a property management agreement. Such assistance includes, without limitation, assisting a client in the hiring of any number of licensed contractors to perform the work. Nothing in this subsection authorizes the performance of any work for which a license is required pursuant to this chapter by a person who is not licensed pursuant to this chapter or the payment of any additional compensation to a person licensed as a real estate broker, real estate broker-salesperson or real estate salesperson for assisting a client in scheduling the work. The provisions of this subsection apply only if a building permit is not required to perform the work and if the value of the work does not exceed $10,000 per residential property during the fixed term of the written brokerage agreement, if the assistance is provided pursuant to such an agreement, or during a period not to exceed 6 months if the assistance is provided pursuant to a property management agreement. As used in this subsection:

(a) "Brokerage agreement" has the meaning ascribed to it in NRS 645.005.

(b) "Property management agreement" has the meaning ascribed to it in NRS 645.0192.

(c) "Real estate broker" has the meaning ascribed to it in NRS 645.030.

(d) "Real estate broker-salesperson" has the meaning ascribed to it in NRS 645.035.

(e) "Real estate salesperson" has the meaning ascribed to it in NRS 645.040.

(f) "Residential property" means:

(1) Improved real estate that consists of not more than four residential units; or

(2) A single-family residential unit, including a condominium, townhouse or home within a subdivision, if the unit is sold, leased or otherwise conveyed unit by unit, regardless of whether the unit is part of a larger building or parcel that consists of more than four units.

[26] NRS 624.031(1).

federal government nor the state agency have to hold a contractor's license to perform work owned by those respective agencies. As is thoroughly discussed in Chapter 6, Public Works Construction, a Nevada state agency must contract with a contractor who is licensed under NRS Chapter 624 to complete the public project over a certain size and nature.[27] Federal works of improvement are completely exempt from any state contractor license requirement.[28]

Second, it should be noted that a person who is building his own residence is not required to be licensed under NRS Chapter 624,[29] however, such person is required to obtain a specific written exemption approval from the Nevada State Contractors Board before doing so.[30] This approval is obtained by filing an Owner-Builder Affidavit with the Contractor's Board.[31] Of critical nature, the approval form obligates the owner-builder to otherwise comply with the laws related to building codes, payment of wages and other requirements.[32] Proof of the owner-builder's eligibility for this exemption is the fact that the owner will not sell or lease the property so constructed within 1 year of its

---

[27] *See* Section 6:5, Pre-qualification of bidders.

[28] NRS 624.031(8).

[29] NRS 624.031(4).

[30] NAC 624.015 provides:

> *To apply for an owner-builder exemption from the provisions of chapter 624 of NRS pursuant to subsection 4 of NRS 624.031, an owner of property must submit an Owner-Builder Disclosure Statement to:*
> *(a) The Board; and*
> *(b) The local building official responsible for issuing the permit for the work that will be the subject of the exemption.*
> *2. If the Owner-Builder Disclosure Statement submitted pursuant to subsection 1 is completed fully and accurately, and signed by the applicant under penalty of perjury, the Board will approve the owner-builder exemption.*
> *3. Unless the Board notifies the applicant within 10 days after he submits the Owner-Builder Disclosure Statement to the Board that the owner-builder exemption is denied, the owner-builder exemption shall be deemed to have been approved by the Board.*
> *4. If the Board denies an application for an owner-builder exemption, the Board will, within 10 days after the applicant submits the Owner-Builder Disclosure Statement to the Board:*
> *(a) Notify the applicant that the owner-builder exemption is denied; and*
> *(b) Set forth the reasons for the denial.*
> *5. If the applicant is notified pursuant to subsection 4 that the owner-builder exemption is denied, the applicant may submit supplemental materials to the Board regarding the application for an owner-builder exemption.*
> *6. If it appears to the satisfaction of the Board that the materials submitted pursuant to subsection 5 satisfy the reasons for the denial of the owner-builder exemption, the Board may approve the owner-builder exemption.*
> *7. As used in this section, “"Owner-Builder Disclosure Statement" means the form adopted by the Board pursuant to NAC 624.017.*

[31] See Form 2-1 in Appendix A.

[32] These Owner-Builder Information page on the Nevada State Contractors Board website: http://www.nvcontractorsboard.com/owner-builder.html

completion. Doing so creates a rebuttable presumption that the work was not constructed for the owner's own personal use, and may subject the owner to liability for contracting without a license.

Third, the provisions of NRS 624.031(5) seem to allow for handyman work without a license, however, there are a number of important terms to focus on in this exemption. Initially, the work cannot be in excess of $1,000 of value including both labor and material. Next, the work cannot require a building permit, or be of a nature of critical importance in the state, which simply means it cannot be either electrical, plumbing, HVAC or fire / life safety work. These types of work must be performed by a person with the proper specialty subcontracting license, regardless of their scope. With these limitations, the handyman repairing a leaky roof for instance would not need a contracting license, so long as the work is not so extensive as to require a permit or exceed the $1,000 limitation. However, because the replacement of a leaking water heater would require a permit by the Las Vegas Department of Building and Safety, a handyman cannot perform it without a license. A word of caution is necessary: Making smaller contracts for the purpose of evading the obligation of the license law is a serious violation.[33] As such, dividing up work for the purpose of evading the law will be a cause of violation of the chapter. For instance, entering into multiple contracts to "repair" a roof in sections for less than $500 each, but which results in the complete replacement of a roof for $5,000 would be seen as a violation of the contractor's license law. Such activities should not be undertaken in any circumstance, including for the purpose of evading a contractor's license bid limitation.

In 2013, the Nevada legislature introduced a new exception for real estate managers who are licensed to perform such management under NRS Chapter 645. NRS 624.031(11) provides an exemption for such managers who coordinate the repair of rental properties for their lease or rental to new tenants or emergency repairs. Such actions will be exempt from licensing so long as the work performed does not require a permit and does not exceed $10,000 in value per property in a 6 month period of time.

It should also be noted that there is a classification C-40 "catch-all" license sub-classification. NAC 624.570 provides for issuing an "unclassified" license to cover work not otherwise included in enumerated classifications. The existence of unclassified license category raises a question on exceptions in general. The safest course of action is

---

[33] NRS 624.3014(2)(b) provides:

> *The following acts, among others, constitute a cause for disciplinary action under NRS 624.300 ...(2) With the intent to evade the provisions of this chapter: ... (b) Combining or conspiring with an unlicensed person to perform an unauthorized act.*

Since the act of bidding or entering into a contract beyond one's license limitation is a unauthorized practice (see NRS 624.3015(2)), entering into multiple contracts with a customer which breakup traditional construction tasks into smaller contracts, with the intent of avoiding the license limitation is usually seen as a violation of this section.

to consult with the NSCB in determining if a license is necessary and what classification before starting work.

2:4 UNLICENSED CONTRACTING AND PENALTIES

As has already been discussed to some degree is the nature of unlicensed contracting. Unlicensed contracting can arise from performing work without a license at all, performing work outside of a scope limitation or classification of a person's license, or from contracting beyond the financial limitations of the license. These parameters are often confusing, even to licensed contractors or the contractor's board's own investigators. A solid understanding of the statutory basis of unlicensed violations is critical for the construction law practitioner.

NRS 624.700 provides:

> *1. It is unlawful for any person or combination of persons to:*
> *(a) Engage in the business or act in the capacity of a contractor within this State; or*
> *(b) Submit a bid on a job situated within this State,*
> *→ without having an active license therefor as provided in this chapter, unless that person or combination of persons is exempted from licensure pursuant to NRS 624.031.*
> *2. The district attorneys in this State shall prosecute all violations of this section which occur in their respective counties, unless the violations are prosecuted by the Attorney General. Upon the request of the Board, the Attorney General shall prosecute any violation of this section in lieu of prosecution by the district attorney.*
> *3. In addition to any other penalty imposed pursuant to this chapter, a person who is convicted of violating subsection 1 may be required to pay:*
> *(a) Court costs and the costs of prosecution;*
> *(b) Reasonable costs of the investigation of the violation to the Board;*
> *(c) Damages he caused as a result of the violation up to the amount of his pecuniary gain from the violation; or*
> *(d) Any combination of paragraphs (a), (b) and (c).*
> *4. If a person submits a bid or enters into a contract in violation of subsection 1, the bid or contract shall be deemed void ab initio.*

Of most important understanding are subsections 1 and 4, which proscribe the conduct of an unlicensed person and then add the civil penalty for unlicensed work in voiding construction contracts. Under subsection 1, a person violates Nevada law by engaging in the business of, acting in the capacity of or submitting a bid to perform a job as a contractor in Nevada without a Nevada issued license to do so. This is of vital importance. A person who does not have a contractor's license in Nevada cannot provide any bid for a project in Nevada, even contingent upon obtaining a Nevada contractor's license. Doing so will cause, at a minimum, an investigation of the act and most likely an administrative fine being imposed upon the unlicensed person.[34] Also, NRS

---

[34] NRS 624.710 provides:

> *1. If any person violates the provisions of subsection 1 of NRS 624.700, subsection 1, 2 or 3 of NRS 624.720 or NRS 624.740, the Board may impose for each violation an administrative fine in an amount that is not less than $1,000 and not more than $50,000.*

624.341(1)(a) require the Board to issue a citation to an unlicensed contractor as well as a fine of at least $1,000.[35] In addition, the Contractor's Board may bar the unlicensed person from qualifying for a license in the future. Therefore, providing any type of bid activity, e.g., soliciting bids from trade contractors, checking lead times, pricing or making inquiries used for the bid is of the utmost in prohibited activities.

Subsection 4 also makes any contract which an unlicensed person enters into for construction work void *ab initio*. This does not equal a total ban on recovery, however. The Nevada Supreme Court has allowed unlicensed contractors to recover for the value of their work on an unjust enrichment basis, even though recovery would seem to be disallowed under NRS 624.700.[36] While this propensity to wink at a loss of all recovery will, to a large degree, subvert the effectiveness of NRS 624.700(4) and undermines the will of the Legislature in forbidding collection for construction work performed without a license, the Supreme Court seems to balance the equities in this situation -- not wanting the prohibition to apply within the context of a fraud or knowing violation of the statute used by a recalcitrant owner for his own benefit.

It is, of course, axiomatic that one cannot recover under a void contract. As one court declared:

> *A contract which is void ab initio, or void from the beginning, may not be enforced. No contractual duty exists, no breach of contract is possible, and no judgment for money damages can be obtained under the contract ... Judicial or equitable doctrines cannot breathe life into such a contract.*[37]

> *2. The Board shall, by regulation, establish standards for use by the Board in determining the amount of an administrative fine imposed pursuant to this section. The standards must include, without limitation, provisions requiring the Board to consider:*
> *(a) The gravity of the violation;*
> *(b) The good faith of the person; and*
> *(c) Any history of previous violations of the provisions of this chapter or the regulations of the Board committed by the person.*
> *3. An administrative fine imposed pursuant to this section is in addition to any other penalty imposed pursuant to this chapter.*
> *4. If the administrative fine and any interest imposed pursuant to NRS 624.300 is not paid when due, the fine and interest, if any, must be recovered in a civil action brought by the Attorney General on behalf of the Board.*
> *5. All administrative fines and interest collected pursuant to this section must be deposited with the State Treasurer for credit to the Construction Education Account created pursuant to NRS 624.580.*

[35] NRS 624.300(3)(c), Cf. NRS 624.302(7).

[36] *Magill v. Lewis*, 74 Nev. 381, 333 P.2d 717 (1958); Kourafas v. Basic Food Flavors, Inc., 120 Nev. 195, 199, 88 P.3d 822 (2004) (abrogated by, Buzz Stew, LLC v. City of North Las Vegas, 181 P.3d 670 (Nev. 2008)).

[37] *Massachusetts Mun. Wholesale Elec. Co. v. Town of Danvers*, 411 Mass. 39, 577 N.E.2d 283, 292-93 (1991) (internal citations omitted).

Still, on occasion, the Nevada Supreme Court has recognized the concept that the holding of a license may be excused or discharged under the "exception" found in *Magill v. Lewis,* 74 Nev. 381, 333 P.2d 717 (1958). In *Magill,* the Nevada Supreme Court ruled that under the predecessor statute to NRS 624.320,[38] an unlicensed contractor, although it may not recover under a contract, may nevertheless recover under unjust enrichment theory in very limited circumstances. Arguably, a review of *Magill* and its progeny demonstrates that the limited circumstances involve active fraud or misrepresentation on the part of the property owner or other person inducing the unlicensed contractor into performing unlicensed work.[39]

2:5 Application for Contractor's License

Qualification for a contractor's license begins with the application process. A potential licensee must meet certain minimum experience requirements and then perform satisfactory on written tests both practically applicable to the specific license classification and administratively on construction law. In summary, the Nevada State Contractor's Board and its administrative offices will investigate the background and qualifications of an applicant to ensure that the person demonstrates the "degree of experience and knowledge required" to be issued a license.[40] Special investigators,

---

[38] NRS 624.320 provides:

> *No person, firm, copartnership, corporation, association or other organization, or any combination of any thereof, engaged in the business or acting in the capacity of a contractor shall bring or maintain any action in the courts of this State for the collection of compensation for the performance of any act or contract for which a license is required by this chapter without alleging and proving that such person, firm, copartnership, corporation, association or other organization, or any combination of any thereof, was a duly licensed contractor at all times during the performance of such act or contract and when the job was bid.*

[39] *See Nevada Equities, Inc. v. Willard Pease Drilling Co.,* 84 Nev. 300, 302, 440 P.2d 122, 123 (1968), wherein the Court cited to *Magill* for the proposition that “"an unlicensed contractor was allowed recovery on a theory of fraud and unjust enrichment, but not on the contract" (emphasis added); *Beggs v. Lowe,* 89 Nev. 547, 549, 516 P.2d 467, 468 (1973) (“"Preclusive statutes [like NRS 624.320 have been held not to bar quantum meruit relief to an out-of-state contractor if deceit and fraud is alleged and established.") (citing *Magill*).

[40] NRS 624.240 provides:

> *1. Under reasonable regulations adopted by the Board, the Board may investigate, classify and qualify applicants for contractors' licenses by written or oral examinations, or both, and may issue contractors' licenses to qualified applicants. The examinations may, in the discretion of the Board, be given in specific classifications only.*
> *2. If a natural person passes the technical examination given by the Board on or after July 1, 1985, to qualify him for a classification established pursuant to this chapter, demonstrates to the Board the degree of experience and knowledge required in the regulations of the Board, and is granted a license, the person is qualified for a master's license, if issued by any political subdivision, in the classification for which the examination was given, if the examination required the person to demonstrate his or her knowledge and ability to:*
> *(a) Utilize and understand;*
> *(b) Direct and supervise work in compliance with; and*

usually retired FBI or law enforcement officers, are often employed for the background and complaint investigation purposes, and they are very well trained in their investigation skills. In 2015, the Nevada legislature authorized the NSCB investigators to review and consider the licensee qualified employee's character and financial history in determining whether a license should issue to a corporate entity. This series of investigations, testing and monetary qualifications have been created to demonstrate that the applicant will be a credible individual, without a history of damaging others by recalcitrant activities as a contractor.

As such, it is not the fact that someone had a failed contractor's business in the past that will disqualify the candidate for a license. Rather, it is reasons why the business failed and whether the applicant's and/or the qualified employee's character is such that his application demonstrates a forthright and honest person, who will do right by his customers. For this reason, it is critical in the application for a license that the applicant be honest, upfront, candid and as fully disclosing of all potentially negative information as possible in his application documentation. The fact that someone has criminal history in their background will not necessarily disqualify the applicant (although those with a history of criminal activity involving moral turpitude will probably not qualify), so long as the history is honestly and fully disclosed for investigation. Therefore, the applicant must at all times be as thorough and honest in the information provided as possible.[41]

> *(c) Perform and apply any calculations required to ensure that work performed is in compliance with, the applicable codes, standards and regulations.*
> *3. If a natural person qualified for a license before July 1, 1985, in accordance with NRS 624.260 in a trade for which a master's license is required by any political subdivision, and if the license is active on or after July 1, 1985, and if the person so qualified wishes to obtain a master's license, the person must pass either the appropriate examination given by the Board on or after July 1, 1985, in accordance with NRS 624.260 and the regulations of the Board, or the examination given by the political subdivision in the trade for which a master's license is required.*

[41] NRS 624.266 which mandates that a license applicant or licensee affirmatively discloses convictions or pleas to certain crimes to the Board. It provides:

> *1. An applicant for a contractor's license or a licensee shall notify the Board in writing if he or she is convicted of, or enters a plea of guilty, guilty but mentally ill or nolo contendre to:*
> *(a) A crime against a child as that term is defined in NRS 179.245;*
> *(b) A sexual offense as that term is defined in NRS 179.245;*
> *(c) Murder as that term is defined in NRS 200.010;*
> *(d) Voluntary manslaughter as that term is defined in NRS 200.050; or*
> *(e) Any other felony or crime involving moral turpitude if the conviction occurred or the please was entered in the immediately preceding 15 years,*
> *in this State or any other jurisdiction.*
> *2. An applicant for a contractors' license or a licensee shall submit the notification required by subsection 1 not more than 30 days after the conviction or entry of the plea of guilty, guilty but mentally ill or nolo contendere.*

The failure of the licensee or applicant to make disclosures under this section constitutes a cause for disciplinary action under NRS 624.3016(11).

As part of that application, a complete and thorough background disclosure will be required of each qualified applicant and each officer involved with the company, if the applicant is a corporate form of entity. The NSCB provides forms for these disclosures and will use the information provided therein for a complete background investigation of the individual.[42] The applicant can expect that the NSCB will contact those who are identified as persons with knowledge of the applicant, and that those people will be further asked for information and individuals who may also provide information. Those individuals subsequently identified will be contacted as well. When information that is considered unacceptable is uncovered, additional information from the applicant will be sought in most cases to resolve those issues. If the information cannot be satisfactorily resolved, the person will not be allowed a license, or will not be allowed to be associated with the licensed entity as a condition of issuing the license.

In addition to the background examination, a number of financial disclosures will be required of the applicant.[43] Likewise, certain types of applicants may have additional financial disclosure requirements than those with other types of licenses.[44] These will directly relate to the monetary bid limitations of the issued license. In short, a contractor's license will only be issued in an amount that the NSCB can justify based on the applicant's financial health and history. For a license limit of $1 million or more, an applicant must provide either an audited or reviewed financial statement from a certified professional accountant. While there is a sliding scale for bid limitations, an unlimited license will usually require the demonstration of at least $1 million in working capital or $2 million in book value. Using the Board's basic formula calculation of 10 times the working capital or 5 times the book value, this amount would give a company a $10 million license limitation, which the Board would consider to be an unlimited license. Any value less than these amounts would result in the limitation calculated by the lesser of the two values.

It should also be considered that upon investigation of complaints based on a violation of the Board imposed bid limitation, the Board investigators will consider both the base contract amount and any change orders that may be issued on the Project. As a result, a contractor bidding a contract at or near its bid limitation should obtain a one-time increase in its license limit, so that there cannot be a violation based on change order

[42] *See* Form 2-1 in Appendix A.

[43] *See* Form 2-2 in Appendix A.

[44] *See for instance*, NRS 624.264, laying out additional financial disclosures for contractors performing primarily residential construction work and the applicant or the qualifying employee has not previously held a contractors' license, a CPA prepared financial statement may be required, along with other mandates such as escrowing all advance payment construction funds, establishing an aggregate monetary limit on all construction projects performed at any one time, or other such requirements the Board may deem advisable.

activity.[45] The Board will consider contracting over the license limitation as contracting without a license, and the penalties can be severe.[46]

The license application form is fairly self-explanatory to complete,[47] however, it is critical that no shortcuts be taken in the thoroughness and completeness of the application itself. Moreover, the application should be submitted with a full list of additional documents beyond the financial statement and background information already discussed. These documents will include copies of certificates of good standing for the applicant from the Nevada Secretary of State (if the licensee is an entity other than an individual); Out of State License Verification Forms[48] for all contractors licenses held by the applicant at any time before or concurrently with the application; Proof of worker's compensation insurance, meeting state law requirements; Background disclosures[49] for all officers, managers and the qualified employee of the company, including their driver's licenses and fingerprints; Resume and four (4) references for the qualified employee; an executed Bank Verification form[50] for the applicant's bank; An organizational chart identifying individuals associated with the applicant's members, if the applicant's members are legal entities other than individuals or a organization chart of the applicant's elected officers, the Financial Statement discussed previously,[51] and the applicable application fee.

Care should also be given to the form of the entity applying for a license, as on occasion conflicts between alternative entity forms and the NSCB regulations and procedures can impact the processing of a license application. For instance, the adoption of limited liability companies in Nevada at one time raised a question on the NSCB license application processing. One major distinction between corporations and limited liability companies is that a corporation must have officers who are "natural persons,"[52] whereas a limited liability company is operated by members or managers, or managing members,[53] which do not have to be natural persons.[54] Tax planning, especially in more

---

45 NRS 624.220(3) provides that an applicant must request a one-time bid limit increase not later than five (5) days before the bid is submitted, and must receive approval from the Board before the bid is actually submitted. This amendment makes it clear that the Board is not tolerant of late applications for one-time bid increases.

46 *See* Section 2:16, Bid Limitations.

47 *See* Form 2-3 in Appendix A.

48 See Form 2-4 in Appendix A.

49 See Form 2-1 in Appendix A.

50 See Form 2-5 in Appendix A.

51 See Form 2-2 in Appendix A.

52 *See* NRS 78.130(3)

53 *See* NRS 86.071

sophisticated corporate structures, will often take advantage of this by having other limited liability companies be the designated managers or managing members of the subsidiary limited liability company. The NSCB procedures required that investigators look for at least one officer listed on the application also be shown as an officer on the Nevada Secretary of State records as an officer. This led to a few license application rejections until the discrepancy was pointed out to the NSCB, and the application procedure was corrected. The point here is that when an application is rejected, working in a positive and productive manner with the NSCB staff is the best way to resolve these issues. The NSCB staff and executives are reasonable and want to resolve matters so that the law is complied with and the applicant or license can move forward with business, so they will often work with a license applicant to resolve issues whenever they can.

2:6 Indemnity and Bonds

In addition to the application and related documents, the contractor applicant may be required to provide a number of indemnification agreements and bonds as a condition of having a license issued. In general, all applicants will need to provide a contractor's license bond.[55] Individual license applications will usually also require some form of individual indemnification agreement,[56] to be issued by the principals of the applicant (if a separate legal entity) or the individual applicant himself. If the applicant is a legal entity with thin capitalization holdings, it may be necessary for a parent or sister company to provide the indemnification to gain the applicant's necessary bid limitations. In this case, the indemnification agreement will be different depending on whether the indemnifying company is a corporation,[57] a general partnership,[58] a limited liability company,[59] a limited partnership,[60] or a trust entity.[61] Depending on the type of indemnifying agency, the NSCB will likewise need a resolution authorizing the indemnification, an executed bank verification[62] for the indemnifying organization and a financial statement in the form discussed above,[63] for the applicant.

---

[54] *See* NRS 0.039

[55] NRS 624.270(1).

[56] *See* Form 2-6 in Appendix A.

[57] *See* Form 2-7 in Appendix A.

[58] *See* Form 2-8 in Appendix A.

[59] *See* Form 2-9 in Appendix A.

[60] *See* Form 2-10 in Appendix A.

[61] *See* Form 2-11 in Appendix A.

[62] *See* Form 2-5 in Appendix A.

[63] *See* Form 2-2 in Appendix A.

As noted above, the applicant will also need to provide certain bonds to obtain the license, once the application is approved. These bonds will at a minimum be a contractor's license bond in an amount to be established by the Board, between $1,000 and $50,000.[64] If the applicant intends to perform construction on swimming pools, additional bonds and information may also be required.[65] The bonds must be issued by a person or entity who is rated by a national rating agency as "A" or better and may be increased or decreased upon renewal of the license, or at any hearing of the Board where evidence of the need for that change is submitted.[66] A cash deposit can be made in lieu of the provision of a bond, though the amount will not be reduced, nor will interest be paid on the cash submitted.[67]

The bonds inure to the benefit of the state of Nevada and those customers, employees, vendors or other persons injured as a result of the acts of the contractor.[68] It should be noted that claims on contractor's license bonds can be prosecuted without filing of a lawsuit,[69] or the surety may wish to interplead the bond sum if there are excessive claims.[70] Pay-outs will reduce the amount of the bond available for protection of the public. Both the surety and the Board are authorized to deduct reasonable attorney's fees and costs from the bond or cash deposit in the event such costs are incurred as a result of investigations made.[71] Such a reduction or even cancellation of the contractor's bond will require the applicant to provide a replacement bond or have his license suspended or even revoked.[72]

---

[64] *See* NRS 624.270(4). It should be noted at the time of authorship, the general bond amount for a new unlimited license is $50,000. However, this authorizing statute does allow for the Board to impose higher limits if necessary, and are currently being considered.

[65] *See* Form 2-13 in Appendix A and NRS 624.276 and NRS 624.270(7) to (9).

[66] *See* NRS 624.270(4).

[67] *See* NRS 624.270(1)(b).

[68] *See* NRS 624.273(1).

[69] NRS 624.273(4).

[70] NRS 624.273(5).

[71] NRS 624.273(4) and (5).

[72] NRS 624.275(3). As a practical matter, the payment of any portion of a surety bond will probably lead to the cancellation of the entire surety bond, unless reimbursement is promptly made by the contractor to his surety and additional requirements are met. Such action by the bond surety can lead to significant problems for the contractor in procuring additional bonds or a replacement contractor's license bond. Therefore, the prosecution of a meritorious contractor's license bond claim can exert significant pressure on the contractor in the litigation context. This can lead to ramifications for the license bond claimant in terms of future business dealings. As such, the construction law practitioner should carefully review the results of such action and weigh the same against the practical effect. If there is a reasonable likelihood of collection, restraint on this bond claim may be the best course of action.

Finally, it should be noted that a contractor can petition to have the requirement of a bond waived.[73] The procedure for obtaining such a waiver is a fairly straight forward process of preparing an application for bond cancellation and providing a proper financial statement.[74]If the Board determines from the application that the contractor meets the eligibility requirements, the bond requirement can be cancelled.

Because of this waiver option, a practitioner should counsel his clients to review the license bond status of contractors before entering into new construction contracts or opening new job accounts for the contractor of any substance. While a license bond is usually a "last resort" source of recovery, the client making a credit decision may want to be aware of the lack of a license bond before extending credit. The bond waiver essentially assumes that the contractor is of such good repute that there is no longer a need for the public or the state to be protected in the event of a violation. The fact that a contractor has not had a complaint filed against him in 5 years, however, is simply not a conclusive determination that the contractor will not be the cause of such violations in the future.

2:7 Approval and Issuance of License

Once the application has been completed and submitted, the Board's licensing staff will review the same and if acceptable, will note for beginning of the investigation. They may also request additional documentation if they believe it is necessary for processing or to explain any negative information on the application or what is discovered during the investigation process. Likewise, when the application is complete, the Board will issue a testing authorization letter to the qualified employee to take the contractor's license examination. The employee must then schedule and pass the contractor's license test offered by an independent testing agency. The Board usually provides a list of these testing agencies with the testing authorization letter.

When the testing and application processing is complete, the Board will issue a contingent approval letter containing a number of contingencies that must be met in order for the actual license to issue. These contingencies will include the posting of the

---

[73] NRS 624.270(5) provides in pertinent part:

> *After a licensee has acted in the capacity of a licensed contractor in the State of Nevada for not less than 5 consecutive years, the Board may relieve the licensee of the requirement of filing a bond or establishing a cash deposit if evidence supporting such relief is presented to the Board. The Board may at any time thereafter require the licensee to file a new bond or establish a new cash deposit as provided in subsection 4:*
> *(a) If evidence is presented to the Board supporting this requirement;*
> *(b) Pursuant to subsection 6, after notification of a final written decision by the Labor Commissioner; or*
> *(c) Pursuant to subsection 7.*
> *If a licensee is relieved of the requirement of establishing a cash deposit, the deposit may be withdrawn 2 years after such relief is granted, if there is no outstanding claim against it.*

[74] See Form 2-12 in Appendix A.

contractor's license bond, payment of the license fee, executing and returning any affidavit of non-performance of residential construction,[75] providing proof of workers compensation insurance and proof of passing the examinations.

When the contingencies have been met, the Board will issue the license and mail the actual hard copy within a short period of time. However, the license is valid upon its issuance and it can be seen on the NSCB website and other pertinent places of public notices. The contractor will then be authorized to bid and perform contracting work within the license specialization and bid limitations.

2:8. Contract Disclosures and Advertising

Once the contractor has been issued a license, his required compliance with various regulations and statutes continues. The contractor must be ever diligent on ensuring strict compliance with the regulations that are applicable to his particular contracting specialization, and to ensure that he provides all relevant disclosures and information in every transaction. The NSCB takes violations seriously, and will not limit its investigations to the specifics of a complaint when filed. In fact, the Board investigators will look at all information gathered during an investigation to find additional violations on which to lodge complaints.

Contractors must provide various disclosures to the public as part of every transaction. Simple requirements that the contractor publish his license number and bid limitation on every advertisement, letter or even his truck if he advertises his business on that, are prosecuted if not strictly complied with at the Board's discretion.[76] Therefore, the contractor should be fully aware and make sure that all of his advertisements, contracts, subcontracts, letterhead, business cards, bid proposals, invoices, and every other business document contain the license number and bid limitations.

---

[75] See Form 2-14 in Appendix A.

[76] The NSCB investigator's argument will begin with NRS 624.3017(2) and (3), which provide:

> *The following acts, among others, constitute cause for disciplinary action under NRS 624.300:*
>
> ...
>
> *2. Advertising projects of construction without including in the advertisements the name and license number of the licensed contractor who is responsible for the construction.*
> *3. Advertising projects of construction beyond the scope of the license.*

Further, the investigators will likewise point to NAC 624.640(5), which provides:

> *Each licensee shall include in all bids he submits or contracts he enters into for construction work within this State, the number of his license and any monetary limit placed upon his license.*

The Board investigators have construed these provisions to require that license numbers and bid limitations be provided on all material which could be considered advertising. While such interpretations may be a stretch of a good face reading of both the statutes and the administrative regulations, there is little benefit in the fighting over such issues with the investigators, as the costs of such legal arguments often exceed the costs of printing the requirement information on all documents used in the business enterprise.

In additional substantial disclosures must be made as part of contractual relations with the public. Initially, a general contractor must provide a Notice to Owner of Mechanics Lien Law form,[77] which provides owners with a brief notice to expect preliminary notices from subcontractors and suppliers on the project. In addition, general contractors entering into contracts with the owner of a single family residence must provide the owner with the name, license number, business address and telephone number of all subcontractors and material suppliers who will provide the project with materials of over $500 or more,[78] as well as a preprinted notice from the NSCB that complies with the requirements of NRS 624.600(3).[79]

In addition to these notice requirements, contractors who are to perform work on residential swimming pools and spas have substantial notice requirements, as well.[80] These requirements cannot be waived or limited by contract or otherwise. The contract that does not meet these requirements is void and unenforceable against the homeowner.

2:9 License Renewals

The NSCB renews contractors' licenses as they expire. They can be renewed for up to 2 years at a time.[81] As the license nears expiration, the NSCB will mail a renewal package

---

[77] *See* Form 8-1 in Appendix A; see also NRS 108.246.

[78] NRS 624.600 provides:

> *A general building contractor shall provide in writing to the owner of a single-family residence with whom he or she has contracted:*
> *1. The name, license number, business address and telephone number of:*
> *(a) All subcontractors with whom he or she has contracted on the project; and*
> *(b) All persons who furnish material of the value of $500 or more to be used in the project.*
> *2. A notice that a person described in subsection 1 may record a notice of lien upon the residence of the owner and any building, structure and improvement thereon pursuant to the provisions of NRS 108.226.*
> *3. An informational form, whose contents must be prescribed by the Board, regarding:*
> *(a) Contractors pursuant to chapter 624 of NRS; and*
> *(b) Mechanics' and materialmens' liens pursuant to chapter 108 of NRS.*

[79] *See* Form 2-15 in Appendix A.

[80] NRS 624.940; see also NAC 624.695, et seq.

[81] NRS 624.283 provides:

> *1. Each license issued under the provisions of this chapter expires 2 years after the date on which it is issued, except that the Board may by regulation prescribe shorter or longer periods and prorated fees to establish a system of staggered biennial renewals. Any license which is not renewed on or before the date for renewal is automatically suspended.*
> *2. A license may be renewed by submitting to the Board:*
> *(a) An application for renewal;*
> *(b) The fee for renewal fixed by the Board;*

to the licensee, which outlines the required information and documents that must be submitted to renew the license for an additional 2 years.[82] If the renewal is not

---

> *(c) Any assessment required pursuant to NRS 624.470 if the holder of the license is a residential contractor as defined in NRS 624.450; and*
> *(d) All information required to complete the renewal.*
> *3. The Board may require a licensee to demonstrate his financial responsibility at any time through the submission of:*
> *(a) A financial statement that is:*
> *(1) Prepared by an independent certified public accountant; or*
> *(2) Submitted on a form or in a format prescribed by the Board together with an affidavit which verifies the accuracy of the financial statement; and*
> *(b) If the licensee performs residential construction, such additional documentation as the Board deems appropriate.*
> *4. If a license is automatically suspended pursuant to subsection 1, the licensee may have the license reinstated upon filing an application for renewal within 6 months after the date of suspension and paying, in addition to the fee for renewal, a fee for reinstatement fixed by the Board, if the licensee is otherwise in good standing and there are no complaints pending against the licensee. If the licensee is otherwise not in good standing or there is a complaint pending, the Board shall require the licensee to provide a current financial statement prepared by an independent certified public accountant or establish other conditions for reinstatement. An application for renewal must be accompanied by all information required to complete the renewal. A license which is not reinstated within 6 months after it is automatically suspended may be cancelled by the Board, and a new license may be issued only upon application for an original contractor's license.*

[82] NAC 624.630 provides:

> *1. The Board will mail to each licensee, at his or her address of record, an application for the renewal of his or her license. Except as otherwise provided in subsection 2, the licensee must return the completed application to the Board not later than the last day of the month in which the license expires. If the Board prescribes a shorter or longer period of validity for the licensee pursuant to NRS 624.283, the Board will notify the licensee of that fact.*
> *2. If the Board has requested that a licensee submit a financial statement with the application for renewal, the licensee must return to the Board, not later than the first day of the month in which the license expires, a completed application, the renewal fee and:*
> *(a) For a licensee whose license is issued before June 30, 2010:*
> *(1) If the monetary limit of the license is less than $1,000,000:*
> *(I) A current financial statement prepared by an independent certified public accountant;*
> *(II) A current financial statement submitted on a form prescribed by the Board and accompanied by an affidavit that verifies the accuracy of the financial statement; or*
> *(III) A current financial statement prepared using accounting software in accordance with generally accepted accounting principles and accompanied by an affidavit that verifies the accuracy of the financial statement; or*
> *(2) If the monetary limit of the license is $1,000,000 or more, a financial statement that is prepared and reviewed or audited by a certified public accountant within 1 year before the filing of the application.*
> *(b) For a licensee whose license is issued on or after June 30, 2010, the financial statement required by NAC 624.593.*
> *3. If a licensee fails:*
> *(a) To renew his or her license before it expires, a late fee will be charged as set forth in NAC 624.130.*
> *(b) To attempt renewal within the first 6 months of the new license biennium, the Board will deny, revoke or refuse to renew the license. In either situation, the licensee must apply for a new license.*

submitted, the license will automatically be suspended, which forbids the licensee from working on any new contracts or submitting additional bids until the license is renewed.[83]

Similar to the application for a new license, the Board will in most cases require a renewal license applicant to provide a current financial statement. Those financial statements will need to be audited or reviewed by a certified public accountant within one year of submission if the licensee's bid limitation is in excess of $1 million. If the licensee fails to return the completed application no later than the 30th day of the month in which the license expires, the Board will charge a late fee. If the licensee does not provide a renewal within 6 months after the license expires, the license will be revoked and a new license application will be needed if the licensee desires to hold a valid license in the state of Nevada.

2:10 Denial and Appeal Options

In the event that the Board denies an applicant for a license to be issued or renewed, the Board is required to notify the applicant of the denial in writing and to also include therewith a notice of the applicant's rights to have the denial reviewed in a hearing before the Board.[84] The applicant must submit his request for a hearing within 60 days

---

> *4. If a licensee has filed a timely application for renewal, accompanied by the required fee, but necessary information is lacking, the Board will conditionally renew the license until the information is received. If the information is not received within a reasonable time, the Board will deny the renewal.*
> *5. If the completed application for renewal contains information which warrants the action, the Board will impose or reduce the limits upon the license, or remove a classification or subclassification from the license.*

[83] *See* NRS 624.302(1).

[84] NRS 624.2545 provides:

> *1. If the Board denies an application for issuance or renewal of a license pursuant to this chapter, the Board shall send by certified mail, return receipt requested, written notice of the denial to the most current address of the applicant set forth in the records of the Board.*
> *2. A notice of denial must include, without limitation, a statement which explains that the applicant has a right to a hearing before the Board if the applicant submits a written request for such a hearing to the Board within 60 days after the notice of denial is sent to the address of the applicant pursuant to this section.*
> *3. If an applicant who receives a notice of denial pursuant to this section desires to have the denial reviewed at a hearing before the Board, he must submit a written request for a hearing before the Board concerning the denial within 60 days after the notice of denial is sent to his address. If an applicant does not submit notice in accordance with this subsection, the applicant's right to a hearing shall be deemed to be waived.*
> *4. Except as otherwise provided in this subsection, if the Board receives notice from an applicant pursuant to subsection 3, the Board shall hold a hearing on the decision to deny the application of the applicant within 90 days after the date the Board receives notice pursuant to subsection 3. If an applicant requests a continuance and the Board grants the continuance, the hearing required pursuant to this subsection may be held more than 90 days after the date the Board receives notice pursuant to subsection 3.*

of the denial notice being sent to the Board. Although it would seem obvious that the Notice of denial should contain reasons for the Board decision, there is no requirement in either the governing statutes or the Board's administrative regulations that mandates such a disclosure. As such, the Board may not provide a denied applicant with as thorough and detailed reasons for the declination as the applicant may desire. There is little authority for forcing the Board to reveal such information, as Nevada law seems to hold that the decision to provide administrative discovery and information lays within the discretion of the administrative agency.[85]

There is no outlined procedure for this hearing in the Nevada Revised Statutes or the Nevada Administrative Code. In practice, these hearings are usually scheduled as agenda items on the Board's ordinary meeting schedule and are handled summarily. While the denied applicant is provided the opportunity to verbally "plead his case" to the Board, there is little opportunity to present evidence or witnesses. As such, unless the Board determines that it will accept additional information based on the pleas of the applicant, the Board's initial determination may be upheld in most cases. While an action for judicial review of any administrative agency decisions is available under Nevada law, great deference is given to the administrative board's position and discretion. It is therefore the rare occurrence that the Board's decision to deny an application for licensure is overturned.

2:11 CLAIMS AGAINST THE NEVADA STATE CONTRACTOR'S RECOVERY FUND

In an effort to further protect consumers from injuries suffered as a result of a contractor's Nevada Contractor's License Law violation, the Nevada legislature established a Construction Recovery Fund to assist the public in recouping money lost by false acts of residential contractors. The fund is financed through licensing fees paid by residential contractors. The fund will only protect members of the general public who own a residence and who have contracted with a residential contractor for construction services and have been injured thereby.[86] There are a number of potentially injured persons, however, who cannot recover from the Recovery Fund. These have expanded in recent years. For instance, the recovery fund cannot be used by a contractor or supplier to recover trade debts.

---

[85] In *Dutchess Business Services, Inc. v. Nevada State Bd. of Pharmacy*, 191 P.3d 1159 (Nev. 2008), the Nevada Supreme Court ruled that the decision to provide any administrative or pre-litigation documentation or investigative notes lies within the discretion of the administrative agency. A practitioner should assume that acquiring a full disclosure of information may not be easily obtained.

[86] *See* NRS 624.400, et seq. This has also been interpreted by the Board as only allowing for the receipt of money from the recovery fund as a result of actions of the contractor with whom the person has contracted directly. A consumer cannot therefore recover for damages caused by a subcontractor, without making a claim against the general contractor. Effectively, this limits the individual to one recovery from the recovery fund of up to $35,000.00. A person may not use the recovery fund to collect multiple payments because multiple subcontractors caused the problems suffered.

The maximum recovery for a person under the recovery fund is $35,000.00.[87] The maximum that may be paid out against any one contractor cannot exceed a total of $400,000.00.[88] In order to prosecute the claim, the owner must submit a complaint to the Board under NRS 624.480, which must be filed within 4 years of the completion of the contractor's work which forms the basis of the recovery,[89] or 2 years after the entry of a judgment against the contractor from a court of competent jurisdiction.[90] The complaint is prepared on a form provided by the NSCB for the public's use.[91] The Board will hold a hearing on the complaint[92] and, upon a finding that the complaint is justified, will issue a check from the recovery fund to the claimant. The Board must take action on the complaint within 6 months of its filing with the Board.[93]

2:12 Bidder Preferences on Public Works

The licensed Nevada contractor who has paid state and local taxes for 60 consecutive months can apply to the NSCB for a certification of eligibility to receive a bidders preference on public works projects.[94] The procedures and requirements for obtaining such certificates are set forth in NAC 624.685 to 624.6899, inclusive. In general, a contractor seeking to obtain a certification for eligibility needs to provide an application therefore, including an affidavit from his accountant attesting to the payment of sales and use taxes in the State of Nevada for the previous 60 consecutive months, in the

---

[87] See NRS 624.510(3).

[88] See NRS 624.510(7).

[89] NRS 624.480 provides:

> *Except as otherwise provided in NRS 624.490, an injured person who wishes to recover from the account must file a complaint with the Board or its designee within 4 years after the completion of qualified services.*

[90] NRS 624.490 provides:

> *Within 2 years after an injured person has obtained a judgment in any court of competent jurisdiction for recovery of damages against a residential contractor for an act or omission of the residential contractor that is in violation of this chapter or the regulations adopted pursuant thereto, the injured person may apply to the Board for satisfaction of the judgment from the account if:*
> *1. The proceedings in connection with the judgment have terminated, including appeals;*
> *2. The injured person submits an application on a form established for this purpose by the Board;*
> *3. The injured person submits proof satisfactory to the Board of the judgment; and*
> *4. Upon obtaining payment from the account, the injured person assigns his or her rights to enforce the judgment to the Board.*

[91] *See* Form 2-16 in Appendix A.

[92] Procedures for the hearing are found in NAC 624.700, et seq., and should be followed as strictly as possible by the claimant.

[93] NRS 624.500(4).

[94] *See* Section 6:10, Certificate of Eligibility for Bidding Preference.

amount of $5,000 or more.[95] The Board will review the application and accompanying affidavits and issue a certificate of eligibility. The certificate is valid for 60 days from the date of issuance. It may thereafter be renewed as the contractor should request, by filing supplemental applications and affidavits from the accountant for the contractor.[96]

The bidder's preference was been encumbered by the passage of the Nevada First Act, in 2011. This Act amended the preference eligibility by requiring the execution of an affidavit certifying that the contractor under take certain obligations to employ Nevada residents. The failure to abide by the obligations after execution of the affidavit and obtaining the project based on the preference will impose potential liquidated damages, loss of public contracting qualification and loss of eligibility for a bidder's preference.[97]

The Board will likewise deny or revoke a certificate of eligibility, and notify all governmental agencies of such revocation, if the contractor is found to have falsified any information on his application or renewal applications for certification.[98] Most instances of revocation will occur when the Board is informed of a successful challenge to a certificate of eligibility presented to a public entity during a bid protest. In such cases, the NSCB will investigate and revoke any certificate that is determined to not have been

---

[95] *See* Form 2-17 in Appendix A. NAC 624.687(1) provides in pertinent part:

> *1. A contractor who wishes to obtain a certificate of eligibility must submit to the Board:*
> *(a) An application on a form provided by the Board;*
> *(b) A notarized affidavit for a certificate of eligibility on a form provided by the Board;*
> *(c) A notarized statement of compliance on a form provided by the Board;*
> *(d) The fee set forth in NAC 624.130; and*
> *(e) Any other documentation required by the Board.*

[96] *See* Form 2-18 in Appendix A.

[97] *See* Section 6:11; The Nevada First Act was substantially amended in 2013 to remove some of the uncertainty it created for both contractors and public entities employing them. However, the actual implementation of the Act and whether it actually will accomplish its goals of getting more Nevadan's employed remains in question. In practice, in order to avoid the seemingly overly burdensome reporting requirements, some public entities have not required the affidavit when the two lowest bidders both qualified for the preference, essentially deciding the preference has no effect so there is no need to require the affidavit.

[98] NAC 624.6893 provides:

> *1. If a contractor who applies to the Board for a certificate of eligibility submits false or misleading information, submits an application which is incomplete or does not comply with this chapter or chapter 338 or 624 of NRS, the Board may:*
> *(a) Deny the application;*
> *(b) If the contractor has received a certificate of eligibility, revoke the certificate of eligibility; or*
> *(c) Take such actions that the Board deems appropriate under the circumstances.*
> *2. In carrying out the provisions of this section, the Board may rely on information contained in the records maintained by the Board and need not conduct any investigation, inquiry or hearing regarding the information contained in those records.*

issued on truthful and correct application information.[99] The contractor who is successfully challenged on the certification will have that certification immediately revoked and is not entitled to any hearing before the revocation is effective.

2:13. Conversions, Changes and Other Alterations

In the course of business, a contractor may have a number of reasons that changes to the license may be necessary. For instance, a person with an individual license may decide to incorporate his construction business. That will require a conversion of the individual license to a corporate license. A contractor operating as a general partnership may need to add or delete a partner, thereby requiring a new license application. Or a contractor may decide that he needs to replace the qualified employee of the company, and again, that requires a change to the license.

Unfortunately, when these changes occur many contractors do not recognize that such business changes mandate notification to the NSCB at a minimum, and may actually invalidate the contractor's current license automatically. Unless the full change is vetted for licensure issues, the contractor may find himself in administrative disciplinary proceedings, paying substantial fines or having his license revoked. Therefore, the construction practitioner should always keep license issues in mind as contracting businesses are changed or major decisions are contemplated.

The change of the contractor's business entity type will almost always require a new contractor's license application. Failing to revise the contractor's license can cause liability for the previous form entity, and can leave the new entity guilty of contracting without a license at all. The most common occurrence is the individual license holder who decides for whatever reason to form a corporation or limited liability company for his business. While the corporation can be formed in short order through the Nevada Secretary of State, the new entity is not automatically licensed because the sole member or sole shareholder holds an individual contractor's license. In fact, the failure to obtain a license in the new entity's name will make the individual license holder personally liable for the work that is performed, as only the licensed entity can legally contract to perform the contracting work. The corporate shell will be easily by-passed in such circumstances.

Likewise, the change of the qualified employee will leave the contractor with only 30 days to obtain a new qualified employee, and submit the proper paperwork to the NSCB

---

[99] NAC 624.6899 provides:

> *1. If a public body determines that a written objection is accompanied by the required proof or substantiating evidence pursuant to subsection 14 of NRS 338.1389 or subsection 14 of NRS 338.147, the public body shall notify the Board in writing of the determination of the public body within 30 days after the date of its determination.*
> *2. Upon receipt of the written documentation from the public body, the Board or its designee will immediately revoke the certificate of eligibility for the contractor. No formal disciplinary hearing is required before revocation of the certificate of eligibility based upon the receipt of the documentation from the public body which received the bid or proposal on a contract for the completion of a public work.*

for approval.[100] If the contractor does not replace the qualifier, the contractor's license can be automatically suspended or even revoked entirely by the NSCB. As such, the contractor should always be proactive in notifying the Board of corporate changes affecting its contractor's license, and to be diligent in the processing of those changes.

2:14. License Limitations and Performance Restrictions

As has been previously mentioned in this Chapter, most licenses are restricted in some fashion or another in Nevada. It is only the Unlimited AB classification license which gives the license holder virtually unlimited ability to construct any project in the State of Nevada,[101] as this classification allows for the construction of any project within both the A,[102] and a B[103] license with unlimited bid limitations. Thereafter, all license

---

[100] NRS 624.285 provides:

> *1. If the natural person qualifying by examination on behalf of another natural person or a firm pursuant to subsection 2 of NRS 624.260 ceases for any reason to be connected with the licensee to whom the license is issued, the licensee shall notify the Board in writing within 10 days after the cessation of association or employment. If a notice is given, the license remains in force for a reasonable length of time to be set by the Board, but not exceeding 30 days after the date of the cessation of association or employment.*
> *2. The licensee shall replace the person originally qualified with another natural person similarly qualified and approved by the Board within the time limited by subsection 1, unless extended by the Board for good cause.*
> *3. If the licensee fails to notify the Board within the 10-day period his license must be automatically suspended. The license must be reinstated upon the replacement of the person originally qualified by another natural person similarly qualified and approved by the Board.*
> *4. If the licensee fails to replace the person originally qualified within the 30-day period, his license may be suspended or revoked.*

[101] NAC 624.180 provides:

> *General building and general engineering. (NRS 624.100, NRS 624.220) The Board will grant a "classification AB" license in the branches of general building and general engineering to persons who are qualified to act as both general building (classification B) and general engineering (classification A) contractors. This classification is limited to those applicants or licensees who can show a sufficient degree of experience and financial responsibility to support an unlimited license in both the A and B classifications.*

[102] NAC 624.150 provides as follows and allows a licensed contractor to perform all of the listed subclassifications as a subcontractor as well:

> *The subclassifications of a license designated classification A and the work authorized for persons licensed in the respective subclassifications are:*
> *1. AIRPORTS (subclassification A-1): The construction, alteration and repair of airports, including any navigational equipment, lights, beacons, markers, taxiways, runways, hangars and terminals.*
> *2. HIGHWAYS (subclassification A-2): The construction of highways, roads, streets and other public ways used for vehicular travel, including any drains, tunnels, bridges and other appurtenances to the construction.*
> *3. DAMS AND RESERVOIRS (subclassification A-3): The construction, whether from earth, masonry, steel or concrete, or any combination of these materials, of dams and reservoirs designed to obstruct, control or use water, including the relocation of existing structures, any necessary excavation and the construction of embankments, foundations, piles, piers, spillways, tunnels, roadways and other incidental work.*

4. BRIDGES (subclassification A-4): The installation, construction, alteration and repair of bridges which are fabricated of steel, masonry, concrete or other suitable materials, and are designed for use by pedestrians or moving traffic, and any abutments, foundations, piles, piers, culverts, roadways and other appurtenances to the bridges.

5. DIAMOND AND CORE DRILLING (subclassification A-5): The obtainment by diamond or core drilling, of concrete, soil and rock.

6. DRILLING OF OIL, GAS AND EXPLORATORY WELLS (subclassification A-6): The drilling, altering and repair of existing or new oil, gas or exploratory wells, including the casing, packing and installation of pumps and other supplemental material, equipment or structures.

7. EXCAVATING AND GRADING (subclassification A-7): The digging, movement and placement of material forming the surface of the earth, other than water, with hand and power tools, machines and explosives to cut, fill, excavate, grade, backfill and perform other similar excavating, grading and trenching operations.

8. SEALING AND STRIPING OF ASPHALTIC SURFACES (subclassification A-8): The filling of cracks and voids in existing asphaltic surfaces, the application of sealants and the installation of precast bumpers, traffic signs, nonelectrical markers and striping on the surfaces.

9. PIERS AND FOUNDATIONS (subclassification A-9): The examination, excavation, drilling, compacting, pumping, sealing and other work necessary to construct, alter or repair piers, piles, footings and foundations placed in the earth's subsurface to prevent structural settling and to provide an adequate capacity to sustain or transmit the structural load to the soil or rock below.

10. COMMERCIAL AND RESIDENTIAL POOLS (subclassification A-10): The construction, alteration and repair of commercial and residential pools and spas, used for swimming, therapy or decoration, including any appurtenant equipment. The sub-subclassifications of this subclassification are:

(a) RESIDENTIAL POOLS (sub-subclassification A-10a): The construction, alteration and repair of residential pools and spas, used for swimming, therapy or decoration, including any appurtenant equipment.

(b) RESIDENTIAL SPAS (sub-subclassification A-10b): The construction and repair of residential spas, including any appurtenant equipment.

(c) REPAIR OF POOLS AND SPAS (sub-subclassification A-10c): The repair and replacement of plaster, coping and coating of pool decks on residential pools and spas.

(d) POOLS AND SPAS OF FIBERGLASS (sub-subclassification A-10d): The construction and repair of residential pools and spas which are made of fiberglass.

(e) MAINTENANCE AND REPAIR OF POOLS AND SPAS (sub-subclassification A-10e): The alteration and repair of plaster, tile, coping, pumps, filters, heaters, decking, pool painting, timers, controls and lights on residential and commercial spas, pools, fountains, waterfalls and ponds.

(f) WATER AND GAS LINES FOR RESIDENTIAL POOLS AND SPAS (sub-subclassification A-10f): The installation of water and gas service lines from the point of service to the pool equipment of the pool or spa of a single-family residence. Work in this sub-subclassification is authorized only for the holder of a certificate as a master plumber, journeyman plumber or journeyman in a plumbing specialty, or an equivalent certificate, issued by the appropriate local building department.

11. RECYCLING ASPHALT (subclassification A-11): The scarifications of existing asphaltic mat, the raking of the asphalt into rows, its pulverization, the incorporation of necessary additives, the aeration, spreading and compacting of the asphalt and the application of a coating composed of such ingredients as asphaltic concrete or slurry.

12. EXCAVATING, GRADING, TRENCHING AND SURFACING (subclassification A-12): All work authorized for a license of subclassification A-7 and the mixing, fabrication and placement of pavement and surfaces consisting of graded mineral aggregates, asphalt or concrete products.

13. WRECKING BUILDINGS (subclassification A-13): The wrecking of existing structures by the use of tools, equipment or explosives, and the raising, cribbing and underpinning of buildings and other structures so that alterations, repairs and new substructures may be constructed under the retained and undisturbed portion of the building or other structure.

14. STEEL ERECTION AND INDUSTRIAL MACHINERY (subclassification A-14): The fabrication and erection of steel shapes and plates, regardless of shape or size, to be used as structural members, including any related riveting, welding and rigging, and the installation of any industrial machinery.

15. SEWERS, DRAINS AND PIPES (subclassification A-15): The laying of cast-iron, steel, concrete, vitreous and nonvitreous pipe for sewers, drains and irrigation, including any related excavating, grading, trenching, backfilling, paving and surfacing, and the fabrication and erection of cesspools and septic tanks.

16. PAVING OF STREETS, DRIVEWAYS AND PARKING LOTS (subclassification A-16): Examination, excavation, grading, compacting, alteration and repair in the application of asphalt to streets, driveways, parking lots, boat ramps, and landing strips and taxiways for an airport.

17. LINES TO TRANSMIT ELECTRICITY (subclassification A-17): The installation, alteration and repair of primary overhead lines which transmit electricity, including the erection of poles, towers, anchors, guys, transformers, substations, circuit breakers and any other related hardware, equipment or systems.

18. FARM IRRIGATION (subclassification A-18): The excavation, fabrication, installation, alteration and repair of pipes, pumps, fixtures and any other material and equipment used in or incidental to systems for irrigating crops.

19. PIPELINE AND CONDUITS (subclassification A-19): The fabrication and installation of electrical conduits only, and pipelines including the trenching, boring, shoring, backfilling, compacting, paving, surfacing and application of protective coatings necessary to complete only the installation of the pipes and conduits. A person who holds a subclassification A-19 may perform any of the work authorized for the following subclassifications:

(a) Water (subclassification A-19a).

(b) Gas (subclassification A-19b).

20. INDUSTRIAL PIPING (subclassification A-20): The fabrication and installation of pipes for the transmission of steam, gases, chemicals and other substances required for industrial manufacturing or commercial operations and any related excavation, trenching and backfilling.

21. FENCING AND GUARDRAILS (subclassification A-21): The assembling, cutting, shaping, fabricating and installing of wood or metal fencing, guardrails, signs and nonelectric markers for highways, equipment for playgrounds and supplemental materials.

22. UNCLASSIFIED (subclassification A-22): Work limited in scope by the Board to a specialty which is supported by the licensee's knowledge and experience in a trade or craft and which is not included in the other subclassifications of a license in classification A.

23. REMOVAL OF ASBESTOS (subclassification A-23): The cleaning, handling, repair, removal, encapsulation, enclosure, hauling and disposal of, or other work with, materials containing asbestos.

24. FOUNTAINS AND OTHER WATER FEATURES (subclassification A-24): The construction, alteration and repair of commercial and residential fountains, waterfalls, ponds and similar water features not intended to serve as swimming pools, including any appurtenant equipment.

25. TELECOMMUNICATION TOWERS (subclassification A-25): The fabrication and erection of towers used to support telecommunication equipment, including any related riveting, welding and rigging, and the installation of electrical components and related equipment.

[103] NAC 624.160 provides:

> *The Board will grant to qualified applicants a license in the branch of general building. The Board designates such a license as a "classification B" license. A person who holds a classification B license may perform the work described in subsection 3 of NRS 624.215.*

and NRS 624.215(3) provides:

> *A general building contractor is a contractor whose principal contracting business is in connection with the construction or remodeling of buildings or structures for the support, shelter and enclosure of persons, animals, chattels or movable property of any kind, requiring in their construction the use of more than two unrelated building trades or crafts, upon which he is a prime contractor and where the construction or remodeling of a building is the primary purpose. Unless he holds the appropriate specialty license, a general building contractor may only contract to perform specialty contracting if he is a prime contractor on a project. A general building contractor shall not perform specialty contracting in plumbing, electrical, refrigeration and air-conditioning or fire protection without a license for the specialty. A person who exclusively constructs or repairs mobile homes, manufactured homes or commercial coaches is not a general building contractor.*

classifications are restrictive on the work that may be performed. If a contractor is uncertain as to whether a type of specific work is authorized under his license classification, it is important to inquire of the NSCB about that work. Some work outside the license classification can be performed which is incidental to the main work of the project under certain circumstances,[104] so long as that out of classification work is merely incidental or supplemental to the work of the classification. Unfortunately, there is no authority or guideline provided by the NSCB that defines incidental or supplemental as it relates to out-of-license-classification work. In practice, allegations of incidental and supplemental work have been a matter of personal judgment of the NSCB investigator based on the circumstances of the case. Therefore, before a contractor relies on the designation of incidental and supplemental, the contractor should seek an advisory opinion from the NSCB.

Of particular importance, however, is the understanding that a general building contractor, i.e., one holding a B classification license, cannot perform work requiring a sub-classification specialty "C" license under the B license unless he is performing two or more specialty sub-classification trades on the project.[105] In no event, however, can the class B general building contractor perform specialty contracting in plumbing, electrical, refrigeration and air-conditioning or fire protection without the specific sub-classification license for that work.[106] Moreover, some jurisdictions with authority have refused to allow contractors holding a class B license from pulling specialty permits, such as demolition, unless the contractor can produce either a construction contract for the entire work of improvement, or a specialty license for the permitted work. Hence, the contractor should be prepared for such eventualities and impediments to their work based on license issues, and take steps to ensure that no such issue may arise.

2:15 Special Rules on Company Names

NRS 624.254 provides:

> *No license may be issued or renewed by the Board under a name which:*
> *1. Is the same as the name of another licensee;*
> *2. So resembles the name of another licensee that the Board determines that it is likely to result in confusion or mistake; or*
> *3. The Board determines is likely to mislead the general public.*

---

[104] NRS 624.220(4) provides:

> *Subject to the provisions of regulations adopted pursuant to subsection 5, nothing contained in this section prohibits a specialty contractor from taking and executing a contract involving the use of two or more crafts or trades, if the performance of the work in the crafts or trades, other than in which the specialty contractor is licensed, is incidental and supplemental to the performance of work in the craft for which the specialty contractor is licensed.*

[105] NRS 624.215(3).

[106] NRS 624.215(3).

As a general rule, if a requested contractor's name may cause any confusion between license holders, the Board will deny the second licensee application until a different name is chosen. The fact that the Nevada Secretary of State has allowed the formation of a corporation or other business entity with the similar name is not relevant to the NSCB. Rather, the NSCB is empowered with 100% discretion in the approval of the name of the licensee. More particularly, the initial decision on name approval will be made by the person processing the license application. Only an appeal to the actual Board will overturn the initial application name decision.

For this reason, as with every issue with the NSCB, care should be taken to discuss any potential rough issues with the processing personnel at the NSCB before the application is submitted. By getting the direction of those processing applications and making adjustments to the application before it is submitted, processing time to new licensure is dramatically reduced and problems can be reasonably overcome. Failure to address obvious issues before submitting the application will require that additional information be obtained and presented or could result in the outright denial of the application.

2:16 Bid Limitations

We have discussed in passing the necessity of keeping contracts within bid limits imposed upon a license by the NSCB and the effect of bidding beyond that limitation, however, it should be understood that the bid limitation is not just a general guideline for contractors to shoot towards in their contracts. The bid limitation is an actual limitation on the contracting ability of the licensed contractor and bidding beyond that license is the legal equivalent of contracting without a license. NRS 624.3015 provides in pertinent part:

> *The following acts, among others, constitute cause for disciplinary action under NRS 624.300:*
>
> ...
>
> *2. Bidding to contract or contracting for a sum for one construction contract or project in excess of the limit placed on the license by the Board.*
> *3. Knowingly bidding to contract or entering into a contract with a contractor for work in excess of his or her limit or beyond the scope of his or her license.*

The NSCB will construe the contract bid to include any change orders that are ultimately provided to the contractor. As such, the NSCB will hold a contractor in violation of these provisions if the total contract at the end of the project exceeds the contractors' bid limitation. It is also important to understand that both the contractor who submits a bid beyond the license limit and the contractor who accepts the bid and enters into a contract with that person are subject to discipline. Discipline will be an administrative citation and a fine of up to $50,000.[107] For this reason it is imperative that if a licensee

---

[107] NRS 624.300(3) provides in pertinent part:

> *If a licensee violates:*

intends to submit a bid beyond his license limitation, the licensee either applies for a full increase in the limitation or a one time increase before the bid is submitted.

A permanent bid limit increase is handled similarly to a new license application in terms of the financial responsibility requirements.[108] An application for permanent bid limit increase needs to be filed with the NSCB,[109] along with the necessary financial information and application fee. The NSCB will evaluate the financial information to determine the new bid limitation, which again will follow the same formulaic system for establishing the original bid limitation.[110]

The licensee can also request a one-time increase in limit for a specific project. In this case, the application[111] and additional documentation must be submitted to and approved by the NSCB at least five (5) days before the licensee submits its bid.[112] It should be noted that the licensee should not submit any bid or sign any contract until the one time increase in limit has been approved Given the ease of submitting a one-time increase application, there is little excuse for not doing so and the NSCB will not view the failure to do so with much leniency.

It should also be noted that clerical errors and other mistakes that lead to violations of the bid limitation prohibitions are not sufficient to defend the licensee from discipline from the Board. The Board's leveling of fines and administrative citations have been

---

> *(a) The provisions of NRS 624.3014, subsection 2 or 3 of NRS 624.3015, subsection 1 of NRS 624.302 or subsection 1 of NRS 624.305, the Board may impose for each violation an administrative fine in an amount that is not more than $50,000.*

108 *See* Section 2:5, Application for Contractor's License.

109 *See* Form 2-19 in Appendix A.

110 *See* Section 2:5, Application for Contractor's License.

111 *See* Form 2-20 in Appendix A.

112 NRS 624.220(3). NAC 624.670 provides:

> *1. A licensee may, in accordance with the provisions of NRS 624.220, submit to the Board a written application requesting an increase, for a single project, in the monetary limit on his or her license. Not more than five such applications may be submitted by a licensee during any 12-month period.*
> *2. A licensee must submit with the application:*
> *(a) The financial statement required by NAC 624.593; and*
> *(b) Any other supporting information the Board requests.*
> *3. The Board will approve the application if it finds that the financial status of the licensee is adequate to justify the increase and if the licensee:*
> *(a) Procures and agrees to maintain any performance or payment bond, or both, that the Board requires; and*
> *(b) Complies with any other conditions the Board finds necessary to protect the public interest.*

routinely upheld by Nevada Courts, even when it was established that if the contractor had created two contracts instead of one, there would have been no violation.[113]

2:17 Discipline and Violations

The primary responsibility of the NSCB's investigation arm is the review of complaints against contractors and the imposition of discipline for proven violations of the licensees under their authority. The NSCB will investigate any and all complaints filed against contractors, and as a result, the filing of a complaint with the NSCB has become a favored method for practitioners to attempt to force payment to subcontractors from higher-tiered contractors.

In general, the NSCB will not attempt to insert itself into disputed issues, if the dispute cannot be substantiated; that is, the NSCB cannot determine that the dispute is not justified by its investigation. However, if there is no genuine dispute the NSCB will use its powers for administrative discipline to force a capitulation by the contractor complained about. Defending the contractor from the NSCB investigation and complaint can be very difficult, as administrative agencies in Nevada are given a great deal of discretion in their actions governing those within their jurisdiction.

Initially, commencing a complaint is a fairly simple process of preparing the complaint form and filing it with the NSCB.[114] The practitioner should fill out the form completely and provide the NSCB with all the necessary documentation to prove the allegations of violations. NSCB prosecutable violations are found at NRS 624.301 to NRS 624.30175. When the practitioner is preparing the complaint, it should be determined what evidence is available to support the complaint and what remedy the complaining party is seeking. The NSCB will not substitute itself for a court of law. Rather, the NSCB will investigate a claim of violation of the law as it relates to a contractor's conduct, and will focus its investigation on that issue. The issues complained about should not require the NSCB to determine who delayed a project or whether a particular item of work was the responsibility between two contractors. Rather, the Board will seek clear violations of the law when there is no legitimate excuse for the failure to do so. If the complaint will require a weighing of evidence, it is unlikely that the NSCB investigator will substantiate the complaint.

Once the complaint is filed, the NSCB will assign an investigator who will review the complaint and send a notice to the accused contractor that a complaint has been filed. They will then seek to obtain information from the accused contractor to verify the complaint and any defense that the contractor may have. In most cases where a claim of lack of payment has been made in the complaint, the NSCB will also demand that the accused contractor provide proof of financial solvency.[115] As such, the practitioner

---

[113] *Gur-Kovic v. State Contractors Bd.*, 95 Nev. 489, 596 P.2d 850 (1979).

[114] *See* Form 2-21 in Appendix A.

[115] NRS 624.323 provides:

should be ready to have its client subject to an investigation be prepared to provide the appropriate financial statements. The NSCB is not limited in any way to the information complained of in the complaint. The NSCB investigator is free to review all information provided and to make determinations of any other violations that result from that investigation, including the review of the contractor's license bid limitation if it is not supported by the newly provided financial statements demanded in the investigation.

If the investigation supports the complaint, the NSCB investigator will hold an informal meeting of the contractor and the complaining party. In most cases, counsel is allowed for both parties to attend. While the meeting must be held promptly, reasonable written requests for continuances are usually granted. The accused contractor should be fully prepared to discuss the complained of issues with the investigator and should provide any evidence that will assist in his defense. The investigator may continue the meeting for the parties or the investigator to obtain additional information, or they may inform the parties of the complaint disposition at that time. If the complaint is not verified, the NSCB investigator will send a notice to the complainant that the claim was not substantiated and closed. If the claim is substantiated and the complainant has suffered damages as a result, the NSCB Investigator will issue a Notice to Correct letter.

The Notice to Correct letter spells out the allegations of violation that the NSCB investigation unit has been able to substantiate. The Contractor is given a period of time, approximately 30 days, to correct the condition cited. The contractor can accept the

---

1. In addition to any other requirements set forth in this chapter, if an investigation is conducted against a licensee and the Board determines that there is cause to proceed with a formal disciplinary proceeding against the licensee, the Board shall require the licensee to submit to the Board:
(a) A financial statement that is:
(1) Prepared by an independent certified public accountant; or
(2) Submitted on a form or in a format prescribed by the Board together with an affidavit which verifies the accuracy of the financial statement; and
(b) A statement setting forth the number of building permits issued to and construction projects completed by the licensee during the immediately preceding year and any other information required by the Board. The statement submitted pursuant to this paragraph must be provided on a form approved by the Board.
2. After providing the licensee with notice and an opportunity to be heard, the Board must determine whether, based on the financial information concerning the licensee, it would be in the public interest to do any or all of the following:
(a) Require the licensee to obtain the services of a construction control with respect to any money that the licensee requires a purchaser of a new residence to pay in advance to make upgrades to the new residence. If the Board imposes such a requirement, the licensee may not:
(1) Be related to the construction control or to an employee or agent of the construction control; or
(2) Hold, directly or indirectly, a financial interest in the business of the construction control.
(b) Establish an aggregate monetary limit on the contractor's license, which must be the maximum combined monetary limit on all contracts that the licensee may undertake or perform as a licensed contractor at any one time, regardless of the number of contracts, construction sites, subdivision sites or clients. If the Board establishes such a limit, the Board:
(1) Shall determine the period that the limit is in effect; and
(2) During that period, may increase or decrease the limit as the Board deems appropriate.
3. The provisions of this section do not limit the authority of the Board to take disciplinary action against the licensee.

notice to correct and repair or undertake steps to complete the correction items. Once completed, the NSCB investigator will usually verify with the complaining party that the corrections have been made and will then close the file as substantiated and resolved. Depending on the severity of the violation, the NSCB investigator may also fine the contractor or issue an administrative citation. The contractor, however, may not be able to comply with the Notice to Correct for any of a number of reasons, including that the complaining party will not allow the contractor to enter into the project to make corrections or may wish to dispute the correction and/or citation requirement altogether. In this case, the NSCB investigator will file a formal complaint against the Contractor, requiring a hearing before a member of the NSCB, sitting as a hearing officer.

Procedures for handling the hearing and subpoenaing witnesses are set forth in NRS 624.327 to NRS 624.372, inclusive, as well as NAC 624.6975 to NAC 624.770, inclusive. The procedures breakdown into two separate types of complaints: administrative citation procedures,[116] and Claims seeking a recovery of monetary damages from the contractor.[117]

---

116 *See* NAC 624.6975 to NAC 624.7296.

117 *See* NAC 624.730 to NAC 624.770.

Chapter 3 Private Works Prompt Payment Act

3:1 Historical context and influence on Nevada contracting

One of the most important concepts affecting Nevada construction law is the application and reach of the Nevada Prompt Payment Act.[118] The Nevada Prompt Payment Act ("PPA") affects virtually every private works construction contract executed in the state of Nevada. The effect of the PPA is to mandate compliance with contractual terms or impose reasonable ones when contract terms don't exist or are over-reaching, regarding construction payments and change orders. The PPA requires an owner or higher tiered contractor to pay its lower tiered contractors by contractual due dates or imposes due dates when a written contract is silent. The PPA will also supersede contract terms dealing with change orders, imposing strict time tables for execution or rejection of change orders which, if not complied with, eviscerate the contractual change order clause and mandate submitted change order requests become part of the contractor's scope and time. Failure to abide by the requirements of the PPA allows the contractor to stop all work on the project and demobilize until the owner or higher-tiered contractor complies with the PPA requirements. Should demobilization not cure the payment or change order issue, the contractor is (in certain circumstances) allowed to terminate the contract and sue the higher-tiered contractor for breach of the now revised contract.

The PPA is another piece of contractor protection legislation that arises out of the perceived injustices of the *Venetian Casino Resort* litigation referenced in Chapter 1, Introduction and Preliminary Matters.[119] Enacted as Senate Bill 274 of the 71st Legislative Session in 2001, the PPA was presented as a joint bill of the Nevada construction industry and focused on the alleged inequity of the *Venetian Casino Resort* case and the perceived escalation of payment issues arising during the 1990's construction surge:

> *Senator O'Connell asked if the Venetian Resort-Hotel-Casino had paid the umbrella contractor for labor, services, and supplies. Mr. Holloway explained the owners of the Venetian had requested and received extras, add-ons, and improvements over and above the original plans. Contractors, subcontractors, and suppliers had most often not been paid for these expenses as well. The bulk of the money owed is to contractors, subcontractors, and suppliers from the original arrangements. He pointed out that in negotiations held between owners and contractors, subcontractors, and suppliers, many in the trades were forced to settle for reduced payment rates, oftentimes for less than 50 cents on the dollar, in order to stay in business or just stave off bankruptcy.*

---

[118] NRS 624.606, et seq.

[119] Minutes of the Senate Committee on Commerce and Labor, 71st Nevada Legislative Session, March 15, 2001.

Chairman Townsend asked how widespread the problem of nonpayment to contractors, subcontractors, and suppliers was overall. Ms. Perkins said the problem was increasingly becoming more and more widespread and was continuing to adversely affect all ongoing projects in Las Vegas, both large and small.

Senator Carlton asked if the problem of nonpayment had developed prior to the Venetian incidents during the past decade of mass expansion in Las Vegas. Mr. Peel said the problem had become more prevalent in the last 4 years. Prior to the building of the Venetian, issues of nonpayment were not a routine matter as they presently are. He said pamphlets describing how owners could avoid paying the full amount to contractors, subcontractors, and suppliers were being circulated in Las Vegas by unscrupulous people. Senator Carlton asked for approximate percentage increases this problem was causing before and after the Venetian problem escalated. Ms. Perkins said nonpayment incidents for her company more than doubled since the Venetian was built from a less than 30 percent incident rate to over 60 percent currently and rising. [20]

The PPA's provisions are far reaching, somewhat draconian and supersede or invalidate contractual provisions which are contrary to its purpose or modify its terms, as will be discussed in ensuing sections. For this reason, a practitioner should always keep the PPA's provisions in mind when drafting contracts or reviewing provisions which reflect upon the concepts addressed in the PPA. Because the PPA is relatively new, no citable case law has been issued examining these statutory provisions.[121] Therefore, contracts must be analyzed purely against the face of the statute and its intent and purpose.

3:2 Applicability

In general, the PPA will not apply to two areas of general contracts: 1) public works and 2) residential projects which are being built under a contract between the general contractor and a person who will own or occupy the home. However, because of the placement of the excepting provisions, there is some question as to whether the PPA only exempts the general contract in these situations. The excepting provisions are only found in NRS 624.622, which is applicable to general contracts, and governs the

---

[120] Minutes of the Senate Committee on Commerce and Labor, 71st Nevada Legislative Session, March 15, 2001.

[121] In late 2015, the Nevada Supreme Court issued an unpublished decision in the case of *Insulation Contracting & Supply, Inc. v. S3H, Inc.*, No. 62856, 2015 WL 5774180 (Nev. Sept. 29, 2015) which discussed the application of part of the PPA, as well as parts of the Nevada Mechanic's Lien Statutes which had also not previously been reviewed. A petition to have *Insulation Contracting* re-issued as a reported decision was filed, but as of the time of publication, no decision on that petition had been issued. Under current Nevada Supreme Court Rule 123, unpublished orders are not citable as authority in state court cases. Nevertheless, where context requires *Insulation Contracting* is referenced. The practitioner is cautioned, however, that until the Nevada Supreme Court rules on the petition for its publication, *Insulation Contracting* may not be cited as controlling authority before Nevada courts.

transactions between the owner and the general contractor. Similar exempting language is not found in NRS 624.624 to 624.628, which govern relations between "higher-tiered contractors" and "lower-tiered contractors."

NRS 624.622(4) of the PPA provides:

> *This section, NRS 624.609, 624.610 and 624.620 do not apply to an agreement between: (a) A prime contractor and a natural person who owns a single-family residence for the performance of qualified services with respect to the residence; or (b) A public body and a prime contractor for the performance of work and labor on a public work.*[122]

Some legislative history does address the exemptions of the statute, but these seem to support the concept that the exemptions only apply to the contracts between exempted owners and their general contractors.

> *Madelyn Shipman, Lobbyist, Assistant District Attorney, Civil Division, Washoe County, offered a proposed amendment to S.B. 274 which she read into the record (Exhibit C). Ms. Shipman's amended language affected section 3, subsection 10, of the proposed legislation and excluded that section of the legislation from applying to a contract between a residential contractor and a person who owns a single-family residence. Also, a public body and a contractor for a public works project would be exempt as well. ... Mr. Holloway said it was not the intent of his organization to include public works or state and local governments from the proposed legislation and therefore those entities would be exempt. Chairman Townsend asked if there were members of Mr. Holloway's organization who might have examples of the State Public Works Board defaulting on payment or not paying for labor, services, and supplies on a timely basis. Mr. Holloway responded in the affirmative and added that was the reason his organization sponsored legislation known as "the prompt pay bill."*[123]

The "prompt pay bill" referred to by Mr. Holloway in the above quote is found at NRS 338.400 to NRS 338.645, inclusive, which is discussed in Chapter 6, Public Works Construction, and applies only to public works construction. Those statutes govern payment relationships between both public owners and general contractors, as well as those between general contractors and their subcontractors and suppliers on public works projects. Arguably then, the comments by Mr. Holloway can be construed as supporting the idea that the PPA exemptions for public works also apply to subcontract agreements on public projects. Had the Legislature intended this PPA to apply to subcontract agreements on public works projects, they would not have enacted NRS 338.400, et seq.

---

[122] NRS 624.622.

[123] Minutes of the Senate Committee on Commerce and Labor, 71st Nevada Legislative Session, March 15, 2001.

While this is a reasonably convincing argument, the fact that the Legislature did not mention subcontract agreements in drafting NRS 624.622(4), and did not insert a corresponding provision in the portions of the PPA applicable to subcontractors (NRS 624.624 to NRS 624.628, inclusive), may also indicate the intent of the Legislature to only exempt public works general contracts from the provisions of the PPA. The fact that the legislative history only specifically discusses contracts between owners and general contractors likewise may indicate the exemptions should only apply to prime contracts.

With residential projects, the question becomes a bit murkier. NRS 624.031(4) exempts residential project owners from the entire scheme of NRS Chapter 624:

> *The provisions of this chapter do not apply to:... An owner of property who is building or improving a residential structure on the property for his own occupancy and not intended for sale or lease. The sale or lease, or the offering for sale or lease, of the newly built structure within 1 year after its completion creates a rebuttable presumption for the purposes of this section that the building of the structure was performed with the intent to sell or lease that structure. An owner of property who requests an exemption pursuant to this subsection must apply to the Board for the exemption. The Board shall adopt regulations setting forth the requirements for granting the exemption.*[124]

The owner's exemption request takes the form an Affidavit issued to the Nevada State Contractor's Board.[125] The form describes, the "owner" in this case is an "owner-builder" who acts as an actual contractor either constructing the work him or herself, or through the hiring and supervision of subcontractors. If the owner instead hires a general contractor to perform the work, the exemption certificate need not be applied for at all. As a result, there is a question of whether the provisions of NRS Chapter 624 would apply to anyone who is not actually acting in the capacity of a contractor. Chapter 624 governs the formation and rules that are applicable to the profession of contracting. Whether or not an individual, or someone who is only tangentially regulated by the rules governing those who interact with that group of persons, can be required to comply with those rules is not clear. Some may reasonably doubt that a statutory obligation under NRS Chapter 624 placed on a person not specifically governed by its provisions would be enforceable. As a practical matter, however, it is doubtful if the Nevada judiciary would focus on such arguments.[126]

---

[124] NRS 624.031(4).

[125] *See* Form 3-1 in Appendix A.

[126] Arguments that a professional licensing statute should not have applicability to those not holding such licenses may have some superficial appeal, however, the more persuasive argument in NRS Chapter 624 is for application to non-licensed owners. While Chapter 624 has outlined exceptions to certain owners of property, Chapter 624 has a scope of applicability which would also include owners of property and developers under certain circumstances.

NRS 624.005 is the legislative declaration for Chapter 624. It "declares that the provisions of this chapter relating to the discipline of licensees are intended to promote public confidence and trust in the competence and integrity of the licensees and to promote the health, safety and welfare of the public." [Emphasis added . The declaration does not state that the chapter is applicable exclusively to licensees nor does it preclude its application beyond licensees. It simply addresses the provisions dealing with the discipline of licensees and the purpose of those provisions. In fact, an attempt to interpret the chapter as only applying to licensed contractors is undermined by NRS 624.700, which states that it is unlawful for an unlicensed person to engage in business or submit bids without a license, and NRS 624.341(1)(a) allowing the NSCB to issue an administrative citation to an unlicensed person. This coupled with NRS 171.17751 (permitting state licensing board's designate to issue citations) demonstrate the chapter's scope of applicability over those individuals not licensed by the contractor's board. See also NRS 624.341(5).

While NRS 624.031 identifies owners that the chapter does not apply to, that exemption is limited. The statute identifies three specific owners who are exempt: "owners building or improving a residential structure..."; "an owner of a complex containing not more than four condominiums, townhouses, apartments or cooperative units..."; and an "owner of property, the primary use of which is an agricultural or farming enterprise." These would not the average project developer, in most cases. NRS 624.609 and NRS 624.610 specifically address duties to be performed by owners of construction projects that are not exempt. These specific requirements are discussed extensively in this Chapter.

In the PPA, we see the legislature's attempt to mitigate harm alleged by contractors and subcontractors, particularly an owner's or developer's failure to pay for work performed. The PPA outlines duties of the owner/developer to pay timely and the contractor's and subcontractor's right to stop work for non-payment. The PPA also outlines the rights of the owner/developer to retain a percentage of the amount owed for work under certain circumstances and the proper procedure for such retention.

In an attempt to interpret the PPA and its applicability to property owners, it is safe to assume that the courts will find that an absurd result would occur in the event that it was held that owners were not governed by the chapter. Two things are clear from the legislative intent: The first is that the legislature intended to protect contractors and subcontractors from owners/developers who failed to pay or pay timely on construction projects. The second was the legislature issued directives on how owners/developers were to conduct themselves in the area of paying their contractors and subcontractors. To remove the owner from the PPA's jurisdiction would cause the PPA to be of no value to the group it is designed to protect-contractors-as owners would be able to shield themselves from litigation for failure to pay. This type of shielding was prevented in Shimrak v. Garcia-Mendoza, 112 Nev. 246, 912 P.2d 822 (1996).

In Shimrak, Plaintiff sued attorney Garcia-Mendoza for services he provided as a private investigator. Ms. Garcia-Mendoza asserted a defense that paying investigator would be in violation of then Nevada Supreme Court Rule 188 ("SCR 188") which prohibits fee splitting with non-lawyers. However, the Court held that the rule was specific in its applicability to lawyers, not to non-lawyers, and violation of the rules subject only an offending attorney to sanctions. Moreover, the Court stated that not enforcing the contract between the parties "would actually endanger the public, because it would allow lawyers to enter into such contracts and then get out of them by invoking SCR 188."

Shimrak illustrates two important issues: First, the specificity of SCR 188 addresses only lawyers. The Court noted this specificity. In the Prompt Pay Act, the statute also is specific in addressing exactly what owners the statute is applicable to, what their obligations are and what exceptions apply. Second, the Court noted one of the purposes of SCR 188 in protecting the public, and apply the rule to the investigator would cause an absurd result. The Court would probably also find an absurd result would occur should

Such concerns, however, do not arise when a subcontractor is attempting to enforce those provisions on a "higher-tiered contractor", who is defined as the prime or general contractor under contract with the owner.[127] Clearly, the "higher-tiered contractor" is governed by the provisions of NRS Chapter 624. As such, a general contractor may be placed in the precarious position of having unenforceable statutory provisions "protecting" him from the actions of an unscrupulous or recalcitrant owner, but having to perform those obligations of payment required by the statute to his subcontractors. A general contractor must comply with the provisions of the PPA as to his subcontractors or face the penalties allowed to the subcontractor and even discipline by the NSCB.[128]

3:3 Requirements

The PPA requires that owners[129] pay their prime contractors[130] within certain time limits, and also limits the number of reasons that full or even partial payment can be

---

owners/developers be permitted to avoid the mandates of the PPA's because the very group the chapter is intended to protect would have no protection at all.

Another case to understand concerning specificity of a statute is Natchez v. State, 102 Nev. 247, 721 P.2d 361 (1986). In Natchez, Dr. Natchez appealed sanctions imposed upon him for violating NRS 636.300 which bars optometrist from being employed by non-optometrist. The Court noted that the legislature specifically provided in the plain language of the statute that ophthalmologist were included in the definition of “"a person not licensed to practice optometry" and “"not an optometrist" for purposes of NRS 636.300(2) and (5). Furthermore, NRS 636.390 provides that the chapter shall not be construed to apply to physicians and surgeons duly licensed to practice in this state.

Lastly, one should be cognizant of how the Nevada Supreme Court will interpret statutes and legislative history. In D.R. Horton, Inc. v. Eighth Judicial Dist. Court ex rel. County of Clark, 123 Nev. 468, 168 P.3d 731 (2007), a homeowners association prepared a pre-litigation notice of construction defect pursuant to NRS 40.645 and, unsatisfied with general contractor's response, filed a constructional defect action. The district court denied the general contractor's motion for a judgment declaring the pre-litigation notice was unreasonable and insufficient. The general contractor filed a petition for a writ of prohibition and mandamus. The dispute surrounded the issue of whether the homeowners association specified in “"reasonable detail" the defects alleged in their pre-trial notice, pursuant to NRS 40.645. In considering the parties' interpretations of the statute the Court concluded that they were both reasonable, but significantly different. The Court indicated that when statutory language is clear and unambiguous, plain meaning must be given unless doing so would violate the spirit of the statutory scheme: "The court reads legislative enactments as a whole in order to understand legislative intent. No part of statute may be rendered meaningless and language should not be read to produce absurd or unreasonable results." D.R. Horton, 168 P.3d at 738. Thus, in interpreting the PPA and its applicability to owners who do not hold contractors licenses, it should be considered that the Nevada courts would most probably apply the PPA to an owner and would interpret the PPA so as to give full effect to the legislative intent to protect contractors from the failure of owners to comply with its requirements.

[127] NRS 624.607.

[128] *See* Chapter 2, Contractor Licensing and Related Issues.

[129] NRS 624.6084 provides:

withheld. These same limitations are passed along to the prime contractors and other "higher-tiered contractors," [131] governing payment relationships with their subcontractors or "lower-tiered contractors."[132]

In addition to regulating payment issues, the PPA also sets out requirements for change order issuance. Essentially, the PPA mandates that a higher-tiered contractor respond to a change order within certain time parameters, or the PPA operates to deem the change order accepted by its terms. In dealing with both payment situations as well as change orders, the burden is shifted to the higher-tiered contractor to take some action relative to a lower-tiered contractor's request, otherwise the law steps in to enforce the lower-tiered contractor's request, regardless of its merit. Only by undertaking the statutorily proscribed procedures can the owner or higher-tiered contractor protect himself and preserve his legal rights.

3:4 Procedures on Payments for Owners

The PPA starts by inserting some terms governing when payments are due, if those terms have not been already negotiated between the Parties. While the parties (owners and prime contractors) are free to establish written payment schedules as they might, failure to define when payment is specifically due in the contract will result in the statutory terms being implemented. In this situation, the owner is required to either

---

> *1. 'Owner' means an owner or lessee of real property or any improvement who enters into an oral or written agreement with a prime contractor pursuant to which the prime contractor agrees to provide work, materials or equipment for a work of improvement.*
> *2. The term includes, without limitation, an owner of a planned unit development who enters into one or more oral or written agreements to construct a work of improvement in the planned unit development in the manner described in subsection 5 of NRS 624.020."*

[130] NRS 624.6087 provides:

> *'Prime contractor' means a contractor who enters into an oral or written agreement with an owner pursuant to which the prime contractor agrees to provide work, materials or equipment for a work of improvement.*

[131] NRS 624.607 provides:

> *'Higher-tiered contractor' means a prime contractor or subcontractor who has entered into an oral or written agreement with a lower-tiered subcontractor pursuant to which the lower-tiered subcontractor has agreed to provide work, materials or equipment for a work of improvement.*

[132] NRS 624.608 provides:

> *'Lower-tiered subcontractor' means a subcontractor who has agreed in an oral or written agreement with a higher-tiered contractor to provide work, materials or equipment for a work of improvement.*

make payment or to inform his prime contractors that payment will not be forthcoming and provide the reasons why.

NRS 624.609(1) provides:

> *Except as otherwise provided in subsections 2 and 4 and subsection 4 of NRS 624.622,*[133] *if an owner of real property enters into a written or oral agreement with a prime contractor for the performance of work or the provision of materials or equipment by the prime contractor, the owner must: (a) Pay the prime contractor on or before the date a payment is due pursuant to a schedule for payments established in a written agreement; or (b) If no such schedule is established or if the agreement is oral, pay the prime contractor within 21 days after the date the prime contractor submits a request for payment.*

The PPA does not define a "schedule for payments." Typically, a construction contract will schedule payment in one of two ways; a set interval based on a percentage of completion determined in a formulaic fashion, or in lump sum amounts based on a timetable of events. Webster's defines "schedule" as "an ordered list of times at which things are planned to occur."[134] The former payment method sets a time during the month when progress will be measured and then the progress payment will be calculated. Once calculated, there is a period of time to deliver the requested payment. However, errors or disputes over the calculation can impact the "date that payment is due" under such formulas, which raises a question as to whether an "ordered list of times at which things are planned to occur" has been established.

Regardless, if a schedule of payments exists, then the PPA requires that payment be made on or before the date that the schedule indicates payment is due. Otherwise, the owner is obligated to pay the prime contractor within 21 days of receipt of the prime contractor's invoice for payment. While this may seem reasonable in the abstract, it is often the case that the owner may dispute the amount the prime contractor claims is due in that invoice. This is certainly the case when payments are based on a percentage of acceptable work in place, and the calculation is subject to the interpretation of the parties involved. In this situation, the owner is obligated to inform the prime contractor of the dispute and any intention to withhold all or any part of the amount that is due to be paid to the prime contractor, whether demonstrated by invoice or by calculated formula.

NRS 624.609(3) provides:

---

[133] NRS 624.622(4) exempts public works and certain residential projects from the PPA. See Section 3:2, Applicability.

[134] Webster's Online Dictionary, http://www.websters-online-dictionary.org/definition/schedule, 2008.

> *If, pursuant to subparagraph (2) or (3) of paragraph (a) of subsection 2 or paragraph (b) of subsection 2, an owner intends to withhold any amount from a payment to be made to a prime contractor, the owner must give, on or before the date the payment is due, a written notice to the prime contractor of any amount that will be withheld. The written notice of withholding must: (a) Identify the amount of the request for payment that will be withheld from the prime contractor; (b) Give a reasonably detailed explanation of the condition or the reason the owner will withhold that amount, including, without limitation, a specific reference to the provision or section of the agreement, and any documents relating thereto, and the applicable building code, law or regulation with which the prime contractor has failed to comply; and (c) Be signed by an authorized agent of the owner.*

As the foregoing quote demonstrates, the burden is on the project Owner who intends to withhold any portion of a payment to inform the prime contractor of that fact in writing before the payment becomes due. Further, this notice must provide certain information about the withholding and the reasons therefore, in order to allow the prime contractor to correct any deficiencies causing the withholding.[135] While there is no case law to explain the extent of these requirements, other provisions of the statute will shed some light on the specific references, such as calculating the amount to be withheld or disclosure of the basis for withholding.

3:5 Calculating the Amount of Payment to be Withheld

NRS 624.609(2) provides:

> *If an owner has complied with subsection 3, the owner may: (a) Withhold from any payment to be made to the prime contractor: (1) A retention amount that, if the owner is authorized to withhold a retention amount pursuant to the agreement, must not exceed 10 percent of the amount of the payment to be made; (2) An amount equal to the sum of the value of: (I) Any work or labor that has not been performed or materials or equipment that has not been furnished for which payment is being sought, unless the agreement otherwise allows or requires such a payment to be made; and (II) Costs and expenses reasonably necessary to correct or repair any work which is the subject of the request for payment and which is not materially in compliance with the agreement to the extent that such costs and expenses exceed 50 percent of the retention amount withheld pursuant to subparagraph (1); and (3) The amount the owner has paid or is required to pay pursuant to an official notice from a state agency or employee benefit trust fund, for which the owner is or may reasonably be liable for the prime contractor or his or her lower-tiered subcontractors in accordance with chapter 608, 612, 616A to 616D, inclusive, or 617 of NRS....*

---

[135] *See* Form 3-2 in Appendix A.

The PPA allows withholding from a prime contractor for three basic reasons: 1) retention, 2) improperly billed for work (unperformed or deficiently performed) and 3) because the prime contractor has failed to pay wages or fringe benefit obligations to its employees. Each of these categories, however, has its own conditions which must be satisfied in calculating the amount to be withheld as a basis thereof.

3:6 Progress Payment Retention

Retention is the amount of money contractually withheld from a contractor by an owner to secure complete performance of the contracted scope of work.[136] As of January 1, 2015, the PPA indicates that an owner may withhold from a prime contractor:

> *(1) A retention amount that, if the owner is authorized to withhold a retention amount pursuant to the agreement, must not exceed 5 percent of the amount of the payment to be made...* [37]

There are two aspects of withholding retention from a prime contractor on progress payments that must be recognized: 1) Retention may only be withheld if doing so is authorized by written agreement, and 2) Retention can never exceed five percent (5%)[138] of the payment to be made.

A written agreement and authorization is necessary in the state of Nevada for an owner to withhold retention from his prime contractor in progress payments. An oral contract will not allow for retention to be withheld, and most pre-printed purchase orders will not contain provisions allowing for the withholding of retention. Therefore, the owner of a project who intends to withhold retention should always insert authorization therefore in his written agreement. While there will be no specific language to authorize such withholding, it is a best practice to leave no ambiguity in the authorization that retention will be intended and expected to be withheld from each and every progress payment.

Likewise, the written agreement should specifically delineate the percentage of the progress payment to be withheld. NRS 624.609(2)(a)(1) restricts this amount to no

---

[136] *Western Landscape Construction v. Bank of America*, 58 Cal. App. 4th 57, 64, 67 Cal. Rptr. 2d 868, 871 (2d Dist. 1997).

[137] NRS 624.609(2)(a)(1).

[138] In the 2015 Legislature the maximum amount of retention that can be held on any construction project in Nevada was reduced from 10% to 5%, effective for every contract entered into on or after January 1, 2016. Since this text was published after that date, the

more than 5% of the total payment made, however, there is no restriction that the retention amount may be less, or may even fluctuate based on job progress or final completion of milestone work. Many construction contracts will seek to have a reduction in progress payment retention during the project, or a complete cessation of retention withholding at some specific milestone. Any of these concepts are authorized, so long as the total amount of any progress payment retention withheld does not exceed 5% of that particular payment.

A strict interpretation of NRS 624.609(3) would seem to require that written notice of the owner's intention to withhold retention be issued for every contractual progress payment made.[139] Given the specific contractual authorization and the intelligent contract drafter's inclusion of authorizing language within the contract agreement itself, additional written notice of withholding retention seems redundant, especially when given the restriction of NRS 624.609(2)(a)(1) that retention may only be withheld if authorized by contractual agreement. In this case, the transmittal of payment reflecting a line-item deduction for retention should be sufficient written notice to comply with the statutory mandate of NRS 624.609(3). A more conservative approach would be to ensure that the retention line-item description indicated the precise section of the contract identifying the provisions of the agreement authorizing the owner to withhold retention. However, strict compliance with the statute would seem to require that a separate written notice be issued to the prime contractor with each payment from which the owner withholds a retention amount.

Subtly different rules apply to payment of retention upon completion of work under NRS 624.620. These shall be discussed later in this Chapter.

3:7 UNPERFORMED OR DEFICIENT WORK

Payment can be withheld for any unperformed work or deficiently performed work as well, only if the contractor has submitted an invoice for its performance. Calculating the amounts for each of these sub-categorize of withholding is somewhat complex, and is different depending on the sub-category involved. Again, strict compliance with the statutory dictates is critical to ensuring that disputes are minimized and the owner is properly protected in its withholding.

3:8 WITHHOLDING FOR UNPERFORMED WORK OR MATERIALS OR EQUIPMENT NOT FURNISHED

Under the PPA, an owner may withhold money from the prime contractor when the payment being requested is for work that remains unperformed or for material or

[139] *See* Section 3:4, *et seq.*

equipment not delivered to the job site. Specifically, NRS 624.609(2)(a)(2)(I) provides that an owner who has provided appropriate notice may withhold:

> *(2) An amount equal to the sum of the value of: (I) Any work or labor that has not been performed or materials or equipment that has not been furnished for which payment is being sought, unless the agreement otherwise allows or requires such a payment to be made;*

This calculation first requires that the contract be free of any obligation of the owner to pay for labor, materials or equipment which is not furnished. Long lead time items or items of special manufacture are often items which must be paid for prior to their actual delivery to the project. Secondly, careful inspection of the project and storage facilities for materials and equipment must be made before withholding for materials or equipment not actually furnished.

Materials and equipment are "furnished" when they are delivered to and are available for the installing contractor's use. They need not be installed in the project to be furnished.[140] Obviously, a factual question arises if materials or equipment are not actually on site as to whether they have been made available for installation and thus payment may not be withheld under the PPA.[141] While this matter should be dealt with at the contract formation stage, it is critical to note that materials and equipment may be available even if they are not actually on site, but rather stored at a project staging location off site or even at a contractor's place of business.

Once the determination of whether materials or equipment have been furnished is determined, the owner must then analyze the contract to ensure that payment for the unfurnished goods is not authorized. Exclusion or contract specific line-items should be reviewed to discover any pre-delivery material or equipment payments, deposits or other such requirements which may impair the owner's ability to withhold funds from the prime contractor. If payment is authorized by the contract, the owner cannot withhold the payment requested from the prime contractor under the PPA.

---

140 *Halbert's Lumber, Inc. v. Lucky Stores, Inc.*, 6 Cal. App. 4th 1233, 1240-1244, 8 Cal. Rptr. 2d 298 (4th Dist. 1992).

141 Some states have questioned whether a supplier's mechanics lien for materials or equipment attaches to the property when materials have been merely delivered or must wait until the materials or equipment are incorporated into the structure. See *Halbert's Lumber, Inc. v. Lucky Stores, Inc.*, 6 Cal. App. 4th 1233, 1240-1244, 8 Cal. Rptr. 2d 298 (4th Dist. 1992) and citations noted therein. However, Nevada's mechanics lien statute allow liens to attach to property for materials or equipment which are merely furnished to or are intended to be furnished to the project. NRS 108.222(1). See Chapter 8, Nevada Mechanic's Liens for a complete discussion of the level of incorporation of materials into a project for a mechanics lien to arise in Nevada.

Withholding for work or labor which has not been performed can be a significantly more abstract question, depending on the method used to calculate payment made. While a payment due upon completion of specific tasks or milestones can be readily ascertained, progress payment based on calculated percentages of completion is inherently subjective and can cause serious disputes. Best practices are for the project manager and the owner's representative to walk the project and review the level of completion of the milestone or task and agree upon a completion percentage before the payment application is submitted. This can also be accomplished after the owner has notified the prime contractor of his intention to withhold, though resolving such issues before payment is requested is preferred. In any case, determination of a percentage of completion is a factual inquiry that requires a fair amount of estimating experience. The retention of a consultant or construction expert should be recommended to the owner for calculation of partial percentage of completion amounts.

3:9 WITHHOLDING FOR DEFICIENTLY PERFORMED WORK

The most complex withholding authorization comes in determining the proper amount to withhold from a prime contractor's payment related to deficiently performed work. NRS 624.609(2)(a)(2)(II) provides that an owner who has provided appropriate notice may withhold:

> *An amount equal to the sum of the value of: ... (II) Costs and expenses reasonably necessary to correct or repair any work which is the subject of the request for payment and which is not materially in compliance with the agreement to the extent that such costs and expenses exceed 50 percent of the retention amount withheld pursuant to subparagraph (1)....*

The initial determination that must be made by an owner in withholding funds from a progress payment is whether or not the prime contractor is requesting payment for work that the owner considers deficient; that is not "materially in compliance with the agreement", and if the contractor fails to correct the deficiency, the owner would be required to correct in order to complete the project. Obviously, one type of work that falls into this category is work that is incomplete, even though the partial work that has been performed is materially in compliance with the contract requirements. Again, this will involve contract payment term analysis. If the contract contemplates payment based on a percentage of completion, it stands to reason that partially completed work is not deficient and payment cannot be withheld as a result. However, when payment is based on completed milestones or completed tasks, failure to achieve such milestones is sufficient reason to withhold funds, calculated within the requirements of the statute.

If the payment requested involves work which the owner contemplates is deficiently completed or is incomplete such that withholding is appropriate, the owner must next calculate the "reasonably necessary" cost to complete the unfinished work or to correct the deficiencies in the completed work, in order to achieve "material compliance with the agreement." Like the calculation of percentage of work complete, the calculation of costs reasonably necessary to correct or repair the work is to a large extent subjective and based on factual analysis of the work in place, cost of labor, materials and other issues, time for repair and impact on failing to repair, and other potential damage elements which are necessarily incurred as a result of the contractor's failure to complete the work.[142] While some may believe this opens a significant door to the owner to withhold funds, the concept of reasonableness will be used to regulate any abuses.

Once the owner has determined that the prime contractor has requested payment for work which is deficient, and has calculated the costs and expenses reasonably necessary to correct that work, the owner must now review the retention reserve for the final amount analysis. The owner may only withhold the amount of his reasonably necessary cost to repair the deficient work that exceeds fifty percent (50%) of the amount of retention the owner has withheld from the prime contractor.[143]

Here some additional ambiguity arises, however, from the statutory construction of NRS 624.609(2)(a), which was not explained in the legislative history of the PPA. A plain reading of the statute would require that the retention amount that is withheld from the *current* payment is the amount used for calculation of the 50% credit requirement. However, retention is usually a cumulative account, which increases as each progress payment is provided. As such, the cumulative retention amount can far exceed the specific payment request as a project continues over time. If NRS 624.609(2)(a) is read as requiring the cumulative retention amount to be used in the calculation of additional cost to be withheld, the ability of an owner to withhold additional sums for deficient

---

[142] Legislative History of the PPA indicates that "reasonably" necessary takes into account all of the circumstances in a case, but the term is not statutorily defined. "Senator Carlton asked what "for reasonable cause" means. ... Mr. Young responded, normally "reasonable cause" is a term the courts use. He said it is something, under all the circumstances of the particular case, deemed to be appropriate and reasonable, or what a reasonably prudent person would do under the circumstances. He noted it is usually not specifically defined. Still, the potential for disputes over the estimate exists. The owner should again be able to factually justify the calculation of repair costs which form the basis of his notice of withholding." Minutes of the Senate Committee on Commerce and Labor, 71st Legislative Session, May 25, 2001, Senate Bill 274.

[143] For example, if one assumes a prime contractor payment request is for $100,000, the prime contract allows for a 10% retention, and the owner reasonably calculates that $20,000 will be necessary to correct deficient work of the prime contractor, the owner is allowed to withhold a total amount of $25,000 from the prime contractor's payment request. This is calculated by subtracting 50% of the retention amount ($10,000 x 50% = $5,000), and deducting this calculated amount from the reasonable estimate of cost to repair ($20,000 - $5,000 = $15,000), and then adding the retention amount and the cost of repair estimate together to achieve a final withholding amount ($10,000 + $15,000 = $25,000). This is an appropriate calculation of the owner's statutorily authorized withholding from the example payment request of $100,000.

work may be entirely eliminated. Conversely, a sizable cost of repair estimate could quickly engulf an entire progress payment if only the specific retention withheld from that specific retention payment is used for the calculation of cost of repair withholding. This is especially true when the deficient condition is discovered later in the project and the cost of repair has substantially increased, either due to a continuing failure to correct the problem, or as a result of impacts to the project if correction is necessary.

Such considerations should be measured against the entirety of the PPA and scheme of the particular statute in question. NRS 624.609 lays out a scheme of action which an owner must follow in order to withhold any portion of a prime contractor's payment. So long as the notice requirement is followed, the owner may withhold as much from the payment request as will reasonably fall within the four categories of allowable withholdings. As such, each of the four is cumulative against the progress payment request. Since the calculation of allowable withholding in NRS 624.609(2)(a)(2)(II) specifically refers to the retention amount allowed to be withheld according to NRS 624.609(2)(a)(1), it is reasonable to infer that the 50% credit is applicable to the specific amount of retention withheld from the specific progress payment request is the correct retention amount against which the 50% credit is calculated. Such an interpretation, however, would militate against the principals of ensuring that the maximum amount of payment flow down to the contractor[144] on which the statute was formulated, and could lead to a result not in keeping with the dictates of the PPA. Careful evaluation of these competing interests must be reviewed within the context of the factual basis giving rise to the withholding of payment.

3:10 LABOR DEPARTMENT AND DEFINED BENEFIT TRUST FUND HOLDS

The final authorized reason that an owner may withhold all or a partial payment to the prime contractor is the receipt by the owner of a notice from a governmental agency or a defined benefit trust fund that the owner may be held responsible for the prime contractor's (or his sub-tier contractors') failure to pay wages or benefits. NRS 624.609(2)(a)(3) provides that an owner who has provided appropriate notice may withhold:

> *The amount the owner has paid or is required to pay pursuant to an official notice from a state agency or employee benefit trust fund, for which the owner is or may reasonably be liable for the prime contractor or his or her lower-tiered subcontractors in accordance with chapter 608, 612, 616A to 616D, inclusive, or 617 of NRS.*

[144] *See* Section 3:1, Historical Context and Influence on Nevada Contracting. See also, *Lehrer McGovern Bovis, Inc. v. Bullock Insulation, Inc.*, 185 P.3d 1055 (Nev. 2008), opinion withdrawn and superseded on denial of reh'g, 197 P.3d 1032 (Nev. 2008) establishing a public policy in favor of payment to contractors.

Initially, the practitioner should realize that the state of Nevada considers all employees working on a construction project to be the employees of the original contractor, so long as the workers are performing functions which are a part of the work the original contractor is licensed and contracted to perform.[145] The basis of these obligations is found within the Nevada statutes governing wages and employment benefits of employees.[146] The obligation to pay into the unemployment compensation fund or for workers compensation claims is a lien upon the property of the employer, including any money owed to him by a third party, such as the owner on a construction project.[147] As such, notice from a state agency or union administered defined benefit trust fund that monies are due and unpaid from the prime contractor is cause for the owner to withhold the amount of the notice from the prime contractor and pay the same to the notifying agency. The PPA allows for this possibility and establishes the ability of the owner to withhold those funds from the next payment request from the contractor and to transmit those funds to the notifying agency.[148]

Critical to the ability to withhold is the actual receipt of a notice of demand from the state agency or defined benefit trust fund. NRS 624.609(2)(a)(3) only allows withholding upon receipt of an "official notice" from the state agency or trust fund that moneys are due. In this situation, the owner merely needs to send the prime contractor written notice that references the official notice received and the amount of the withholding that will occur.

3:11 Progress Payment Releases

The provisions of the PPA likewise allow the owner to condition payment to the prime contractor on the provision of progress payment releases. NRS 624.609(2)(b) provides:

> *If an owner has complied with subsection 3, the owner may:... (b) Require as a condition precedent to the payment of any amount due, lien releases furnished by the prime contractor and his or her lower-tiered subcontractors and suppliers in accordance with the provisions of paragraphs (a) and (c) of subsection 5 of NRS 108.2457.*

Nevada has set forth specific forms for progress and final payment releases in its mechanics lien statutes at NRS 108.2457(5). These are discussed in detail in §8:29,

---

145 *Richards v. Republic Silver State Disposal, Inc.*, 122 Nev. 1213, 148 P.3d 684 (2006); *Tucker v. Action Equipment and Scaffold Co., Inc.*, 113 Nev. 1349, 951 P.2d 1027 (1997) holding modified by, *Harris v. Rio Hotel & Casino, Inc.*, 117 Nev. 482, 25 P.3d 206 (2001) and overruled by, *Richards v. Republic Silver State Disposal, Inc.*, 122 Nev. 1213, 148 P.3d 684 (2006)).

146 *See, e.g.*, NRS 608.150.

147 *See, e.g.*, NRS 612.680.

148 NRS 612.686.

Notice of non-responsibility, however, it must be noted at this juncture that the PPA only allows conditioning payment on receipt of the specific conditional waiver and release on progress payment form (NRS 108.2457(5)(a)) or *conditional* waiver and release on final payment form (NRS 108.2457(5)(c)).[149] Conditioning payment on receipt of any unconditional waiver and release is not authorized by the PPA and would be a legitimate cause of the prime contractor to stop work.

Additionally, the specific form language must be used as set forth in NRS 108.2457(5), and should not be substantially altered or the limited legal utility of the form could be lost. As is discussed in Section 8:29, Notice of non-responsibility, the statutory effect of any Nevada progress or final payment release is limited and conditional regardless of its language. Even unconditional releases are subject to the condition that the payment given in exchange for them actually clear the back on which it is drawn.[150] This is unusual and appears to be unique to the laws of the state of Nevada. The owner in this case is somewhat constantly at risk of mechanics liens or payment claims, even when he has received unconditional waivers and releases on progress or final payments. Nevertheless, the owner should use and obtain progress and final payment releases from the prime contractor and his sub-tier subcontractors and suppliers, and issue joint checks according to the owner's best practices.

While the owner's payment to the prime contractor may be conditioned on receipt of conditional payment releases, the owner may not withhold payment on this ground unless the owner notifies the prime contractor in writing of its failure to meet with this requirement as provided in NRS 624.609(3). However, nothing in the PPA requires any calculation of amount that can be withheld on the basis of missing release forms. Withholding on the unmet condition of providing conditional releases falls outside the withholding amount calculation provisions required under NRS 624.609(2)(a). Therefore, the failure to provide one conditional release from a single supplier or subcontractor is justification to withhold the entire payment from the prime contractor.[151]

3:12 Description of Basis for Withholding Payment

Once the amounts of withholding are calculated and the reasons for withholding are determined to be valid, the owner's notice of withholding to the prime contractor must be drafted to include a reasonably detailed description of the basis to withhold. NRS 624.609(3) provides:

---

[149] *See* Forms 8-7 and 8-9 in Appendix A.

[150] *See* NRS 108.2457(5)(e).

[151] *See* Form 3-2 in Appendix A.

The written notice of withholding must: ... (b) Give a reasonably detailed explanation of the condition or the reason the owner will withhold that amount, including, without limitation, a specific reference to the provision or section of the agreement, and any documents relating thereto, and the applicable building code, law or regulation with which the prime contractor has failed to comply....

The purpose of the detailed description is to provide the prime contractor a specific cause for the withholding to enable the prime contractor to correct the unmet condition as soon as possible, thereby releasing payment. Therefore, a properly described withholding cause will set out the precise location of and the exact deficiency with which the owner is concerned to withhold payment. Thereafter, there should be a reference to the provision of the prime construction contract or applicable law under the PPA that authorizes the withholding of the problem. Likewise, if withholding is due to a notice from any state agency, that notice should be referenced and, in good practice, a copy provided to the prime contractor.

While the actual content of the description is left to a "reasonableness" standard,[152] the owner directing the notice of withholding should endeavor to provide the prime contractor with sufficient information to allow a quick investigation and correction.

3:13 Execution of the Withholding Notice

The final element of the written notice of withholding is a signature. NRS 624.609(3)(c) provides *"The written notice of withholding must:... (c) Be signed by an authorized agent of the owner."* The purpose of the signature by an authorized agent is to provide corporate effect to the notice. Issuing the notice of withholding begins a process of actions which has binding legal effect upon both the owner and the prime contractor. Therefore, it is necessary that the owner be bound by the decision to withhold. Hence, the necessity of an authorized agent issuing any notice of withholding and executing that notice indicating that the company has been bound by the decision to withhold and the effects of the PPA that are carried by that act.

This could also be seen as an argument against electronic mail notification. Nevada's subscription to the Uniform Electronic Transactions Act[153] may eliminate some of the

---

[152] Legislative History of the PPA indicates that "reasonably" necessary takes into account all of the circumstances in a case, but the term is not statutorily defined. "Senator Carlton asked what "for reasonable cause" means. ... Mr. Young responded, normally "reasonable cause" is a term the courts use. He said it is something, under all the circumstances of the particular case, deemed to be appropriate and reasonable, or what a reasonably prudent person would do under the circumstances. He noted it is usually not specifically defined. Still, the potential for disputes over the estimate exists. The owner should again be able to factually justify the calculation of repair costs which form the basis of his notice of withholding." Minutes of the Senate Committee on Commerce and Labor, 71st Legislative Session, May 25, 2001, Senate Bill 274.

argument that since the email is not signed as required by the PPA, and so cannot be effective. This argument, like most of the PPA, has not yet been tested by judicial review.

3:14 Correction of Causes for Withholding or Disputes over Withholding Basis

Once the decision to withhold has been made and the prime contractor notified in writing of that decision, the prime contractor has several options in responding. These options are set forth inNRS 624.609(4), which provides in pertinent part:

> *A prime contractor who receives a notice of withholding pursuant to subsection 3 ... may: (a) Give the owner a written notice and thereby dispute in good faith and for reasonable cause the amount withheld, or the condition or reason for the withholding; or (b) Correct any condition or reason for the withholding described in the notice of withholding and thereafter provide written notice to the owner of the correction of the condition or reason for the withholding. The notice of correction must be sufficient to identify the scope and manner of the correction of the condition or reason for the withholding and be signed by an authorized representative of the prime contractor....*

The first option available to the prime contractor is to provide the owner with a written notice that the prime contractor disputes the reason for withholding in good faith.[154] This notice would then lead directly to resolution of the dispute by the contractually agreed to alternative dispute resolution procedures or to filing a lawsuit to resolve the matter. Likewise, the prime contractor is authorized to undertake steps set forth in the PPA to stop work on the project, as set forth in NRS 624.610. These procedures are discussed in detail later in this Chapter.

The second option is to correct the condition or reason for the withholding and resubmit the situation to the owner for approval.[155] In this case, the prime contractor is charged with the actual correction of the deficiency causing the withholding, and the reporting not only that the condition has been corrected, but to provide the owner with a written notice which sufficiently identifies the scope and manner of the correction. How much detail is required for this notice is not clear, but should again be governed by the reasonableness standard.[156]

---

[153] NRS 719.010, et seq. NRS 719.220(2) indicates that the argument to use electronic transmissions for notice can be determined by conduct of the parties. Given this view, careful consideration can be given to the actions of the parties during the course of the project to demonstrate that notice of different issues between them took place by electronic transmission and so notice under the PPA should not be objectionable. To ensure that email is acceptable notice under the PPA, however, the parties' contract should allow for email transmission notice. *See* NRS 624.662(3)(d).

[154] *See* Form 3-3 in Appendix A.

[155] *See* Form 3-3 in Appendix A.

[156] *See* Section 3:12, Description of Basis for Withholding.

Once again, the prime contractor's response to the owner must be executed by an authorized agent of the prime contractor. Similar to the notice to withhold, the notice of good faith dispute or notice of correction will bind the prime contractor legally to the provisions of the PPA. Such decisions must be made by authorized agents of the prime contractor to be effectual.

3:15. Responding to Prime Contractor's Notice of Correction

Once the prime contractor has responded to the owner's notice of withholding by correcting the reason for withholding and providing a notice of correction to the owner, the owner has two options to respond. These are set forth in the continuation of NRS 624.609(4)(b):

> *If an owner receives a written notice from the prime contractor of the correction of a condition or reason for the withholding pursuant to this paragraph, the owner shall: (1) Pay the amount withheld by the owner for that condition or reason for the withholding on or before the date the next payment is due the prime contractor; or (2) Object to the scope and manner of the correction of the condition or reason for the withholding, on or before the date the next payment is due to the prime contractor, in a written statement which sets forth the condition or reason for the objection and which complies with subsection 3. If the owner objects to the scope and manner of the correction of a condition or reason for the withholding, the owner shall nevertheless pay to the prime contractor, along with the payment to be made pursuant to the prime contractor's next payment request, the amount withheld for the correction of the condition or reason for the withholding to which the owner no longer objects.*

The owner who received a notice of correction must inspect the corrected condition for actual correction of the reason withholding was necessary in the first place. If the condition has been acceptably corrected, the owner must pay the withheld portion of the previous payment request on or before the date the next payment is due to the prime contractor. If the condition has not been corrected, the owner may not rely on the sufficiency of the previous notice to withhold, but must actually respond again to the prime contractor objecting to the correction. Otherwise, the prime contractor must be paid or the remedies available to the prime contractor, i.e., stopping work on the project, may be enforced by the prime contractor with legal impunity.

If the owner's inspection reveals that the correction of the condition leading to withholding has not been properly corrected after receipt of a notice of correction, the owner must deliver to the prime contractor a written notice of objection to the correction. This notice of objection must set out the reason for the objection in the same manner as a notice of withholding, and otherwise comply with the requirements of a notice of withholding under NRS 624.609(3). This notice of objection must again be delivered to the prime contractor on or before the date the next payment is due to the prime contractor under the contract schedule of payments or would be due under the provisions of the PPA. As part of the written notice of objection, however, the owner must pay to the prime contractor any withheld funds which are no longer included in the calculation of the amount reasonably necessary to correct the deficient condition. This means that the owner must again review the allegedly "corrected" work, calculate a reasonable estimate of the cost to correct the now "corrected" condition, and determine again how much of this revised reasonable estimate exceeds 50% of the current draw retention.[157] This amount must then be deducted from the previously withheld amount, and the balance paid to the prime contractor on or before the next scheduled payment is due.

Once the notice of objection is received by the prime contractor, the prime contractor may respond to the notice of objection in the same manner as to a notice of withholding.[158] In turn, the owner must respond again to the second notice of correction as previously discussed.[159] This cycle of written notices continues until the issue is fully resolved, or the prime contractor issues a notice of good faith dispute and moves on to the remedies that are available to the prime contractor under the PPA.

3:16 Procedures on Payments for Higher-Tiered Contractors

The PPA also contains separate procedures for withholding payment between a "higher-tiered contractor" and a "lower-tiered subcontractor", as these terms are defined within the PPA. Most of these procedures found in NRS 624.624 are identical to those between an owner and a prime contractor set forth in previous sections of this Chapter, with the higher-tiered contractor obligated to perform the same procedures as the owner, and the lower-tiered subcontractor obligated to respond the same manner as a prime contractor. As these actions are similar to those already discussed, their functions will be summarized in this section with reference to the details set forth in previous sections. There are a number of differences, however, when dealing with concepts such as a pay-when-paid or a paid-if-paid provision or when payment has been received by the higher-tiered contractor which affect the obligations specifically. These will be detailed in this section.

---

[157] *See* Section 3:9, Withholding for deficiently performed work.

[158] *See* Section 3:14, Correction of causes for withholding or disputes over withholding basis and Form 3-3 in Appendix A.

[159] *See* Form 3-4 in Appendix A.

3:17 DEFINITIONS

The definitions of "higher-tiered contractor" and "lower-tiered subcontractor" were added to the PPA in 2005, and are found at NRS 624.607 and NRS 624.608, respectively. These sections provide as follows:

> *NRS 624.607: "Higher-tiered contractor" means a prime contractor or subcontractor who has entered into an oral or written agreement with a lower-tiered subcontractor pursuant to which the lower-tiered subcontractor has agreed to provide work, materials or equipment for a work of improvement.*
>
> *NRS 624.608: "Lower-tiered subcontractor" means a subcontractor who has agreed in an oral or written agreement with a higher-tiered contractor to provide work, materials or equipment for a work of improvement.*

The language is somewhat clumsy, but is generally trying to define terms that mean any relationship on a construction project where a prime contractor or any subcontractor enters into a contractual relationship with anyone else to perform a portion of that contractor or subcontractor's work. Regardless of the contractual level (or "tier") at which that contract is executed, the PPA will apply to that contractual relationship, including a contractual relationship that includes a material supplier or equipment supplier.

3:18 WITHHOLDING PAYMENTS TO LOWER-TIERED SUBCONTRACTORS

The PPA sets forth the procedures for a higher-tiered contractor to withhold payment to a lower-tiered subcontractor in NRS 624.624. Similar to the procedures for an owner to withhold payment to a prime contractor,[160] the PPA supersedes contractual provisions for payments where there is no actual written schedule of payments provided, and establishes a requirement that payment be made to a lower-tiered subcontractor on or before the date contractually scheduled therefore or imposes a 30 day time period after presentment of the lower-tiered subcontractor's invoice within which payment must be received.[161] However, both the schedule of payments and the 30 day after invoice period

---

[160] *See* Section 3:4.

[161] NRS 624.624(1) provides:

> *Except as otherwise provided in this section, if a higher-tiered contractor enters into:*
> *(a) A written agreement with a lower-tiered subcontractor that includes a schedule for payments, the higher-tiered contractor shall pay the lower-tiered subcontractor:*
> *(1) On or before the date payment is due; or*
> *(2) Within 10 days after the date the higher-tiered contractor receives payment for all or a portion of the work, materials or equipment described in a request for payment submitted by the lower-tiered subcontractor,*
> *whichever is earlier.*

are also shorted to 10 days after the higher-tiered contractor receives payment intended for the lower-tiered subcontractor. Thus, there are no payment terms on which a higher-tiered contractor may rely to float, delay or spread out payments to a lower-tier subcontractor. Any payment received by a contractor or subcontractor of any tier for a lower-tier subcontractor or supplier must be delivered to that lower-tier subcontractor or supplier within 10 days of receipt, unless the higher-tiered contractor intends to and actually complies with the requirements necessary to withhold payment.

The higher-tiered contractor's obligations and requirements for withholding payment to a lower-tier subcontractor are set forth in NRS 624.624(3),[162] and are identical to those required to be followed by an owner when withholding payment to a prime contractor.[163] The higher-tiered contractor may only withhold payment for the same basic reasons as an owner: retention;[164] unperformed work, undelivered materials or deficient work product;[165] notice of failure to pay wages or fringe benefits,[166] and/or

---

> *(b) A written agreement with a lower-tiered subcontractor that does not contain a schedule for payments, or an agreement that is oral, the higher-tiered contractor shall pay the lower-tiered subcontractor:*
> *(1) Within 30 days after the date the lower-tiered subcontractor submits a request for payment; or*
> *(2) Within 10 days after the date the higher-tiered contractor receives payment for all or a portion of the work, labor, materials, equipment or services described in a request for payment submitted by the lower-tiered subcontractor,*
> *whichever is earlier.*

[162] NRS 624.624(3) provides:

> *If, pursuant to subparagraph (2) or (3) of paragraph (a) of subsection 2 or paragraph (b) of subsection 2, a higher-tiered contractor intends to withhold any amount from a payment to be made to a lower-tiered subcontractor, the higher-tiered contractor must give, on or before the date the payment is due, a written notice to the lower-tiered subcontractor of any amount that will be withheld and give a copy of such notice to all reputed higher-tiered contractors and the owner. The written notice of withholding must:*
> *(a) Identify the amount of the request for payment that will be withheld from the lower-tiered subcontractor;*
> *(b) Give a reasonably detailed explanation of the condition or the reason the higher-tiered contractor will withhold that amount, including, without limitation, a specific reference to the provision or section of the agreement with the lower-tiered subcontractor, and any documents relating thereto, and the applicable building code, law or regulation with which the lower-tiered subcontractor has failed to comply; and*
> *(c) Be signed by an authorized agent of the higher-tiered contractor.*

[163] *See* Sections 3:4 to 3:13.

[164] *See* Sections 3:6 Progress payment retention.

[165] *See* Section 3:7, Unperformed or deficient work.

failure to provide conditional waivers and releases.[167] Likewise, the higher-tiered contractor must prepare and deliver his notice of withholding in the same manner that an owner is required to do so.[168]

The lower-tiered subcontractor must respond to a notice to withhold in the same manner that a prime contractor would respond to the owner. NRS 624.624(4)[169] sets out the identical procedures for providing a notice of good faith dispute, or correcting the deficiency causing withholding and providing the higher-tiered contractor with notice of that correction.[170] Likewise, the higher-tiered contractor can object to the correction, but must recalculate the withholding amount to account for any actual

---

[166] *See* Section 3:10, Labor department and defined benefit trust fund holds.

[167] *See* Section 3:11, Progress payment releases.

[168] *See* Sections 3:13 to 3:14 and Form 3-2 in Appendix A.

[169] NRS 624.624(4) provides:

> *A lower-tiered subcontractor who receives a notice of withholding pursuant to subsection 3 or a notice of objection pursuant to subparagraph (2) of paragraph (b) may:*
> *(a) Give the higher-tiered contractor a written notice and thereby dispute in good faith and for reasonable cause the amount withheld or the conditions or reasons for the withholding; or*
> *(b) Correct any condition or reason for the withholding described in the notice of withholding and thereafter provide written notice to the higher-tiered contractor of the correction of the condition or reason for the withholding. The notice of correction must be sufficient to identify the scope and manner of the correction of the condition or reason for the withholding and be signed by an authorized representative of the lower-tiered subcontractor.*
> *If a higher-tiered contractor receives a written notice from the lower-tiered subcontractor of the correction of a condition or reason for the withholding pursuant to this paragraph, the higher-tiered contractor shall:*
> *(1) Pay the amount withheld by the higher-tiered contractor for that condition or reason for the withholding on or before the date the next payment is due the lower-tiered subcontractor; or*
> *(2) Object to the scope and manner of the correction of the condition or reason for the withholding, on or before the date the next payment is due to the lower-tiered subcontractor, in a written statement which sets forth the condition or reason for the objection and which complies with subsection 3.*
> *If the higher-tiered contractor objects to the scope and manner of the correction of a condition or reason for the withholding, he shall nevertheless pay to the lower-tiered subcontractor, along with payment to be made pursuant to the lower-tiered subcontractor's next payment request, the amount withheld for the correction of the conditions or reasons for the withholding to which the higher-tiered contractor no longer objects.*

[170] *See* Section 3:14 Correction of Causes for Withholding or Disputes over Withholding Basis, *and see* Form 3-3 in Appendix A.

diminishment of the reasonable estimate to repair or to deal with any increase in withheld retention amounts.[171] This cycle again may repeat until the lower-tier subcontractor issues a notice of good faith dispute or the withholding issue is corrected and the withheld money is paid out.

3:19. Effect of a Pay-When-Paid or Pay-If-Paid Contractual Provision

Contrary to the beliefs of some Nevada practitioners, the PPA does not either impliedly or explicitly outlaw contractual provisions making payment to a lower-tier subcontractor conditional based on receipt of payment from an owner or other higher-tiered contractor. The idea that the PPA outlawed use of contingency payment agreements is based a selective reading of the PPA itself.[172] Instead, the PPA is probably more likely to support their enforcement, while maintaining the rights of subcontractors to stop work even under their application. While this is not a typical approach, the PPA actually accomplishes both goals for the benefit of both subcontractors and general contractors; allowing the unpaid subcontractor to stop work, while allowing the unpaid general contractor protection from illegitimate mandates that it finance the project when the owner fails to pay.

3:20. Prompt Payment Act Effect on Change Order Requests

Uniquely, the PPA also makes a significant impact on the methods for dealing with change order requests between the owner and prime contractor, and a slightly different impact on how a higher-tiered contractor deals with change order requests from lower-tiered subcontractors. In practical application, the PPA's change order requirements only work correctly when there are few tiers of contractors within which the project is built. These provisions cause significant dilemmas for larger construction projects, however, where many levels of subcontractors may exist and communication of change order requests and the necessary back up and support for them cannot be quickly exchanged between all tiers involved. In these cases, serious contractual disputes can, and traps for the unwary do, exist which can result in large lawsuits.

In essence, the PPA mandates that the owner or higher-tiered contractor who receives a change order request[173] must respond to it in writing within 30 days of receipt. If that

---

[171] *See* Section 3:15 Responding to prime contractor's notice of correction.

[172] For a complete discussion of the arguments for and against enforcement, *see* Section 4:14 Contingency Payment Clauses.

[173] It should be noted that the PPA will probably apply to any document that requests a change in the contract time or price, regardless of what term is used for that request in a given construction project scheme. Thus, calling a change order request a "request for change," "extra work authorization proposal" or some other nomenclature will probably have little effect, if any, on the applicability of the PPA or the timing of a response to that document, thereunder.

owner or higher-tier contractor fails to act upon the change order request within that time period, the change order request becomes a part of the applicable construction contract or subcontract by operation of law. The price and scope of the work is accordingly increased and the time requested in the change order request is granted to the presenting party, regardless of the merit of the change order request. The prime contractor or lower-tier subcontractor who presented the request is allowed to bill against the now legally enforceable change order request and if payment is not received thereon (or if the owner or higher-tier contractor does not provide notice of withholding as previously discussed), the prime contractor or lower-tiered subcontractor may stop work on the project with legal impunity.

Probably reflective of their later inclusion in the PPA through legislative amendment in 2005, the provisions affecting change order requests between owners and prime contractors and those between higher-tier contractors and lower-tier subcontractors are actually found within the remedy provisions of NRS 624.610 and NRS 624.626, respectively. These sections outline the procedures for a prime contractor and lower-tier subcontractor to stop work, as opposed to the procedures necessary to affect payment found in NRS 624.609 and NRS 624.624. Regardless, the procedures for dealing with change order requests should be followed with care to best protect against being legally obligated for unauthorized or questionable change order requests.

As affecting contracts between owners and their prime contractors, NRS 624.610 reads in pertinent part:

> *1. If:... (d) Within 30 days after the date that a written request for a change order is submitted by the prime contractor to the owner, the owner fails to:(1) Issue the change order; or (2) If the request for a change order is unreasonable or does not contain sufficient information to make a determination, give written notice to the prime contractor of the reasons why the change order is unreasonable or explain that additional information and time are necessary to make a determination, the prime contractor may stop work after giving written notice to the owner at least 10 days before stopping work. ...*
>
> *...*
>
> *3. If an owner fails to issue a change order or give written notice to the prime contractor pursuant to the provisions of paragraph (d) of subsection 1: (a) The agreement price must be increased by the amount sought in the request for a change order; (b) The time for performance must be extended by the amount sought in the request for a change order; (c) The prime contractor may submit to the owner a bill or invoice for the labor, materials, equipment or services that are the subject of the request for a change order; and (d) The owner shall pay the prime contractor for such labor, materials, equipment or services with the next payment made to the prime contractor.*

As between owners and prime contractors, the submission of a change order request to the owner begins a 30 day clock running for response to the change order. NRS

624.610(1)(d), while seeming to acknowledge two acceptable responses, actually sets out three: 1) issue the change order according to the terms of the request; 2) issue a written objection to the change order request that it is unreasonable and the reasons therefor; or 3) issue a written notice to the prime contractor that additional time and/or information is needed to process the change order.[174] If the owner fails to take any of these steps, the prime contractor may stop work, by following the procedures outlined for doing so.[175] But failing to act according to NRS 624.610(1)(d) likewise carries with it an additional penalty: making the change order request valid and enforceable by operation of law.

Under NRS 624.610(3), failing to respond in writing to a change order request within 30 days causes the prime contract to be altered by the written change order as submitted by the prime contractor. The contract price is increased and the time for performance is extended by the change order requests terms. The prime contractor is thereafter authorized to bill against the change order request and the owner must pay the request for payment against the change order in the next draw request. It is fair to say that this provision in the law would be disallowed under most standard construction contracts. As the PPA voids any contractual provision which conflicts with its mandates,[176] however, there is little that may be contractually used to avoid the harsh results of this provision. Short of a successful constitutionality challenge to the PPA, the only protection for an owner is to ensure that every change order is responded to in writing within 30 days of its receipt.

As between higher-tiered contractors and lower-tiered subcontractors, the provisions affecting change order requests are slightly different. NRS 624.626 provides in pertinent part:

> *1. If:... (e) Within 30 days after the date that a written request for a change order is submitted by the lower-tiered subcontractor to the higher-tiered contractor, the higher-tiered contractor fails to: (1) Issue the change order; or (2) If the request for a change order is unreasonable, give written notice to the lower-tiered subcontractor of the reasons why the change order is unreasonable, the lower-tiered subcontractor may stop work under the agreement until payment is received if the lower-tiered subcontractor gives written notice to the higher-tiered contractor at least 10 days before stopping work.*
>
> ...
>
> *3. If a higher-tiered contractor fails to issue a change order or fails to give written notice pursuant to paragraph (e) of subsection 1: (a) The agreement price must be increased*

---

[174] *See* Form 3-5 in Appendix A.

[175] These steps are discussed in Section 3:21 Stopping work.

[176] NRS 624.622(2).

by the amount sought in the request for a change order; (b) The time for performance must be extended by the amount sought in the request for a change order; (c) The lower-tiered subcontractor may submit to the higher-tiered contractor a bill or invoice for the labor, materials, equipment or services that are the subject of the request for a change order; and (d) The higher-tiered contractor shall pay the lower-tiered subcontractor for such labor, materials, equipment or services with the next payment made to the lower-tiered subcontractor.

As affecting change order requests between higher-tiered contractors and lower-tiered subcontractors, the PPA allows a higher-tiered only two ways to respond to a lower-tiered subcontractor's change order requests: 1) issue the change order request according to its terms; or 2) reject the change order request as unreasonable, providing written notice of the reasons why the change order request is considered unreasonable by the higher-tiered subcontractor.[177] There is no discussion in the legislative history of the PPA of any reason that the higher-tiered contractor is not allowed to inform the lower-tiered subcontractor that additional time or information will be necessary to process the change order request, as the owner is authorized to do under NRS 624.610(1)(d).[178] Therefore, the PPA poses a trap for the unwary general or higher-tiered contractor who is faced with change order requests that are submitted by lower-tiered subcontractors but must be approved by the owner or other prime contractor before the subcontract may be altered. The general or higher-tiered contractor must take steps to deal with the lower-tiered subcontractor's change order request while the owner is processing it, or risk the situation where the owner rejects the change order request but the PPA has operated to make the change order request enforceable against him.[179]

---

[177] *See* Form 3-6.

[178] The reason for the absence of any discussion on this subject is because the lack of an option for the higher-tiered contractor to request additional time and information is probably a drafting error by the Legislature. The author of this book was involved in the review and negotiations over the 2005 amendments to the PPA, which inserted this change order request language in its terms. The draft bills presented to the Legislative Counsel Bureau for conformance with the submission requirements to the Legislature included identical provisions in the sections that became NRS 624.610(1)(d) and NRS 624.626(1)(e) respectively, and both included the provisions allowing the higher-tiered party the ability to respond to a change order request with notice that additional time and information would be necessary. Somewhere in the process of the amendments and changes the language was dropped from NRS 624.626(1)(e) and this alteration was apparently not caught by those involved in reviewing the final bill drafts approved by the Legislature in 2005.

[179] In the unpublished decision of *Insulation Contracting & Supply, Inc. v. S3H, Inc.*, No. 62856, 2015 WL 5774180 (Nev. Sept. 29, 2015), a divided Nevada Supreme Court panel determined that a written notice to a lower tier contractor stating that approval of the change order request was contingent upon the Owner approval and until such approval the lower tier contractor should assume and conclude the change order request was unreasonable was sufficient to prevent the change order from becoming part of its subcontract under the PPA. While not citable as authority for this proposition, the case does indicate what type of notice may be effective in these situations.

3:21 STOPPING WORK

As mentioned in passing, the ultimate remedy of the PPA is to allow an unpaid prime contractor or lower-tiered subcontractor to stop work on the project while payment issues are being worked out with the owner or higher-tiered contractor. The procedures for doing so are fairly simple, though in practice they have some significant impacts to the project and to the cost for the involved contractors.

Initially, there must be a lack of payment that has either been met with a notice of good faith dispute from the affected prime contractor or a failure of the owner or higher-tier contractor to provide required notices of withholding or rejection of a change order request as previously discussed.[180] Once that situation arises, the prime contractor or lower-tiered subcontractor must provide written notice of his intention to stop work.

---

[180] NRS 624.610 provides:

> *1. If: (a) An owner fails to pay the prime contractor in the time and manner required by subsection 1 or 4 of NRS 624.609; (b) An owner fails to give the prime contractor written notice of any withholding in the time and manner required by subsection 3 or 4 of NRS 624.609; (c) After receipt of a notice of withholding given pursuant to subsection 3 or 4 of NRS 624.609, the prime contractor gives the owner written notice pursuant to subsection 4 of NRS 624.609 and thereby disputes in good faith and for reasonable cause the amount withheld or the condition or reason for the withholding; or (d) Within 30 days after the date that a written request for a change order is submitted by the prime contractor to the owner, the owner fails to: (1) Issue the change order; or (2) If the request for a change order is unreasonable or does not contain sufficient information to make a determination, give written notice to the prime contractor of the reasons why the change order is unreasonable or explain that additional information and time are necessary to make a determination, the prime contractor may stop work after giving written notice to the owner at least 10 days before stopping work.*

NRS 624.626 provides:

> *1. If: (a) A higher-tiered contractor fails to pay the lower-tiered subcontractor within the time provided in subsection 1 or 4 of NRS 624.624; (b) A higher-tiered contractor fails to pay the lower-tiered subcontractor within 45 days after the 25th day of the month in which the lower-tiered subcontractor submits a request for payment, even if the higher-tiered contractor has not been paid and the agreement contains a provision which requires the higher-tiered contractor to pay the lower-tiered subcontractor only if or when the higher-tiered contractor is paid; (c) A higher-tiered contractor fails to give the lower-tiered subcontractor written notice of any withholding in the time and manner required by subsection 3 or 4 of NRS 624.624; (d) After receipt of a notice of withholding pursuant to subsection 3 or 4 of NRS 624.624, the lower-tiered subcontractor gives the higher-tiered contractor written notice pursuant to subsection 4 of NRS 624.624 and thereby disputes in good faith and for reasonable cause the amount withheld or the condition or reason for the withholding; or (e) Within 30 days after the date that a written request for a change order is submitted by the lower-tiered subcontractor to the higher-tiered contractor, the higher-tiered contractor fails to: (1) Issue the change order; or (2) If the request for a change order is unreasonable, give written notice to the lower-tiered subcontractor of the reasons why*

The written notice of the prime contractor or lower-tiered subcontractor to stop work must be served upon the owner or higher-tier contractor a full 10 calendar days before actually stopping work and demobilizing. There is no critical language for a written notice that the prime contractor or the lower-tiered subcontractor intends to stop work, though good practice would include identification of the precise payment dispute and setting forth an actual date of anticipated work stoppage.[181] Like all other notices under the PPA, the notice of intent to stop work must be delivered to the owner or higher-tiered contractor as specified in NRS 624.622(3) or NRS 624.628(4) respectively, which is discussed in §3:29, Delivery of Notices Under the Prompt Payment Act.

3:22. STOPPING WORK UNDER A PAY-WHEN OR PAY-IF-PAID CLAUSE

Somewhat differently than stopping work due to a dispute with the higher-tiered contractor, when a lower-tiered subcontractor has not been paid because there is a valid pay-if-paid clause or a valid pay-when-paid clause in its subcontract, and the owner has not paid the higher-tiered contractor for the lower-tiered subcontractor's work, the lower-tiered subcontractor may still stop work under the PPA. This is not because the PPA outlaws such contingency payment clauses, but rather they are contemplated by the PPA. Instead, the PPA provides for a procedure to stop work, even in light of such a contractual clause. In this case, the timeframe within which the payment must be made is different than under the usual PPA timelines for notice of withholding. NRS 624.626(1) provides in pertinent part:

> *If:... (b) A higher-tiered contractor fails to pay the lower-tiered subcontractor within 45 days after the 25th day of the month in which the lower-tiered subcontractor submits a request for payment, even if the higher-tiered contractor has not been paid and the agreement contains a provision which requires the higher-tiered contractor to pay the lower-tiered subcontractor only if or when the higher-tiered contractor is paid ... the lower-tiered subcontractor may stop work under the agreement until payment is received if the lower-tiered subcontractor gives written notice to the higher-tiered contractor at least 10 days before stopping work.*

In this lack of a pre-requisite payment from the owner situation, there is no burden on the higher-tiered contractor to provide notice of any intention to withhold. Obviously, this is because none exist; the higher-tier contractor would gladly pay the lower-tiered subcontractor, except that the condition to that payment--owner's payment to the higher-tier contractor for the lower-tiered subcontractor's work--has not occurred. In

---

> *the change order is unreasonable, the lower-tiered subcontractor may stop work under the agreement until payment is received if the lower-tiered subcontractor gives written notice to the higher-tiered contractor at least 10 days before stopping work.*

[181] A sample Notice of Intent to Stop Work has been provided at Form 3-7 in Appendix A.

this situation, however, the lower-tiered subcontractor does not need to continue working without payment. Instead, he must calculate the date by which his ability under the PPA to stop work arises, and then send his 10 day notice of intent to stop work to the higher tiered contractor.

The calculation of the date for which a notice may be sent is essentially 46 to 71 days from the date the lower-tiered subcontractor submitted his unpaid invoice to the higher-tiered contractor, and fluctuates based on the date of the month the invoice was actually submitted. For instance, if the lower-tiered subcontractor submits his invoice on the 15th day of the month, then the day on which he may submit his 10 day notice of intent to stop work based on a lack of payment of that invoice would be 55 calendar days later.[182] If payment is not received within that 10 day time frame, the lower-tiered subcontractor may stop work without liability imposed based on the language of the subcontract agreement.

3:23 Termination of Contracts under the Prompt Payment Act

The PPA provides vehicles for the prime contractor or the lower-tiered subcontractor to terminate their contracts under certain circumstances. These circumstances can vary with the type of situation encountered by the contractor or the acts of the owner, and also the cause for withholding payment. The rights to terminate between the prime contractor and the lower-tiered subcontractors vary sufficiently, that separate treatment of each is warranted.

3:24 Termination of or by the Prime Contractor

Termination of the prime contract can be accomplished by the prime contractor under the PPA for two distinct causes, with certain subcategories: 1) Failure of the owner to make payment and/or comply with the notice requirements of the PPA, and 2) The owner causes the work to be stopped for 15 or more days through its own or its agent's actions or neglect.[183] How termination is accomplished and what the prime contractor may recover in any lawsuit filed thereafter is based on the cause for termination.

For termination based on payment related issues, NRS 624.610(2) provides:

> *If a prime contractor stops work pursuant to paragraph (a), (b) or (c) of subsection 1, the prime contractor may terminate the agreement by giving written notice of termination to the owner after stopping work but at least 15 days before terminating the agreement. If the prime contractor is paid the amount due before the date for*

---

[182] ((15th to the 25th = 10 days) + 45 days = 55 days from the date of invoice). See Form 3-7 in Appendix A.

[183] *See* Form 3-8 in Appendix A.

termination of the agreement set forth in the written notice, the prime contractor shall not terminate the agreement and shall resume work.

Initially, it should be pointed out that the failure to execute, reject or request additional time and information to process a change order request for extra work is excluded from the lists of reasons that a prime contractor may terminate his contract. However, as previously discussed the failure to timely process or respond to a change order request causes that change order request to become part of the contract. A subsequent failure to pay on the then revised contract amount would allow the prime contractor to stop work and terminate the agreement for lack of payment under the provisions of NRS 624.610(2).

Termination of the prime contract then can also only occur after the prime contractor has stopped work in accordance with NRS 624.610(1). In this case, the prime contractor must give the owner an additional written notice of its intention to terminate the contract. This notice must be delivered to the owner 15 days before the prime contractor may consider the contract terminated. If the owner makes the payment due to the prime contractor, the prime contractor must re-commence work under the contract and may not terminate it.

Stopping work under the PPA is not without its risks, however, as the owner has a reciprocal right to terminate a prime contract if the prime contractor stops work. NRS 624.610(5) provides: "If a prime contractor stops work pursuant to subsection 1, the owner may terminate the agreement by giving the prime contractor written notice of his intent to terminate at least 15 days before terminating the agreement." Thus, if the owner feels that its cause for withholding payment from the prime contractor is legally valid, such that the prime contractor's stopping work is not in good faith or is not justified under the PPA, the owner may terminate the prime contractor on the project and also sue for damages. While the PPA does provide some protection to the prime contractor in this situation,[184] the prime contractor is not completely immune from liability for an owner's damage. The PPA does not limit liability when the prime contractor's work stoppage is not reasonable. In such a circumstance, the prime contractor may be subject to any damages for delay, disruption or other impact on the project as a result of his work stoppage.

The PPA also allows a prime contractor to stop work if the owner or his agents cause the work to be stopped for a period of 15 days or more. NRS 624.610(4) provides:

If the owner through his or her own act or neglect, or through an act or neglect of his or her agent, excluding acts of God, floods, fires, labor disputes, strikes or reasonable adjustments to work schedules, causes the work to be stopped for a period of 15 days or

---

[184] *See* Section 3:26 Protection from Liability for Stopping Work and Terminating Contracts.

more, the prime contractor may terminate the agreement if: (a) The prime contractor gives written notice of his or her intent to terminate to the owner at least 10 days before terminating the agreement; and (b) The owner fails to allow work to resume within the time set forth in the written notice given pursuant to paragraph (a).

The owner or his agent will need to be the primary cause of the work stoppage. This can be through loss of funding, economic factors militating against the project, failing to achieve owner delivered milestones, procurement issues of owner deliverables or other issues which are not the fault or cause of the prime contractor. Issues which are not within the control of the owner are not causes to terminate the prime contract. In these cases, after a 15 day work stoppage the prime contractor may send the owner a 10 day notice of intent to terminate the contract and the owner will have that 10 day period to allow the work to continue. In this case the prime contractor is not held to a 10 day time period, and may make the time for restart of the work based on a longer period of time. Nevertheless, termination is often necessary as the elapse of time will cause the prime contractor difficulty in maintaining material commitments and subcontractor cost escalations.

3:25 Termination of or by the Lower-Tiered Subcontractor

Once the prime contractor has stopped work, or in the case of the lower-tiered subcontractor when he stops work based on a disputed withholding of funds, the prime contractor or the lower-tiered subcontractor may terminate their agreements on the project. This right of termination is reciprocal; that is, the owner or higher-tiered contractor may terminate the agreement as well. The law governing this situation is again similar to the termination of an owner / prime contractor agreement by a prime contractor, however, neither the higher-tiered contractor, nor the lower-tiered subcontractor may terminate a contract if payment has not been made by the owner and the lower-tiered subcontractor's agreement contains a pay-if-paid or pay-when-paid clause, and this is the sole reason for lack of payment. NRS 624.626(2) provides:

If a lower-tiered subcontractor stops work pursuant to paragraph (a), (c) or (d) of subsection 1, the lower-tiered subcontractor may terminate the agreement with the higher-tiered contractor by giving written notice of the termination to the higher-tiered contractor after stopping work but at least 15 days before the termination of the agreement. If the lower-tiered subcontractor is paid the amount due before the date for termination set forth in the written notice, the lower-tiered subcontractor shall not terminate the agreement and shall resume work.

As can be seen in the quotation, the provisions of NRS 624.626(1)(b) authorizing stoppage of work in the face of a pay-if-paid or pay-when-paid clause is not listed among the basis for stopping work where termination of the contract is allowed. Consequently, a lower-tiered subcontractor should not use the failure of the owner to pay the higher-tiered contractor for the lower-tiered subcontractor's work as a reason to terminate the subcontract agreement. This will expose the lower-tiered subcontractor to liability for wrongful termination of contract and potentially damages outside the protections of the PPA.

Likewise, the lower-tiered subcontractor is not allowed to terminate a contract solely due to the failure of the higher-tiered contractor to execute or respond to change order requests. The lower-tiered subcontractor must take the additional steps of submitting payment for the change order request work that has become part of the contract by operation of NRS 624.626(3), and failing to receive payment therefore may stop work and terminate the agreement under that circumstance.

One potential problem for the lower-tiered subcontractor is exposed in this situation. While the higher-tiered contractor may have allowed the change order request to become part of the contract by failure to object timely, the higher-tiered contractor may reject payment against the change order request under the pay-if-paid language of the subcontractor's agreement. While this still allows the lower-tiered subcontractor to stop work, it prevents the lower-tiered subcontractor from terminating the subcontract agreement, thereby allowing the higher-tiered contractor additional time to resolve the situation with the owner.

3:26 Protection from Liability for Stopping Work and Terminating Contracts

The prime contractor or the lower-tiered subcontractor who stops work due to a lack of payment and otherwise complies with the requirements of the PPA is immunized from liability for any damages that result from the work stoppage or termination. As applicable to prime contractors, NRS 624.610(9) provides:

> *No prime contractor or his lower-tiered subcontractors or suppliers, or their respective sureties, may be held liable for any delays or damages that an owner may suffer as a result of the prime contractor or lower-tiered subcontractors or suppliers stopping their work or the provision of materials or equipment or terminating an agreement for a reasonable basis in law or fact and in accordance with this section or reasonable cause and in accordance with this section or NRS 624.626.*

As applicable to lower-tiered subcontractors, NRS 624.626(9) provides:

> *No lower-tiered subcontractor or his or her lower-tiered subcontractors or suppliers, or their respective sureties, may be held liable for any delays or damages that an owner or higher-tiered contractor may suffer as a result of the lower-tiered subcontractor and his or her lower-tiered subcontractors and suppliers stopping their work or the provision of materials or equipment or terminating an agreement for a reasonable basis in law or fact and in accordance with this section.*

These statutory provisions, however, only offer protection if the prime contractor or the lower-tier subcontractor has properly complied with all notice requirements of the PPA, *and* has correctly demonstrated that the facts support the stoppage of work and termination. The protection only is enforced if the terminating contractor or subcontractor has a "reasonable basis in law or fact" to stop work and terminate the agreement. If the stopping and terminating contractor or subcontractor has done so without reasonable cause, there will be significant liability for abandonment of the contract and could expose that contractor or subcontractor to significant project damages. Therefore, the decision to stop work and/or terminate should be carefully considered as an option of last resort.

3:27 Final Payment and Withholding from Prime Contractors

As with progress payments, the PPA attempts to mandate timing of final payment to prime contractors. An owner who wishes to retain some final payment money from the prime contractor, however, may do so again under limited circumstances and upon certain conditions. These conditions and regulations are set forth in NRS 624.620. Subsection 1 of NRS 624.620 lays out the timing when final payment must be made to the prime contractor:

> *Except as otherwise provided in this section, any money remaining unpaid for the construction of a work of improvement is payable to the prime contractor within 30 days after: (a) Occupancy or use of the work of improvement by the owner or by a person acting with the authority of the owner; or (b) The availability of a work of improvement for its intended use. The prime contractor must have provided to the owner: (1) A written notice of availability on or before the day on which the prime contractor claims that the work of improvement became available for use or occupancy; or (2) A certificate of occupancy or a temporary certificate of occupancy issued by the appropriate building inspector or other authority.*

Under the PPA, timing of final payment to the prime contractor is arguably not regulated by contractual terms, but rather by notice to the Owner that the work is available for use, or provision of a temporary or permanent certificate of occupancy.[185] It should be noted that this is not necessarily substantial completion as would be defined by most contracts or court determinations.[186] Rather, this statute is triggered not by the act of the owner occupying or using the work, but by the delivery of notice or the certificate of occupancy to the owner that the work is available for such occupation or use. Thus, once again the owner needs to be aware of and anticipate the receipt of the prime contractor's notice or the certificate of occupancy in order to provide notice of any need to withhold additional payment from the prime contractor.

---

[185] *See* Form 3-9 in Appendix A.

[186] *See* Bruner & O'Connor on Construction Law, Section 8:23.

Furthermore, the partial use or occupancy of the project by the owner or his agent must be compensated in direct proportion to the amount of the project so used or occupied, if the completion is only partial.[187] NRS 624.620(5) provides:

> *The partial occupancy or availability of a building requires payment in direct proportion to the value of the part of the building which is partially occupied or partially available. For works of improvement which involve more than one building, each building must be considered separately in determining the amount of money which is payable to the prime contractor.*

In this case, the prime contractor should calculate the amount of his final payment that is necessarily due and include the same with the notification that the project is partially available for use or occupancy. Conversely, the owner should likewise calculate the availability of the project and be prepared for a request for payment from the prime contractor in proportion to the space reasonably available.

The fact that the PPA authorizes proportional payment for partial occupancy or availability raises the question of the amount of payment due when the jurisdictional authority issues a temporary certificate of occupancy for the project. In general, a temporary certificate of occupancy does not allow complete operations of the facility in question, but will allow the owner to begin some limited operations while the missing items for final completion are being worked out. Nothing in the PPA contemplates use of a temporary certificate of occupancy for payment purposes.

Once the notice of availability or certificate of occupancy is delivered to the owner, the owner must pay all remaining funds to the prime contractor withheld by the owner within 30 calendar days. This would include all retention and other funds withheld for any other purpose. If the owner determines that some or all of the withheld funds need to be retained, the owner must provide written notice to the prime contractor of that fact and the reasons therefore on or before the 30th day after receipt of the notice of availability or certificate of completion. NRS 624.620(3) provides:

> *If, pursuant to paragraph (a) of subsection 2, an owner intends to withhold any amount from a payment to be made to a prime contractor, the owner must, on or before the date the payment is due, give written notice to the prime contractor of any amount that will be withheld. The written notice of withholding must: (a) Identify the amount that will be withheld from the prime contractor; (b) Give a reasonably detailed explanation of the condition for which or the reason the owner will withhold that amount, including, without limitation, a specific reference to the provision or section of the agreement with the prime contractor, and any documents relating thereto, and the applicable building*

---

[187] *See* Form 3-10 in Appendix A.

code, law or regulation with which the prime contractor has failed to comply; and (c) Be signed by an authorized agent of the owner.

The requirements for withholding all or a part of the final payment due a prime contractor are essentially identical to those for withholding progress payments as previously discussed. The owner must provide written notice of the amount that will be withheld from the prime contractor, provide a reasonably detailed description of the reasons for withholding. This description should also include the legal or contractual basis for the withholding of funds. The amount withheld should be calculated as previously discussed in Sections 3:5 to 3:10, but should not include any amount for retention. The calculation method is set forth in NRS 624.620(2), which provides:

If the owner has complied with subsection 3, the owner may: (a) Withhold payment for the amount of: (1) Any work or labor that has not been performed or materials or equipment that has not been furnished for which payment is sought; (2) The costs and expenses reasonably necessary to correct or repair any work that is not materially in compliance with the agreement to the extent that such costs and expenses exceed 50 percent of the amount of retention being withheld pursuant to the terms of the agreement; and (3) Money the owner has paid or is required to pay pursuant to an official notice from a state agency, or employee benefit trust fund, for which the owner is liable for the prime contractor or his or her lower-tiered subcontractors in accordance with chapter 608, 612, 616A to 616D, inclusive, or 617 of NRS. (b) Require, as a condition precedent to the payment of any unpaid amount under the agreement, that lien releases be furnished by the prime contractor and his or her lower-tiered subcontractors and suppliers in accordance with the provisions of paragraphs (a) and (c) of subsection 5 of NRS 108.2457.

Once again, the prime contractor's payment may be conditioned on receipt of conditional lien releases in the form set forth in NRS 108.2457(5)(a) and (c).[188] Payment requested without provision of the conditional lien releases from all levels of lower-tiered subcontractors may be withheld until such releases are provided. Once again, however, the final payment cannot be withheld based on the failure to provide unconditional release forms. The owner is therefore at risk that the prime contractor would fail to provide final payment to all subcontractors and suppliers. An owner should carefully consider the use of joint checks to ensure payment reaches all levels of the construction project organizational chart.

3:28 FINAL PAYMENT AND WITHHOLDING FROM LOWER-TIERED SUBCONTRACTORS

Final payment to lower-tiered subcontractors is governed by the provisions of NRS 624.624 and NRS 624.626 discussed within the topic of progress payments discussed in Sections 3:19 to 3:26, inclusive. However, the higher-tiered contractor is again provided

---

[188] *See* Forms 8-7 and 8-9 in Appendix A.

the additional option of withholding if the higher-tiered contractor is not paid and there exists a valid pay-if-paid or pay-when-paid clause in the subcontract.[189] No separate provisions regarding final payment to lower-tiered subcontractors is provided within the PPA. This raises a number of concerns for lower-tiered subcontractors seeking to recover their retention payments when the project is of any substantial duration.

In some instances, final payment of retention and other withheld amounts may be extended by the owner through the issuance of change orders to the prime contractor or simply because the affected lower-tiered subcontractor's work was complete early on in the construction process. In these cases, final payment to the prime contractor will not be made for a substantial period of time and the lower-tiered subcontractor may face the prospect of not receiving his final payment months or sometimes even years after his work is complete. While some efforts to rectify this perceived inequity have been unsuccessfully made at the legislative level in recent years,[190] there is currently no legal impediment to contractually retaining a lower-tiered subcontractor's final payment until final completion of the entire project. This should be a matter of negotiation between the lower-tiered subcontractor and the higher-tiered contractor at bid time.

3:29 Delivery of Notices under the Prompt Payment Act

As the PPA is driven by notice to the various parties, the PPA does proscribe the methods in which notice must be provided under its provisions. These notice requirements are found in NRS 624.622 affecting notice between owners and prime contractors and NRS 624.628 as affecting relationships between higher-tiered contractors and lower-tiered subcontractors. NRS 624.622 provides in pertinent part:

> *1. A prime contractor shall provide a copy of any notice given to an owner pursuant to subsection 1 or 2 of NRS 624.610 to each lower-tiered subcontractor with whom the prime contractor has entered into an agreement. Upon receipt of payment pursuant to NRS 624.609, the prime contractor shall notify all such lower-tiered subcontractors in writing of his receipt of payment.*
>
> ...
>
> *3. All notices required pursuant to this section, NRS 624.609, 624.610 and 624.620 must be: (a) Delivered personally, in which case the prime contractor shall obtain a notarized*

---

189 It should be kept in mind by the higher-tiered contractor, however, that the Nevada State Contractor's Board has taken the position from time to time that when a higher-tiered contractor has the capacity to pay his lower-tiered subcontractors, the failure to do so is a violation of NRS 624.3012(2) regardless of any subcontract language and/or the fact that the higher-tiered contractor has not been paid. A lower-tiered subcontractor has been able to make complaint to the contractor's board in this instance, which can result in an order by the NSCB to pay the lower-tiered subcontractor or risk administrative citation or fine. In 2009, however, the NSCB changed its policies for investigators, allowing for the review and consideration of pay-if-paid clauses as part of the investigating process.

190 *See* Senate Bill 181 of the 74th Nevada Legislative Session (2007) for example.

statement from the person who delivered the notice as proof of delivery; (b) Sent by facsimile and delivered by regular mail, in which case the prime contractor shall retain proof of a successful transmission of the facsimile; (c) Delivered by certified mail; or (d) Delivered in the manner provided for in the agreement.

Similarly, NRS 624.628 provides in pertinent part:

> *1. A lower-tiered subcontractor shall provide a copy of any notice given to a higher-tiered contractor pursuant to this section or NRS 624.624 or 624.626 to each lower-tiered subcontractor with whom the lower-tiered subcontractor has entered into an agreement and who has not fully performed under the agreement. Upon receipt of payment pursuant to NRS 624.624, the lower-tiered subcontractor shall notify all of his or her lower-tiered subcontractors in writing of receipt of payment.*
> *2. A lower-tiered subcontractor shall provide a copy of any notice given to a higher-tiered contractor pursuant to this section or NRS 624.624 or 624.626 to all other higher-tiered contractors and the owner, if known. The failure of a lower-tiered subcontractor to comply with this subsection does not invalidate any notice otherwise properly given.*
> ...
> *4. All notices required pursuant to this section or NRS 624.624 or 624.626 must be: (a) Delivered personally, in which case the lower-tiered subcontractor shall obtain a notarized statement from the person who delivered the notice as proof of delivery; (b) Sent by facsimile and delivered by regular mail, in which case the lower-tiered subcontractor shall retain proof of a successful transmission of the facsimile; (c) Delivered by certified mail; or (d) Delivered in the manner provided in the agreement between the higher-tiered contractor and the lower-tiered subcontractor.*

In these statutes, the PPA makes it clear that when a prime contractor or lower-tiered subcontractor provides a notice to the owner or the higher-tiered contractor of his intention to stop work or his intention to terminate a contract, he must likewise provide a copy of that notice to those who are working on the project along with him. For the prime contractor, a notice to the owner of his intention to stop work must be provided to all of his lower-tiered subcontractors. In turn, those lower-tiered subcontractors must provide a copy of that notice to all their lower-tiered subcontractors.

When a lower-tiered subcontractor provides such a notice to stop work or terminate a contract to his higher-tiered subcontractor, he must provide a copy of that same notice not only to his lower-tiered subcontractors but also to all other higher-tiered contractors and to the owner. Of course, there is no risk to the lower-tiered subcontractor for failing to do so. For the prime contractor, however, no such protection is provided in the statute. The absence of the protectionist language from NRS 624.622(1) may indicate a legislative intent not to protect the prime contractor from losing protections against lower-tiered subcontractor claims or owner claims under the PPA.

In any case, all notices must be delivered, whether by the owner or prime contractor under NRS 624.609 and NRS 624.610 or by the higher-tiered contractor and lower-tiered subcontractor under NRS 624.624 and NRS 624.626, in the same four acceptable manners:

1) personal delivery;
2) facsimile transfer and regular mail;
3) via certified mail or
4) any other manner agreed to in the contract between the parties involved.

In the instance of personal delivery, a notarized statement attesting to delivery must be provided by the person delivering the notice.[191] For facsimile delivery, it is important that the person making the facsimile transfer be able to both prove the facsimile was successfully made by obtaining a proof of successful transmission from the sending facsimile machine and to also be able to prove that the notice was placed in the regular mail. Although such proof may be provided in many ways, a written notarized statement can also be used for this purpose.[192] The Notice may also be delivered by certified mail. In this case, no need to have a return receipt card for the certified mail is required, though paying for and obtaining the same is the best evidence of such delivery.

Finally, the parties can agree that notice under this section can be made in any other manner. This would include notice by electronic mail or other specific method of delivery.[193] A contract provision allowing for this type of transmission method should be followed with the utmost care and should also be capable of generating proof that the method was complied with and notice was actually made in this manner. Any method that compliance cannot later be proven in court should be discarded and not used as a contractual method of delivering notice for any purpose, especially for notices required under the PPA.

3:30 INFORMATION SHARING AND OTHER MISUNDERSTOOD CONCEPTS

---

[191] *See* Form 3-11.

[192] *See* Form 3-11.

[193] An argument can be made that the PPA requirement for notices to be signed could eliminate the use of email or other electronic delivery of notices not specifically authorized by statute or contract. This argument, however, needs to be balanced against the provisions of the Uniform Electronic Transfers Act (adopted in Nevada at NRS 719.010, et seq.); for instance, NRS 719.220(3) allowing for the consideration of the common practices between the parties to determine whether the intent to be bound by electronic transactions may eliminate some of the potency of such arguments. There seems to be little substance in the requirement for a written signature when the historical dealing between an owner and contractor is through an electronic medium.

Under the PPA, there is a sense that information regarding payments made to higher-tiered contractors or prime contractors is to be shared with anyone affected by such information, regardless of their contractual or hierarchal position in the construction project organization chart. Whether payment has been made to a higher-tier contractor is critical to the lower-tier subcontractor who has not been paid and who may be entitled to either force a payment to be made by a recalcitrant prime contractor or to exercise his right to stop work or terminate his contract. As a result, the PPA requires those in a position to have such payment information to provide the same to the lower-tiered subcontractor upon written request. NRS 624.628(5) provides in pertinent part:

> *Within 5 days after the owner or any higher-tiered contractor receives a written request for the information set forth in paragraphs (a), (b) and (c) from a lower-tiered subcontractor with respect to an agreement that has not been fully performed, the owner or higher-tiered contractor shall notify the lower-tiered subcontractor in writing of the following: (a) The date the owner or higher-tiered contractor made a specified payment to the prime contractor or lower-tiered subcontractor: (b) Whether the owner or higher-tiered contractor has paid the prime contractor or lower-tiered subcontractor the entire amount of a specified payment; and (c) The amount withheld by the owner or higher-tiered contractor of a specified payment to his or her prime contractor or lower-tiered subcontractor and the condition or reason for the withholding.*

Often times the higher-tiered contractor or prime contractor will object to his lower-tiered subcontractor's request for such payment information, claiming that such information is privileged or subject to some type of proprietary and confidential claim. This is not correct. The PPA's mandate that this information be provided to the lower-tiered subcontractor, coupled with the provisions of the PPA demonstrating that any contractual obligation of confidentiality conflicting with this requirement for information sharing is unenforceable as against the State's public policy, clearly indicate that the information must be shared when requested regardless of any party's claim that the information is confidential. While what penalty the owner may suffer by failing to comply with this information is in some doubt, there is exposure of any licensed contractor to administrative citation and fine by the Nevada State Contractor's Board for failing to abide by these requirements.[194] It is therefore imperative that licensed contractors comply with any request for information timely under the PPA requirements.

The PPA also does not in itself create a cause of action for its violation. Rather, the PPA merely provides additional rights to a prime contractor or lower-tiered contractor to stop work and terminate a contract, and then proceed to exercise existing rights in law or equity to recover for the value of its work and the damages it suffers.[195] The

---

[194] *See* NRS 624.300(1).

[195] *See* NRS 624.610(8) and NRS 624.626(8), respectively.

legislative history of the PPA would also support the concept that no new causes of action are being created by the enactment of the PPA.[196] Normally, such an argument would be prevailing however, Nevada case law has expanded the effects of statutory language such as this which adds to the list of rights available to an aggrieved party, finding in at least one case that such language actually did create a cause of action under the particular statute.[197] Some have attempted in practice to construct a negligence per se argument for violations of the PPA, where damages may be presumed. Actual damages for violations of the PPA are difficult to justify beyond contractual damages and therefore may be seriously questioned.

Finally, as previously discussed in Section 3:19, Effect of a pay-when-paid or pay-if-paid contractual provision, the PPA does not eliminate the validity of a sufficiently crafted pay-if-paid contractual provision or a pay-when-paid contractual provision. In fact, the PPA can be seen as supporting the concept that such provisions are legislatively viewed as enforceable by the fact that the PPA recognizes those provisions and allows for a lower-tiered subcontractor to stop work despite its contractual validity. The PPA should not be the only basis for a lower-tiered subcontractor to assert that such payment provisions are invalid.[198]

3:31 INTEREST ON WITHHELD PAYMENTS

The PPA also modifies the standard statutory pre-judgment interest rate in Nevada, which may be applicable to a construction dispute over payment. NRS 624.630 provides:

> *Any money which is payable to a prime contractor, higher-tiered contractor or lower-tiered subcontractor pursuant to NRS 624.609, 624.610, 624.620, 624.624, 624.626 or 624.628 accrues interest from the time it becomes due at a rate equal to the higher of: 1. The rate agreed upon in the agreement between the parties; or 2. The rate equal to the prime rate at the largest bank in this State, as determined by the Commissioner of Financial Institutions on January 1 or July 1, as the case may be, immediately preceding: (a) The time at which the agreement was signed; or (b) If the agreement was oral, the*

---

[196] *See* Minutes of the Senate Subcommittee on Commerce and Labor, 71st Legislative Session, April 21, 2001. In discussing this section, one of the drafters of the legislation stated: "The intent of the provision was not to create rights that do not otherwise exist. It was intended to preserve the mechanic's lien rights, and also to preserve whatever rights may be provided by contract. It is similar language to what we used in the "prompt pay" statute to preserve the right to arbitrate. As long as the rights are not impaired and the contractor or subcontractor in the respective sections can pursue those claims or rights they have "at law or equity," we would not have an objection to modifying the language in some fashion so it would be fair to all parties."

[197] *See Olson v. Richard*, 120 Nev. 240, 243-244, 89 P.3d 31 (2004).

[198] *See Lehrer McGovern Bovis, Inc. v. Bullock Insulation, Inc.*, 197 P.3d 1032, fn. 50 (Nev. 2008).

time at which the terms of the agreement were agreed to by the parties, plus 4 percent until the date of payment.

Thus, a calculated interest rate in the construction contract between the disputing parties will be enforced. However, in the absence of such a rate, the applicable interest rate will be determined at the prime rate, plus *four* percent. The standard prejudgment interest rate in Nevada is prime rate plus *two* percent.[199] As such, the PPA makes failure to pay a contractor more onerous than any other breach of contract.

3:32 Waiver, Modification and Alterations

The catch-all provisions of the PPA found in NRS 624.622 and NRS 624.628 also block any attempts by owners or higher-tiered contractors to modify the rights established by the PPA or to have such lower-tiered contractors seeking to assert those rights waive their applicability. NRS 624.622(2) provides in pertinent part:

> *A condition, stipulation or provision in an agreement which: (a) Requires a prime contractor to waive any rights provided in this section, NRS 624.609, 624.610, 624.620 or 624.630, or which limits those rights; (b) Relieves an owner of any obligation or liability imposed pursuant to NRS 624.606 to 624.630, inclusive ... is against public policy and is void and unenforceable.*

Likewise, NRS 624.628(3) provides in pertinent part:

> *A condition, stipulation or provision in an agreement which: (a) Requires a lower-tiered subcontractor to waive any rights provided in this section or NRS 624.624, 624.626 or 624.630 or which limits those rights; (b) Relieves a higher-tiered contractor of any obligation or liability imposed pursuant to this section, NRS 624.624, 624.626 or 624.630; ...is against public policy and is void and unenforceable.*

As these provisions demonstrate, any attempt to modify or waive the rights conferred within the PPA on those who might seek to enforce those rights, as well as any attempt to relieve the party who is obligated or liable for the failure to perform under the PPA cannot be enforced. Indeed, the legislature has declared the effort to do so against the public policy of the state, which has been held by the Nevada Supreme Court to be definitive.[200] As such, the PPA must be considered at every level of private works contracting within the State of Nevada.

---

[199] NRS 17.130(2).

[200] *See Dayside Inc. v. First Judicial Dist. Court of State of Nevada, in and for Carson City,* 119 Nev. 404, 408, 75 P.3d 384, 387 (2003) (overruled by, *Lehrer McGovern Bovis, Inc. v. Bullock Insulation, Inc.*, 197 P.3d 1032 (Nev. 2008)).

Chapter 4 Nevada Construction Contracts

4:1 Introduction to Nevada construction contracts

The use of construction contracts is of critical importance in the performance of construction work and in the minimization of disputes. In general, no work should be performed until a specific and written construction contract has been prepared and executed. While this is not always the case in real world environments, the construction parties should use their best efforts to obtain a complete contract or at least determine what written documentation has been prepared and executed, in order to ascertain whether a written record of the transaction exists before starting work. Whether all the terms of a contract are included in the writing is not as important as ascertaining that there is some writing that, at a minimum, contains a scope of work, a price or method to determine the price of the work and an indication of an intent to be bound by the scope and payment terms.

Beyond mere scope of work and payment terms, certain specific preventive measures may be taken to minimize or avoid disputes in construction projects through the construction contract. These measures not only include ensuring that proper and common issues of construction are contractually resolved, but other activities as well; thoroughly reviewing the contract and bid documents, including the wording of the invitation to bidders and/or contractor's proposal, taking the steps necessary to obtain bond and insurance protection, evaluating potential and actual problems as they arise, maintaining an adequate record keeping system, involving the attorney and other consultants early, and properly documenting problems as they occur.

The initial decision by the owner should be the preparation of a project program, which is essentially a listing of all the uses of the construction project when finished, the desired features of the project and the specifications to which the project should function. The more detailed the project program is from the owner, the more accurate will be the design and ultimately the construction of the project in order to meet the owner's expectations.

4:2 Project delivery methods

Once the project is programmed and meets the owner's needs, the method by which the project is delivered needs to be selected. Project delivery involves planning, funding, programming, scheduling, designing, selecting the site, obtaining governmental approvals, and many other factors as well as the method for constructing the project. In today's highly competitive and specialized market, many "traditional" architectural and construction firms are looking to expand their scope of services and client base by offering unified, one stop shopping as an alternative to the traditional design-bid-build method of project delivery. Moreover, private owners and public entities increasingly seek to expedite project completion and control costs and claims. These factors have facilitated the increased use of construction management, multiple prime, fast-track and design-build contracting, integrated design or "integrated project development" and other delivery methodologies which help to alleviate the tensions that arise through the traditional design-bid-build model.

The selection of a project delivery method depends on the unique circumstances of each project. The parties should consider all potential project delivery systems to make an informed decision as to the most appropriate method. Public entities must adhere to specific rules when selecting methods of project delivery. Private entities are not bound by such considerations. The following are some examples of more popular construction delivery methods and their advantages and disadvantage. This is by no means an exhaustive list of the potential delivery methods.[201]

4:3 Design-bid-build

Under the three-part design-bid-build method of project delivery, an owner either uses in-house architects or solicits proposals for programming, schematic design, design development, complete construction drawings and specifications and costs estimates. The architect is selected on the basis of qualifications and demonstrated competence. Price is usually a secondary consideration or is a factor only in negotiating the terms of the contract. Usually, 100% complete construction documents are to be submitted to one or more contractors for competitive bidding or a negotiated construction contract, though this is often not the case.

In this traditional setting, the architect's role is a collaborative relationship with the owner to design a project that meets the owner's needs and to act as the owner's agent to ensure the contractor precisely follows the drawings and specifications. The architect is responsible for the efficacy of the design and for code compliance, particularly disabled access and environmental compliance, unless expressly agreed otherwise. The architect interprets documents and accepts or rejects construction as complying or not complying with the contract documents. The architect can also act as an arbiter of disputes between the owner and the contractor.

The architect is held to a standard of professional negligence, i.e., it must perform design services in the same manner as architects in the same field and with the same training would under similar circumstances. Architects may also be held to be responsible for express warranties set forth in the contract with owner, e.g., the plans will be free from

[201] For an exhaustive discussion of the issues in construction contracting on a global scale, refer to Bruner & O'Connor on Construction Law, Chapter 2.

defects, or the architect will modify the design, without cost to the owner if all bids exceed the architect's estimate of construction cost. Unless the contract contains such express warranties, however, an architect does not guarantee that the plans will be free of defects or even that the design will produce a project that is fit for its intended use.

Under the design-bid-build method of project delivery, a single contractor is selected who furnishes construction. In turn, the contractor enters into subcontracts with trade contractors and suppliers. The contractor's role is to comply with the drawings and specifications and other contract requirements. The contractor is responsible for means, methods, techniques and sequence of construction, construction cost, quality and schedule. Unless contractually required to do value engineering, the contractor generally will only suggest changes that benefit it. The contractor is responsible to strictly meet the contractual promises and various express and implied warranties in the contract, e.g., the materials are new, of good quality and the work is free of defects.

The owner must provide access to the site, make prompt payments and impliedly warrants that the project can be constructed from the plans and specifications. The Nevada Supreme Court appears to have signaled its intention to adopt the holding of *Spearin v. United States*, 248 U.S. 132, 54 Ct.Cl. 187, 39 S.Ct 59 (1918),[202] while the doctrine has been recognized and applied by the 9th Circuit as in keeping with Nevada law.[203] Due to the *Spearin* doctrine, an owner's liability to the contractor for defects in the plans and specifications is often greater than the liability of the architect who furnished the plans to the owner.

The design-bid-build model provides clear lines of authority among owner, architect and contractor and clear standards and divisions of legal and contractual responsibilities. The contractor looks to the owner to provide a constructible set of plans, who in turns looks to the architect to coordinate the design and answer the questions posed by the contractor. The architect and the contractor provide checks and balances to each other's work, and the owner is allowed to rely on the Architects work product and has the architect to verify the contractors work is complete and accurate.

Unfortunately, the design-bid-built model has numerous disadvantages as well. A significant time delay occurs between the design and the construction, which often results in lost cost saving opportunities through value engineering. Since each of the three players are solitary and independent of each other, the method does not give support to a team atmosphere, which can breed disputes over change orders, requests

---

[202] *Halcrow, Inc. v. Dist. Ct.*, 129 Nev.Adv.Op. 42, 302 P.3d 114, 1154, fn 3 (2013), *see also Home Furniture, Inc. v. Brunzell Construction Co.*, 84 Nev. 309, 313-14, 440 P.2d 398, 401-02 (1968).

[203] *See Frank Briscoe Co., Inc. v. Clark County*, 857 F.2d 606, 612, 12 Fed. R. Serv. 3d 1307 (9th Cir. 1988).

for information and can result in prolonged disputes and protracted litigation. To avoid these disadvantages, other delivery methods have been created with varying degrees of success.

4:4 Construction Management

Construction management, which gained popularity in the 1970's, and has been expanding ever since, was one of the first methods of realigning the traditional project relationships by severing the management function from both the architect and the contractor. The scope of services of a construction manager varies widely, so it is hard to precisely define. It has been said that a construction manager is whatever the contract with the owner says it is. In general, construction management is the process of professional management applied to a construction program, from concept to completion, for the purpose of controlling cost, time and quality, including planning, scheduling, bidding, contracting, cost estimating, quality control, cost control, risk management and construction productivity. There is relatively little case law interpreting this relationship (none in Nevada), so legal liability of construction managers is often unclear. In general, the liability of a construction manager flows from the services performed and the type of contract. Construction managers typically fall into three groups: 1) Construction Manager as at-risk contractor; 2) Construction Manager as design professional; and 3) Construction Manager as agent/advisor to owner. Regardless of the type of Construction Manager, Nevada law will require he be either a licensed general contractor, a licensed professional engineer or a registered architect.[204]

Contractors were the first to call themselves construction managers in response to the complexities of construction techniques and the difficulty in managing highly specialized

---

[204] NRS 624.020 provides in pertinent part:

> *1. "Contractor" is synonymous with "builder."*
> *2. A contractor is any person, except a registered architect or a licensed professional engineer, acting solely in his professional capacity, who in any capacity other than as the employee of another with wages as the sole compensation, undertakes to, offers to undertake to, purports to have the capacity to undertake to, or submits a bid to, or does himself or by or through others, construct, alter, repair, add to, subtract from, improve, move, wreck or demolish any building, highway, road, railroad, excavation or other structure, project, development or improvement, or to do any part thereof, including the erection of scaffolding or other structures or works in connection therewith. Evidence of the securing of any permit from a governmental agency or the employment of any person on a construction project must be accepted by the Board or any court of this State as prima facie evidence that the person securing that permit or employing any person on a construction project is acting in the capacity of a contractor pursuant to the provisions of this chapter.*
> *4. A contractor includes a construction manager who performs management and counseling services on a construction project for a professional fee.*

subcontractors. NRS 624.020(4) sets forth contractor licensing requirements and for purposes of that chapter defines "contractor" to include a construction manager who performs management and counseling services on a construction project for a professional fee. The Associated General Contractors of America ("AGC") treats construction management as project planning, design and construction as integrated tasks, assigned to team members to maximize value to the owner. Construction management is viewed as professional services, with construction services as one component of the total Construction Management package. A Construction Manager is "at-risk" if it guarantees the cost of the work (by lump sum or guaranteed maximum price) and time for construction.

There are many inherent conflicts of interest in the at-risk form of construction management. If the Construction Manager is at-risk and retains the right to perform work with its own forces, it may seek to maximize its profits after the trades are bid by self-performing work. Moreover, a Construction Manager cannot be expected to make strict inspections of its own work. If the method of compensation for a Construction Manager at risk is cost of the work plus a fee with no guaranteed maximum price, the Construction Manager has no incentive to control costs. From the Construction Manager's perspective, if the Construction Manager is at risk, it has the traditional adverse relationship with the owner, but in providing professional services, the Construction Manager has assumed new responsibilities and liabilities that arise from the relationship.

Design professionals entered the construction management business who, like contractors, viewed themselves as already performing management functions and sought to avoid the loss of some of their traditional services to other firms. NRS 623.023 defines the practice of architecture to include "administration of construction, consultations, evaluations, investigations, contract documents, advice and direction." Most design professionals seeking to take on a management role refer to themselves as project managers, not construction managers, emphasizing their role at the beginning of the project. In addition to conflict of interest problems, a Construction Manager acting as design professional may face licensing problems, particularly if the Construction Manager is also responsible for construction.[205]

When the construction manager is functioning as the agent of or advisor to the owner, the construction manager performs its functions for a fee, without any business risk and is not in a contractual relationship with any of the trades or designers on the project. In this role, the construction manager functions as an independent professional. The construction manager does not perform significant design or construction, although, it

---

[205] *See* NRS 624.020(4); *cf. Kourafas v. Basic Food Flavors, Inc.*, 120 Nev. 195, 88 P.3d 822 (2004) (abrogated by *Buzz Stew, LLC v. City of North Las Vegas*, 181 P.3d 670 (Nev. 2008)).

may provide "general conditions" of the site. Regardless, the construction manager as agent must conform to Nevada law as to licensing authority.[206]

Nevada law requires caution here. As a delivery method, Nevada does *not* allow Construction Management where an unlicensed owner directly holds the risk of trade (i.e., subcontractor) liability while retaining a construction manager as its agent to overview and supervise the construction. In a somewhat twisted legal argument, the NSCB takes the position that holding the trade subcontracts puts the owner in the position of acting as an unlicensed contractor.[207] This position essentially means that the delivery of a private work project via the construction manager as agent delivery method is illegal in Nevada, unless the owner itself holds the appropriate general contracting license, or also retains a licensed general contractor to perform the actual construction, and the construction manager purely as the owner's representative on the project.

Each type of construction management contracting has its own advantages and disadvantages, however, certain general statements can be made. Construction management is well suited where Owner does not have in house staff with expertise to manage a job, multiple primes or competitive bidding or fast track design is involved. Early input on price and constructability before bidding the work prevents change orders and should result in lower construction costs, and construction management provides checks and balances on architect. Fostering a close working relationship among construction management designer and owner can eliminate surprises in cost, design and time.

Similarly, each type of construction management has its own disadvantages. For construction management as agent, since prime and trade contractors do not sign a

---

[206] *See* NRS 624.020(4).

[207] This argument is a bit convoluted, but essentially runs as follows: An owner who undertakes to build a project through a construction manager as agent ("CMAA"), while holding all of the trade contracts, is "himself or herself or through others, construct[ing ... an ... improvement..." under NRS 624.020(2), and in holding 2 or more unrelated trade contracts is performing as a "general building contractor" under NRS 624.215(3). Since the owner does not hold a class B license, in holding the trade contracts directly he is therefore unlawfully "act[ing in the capacity of a contractor" which is a violation of NRS 624.700(1)(a). This is buttressed by the outright prohibition on owners "contract[ing with a specialty or other contractor directly pursuant to an agreement with the managing contractor without first obtaining the appropriate ... license" found in NAC 624.580(5). This is somewhat perplexing, since the owner has retained a licensed general contractor to manage and supervise the construction, but has merely decided to minimize the risk of payment diversion by holding the subcontracts directly. Given the risks for owners using the mandatory payment release forms under NRS 108.2457, use of construction management as agent as a delivery method would be beneficial. Likewise, the owner holding trade contracts directly benefits the trades by allowing payment to be received promptly and without potential diversion by the general contractor. Nevertheless, such benefits have not been sufficient to prompt the NSCB to seek revision of these rules.

contract with construction management, such contractors can still blame each other or the construction manager for schedule or coordination problems. Since the construction manager as agent is merely the agent of the owner, defaults by the construction manager places the owner at increased risk and exposure for such construction errors made by the construction manager as agent. Further, the construction management advisor has no leverage to force prime or trade contractors to perform without contractual privity. They can only act as the owner's agent in attempting to demand compliance.

The construction manager as agent overlaps its duties with architect's or contractor's services, which only adds expense without liability unless the construction manager is at-risk. Therefore, the use of a construction manager as agent can merely increase cost to the project, without any significant benefit. If construction management emphasizes value engineering it may create or exacerbate an adversarial relationship with architect.

Nevada also allows construction management in public works construction. As discussed in Chapter 6: Public Works Construction, construction management in public works has been under attack, primarily because of public entity affinity for this delivery method and the perception that construction management limits the number of contractors able to win public works construction contracts.

4:5. Design-build

In design-build contracting, one entity performs both design and construction under a single contract with the owner. Typically, the design-builder is a licensed general contractor that employs its own architects and engineers or retains them as sub-consultants, or the design-builder is a joint venture between a general contractor and a design firm which engages its own contractor's license. With this method of project delivery, owners seek to avoid the conflicts that arise between designers and contractors when there are errors or omissions in the design or where the contractor fails to adequately inspect the site, or coordinate the plans. Most owners also seek to expedite the schedule and thereby save costs with design-build.

Design-build does not reduce the tasks required to complete a project but reallocates responsibilities and risks in a different manner than the traditional three-part design, bid, build system. Since the design-build process eliminates the separate design contract with the owner, the owner's *Spearin* doctrine liability for design is also eliminated. Time to process design changes or questions about the design from the contractor is drastically reduced and the number of change orders and cost increases to the owner due to design errors should also be limited, since there is only one source of both construction and design.

There are also numerous advantages to the Design-Builder / Contractor. The use of design-build allows for a faster construction process and reduces repetitive tasks, thereby decreasing general conditions and overhead expenses. Theoretically, the design-build process should also reduce scheduling problems caused by lags in design and building communication, as well as job site disputes. These advantages should allow for a higher profit margin and reduced construction expenses.

Along with the advantages, there are a number of disadvantages. For the owner, design-build contracting can cause a number of unforeseen risks. Weakness in the abilities of the design-builder can be found in that the design-builder may have emphasized one discipline over the other, leaving a weak link the process. For instance, if the design-builder is a contractor who has added a design service to his business, the design may suffer from a lack of experience in the design discipline. Conversely, if the design-builder was a design firm that added construction services to their work product, the construction work may suffer, as well as the cost may escalate due to a lack of construction experience. Furthermore, the design build process leaves the owner out of as much of the decision making process as possible, leaving the project to the design-builder. As the owner's input grows, the owner takes on more and more liability for interfering with the design-build process which can lead to the owner's increased legal liability. Finally, the design-build team may have difficulty in obtaining the best quality insurance and bonding of the various disciplines, thereby reducing the owner's protection in the event of a default.

There are disadvantages for the design-build contractor as well. Taking on the obligations of both design and construction assumes a much greater risk that a single discipline is required to hold. The design-builder will be responsible for the costs of design errors and bid busts that they ordinarily might have contractual or indemnity shields from under more traditional delivery methodologies. Likewise, the design-build team must be licensed as both a designer and a contractor, and provide the appropriate errors and omissions insurance and commercial general liability insurance which the individual designer or contractor would not otherwise be required to provide. Insurers and bonding companies may not be receptive to providing the design-builder with these policies if there is a perceived weakness in one of the disciplines.

4:6 Integrated Design / Integrated Project Development

In the 2000's, Leadership in Energy and Environmental Design ("LEED") construction certifications became a building standard within public and private works construction and Nevada saw a significant number of public and private LEED certified projects constructed. Issued by the United States Green Building Counsel (USGBC), LEED certification reflects the efforts of developers, designers and contractors to deliver a new building (or retrofit an existing building) in a manner which reduces the impact of the construction and/or operation of the structure on the existing environment, resulting in a building that is constructed and operated in an efficient and "sustainable" manner. As an incentive to undertake such efforts, NRS Chapter 701A Energy-Related Tax

Incentives, was established to offer certain tax breaks and incentives for "green" building which achieve LEED certification at the silver, gold or platinum levels. These incentives resulted in large scale projects seeking LEED certification status, and hence a lower tax obligation. Most notably, City Center Resort on the Las Vegas Strip is one of the largest new construction projects to earn LEED certification in the world. Likewise, existing facilities such as the Sands Convention Center have sought and obtained LEED certification for their existing "green" building operation and maintenance programs.

As the Great Recession took hold and persisted through the early 2010s, public entities in Nevada began to see tax revenues drop from LEED certified construction. Likewise, as using "sustainable" construction methods and operations became more standardized, the need for LEED certification (and the significant cost related merely to the certification itself) dropped off in favor of simply designing and building in a "green" manner. In recognition of these two effects, the 2013 Nevada Legislature revised NRS Chapter 701A to allow incentives to be available for LEED "or other equivalent rating system" compliant projects. Likewise, the tax incentives were lessened for meeting those "green" criteria. As a result, the number of construction projects actively seeking LEED certification dropped off significantly, while "green" construction has continued to become the standard of the industry in new construction.

"Green" building incentives are the responsibility of the Nevada Office of Energy ("NOE"). NRS Chapter 701A establishes certain criteria which a private work construction project must meet in order to obtain the tax breaks for "green" building. While the legislation and enacted regulations for obtaining these tax incentives are voluminous, the tax incentives can be reasonably summarized. Essentially, the director of the NOE now establishes its own criteria for achieving a green building rating, which are identified as silver, gold or platinum levels. NRS 701A.110 provides partial abatements of property tax obligations imposed under NRS Chapter 361 in the amounts of 25 percent, 30 percent or 35 percent, respectively, but cannot exceed the amount of $100,000 per year. The property tax abatements apply to all such taxes, except those imposed for support of public education. These abatements will continue for at least 10 years, so long as the building continues to meet the "green" certification standards in the determination of the NOE. In addition, under NRS 701A.200 further abatements to real property taxes imposed by NRS Chapter 361 are available to businesses using a system for the provision of climate control, water or electrical services by use of wind, solar, geothermal, conversion of solid waste or waterpower.

While these partial tax abatements are welcome in theory, they are in reality offsets for the increased cost of construction and maintenance caused by "green" building products. As "green" building is a relatively new concept in wide application, materials and supply techniques meeting the rigorous requirements for "green" certification have been in short supply and had limited testing to demonstrate their effectiveness in long term use.

Some "green" materials simply do not meet minimum specifications for use in particular designs, which requires the use of non-"green" materials as substitutes. Over the last several years, however, innovation and demand have increased ready available "green" materials, and availability appears to no longer be a weak link in the "green" building chain for success. Whether the long term sustainability and functionality of those materials will meet the goals of "sustainability" remains to be seen.

A key component of LEED certification under LEED version 3 is construction by use of the Integrated Design or Integrated Project Development ("IPD") management model. IPD has been defined as "a project delivery approach that integrates people, systems, business structures, and practices into a process that collaboratively harness the talents and insights of all participants to reduce waste and optimize efficiency through all phases of design, fabrication and construction."[208] While the goals of IPD as stated in this definition are laudable, in order to properly function, a complete shift of the adversarial mindset that is built into the design-bid-build construction delivery model has to occur. While CMAR, Design-Build and other alternative delivery methods seek to create a more conducive construction model that reduces delivery costs and time by reducing disputes between the owner, designer and contractor, the system is still plagued by the idea of shifting liability to the other parties in the construction paradigm. As a result, there is still significant opportunity for waste, inefficiencies and resulting cost increases and disputes to arise.

Alternative delivery methods such as CMAR reduce inefficiencies by early involvement of the contractor in preconstruction activities. They also intend that key trade subcontractors will be involved as design progresses, in order to achieve and maximize project cost savings through value engineering and thoroughness of design constructability review. The adoption of Design-Build and CMAR delivery methods for Nevada public works construction were at least in part intended to reduce liability for the State for construction cost increases resulting from deficient design coordination. Huge public government liabilities for construction project claims, such as on the Regional Justice Center in Clark County, have demonstrated the need for early involvement of construction professionals into the design process. These concepts fit perfectly within the parameters of an IPD delivery method.

Nevada public entities routinely use AIA form contract documents for their projects and the AIA have formulated form contracts using the IPD project management strategies the AIA A195, B195 and A295 form agreements. As one author described the documents:

[208] IPD Definition Task Group, 2007, which is an interdisciplinary group sponsored by the American Institute of Architects California Council and McGraw-Hill Construction.

> *Unlike traditional AIA agreements,[the new IPD AIA Documents], B195 and A195 do not include a scope of services; instead, this is spelled out in A295 General Conditions, which also establish a collaboration process for the owner-architect-constructor team. ...[The] A295 writes up a process for early involvement on the part of the contractor, working with the architect through design development, providing constructability reviews, and developing a guaranteed maximum price. This approach changes only a little from the traditional risk-and-reward model.*[209]

The model for IPD within the mentioned AIA form documents may complement well the existing CMAR process outlined in NRS 338.169, *et seq*. But what makes IPD the game changer is the use of Building Information Modeling ("BIM") and the concept of inter-discipline liability waiver.

IPD finds its stride with the use of BIM to construct the project digitally on a computer *before* the shovels are placed in the ground. As described by the National Institute of Building Sciences:

> *A [Building Information Model, or] BIM is a three-dimensional digital representation of the physical and functional characteristics of a building. It is a shared resource of knowledge about a facility that can be used to make decisions about the building throughout its life-cycle, from the initial idea, to design and construction, through daily operations and eventual demolition. [¶] Using BIMs effectively can resolve problems and reduce expense and frustration. For example, when designing a building, there are floor plans, plumbing plans and heating, ventilation and air conditioning (HVAC) plans, often prepared by different people. Without effective communication, the designers risk having pipes, vents and beams colliding in the same space. A BIM allows all of the plans to be stored in a digital format together, so problems can be caught before construction begins.*[210]

When viewed in this light, the value of BIM and IPD to a construction project, including a Nevada public construction project functioning under the Construction Manager at Risk model,[211] begins to take visible form. In field construction design conflicts, failed or lack of coordination issues, requests for information, change order requests and negotiation, and the attendant legal disputes that follow, can potentially be eliminated, as the actual computer driven BIM demonstrates the conflicts that give rise to these efficiency-robbing disputes in electronic 3D images. Solutions can be coordinated in the construction trailer between the designer and affected trade subcontractors long before

---

[209] *New AIA Agreements Support Integrated Project Delivery*, B.J. Novitski, Architectural Record, The McGraw-Hill Companies, Inc., July, 2008.

[210] National Institute of Building Sciences, *2009 Annual Report to the President of the United States*, pg. 28; www.nibs.org/client.assets/files/nibs/NIBS 2009AnnualReport.pdf.

[211] *See* Section 6:21 Construction Manager at Risk

they materialize in the field. So long as the data input is handled competently and cooperatively, the slow down or actual stoppage of construction work to navigate the RFI, Response, Change Order path is eliminated.

While the risks and rewards of BIM pose unique and knotty legal questions that must be vetted in detail (and in many cases have not yet even been considered), the potential value of these liability eliminating concepts cannot be denied. For this reason, a well constructed IPD agreement will require involvement of all key construction team players at the outset of project concept, and include inter-construction team liability waivers for contractual breach, except for willful misconduct.

Such legal concepts are antithetical to current construction contract drafting focus. In order to achieve workable IPD construction contracts, however, cooperative negotiations rather than adversarial blame-shifting must be adopted. Construction lawyers need to learn to seek solutions outside of the traditional liability shifting contract articles drafted to protect clients in the context of litigation, and embrace the more business oriented concepts of making business deals work through cooperative approaches to dispute resolution, sharing of responsibility for project deficiency and the sharing of proprietary information within the development team. The resulting savings in time, cost and legal expenses will serve all members of the development team well in this time of economic recession.

Because of the limited nature of contract term negotiation within the Nevada Public Works system of bid solicitation, public projects may have the easiest ability to incorporate IPD into their construction projects. At present, nothing within the parameters of NRS Chapter 338 would appear to either expressly forbid or expressly authorize the use of IPD and BIM management tools within the constructs of the CMAR or other project delivery protocols authorized for Nevada public works construction. While the obligation of the CMAR to assume overall responsible for satisfactory completion of the preconstruction and actual construction services under NRS 338.1698(4) may impliedly undermine the liability sharing concept of IPD, careful drafting of the responsibility provisions should avoid this complication. So long as the formal steps of CMAR selection are complied with, the use of IPD management techniques should not be disallowed, and in fact should be sought for the reduction of liability for all parties.

The adoption of such cooperative contract measures will require forward and innovative thinking to take most advantage of this new management technique. The benefits to Nevada in reduction of cost, environmental impact, time and disputes will be welcome rewards for such efforts.

4:7 Review of Contract Documents / Use of Standard Form Contracts

Only by a thorough review of the contract documents can the owner or contractor be fully aware of any risks they are assuming over and above those normally expected on a construction project. These risks might result from a poorly drafted scope of work clause, a "contingent pay" provision, a "no damages for delay" clause, a high retention provision, an unusual change or disputes clause, a termination for convenience clause, a liquidated damages clause, an unreasonable notice clause or several other unique construction contract clauses which can shift liability unexpectedly. Because Nevada in general will enforce contracts as written,[212] the contractor and owner must evaluate each of these contingencies to properly estimate the cost of performance.

On private projects, the contractor may want to make its proposal dependent upon certain changes in the contract documents. Of course, this option is not available if the proposal is submitted pursuant to public works competitive bidding statutes. If in submitting a proposal, the contractor fails to condition the proposal upon certain changes in the contract documents, the contractor may have waived its right to object to the contract provisions. The contractor may also be bound to the original contract documents at the price in the proposal, i.e., if the owner accepts the proposal. On the other hand, including conditions in the proposal will place the vigilant contractor in a good position to negotiate the provisions prior to executing the contract. In most cases, it is possible to negotiate more favorable general conditions which better protect your rights but are still fair to both parties.

4:8 Contract Work Scope Provisions

A Contractor's work is defined within his contract as his scope. Scope of work provisions will vary on a job-by-job basis, and for that reason, the scope provisions of every new contract should be carefully reviewed to ensure that the scope of work to be performed under the contract equates with the scope of work provided for in the bid. Most contracts will specifically define the "Work" or the "Scope of Work" provided under the contract, and will include the defined term "Contract Documents." Usually, the Contract Documents consist of the Contract, the Drawings and Specifications, and may include other such documents and particular descriptions of the work provided by the architect or owner. In many cases, the Work will be generally and broadly defined. A typical form construction scope of work might read as follows:

> *The term 'Work' means the construction and services required by the Contract Documents, whether completed or partially completed, and includes all other labor,*

[212] *Dayside Inc. v. First Judicial Dist. Court of State of Nevada, in and for Carson City*, 119 Nev. 404, 75 P.3d 384 (2003) (overruled on other grounds by, *Lehrer McGovern Bovis, Inc. v. Bullock Insulation, Inc.*, 197 P.3d 1032 (Nev. 2008)).

materials, equipment and services provided or to be provided by the Contractor to fulfill the Contractor's obligations. The Work may constitute the whole or a part of the Project.[2 3]

In general, this definition includes the work of subcontractors, sub-subcontractors and material suppliers to the Project. The owner and contractor should always review the Work definitions to be certain that the bid scope is the same obligation she is contracting for the agreed upon price. If those work scope provisions are excessive or include work not within the contemplated scope of the bid, or that were otherwise excluded, the scope provisions should be modified or an exclusions list should be attached to the contract to clarify these exceptions.[214]

The contract documents should always include at least drawings and specifications contained therein, and may include other documents as well. Most contracts will specifically define at least the list of drawings on which the contract sum was based, and care should be taken to make sure this list is accurate to that available to the contractor when it developed its price for the work. Depending on the size of the project, specifications may be found in the drawings themselves or will be bound in a separate book and provide to the contractor all the exact qualities and requirements for materials, equipment, systems, standards and workmanship issues. They should be reviewed carefully in conjunction with the various warranties provided by the contractor before executing his contracts. Specifications should be clear and be coordinated with the drawings. Be certain that the specifications are thoroughly reviewed for all requirements for performance when advising contractors on bid preparation. Care should always be taken to ensure that there are no inconsistencies between the drawings, specifications and the work definitions, either between them or within their own specifics. Many problems arise in construction projects due to a lack of

---

[213] AIA Form 1997-A201, Section 1:1:3.

[214] It should also be noted that NRS 108.22184 provides:

> *"Work" means the planning, design, geotechnical and environmental investigations, surveying, labor and services provided by a lien claimant for the construction, alteration or repair of any improvement, property or work of improvement whether the work is completed or partially completed.*

This definition is not intended to be a contract scope requirement for the work, but rather is a statutory definition of work to be included in a mechanics' lien claim. For a contractor, such a definition would not be acceptable as the term would obligate the contractor to perform many tasks beyond their expertise and, indeed, beyond their license limitations. Therefore, the drafter of a scope of work should attempt to keep the contract scope to the precise work the contractor has agreed to provide and not seek definitions in other legal contexts.

coordination between the various design professionals on a Project. Drawings should be carefully scrutinized before commencement of construction to look for conflicts and missing information. When such conflicts are found, the contractor should always respond with a specific request for information or "RFI" to the owner or architect.

4:9. Exclusions from the contract

Not only is it important for the parties to a construction contract to know what he or she is required to construct or should expect to be constructed under the contract, it is equally important (or more so) to define and specify what is not included in the contract. Most construction bids are made subject to certain conditions and exclusions. For instance, a contractor may bid a project cost, but not take into account the costs and/or delays encountered in obtaining specific building permits through the county. Often these costs or delays are difficult to measure. Therefore, some contractors may place the burden for obtaining certain permits upon the owner and/or the architect who is responsible for the design. Such exclusions must be specifically spelled out in the contract documents.

As a general rule, the definition of "work" will always require the contractor to take all necessary steps to complete the Project. If the Project does not specifically exclude certain items, and those items are necessary for the completion of the project, the contractor may be liable for their provision, even if they were not included in the contractors bid. The contractor should therefore carefully explain in the contract all appropriate and agreed to exclusions from the scope of work.

4:10. Warranties & indemnity

Most construction contracts will require the contractor to provide warranties for her work, along with indemnification for certain potential damages arising from the contractor's performance under the contract. Typical warranties will require the contractor to warrant that all materials are new, are fit for their intended purpose, and are free from defects in materials or workmanship. Some warranties may or should be excluded especially when the contractor has little or no control over the source of materials. For example, if an owner is supplying lighting fixtures to the project for the contractor to install, the contractor should not warrant and should specifically exclude, warranties for materials and workmanship on those fixtures.

Many contracts will force the unsuspecting contractor to warrant that the work will "strictly comply with the plans and specifications." Other contracts will require that the contractor warrant his performance will "be performed in a good and workmanlike manner." While the language of these two typical clauses may seem alike, the legal effects are dramatically different. "Strict compliance with plans and specifications" requires that the contractor perform to the exact tolerances of the plans and specifications, no matter how unreasonable or extraordinary. Requiring the contractor to perform in a "good and workmanlike manner," however, merely requires the contractor to perform to the usual standards and practices in the community where the contract is performed.

Historically, Nevada has not recognized any limitation on contractual indemnity provisions. In general, the case law recognizes three "types" of indemnity provisions, which are generally recognized as "Type 1," "Type 2." and "Type 3" indemnity provisions. As applied in the context of construction, a *Type I Indemnity* is all-inclusive, which would require a contractor to hold harmless and indemnify an owner against any and all liability, regardless of whether it involves the sole negligence of the contractor/owner, or even gross negligence and willful misconduct of the contractor/owner. *Type II Indemnity* would require a Subcontractor to hold harmless and indemnify a contractor/owner against any and all liability, except that which results from the gross negligence or willful misconduct of the contractor/owner. Under this type of provision, a Subcontractor would still be charged with a duty to indemnify a contractor/owner for their sole negligence, as long as it does not amount to gross negligence or willful misconduct. *Type III Indemnity* would limit indemnification solely to those circumstances created by the contractor himself, as well limiting the amount of indemnification to the amount of fault attributable to the contractor, essentially treating indemnity as contribution, rather than a total shift of fault.

In recent years, public policy has recognized that lower-tiered construction participants generally cannot effectively bargain away broad indemnity agreements. As such, anti-indemnity statutes have come into effect to afford additional protection to these parties. Essentially, the public policy concern is to protect workers and the public from attempts to avoid liability through the use of indemnity agreements and to encourage worksite safety.[215] Except in relation to residential construction defect claims[216], these anti-indemnity statutes have not reached Nevada in any substantial way yet.

Of the states that have addressed indemnity provisions within the context of construction contracts by statute, the universal position is that Type I indemnity provisions are prohibited. It appears that Florida is the only state that, by statute, may permit Type II indemnity provisions, while the remaining states appear to prohibit Type II indemnity provisions. Finally, states that have addressed indemnity provisions appear to universally permit Type III provisions, as Type III provisions do not run the risk of encouraging a lack of due care in the performance of work. Presumably, the states that

[215] *See e.g. American Pecco Corp. v. Concrete Bldg. Systems Co.*, 392 F. Supp. 789 (N.D. Ill. 1975); *Estate of Willis v. Kiferbaum Const. Corp.*, 357 Ill. App. 3d 1002, 294 Ill. Dec. 224, 830 N.E.2d 636 (1st Dist. 2005).

[216] *See* Chapter 7: Residential Construction Defect Claims

have not addressed the issue of indemnity provisions by statute would permit Type I, II, and III indemnity provisions.

In 2010, the Nevada Supreme Court addressed the contractual language necessary to create Type I indemnity. As a general proposition, Nevada's Supreme Court usually enforces contracts as written, but has not addressed directly the effectiveness of a Type I indemnity agreement. The recent case of *George L. Brown Ins. v. Star Ins. Co.*, 237 P.3d 92, 126 Nev. Adv. Op. No. 31 (Nev. 2010), however, places specific limits on the language of a Type I indemnity agreement in order to make that obligation enforceable in Nevada. While the case is set within the context of insurance company/agent indemnity, the same analysis may apply to other industry indemnity agreements, including construction.

In the case, the Brown Agency and its individual agents ("Agents") were authorized independent insurance agents for Star Insurance ("Star"), as well as other insurance companies. The contract between the Agents and Star contained an indemnification provision requiring the Agents to indemnify Star for losses arising from the Agents' performance. Specifically, the indemnity provision stated:

> *[Brown] shall defend, indemnify and hold harmless [Star] for any and all damages, losses, liabilities, fines, penalties, costs, and all other expenses reasonably incurred by [Star] including reasonable attorney's fees, for liabilities imposed upon [Star] in connection with or arising out of any claim, suit, hearing, action or proceeding, or threat thereof in which [Star] is involved by reason of [Brown] having performed services for [Star] under this Agreement, or having failed to perform services required under this Agreement.*[217]

At some point, the Agents assisted a third party contractor in obtaining workers' compensation coverage from Star. The Agents indicated that the policy issued by Star would only cover the contractor's employees who worked in Nevada or who resided in Nevada but worked temporarily in other states. After the policy was issued, one of the contractor's workers was injured hauling materials from California to Nevada. A claim was made against the insurance policy issued by Star which Star denied, claiming the policy did not cover workers performing work outside Nevada. The workers' compensation claim was appealed to the California Workers' Compensation Appeals Board, who referred the matter to arbitration for resolution. The Arbitrator found that coverage existed, as did the California Court of Appeal and the California Supreme Court, based in part on the Agents' representations to the Contractor of the extent of coverage.

---

[217] *George L. Brown Ins. v. Star Ins. Co.*, 237 P.3d 92, 94, 126 Nev. Adv. Op. No. 31 (Nev. 2010).

Without further recourse, Star was forced to pay the workers compensation benefits to the injured worker.

Star then commenced an action in Nevada against the Agents, seeking indemnity for the cost of the lawsuits, appeals and the workers' compensation payments. Star was granted summary judgment against the Agents on the basis that the general "any and all liability" language of the contractual indemnity clause required the Agents to indemnify Star for Star's own negligent acts, despite the fact that the indemnity provision did not expressly state that the Agents were doing so. On appeal, the Nevada Supreme Court reversed, specifically holding that a Type I indemnity must specifically state that the indemnitor is indemnifying the indemnitee from its own negligence to be enforceable.

The Court determined that Nevada should follow the traditional "majority rule" in dealing with Type I indemnity, which requires such specific intention to be contractually expressed. The Court determined that the traditional majority rule is more appropriate because "a general clause is not sufficient to impose such an extraordinary remedy" as indemnifying a person from its own negligent act. Thus, the Court stated:

> *... an express or explicit reference to the indemnitee's own negligence is required to indemnify an indemnitee for his or her own negligence-because "the character of [such an] indemnity [is] so unusual and extraordinary, that there can be no presumption that the indemnitor intended to assume the responsibility unless the contract puts it beyond doubt by express stipulation, and no inference from words of general import can establish it."*[218]

In so holding, the Nevada Supreme Court expressly rejected the "modern minority rule" which allowed general statements such as "any and all claims" standing alone to be sufficient to establish Type I indemnity obligations. According to the Court, the minority view allowed "too much to be read into the terms of a contract that the parties may not have intended and could substantially benefit one party to the extreme detriment of the other."[219] As such, the trial court must now "make a finding of whether [the indemnitee] was negligent before it can determine the applicability of the indemnification clause."[220]

In 2011, the Nevada Supreme Court extended this "expressly or explicitly provided" test to Type II indemnity provisions, i.e., those indemnity provisions allowing for complete indemnification of the indemnitee, even in the circumstance of contributory negligence of the indemnitee. In *Reyburn Lawn & Landscape v. Plaster Dev. Co., Inc.*, 127 Nev.Adv.Op.

---

[218] *George L. Brown Ins. v. Star Ins. Co.*, 237 P.3d 92, 97, 126 Nev. Adv. Op. No. 31 (Nev. 2010) (quoting 41 Am. Jur. 2d Indemnity §16 (2005)).

[219] *George L. Brown Ins. v. Star Ins. Co.*, 237 P.3d 92, 97, 126 Nev. Adv. Op. No. 31 (Nev. 2010).

[220] *George L. Brown Ins. v. Star Ins. Co.*, 237 P.3d 92, 98, 126 Nev. Adv. Op. No. 31 (Nev. 2010).

26 (June, 2011), a homeowner's association made a claim for construction defects against the developer/general contractor of a single family home community, arising from the design, preparation and construction of retaining and boundary walls in the communities. The developer made indemnity claims against the retaining wall subcontractor and the landscape subcontractor, based on general indemnity provisions in the construction subcontracts. After the wall subcontractor settled out its liability, the case proceeded to trial with the plaintiff, the general contractor and landscape subcontractor on indemnity claims. During the trial, the subcontractor's president testified in essence that if his company did a certain act, that it would have been "a mistake". Based on this testimony, the general contractor made an oral motion for the entry of judgment on the indemnity obligation against the subcontractor. The district court granted that motion, finding that the subcontractor president's testimony amounted to a judicial admission of liability, and refused to allow the subcontractor to present any exculpatory evidence to the jury. Without the ability to determine the relative fault of the subcontractor, the jury returned a verdict in favor of the plaintiff, finding the general contractor 99% liable for the defects and the plaintiff 1% liable. Because the district court had already entered judgment on the indemnity obligation against the subcontractor, the district court ordered the subcontractor liable for the plaintiff's judgment against the general contractor and awarded interest, attorneys' fees and costs against the subcontractor. The subcontractor appealed.

The Nevada Supreme Court, however, reversed the district court's ruling in its entirety. The court noted that just as in Type I sole indemnity obligations under *Brown Insurance,*[221] an indemnification clause must explicitly or expressly state that the indemnitor will indemnify the indemnitee for the indemnitee's contributory negligence. A general statement of indemnity will not suffice. Contributory Negligence indemnity is governed by the parties' agreement, and because Nevada has not adopted an anti-indemnity statute, the parties are free to contract for the allocation of indemnification responsibilities to each other.

In *Reyburn,*[222] because the indemnification clause did not expressly or explicitly indicate that the subcontractor would indemnify the general contractor for the general contractor's contributory negligence, the extent of the subcontractor's obligation to indemnify would be limited to the damages occurring from the subcontractor's scope of work. Unfortunately, the district court did not allow the jury to review evidence of any construction defect arising from the subcontractor's scope of work; the supreme court was obligated to review that determination to decide if a new trial was appropriate.

---

221 *George L. Brown Ins. v. Star Ins. Co.,* 237 P.3d 92, 98, 126 Nev. Adv. Op. No. 31 (Nev. 2010).

222 *Reyburn Lawn & Landscape v. Plaster Dev. Co., Inc.,* 255 P.3d 268, 127 Nev.Adv.Op. 26 (2011)

The court then determined that only testimony that is deliberate, clear, and unequivocal will support a finding of judicial admission. Anything less is evidentiary admission and must be weighed as evidence by the trier of fact. Since the testimony of the subcontractor's president that hypocritically a mistake had been made, that testimony was not a sufficient statement to constitute a judicial admission of liability. As such, the district court should have allowed the testimony to go to the jury for determination.

Finally, as to the award of attorneys' fees and costs as a result of the indemnity, the court determined that without an express or explicit indemnity for the indemnitor's own or contributory negligence, any award of attorneys' fees based on a breach of indemnity agreement must be limited to those fees incurred in defending the causes of action involving the indemnitor's work. Again, since the jury was not allowed to make any determination or weigh evidence of the subcontractor's own actions or damages arising therefrom, the case had to be reversed and remanded back to the district court for a new trial.

The *Reyburn* case is further evidence that the Nevada Supreme Court is limiting the ability of developers and general contractors to obtain complete indemnity under Type I indemnity obligations, by extending the express contractual requirement to Type II indemnity agreements. In these situations, the developer / general contractor indemnity obligations apparently must expressly and explicitly provide for indemnity and defense, including attorneys' fees and costs incurred, in order to pass those liabilities to subcontracting companies.

More generally, the anti-indemnity statutes vary from state to state, employing different language in regard to the type of negligence involved. For example, California specifically prohibits any provision purporting to indemnify the contractor/owner for any loss arising from the "sole negligence" or "willful misconduct" of the contractor/owner.[223] Many other states, including Michigan, simply prohibit indemnification for the contractor/owner's "sole negligence," without specifying any gross negligence or willful misconduct.[224]

Still, other statutes prohibiting indemnification do not specify that such negligence must be solely on behalf of the contractor/owner, rather the statutes state that an agreement to indemnify "another person from that person's own negligence"[225] or "caused partially or solely"[226] by the contractor/owner's negligence is against public policy and is void

[223] Cal. Civ. Code &s;§2 782.

[224] Mich. Comp. Laws Ann. &s;§691.991.

[225] 740 Ill. Comp. Stat. 35/1.

[226] Del. Code. Ann. tit. 6, &s;§2704.

and unenforceable. This final group appears to most strongly support Type III indemnity provisions, as these provisions limit indemnity to the extent of the contractor's own fault.

Florida appears to be the only state that has a statute that could be read to permit Type II indemnity provisions.[227] Under a Type II provision, the subcontractor would be liable to indemnify the contractor/owner, even for their sole negligence, as long as there is no evidence of gross negligence or willful misconduct. As such, the states listed in the previous section, except for Florida, would also void a Type II provision as against public policy because a Type II provision still contemplates indemnifying the Contractor/owner for its sole negligence, which is strictly prohibited by statutory language.

The initial portion of this statute appears to be fairly standard, prohibiting a contractor/owner from seeking indemnity from a subcontractor for its own negligence.

---

[227] Florida has a unique statute, which provides in relevant part:

> *(1) Any portion of any agreement or contract for or in connection with, or any guarantee of or in connection with, any construction, alteration, repair, or demolition of a building, structure, appurtenance, or appliance, including moving and excavating associated therewith, between an owner of real property and an architect, engineer, general contractor, subcontractor, sub-subcontractor, or materialman or any combination thereof wherein any party referred to herein promises to indemnify or hold harmless the other party to the agreement, contract, or guarantee for liability for damages to persons or property caused in whole or in part by any act, omission, or default of the indemnitee arising from the contract or its performance, shall be void and unenforceable unless the contract contains a monetary limitation on the extent of the indemnification that bears a reasonable commercial relationship to the contract and is part of the project specifications or bid documents, if any. Notwithstanding the foregoing, the monetary limitation on the extent of the indemnification provided to the owner of real property by any party in privity of contract with such owner shall not be less than $1 million per occurrence, unless otherwise agreed by the parties. Indemnification provisions in any such agreements, contracts, or guarantees may not require that the indemnitor indemnify the indemnitee for damages to persons or property caused in whole or in part by any act, omission, or default of a party other than:*
> *(a) The indemnitor;*
> *(b) Any of the indemnitor's contractors, subcontractors, sub-subcontractors, materialmen, or agents of any tier or their respective employees; or*
> *(c) The indemnitee or its officers, directors, agents, or employees. However, such indemnification shall not include claims of, or damages resulting from, gross negligence, or willful, wanton or intentional misconduct of the indemnitee or its officers, directors, agents or employees, or for statutory violation or punitive damages except and to the extent the statutory violation or punitive damages are caused by or result from the acts or omissions of the indemnitor or any of the indemnitor's contractors, subcontractors, sub-subcontractors, materialmen, or agents of any tier or their respective employees ...F.S.A. §725.06 (emphasis added).*

However, the prohibition is qualified by an exception, wherein the indemnity provision will be valid, as long as there is a monetary limitation to the amount of indemnification. This qualification is not unique to Florida's statute. In addition to the qualifying language, a further reading of the statute reveals that a Contractor/owner could legitimately seek indemnification for the subcontractor's negligence, F.S.A §725.06(1)(a), employees or agents of the contractor, F.S.A. §725.06(1)(b), and the negligence of the Contractor/owner, F.S.A. §725.06(1)(c), provided that the Contractor/owner's acts did not amount to gross negligence, or willful, wanton, or intentional misconduct.

As such, Florida's statute is worded in a manner that seemingly would allow a Type II indemnity provision to survive, provided that it included a monetary limit as to the amount of the indemnification that may ultimately be sought.

With the exception of Florida, the list of states prohibiting Type I indemnity provisions equally applies to Type II indemnity provisions. The remaining states prohibit indemnification where the contractor/owner is negligent, whether partially or solely. Therefore, because a Type II indemnity provision would still contemplate indemnification of the contractor/owner for its own negligence, such a provision would be void and unenforceable as against public policy. As mentioned in the introduction, the states with anti-indemnity statutes utilize different terms of art and focus on different types of negligence to determine what type of indemnity is permissible in the context of construction contracts.

Type III indemnity provisions limit indemnity to any liability arising from acts or occurrences on behalf of the Subcontractor. Because the public policy concern is to avoid the allocation of responsibility to non-responsible parties who are not in a position to bargain away such indemnity provisions, Type III provisions do not create any significant issues. A Type III provision falls in line with the public policy of seeking to maintain responsibility with the party that created the situation or circumstances giving rise to the liability. Under this analysis, a Type III provision would likely be upheld and enforceable in every state, including Nevada.

A review of the indemnity provisions of the contract should be undertaken carefully, and the drafter should attempt to craft language that will ultimately benefit his client in the most judicious manner possible. While Nevada has not decided that a Type I indemnity is not enforceable, the construction law practitioner needs to fully advise his client of the risks a Type I indemnity will cause to him.

4:11 CONTRACT CHANGES

The biggest generator of construction disputes is the assertion that the scope of work has changed on the project beyond the original scope of the construction contract, i.e., that there has been extra or different work performed and that work should be compensated. In correct terminology, a "change" typically will involve alteration of the work within the existing scope of the contract which alters materials, methods or designs which the contractor had expected to perform at the time of bid. Extras, on the other hand, typically increase the scope of work inasmuch as they involve work outside of the contract and were not originally contemplated by the parties at the time of bid.

Most construction contracts permit the owner to unilaterally change the scope of work or request additional work to be performed without invalidating the contract. This is an important part of contract law because the clause allows the owner to direct the contractor to perform additions to or deletions from the work without bringing the project to a halt pending resolution of the directive in the courts. Most "changes" clauses also contain administrative procedures whereby the contractor may obtain reimbursement for the costs associated with the changed work. If a contract did not contain a "changes" clause, the addition or deletion of work from the contract would violate the agreement between the parties which contemplated a defined scope of work. Under these circumstances, the contractor would be entitled to sue for breach of contract if he was ordered to perform a "change."

Obviously, changes in the work may affect the cost of performing the work. The costs associated with the change are usually reflected in a written change order by and between the owner and contractor and may include the architect as well. In certain instances, the owner has the right to direct a change in the work, absent an agreement with the contractor if the change is within the scope of the contract. If the change is such that it is beyond the scope of the contract contemplated between the parties, the contractor may have the right to refuse to perform the change order work, claiming that the direction would be "cardinal change" to the contract.

Most contracts also provide that the contractor will be compensated for extra work. When the owner, architect and contractor all agree that a specific item of work is an extra, the owner should issue a written extra work order. In instances where there is a complete agreement, the extra work order will include the amount of the contractor's additional compensation for the extra work. In cases of disagreement, the contractor may be directed to perform the work without a written change order. This is entirely an option to the contractor to perform, and typically Nevada law will favor the contractor. Therefore, the owner and contractor should endeavor to work out disputes over change orders before the work is commenced.

4:12 Time, Time Extensions and/or Delays

Contract provisions dealing with time for performance, extensions of time for performance, delay, disruptions and acceleration claims are a routine provision in most construction contracts. Most contracts will include a clause making time of the essence of the agreement. As a result, the failure of one party to perform on a timely basis results in a material breach of the contract.[228] Thus, if a contractor fails to timely perform on a construction contract, the best defense is to show that the failure to timely perform was excused, through the activities of some other party over whom the contractor had no control or responsibility. To remedy this possibility, a contract may provide that no time extensions will be granted at all, or will only be granted upon the showing that the responsibility for the failure to perform on time is the responsibility of someone other than the contractor failing to perform. Along with this same provision, then, a contractor may also submit a claim for additional time and compensation, because the reasons for his delay are the fault of another party. In general, this is known as an "impact claim."[229] A contractor who accepts that provision must evaluate the risks and potential extra expenses associated with completing the project within the specified contract time if delays occur (i.e., accelerating the performance). Any delays, disruptions, accelerations or other impacts should be calculated in the bid and anticipated in the construction process.

One common contract clause often found in construction contracts is the contract term limiting a contractor's right to recover damages for delay to a mere extension of time to complete the project, and waiving any claim for monetary damages. This type of clause is often referred to as a "no-damage-for-delay-clause," and may read something like this:

> *If the Contractor is delayed at any time in the commencement or progress of the Work by an act or neglect of the Owner or Architect, or of an employee of either, or of a separate contractor employed by the Owner, or by changes ordered in the Work, or by labor disputes, fire, unusual delay in deliveries, unavoidable casualties or other causes beyond the Contractor's control, or by delay authorized by the Owner pending mediation and arbitration, or by other causes which the Architect determines may justify delay, then the Contract Time shall be extended day for day corresponding to the actual days that Contractor was unable to perform any work on the project. However, Contractor shall not be entitled to any economic damages or extra costs for general conditions, home office overhead, lost profits, increased operating costs, rent or any other damage whatsoever beyond a mere extension of the time for completion of the work.*[230]

---

[228] *See* Section 3:20, Prompt Payment Act Effect on Change Order Requests, for a complete discussion of the effect of the Nevada Prompt Payment Act on change orders and the ability of contractors to stop work when changes are disputed.

[229] For a complete discussion on impact claims and how they are presented, see *Bruner & O'Connor on Construction Law.*

[230] Section 8:3:1 of the AIA 1997 A201 General Conditions form contract, as modified.

Such no-damage-for-delay clauses have been seen by many states as a unfair violation of the contractor's right to recover damages, and have interpreted such clauses strictly to allow the contractor to claim that the damages suffered were caused by other circumstances such as disruption to the project schedule forcing the contractor to perform out of sequence work. Some states have found that such clauses are void as against public policy. In Nevada, the Legislature has taken somewhat of a hybrid view by making such a clause void and unenforceable under certain circumstances only. NRS 108.2453(2)(e) provides:

> *2. A condition, stipulation or provision in a contract or other agreement for the improvement of property or for the construction, alteration or repair of a work of improvement in this State that attempts to do any of the following is contrary to public policy and is void and unenforceable: ... (e) Require a prime contractor or subcontractor to waive, release or extinguish a claim or right that the prime contractor or subcontractor may otherwise possess or acquire for delay, acceleration, disruption or impact damages or an extension of time for delays incurred, for any delay, acceleration, disruption or impact event which was unreasonable under the circumstances, not within the contemplation of the parties at the time the contract was entered into, or for which the prime contractor or subcontractor is not responsible.*

In this case, owner or prime contractor who may be the cause of any delay or other impact suffered by the contractor or subcontractor will want to draft the provisions of any no damage for delay clause to make as many potential causes of delay, disruption, acceleration or other impact as clearly within the contemplation of the parties at the time of contracting as possible. This is not necessarily that difficult to do, in that contracting as a general business proposition is filled with events that can and usually will cause delay or impacts on any construction project. For instance, it is a usual event that the governing authority with jurisdiction over some aspect of the project will reject inspections or require plans to be revised. These actions can cause delays to the work. Since these are fairly common actions, it can be reasonably stated in a contract that delays for this type of problem are contemplated by the parties when contracting, and therefore are not compensable. However, to avoid the prohibition of NRS 108.2453(2)(e), the contract clause should specify types of impacts that are within the contemplation of the parties.

Finally, the vigilant contractor should review what events are listed as grounds for a time extension (i.e., an excusable delay) and what procedures must be followed to submit the request for a time extension (i.e., the notice provision). Many times requiring the contractor to submit a schedule analysis (or *"fragnet"* in the industry terminology) demonstrating the delay and impact can be helpful to determining the actual impact and the cause of that impact in the overall schedule. Moreover, it is also helpful to require a time for providing notice of such claims, though the lack of provision of such notice is not necessarily detrimental to the claim.[231] Still, the party providing notice should always make a substantial and good faith effort to comply with the notice provisions of the contract whenever possible, or to comply with the statutory provisions for notice, if any exist.

4:13 Scheduling

As discussed previously, it is critical for a construction contract that time be of the essence of the agreement. In conjunction with such a clause, the responsibilities for preparing and/or adhering to a construction schedule need to be fully understood by all the parties to a construction contract. In most cases, the project owner or designer are not the parties to perform scheduling work for the project. This work is usually determined to be part of the contractor's "means and methods" of construction, which is most cases will be reserved to the contractor by the construction contract. Still, the time and method of the scheduling itself and the updating of that schedule is something that can and should be required by the owner to facilitate the owner's timing for moving, staff training or any other obligations that the owner should need or be required to perform. Likewise, the subcontractors will need to be coordinated in their construction work, and the contractor should again be responsible for that coordination with the subcontractor obligated to fully and cooperate in the scheduling process.

Construction scheduling is a function within the realm of experts. From a legal standpoint, a contractor should prepare and follow a construction schedule for every project and ensure that all parties to the construction contract are reviewing and approving a construction schedule. For litigators, the most crucial element of a construction claim is what is known as a "baseline" schedule; that is, a schedule at the beginning of the job that all the parties to the construction contract agree with and approve. While initial schedules attached to the original construction schedule are rarely sufficient to serve as a baseline schedule, the construction contract should at least set forth a requirement for a construction schedule to be prepared as part of the mobilization of the contractor on site and that schedule be approved by the owner before the contractor is obligated to perform.

The baseline schedule should be updated on a periodic basis as necessary. Many contractors will use what is known in the construction trade as "look ahead" schedules, which are usually distributed at weekly job site meetings with the construction team members. While "look ahead" schedules may be helpful for in the field coordination of the work they are not sufficient as periodic updates to construction scheduling which should be required contractually. Contract scheduling provisions should require the

---

231 *Eagle's Nest Ltd. Partnership v. Brunzell*, 99 Nev. 710, 669 P.2d 714 (1983).

scheduling party to review and update the actual progress of the work against the baseline schedule to demonstrate where the work is progressing properly or to determine where the progress is being held up. For more sophisticated jobs, the scheduling party can be required to provide a schedule update narrative report, to discuss changes to the schedule for the update and to discuss why there are any delays. These documents become critically important if a dispute arises between the parties over delays, disruptions or other impacts to the construction schedule.

If the scheduling party anticipates using electronic scheduling software to perform the scheduling function, it is also then critical that the schedule updates are provided electronically as well as in written form. Electronic scheduling software allows the scheduler to change relationships between events, force specific dates of completion that may not be accurate and otherwise enter software manipulations into the schedule data that may cause the schedule to appear different than the actual construction project is proceeding. Only by reviewing the scheduling party's manipulation of the electronic data can these false constraints and manipulations be found. Therefore, the construction contract provisions should be drafted to require not only the provision of scheduling data, but the retention of the scheduling data for the baseline schedule and all subsequent updates in final electronic form without deletion or overwriting.

Schedules for the project should not only reference the contractor's performance obligations but also the performance obligations of the owner or any other third parties on whom the construction project depends. If the owner is going to supply certain materials for use in the construction process, the date of actual delivery of those items needs to be spelled out in the schedule and the owner notified and approve of the same. Likewise, should any third party contractor that the owner or other party retain separately from the work of the contractor be necessary to complete the contractor's work, that work should be coordinated with the overall project schedule and updated as the project progresses.

Finally, it should also be kept in mind while drafting scheduling clauses that change orders, request for information or any other type of activity may impact the schedule during the work progress. Thought should be provided to those schedule impacts when addressing notice requirements for change order requests or other impact demands by subcontractors or contractors. Allowing a subcontractor to reserve a claim for additional time by stating that time impact is "to be determined" (or "TBD" in construction lingo) is rarely helpful to keeping the project on schedule or reviewing the project for potential claims. Therefore, strict contractual obligations for specific time impact analysis are helpful inclusions in construction contracts.

Some inventive owners will also occasionally attempt to draft the construction contract to make the contractor waive his rights to assert mechanics liens on the project as consideration for the contract itself or otherwise. Such clauses should be deemed void under the Nevada legislative statutes, but recent case law has allowed some doubt in this area.

NRS 108.2453(2)(a) provides:

> *A condition, stipulation or provision in a contract or other agreement for the improvement of property or for the construction, alteration or repair of a work of improvement in this State that attempts to do any of the following is contrary to public policy and is void and unenforceable: (a) Require a lien claimant to waive rights provided by law to lien claimants or to limit the rights provided to lien claimants, other than as expressly provided in NRS 108.221 to 108.246, inclusive.*

While this language is fairly definitive, the Nevada Supreme Court allowed for such waivers to be reviewed on a case-by-case basis for their potential violation of public policy. In *Lehrer McGovern Bovis, Inc. v. Bullock Insulation, Inc.*,[232] the project owner and an out of state general contractor used a poorly worded waiver of the subcontractor's mechanics lien right to argue that neither had an obligation to pay the subcontractor for its work. The Supreme Court disagreed. The project owner's argument was the mechanics lien waiver provision did not violate Nevada public policy and therefore the trial court was in error. The Supreme Court, noting that the Nevada legislature had made contractual mechanics lien waivers void and unenforceable in 2003,[233] disagreed and held that trial courts must review each mechanics lien waiver on a case-by-case basis to determine whether the waiver violates public policy. The Court reasoned that:

> *A contractor has a statutory right to a mechanics lien for the unpaid balance of the price agreed upon for labor, materials and equipment furnished. 'The object of the lien statutes is to secure payment to those who perform labor or furnish material to improve the property of the owner.' This court has held on numerous occasions 'that the mechanics lien statutes are remedial in character and should be liberally construed.'*
>
> ...
>
> *Underlying the policy of preserving laws that provide contractors secured payment for their work and materials is the notion that contractors are generally in a vulnerable position because they extend large blocks of credit; invest significant time, labor, and*

[232] *Lehrer McGovern Bovis, Inc. v. Bullock Insulation, Inc.*, 185 P.3d 1055 (Nev. 2008), opinion withdrawn and superseded on denial of reh'g, 197 P.3d 1032 (Nev. 2008).

[233] *See* NRS 108.2453(2)(a).

> *materials into a project; and have any number of workers vitally depend upon them for eventual payment.*
>
> ...
>
> *[W]e now ... conclude that it is appropriate for the district court to engage in a public policy analysis particular to each lien waiver provision that the court is asked to enforce. In doing so, we emphasize that not every lien waiver provision violates public policy. The enforceability of each lien waiver clause must be resolved on a case-by-case basis by considering whether the form of the lien waiver clause violates Nevada's public policy to secure payment for contractors.*
>
> *In this case, the lien waiver provision applies regardless of whether [the subcontractor] received any payment. We conclude that such a provision violates public policy, as it fails to secure payment for [the subcontractor].*[234]

This analysis is problematic for higher-tiered contractors and owners for several reasons: First, by creating a "public policy to secure payment for contractors," the Nevada Supreme Court seems to have created significant barriers to challenge a mechanics lien's validity for technical errors or omissions in the mechanics lien statutory scheme. This would seem to violate the Nevada legislature's directive that *"Except as otherwise provided in NRS 108.221 to 108.246, inclusive, a person may not waive or modify a right, obligation or liability set forth in the provisions of NRS 108.221 to 108.246, inclusive"*[235] If there is a public policy to secure payment for contractors, it is possible rejecting a mechanic's lien for the failure of the contractor to serve the mandatory "Notice to Owner of Right to Lien" under NRS 108.245 would violate public policy, rendering the statute unenforceable. Second, since the effect of any mechanics lien waiver, including those set forth in NRS 108.2457(5), is to waive mechanics lien rights, such waivers given without corresponding payment may likewise be invalid. Current Nevada mechanics lien statutes seem to disallow such a situation.[236] While the Nevada legislature has obviously created a scheme whereby contractors can secure their right to payment,[237] it is difficult to understand when a lien waiver without an actual corresponding payment or enforceable promise to pay would ever be effective under the court's creation of a public policy of securing payment. As such, there seems to be little value in the court directing trial courts to perform a case-by-case analysis. As such, this tension in the law should be kept in mind while drafting mechanics lien waiver provisions.

---

[234] *Lehrer McGovern Bovis, Inc. v. Bullock Insulation, Inc.,* 185 P.3d 1055, 1063, (Nev. 2008), opinion withdrawn and superseded on denial of reh'g, 197 P.3d 1032 (Nev. 2008).

[235] NRS 108.2453(1).

[236] *See* NRS 108.2457(2)(a).

[237] *See* Chapter 8, Nevada Mechanic's Liens.

4:15 PAY-IF OR PAY-WHEN-PAID CLAUSES

Similar to mechanics' lien waiver provisions, and no damage for delay clauses, many construction subcontracts will include a provision that makes payment from an owner to the contractor a condition precedent to the contractor's obligation to make payment to the subcontractor. This clause is generally known as a pay-if-paid clause, and might typically be worded as follows:

> *Subcontractor agrees that Contractor's obligation to make payment to subcontractor shall be expressly conditioned upon the receipt of payment from the Owner on behalf of Subcontractor by Contractor and that receipt of such payment from the Owner is an express condition precedent to funds becoming due and payable to Subcontractor from Contractor. Subcontractor warrants and agrees that in entering into this subcontract Subcontractor is relying solely on the credit worthiness of the Owner and not the Contractor and Subcontractor agrees in the event of non-payment to look solely to the Owner for payment.*

Alternatively, a construction contract may contain a clause not entirely eliminating the subcontractor's ability to seek payment from the contractor, but rather providing a period of time for the contractor to seek payment from the owner before the subcontractor may pursue the contractor for payment based on the contract. Such a clause is known as a "pay-when-paid" clause and might typically be worded as follows:

> *Subcontractor agrees that Contractor's obligation to make payment to Subcontractor will not come to fruition until Contractor has received payment from Owner for Subcontractor's work. In the event that Owner fails to make timely payment to Contractor for Subcontractor, Subcontractor agrees that it will refrain from proceeding in any litigation or other dispute resolution method against Contractor until Contractor has had sufficient time to pursue collection of payment from Owner. Nothing in this paragraph shall prevent Subcontractor from enforcing any independent right to recover directly from Owner, including but not limited to asserting any mechanics lien right belonging to Subcontractor.*

In Nevada, until recently it was understood that pay-if and pay-when-paid clauses were enforceable and that existing statutory law did not prevent such analysis. However, recent Nevada case law initially brought some doubt to the enforceability of such clauses. In *Lehrer McGovern Bovis, Inc. v. Bullock Insulation, Inc,*[238] the Nevada Supreme Court initially held that contingency payment clauses were void-having dealt with the mechanics lien waiver issue[239] and based thereon recognized a new public policy to

---

[238] *Lehrer McGovern Bovis, Inc. v. Bullock Insulation, Inc.*, 185 P.3d 1055 (Nev. 2008) ("*Bovis I*"), opinion withdrawn and superseded on denial of reh'g, 197 P.3d 1032 (Nev. 2008) ("*Bovis II*").

[239] *See* Section 4:13, Mechanics lien waivers.

secure payment to contractors, the Nevada Supreme Court turned to the general contractor's argument that the pay-if-paid provision should have been enforceable. With no more analysis of pay-if-paid provisions than one paragraph, the court struck them down seemingly without exception:

> *At the time the parties entered into the agreement and subcontract, the Legislature had not yet proclaimed pay-if-paid provisions unenforceable,[33] and this court had not previously addressed the enforceability of such provisions. Because a pay-if-paid provision limits a subcontractor's ability to be paid for work already performed, such a provision impairs the subcontractor's statutory right to place a mechanic's lien on the construction project.[34] As noted above, Nevada's public policy favors securing payment for labor and material contractors.[35] Therefore, we conclude that pay-if-paid provisions are unenforceable because they violate public policy.*
>
> *[[33]We note that in 2001, the Legislature amended NRS Chapter 624 to include the prompt payment provisions contained in NRS 624.624 through 624.626, which make pay-if-paid provisions entered into subsequent to the Legislature's amendments unenforceable. 2001 Nev. Stat., ch. 341, §§5-6, at 1615-18. This amendment does not affect our analysis here because it is not retroactive. See McKellar v. McKellar, 110 Nev. 200, 203, 871 P.2d 296, 298 (1994).*
>
> *[34]See Wm. R. Clarke Corp., 64 Cal.Rptr.2d 578, 938 P.2d at 376 (concluding that a pay-if-paid provision "has the same practical effect as an express waiver of [mechanic's lien] rights").*
>
> *[35]See Schofield v. Copeland Lumber, 101 Nev. 83, 85, 692 P.2d 519, 520 (1985) (explaining that "[t]he object of the lien statutes is to secure payment to those who perform labor or furnish material to improve the property of the owner").]*[240]

Subsequently, the Nevada Supreme Court withdrew this opinion and changed this statement to seem to allow for enforcement, but it is important to discuss the language of the original opinion as it demonstrates a common error (in this author's opinion) often made by Nevada practitioners. First, contrary to the withdrawn opinion's assertion in footnote 33, the Nevada Legislature did not proclaim pay-if-paid provisions unenforceable in NRS 624.624 through NRS 624.626. In fact, NRS 624.626(1)(b) expressly recognizes that a subcontractor may stop work "even if the higher-tiered contractor has not been paid and the agreement contains a provision which requires the higher-tiered contractor to pay the lower-tiered subcontractor only if or when the higher-tiered contractor is paid." Nothing in either the legislative history of NRS 624.624 through 624.626 or in the statutes themselves indicate that a pay-if-paid provision is invalid; indeed, the provision itself implies they are enforceable. Since the withdrawn opinion expressly states that the particular issue was not necessary to decide the case

240 NOTE: The original footnotes are included here within the bracketed text, with their original numbers.

before the Court, it is difficult to understand why is made at all. For this reason, it might be argued as merely dicta. Nevertheless, in a state famished for Court interpretation of these statutes, such a casual remark will have significant practical effect on thousands of cases and transactions throughout this state.

Likewise, it is not reasonable to assert generally that all pay-if-paid clauses would eliminate a subcontractor's right to a mechanics lien. Each clause must be evaluated on its own terms. There is no reason a subcontractor cannot agree that a general contractor's obligation to pay the subcontractor is contingent upon the general contractor receipt of the owner's payment, while still preserving to the subcontractor his mechanics lien rights. All that is necessary is careful subcontract drafting. While the particular provision in *Bovis I & II* may have been drafted to eliminate the subcontractor's mechanics lien right, not all of them will. As such, the Court should allow trial courts to conduct a public policy analysis of such provisions on a case-by-case basis, as well.

Bovis I also completely ignored the corresponding right of a general contractor to secure payment from the owner, and the unreasonable burden placed on that contractor to have to pay subcontractors regardless of the owner's payment. Under the *Bovis I* language, the general contractor becomes a *de facto* lender to the owner for the work of improvement. Further, the opinion did not deal with the situation when a lender decides not to fund the owner of a project for the contractor's work. The lender can still foreclose on the project, rendering the general contractor's mechanics lien invalid, but requiring the general contractor to pay the subcontractor. Whether the unpaid general contractor would have a claim for unjust enrichment against the lender has not been clearly determined.

Fourth, the Nevada Supreme Court's withdrawn opinion did not recognize the substantial difference between Nevada's mechanics lien law and that of California. California has a mechanics lien right that is guaranteed under the state's constitution.[241] There is no such corresponding constitutional right to a mechanic's lien in Nevada. As such, the Nevada Mechanics Liens should be strictly applied according to the rules of the legislative enactment.[242] While these rules may be liberally construed to affect their purpose, California law should not merely be applied to Nevada Mechanics lien statues without substantial review, as the Nevada Mechanics Lien statutes (especially after the 2003 and 2005 legislative amendments) are now unique.[243] The Nevada Supreme Court's citation to the 1992 case of *William R. Clarke Corp. v. Safeco Ins.*, 938 P.2d 372

---

[241] Cal. Const., Art. 14, §3.

[242] NRS 108.221 to 108.246, inclusive.

[243] *In re Fontainebleau Resort Las Vegas*, 128 Nev.Adv.Op. 53, 289 P.3d. 1199, 1207 (2012).

(Cal.1992) is the perfect example. Unlike Nevada's Supreme Court which concludes that "not every lien waiver provision violates public policy," the *Clarke* case expressly states that any lien waiver other than those provided for by statute *does* violate California's constitutional right to a mechanics lien and is, therefore, void.

Finally, the Nevada Supreme Court has previously held that even if a mechanics lien is not available, a subcontractor has a right to a claim against the owner for unjust enrichment.[244] As such, a subcontractor need not record a lien at all, but may directly pursue the owner of a project when he has refused to pay the general contractor for the subcontractor's work without a mechanics lien claim.

Shortly after the release of *Bovis I*, the Nevada Supreme Court withdrew the opinion and issued *Bovis II*. Among other things, *Bovis II*[245] specifically limited the effectiveness of the opinion to contracts entered into before the legislative changes in 2001 to NRS Chapter 624 and in 2003 to NRS Chapter 108. *Bovis II* declared that a pay-if-paid provision protects the subcontractor's right to receive payment from the owner, the provision may be enforceable under certain circumstances.[246] Once again, the Court begins its analysis indicating that at the time the parties entered into the agreement, the legislature had not declared such provisions unenforceable and the court had not previously addressed the issue. Again, the Court footnotes its discussion to state that the legislature amended Chapter 624 in 2001 to revise NRS 624.624 through 624.626, but changes its previous statement that these provisions rendered pay-if-paid clauses unenforceable. Instead, the *Bovis II* Court states in footnote 50:

> *Pay if paid provisions entered into subsequent to the amendments are enforceable only in limited circumstances and are subject to the restrictions laid out in these sections.*

Thus, there is an acknowledgement that pay-if-paid provisions *are* enforceable under certain circumstances. The Court does not, however, specify what those circumstances are. Nevertheless, the context of this opinion seems to indicate that the circumstances

---

244 *See Leasepartners Corp. v. Robert L. Brooks Trust Dated November 12, 1975,* 113 Nev. 747, 942 P.2d 182 (1997).

245 *Lehrer McGovern Bovis, Inc. v. Bullock Insulation, Inc.*, 197 P.3d 1032 (2008); For purposes of this discussion, it should be noted that the Nevada Supreme Court rules, *Bovis I* is not citable as precedent, however, comparison between the cases in dealing with the issue of enforceable contingency payment clauses cases is noteworthy. As such, we will discuss both in this section with the case names noted above where necessary.

246 It should be noted here that the Court does not address a pay-when-paid provision, however, it is believed that the Court's analysis would probably be similar as a pay-when-paid clause is actually less draconian to a unpaid contractor's position than a pay-is-paid clause in practical effect.

will be whether the pay-if-paid clause affects the subcontractor's right to recover payment from the owner.

Bovis II goes on to specify that because a *"pay-if-paid provision limits the subcontractors ability to be paid for work already performed, such a provision impairs the subcontractor's statutory right to place a mechanics lien on the project."* This determination is probably based in the specific contract language being analyzed, the opinion is not clear. But we can surmise that because public policy favors securing payment for labor and material contractors, however, a pay-if-paid clause that fails to support that public policy is unenforceable. Footnote 52 of *Bovis II* seems to support this: *"the object of the lien statutes is to secure payment to those who perform labor or furnish material to improve the property of the owner."*

An interesting turn of events: The Nevada Supreme Court actually considered its previous opinion on these issues and reversed itself, *sua sponte*. It is clear the Court's contingency payment clause analysis in *Bovis I* and *Bovis II* only applies to contracts executed prior to the 2001 / 2003 legislative changes. Certainly the Supreme Court was correct to withdraw its matter-of-fact analysis of Nevada's Prompt Payment Act. But the Court has opened a new debate by not providing what "special circumstances" must exist to make a contingency payment clause enforceable, and perhaps because there are few clues in the statutes themselves. What the Prompt Payment Act allows is a lower-tiered subcontractor to stop work when he is not paid, even when a valid pay-if-paid clause exists in its contract with the higher-tiered contractor, if certain written notices are given with certain deadlines. Still, *Bovis II* does appear to allow for the properly drafted pay-of-paid clause to be enforced, so long as the affected subcontractor's right to enforce a mechanics lien on the property for unpaid work is maintained. Hence, it seems the Nevada Supreme Court has left the door open to enforcing a pay-if-paid provision.

This possibility creates large rifts within the construction industry. Some cannot under any circumstances believe that the law would allow a party to perform work but not be entitled to payment for it. In order to state that the payment time restrictions of NRS 624.624(1) are an implicit denunciation of the contingency payment clause one has to ignore major portions of the PPA, which is not proper statutory interpretation. But arguments usually put forth in support of the position against enforceability do just that; making perfunctory stabs at reconciliation between the actual PPA language and traditional rules of statutory interpretation. The most difficult to explain is the divergent acts required to stop work when the basis for lack of payment includes a contingency payment clause and when it does not.

Initially, the Nevada Supreme Court's rules for statutory interpretation should be understood. Specifically, a statutory scheme must be interpreted as a whole, give effect to all of its provisions.[247] Rather, one must look at the entire scheme of enacted legislation and give effect to all of its meaning, without reaching an absurd result.[248] The arguments for unenforceability generally violate this rule by focusing solely NRS 624.624(1) and ignoring the enacting provisions of NRS 624.626(1) which specify what a lower-tier subcontractor must do under specific circumstances to take advantage of the PPA's rights. There are different requirements depending on the basis for lack of payment. Contingency payment clause situations differ from disputed work situations. The differences are significant. Contrary to popular belief, the Prompt Payment Act regulates what a higher-tiered contractor must to withhold payment from a lower-tiered subcontractor after the higher-tiered contractor has been paid. It does *not* dictate that the lower-tiered subcontractor has to be paid when the higher-tiered contractor has not been paid.

NRS 624.624(1) provides in pertinent part:

> *Except as otherwise provided in this section, if a higher-tiered contractor enters into:*
> *(a) A written agreement with a lower-tiered subcontractor that includes a schedule for payments, the higher-tiered contractor shall pay the lower-tiered subcontractor:*
> *(1) On or before the date payment is due ....*[249]

In general, a "pay-if-paid" clause will state that payment is *not due* from the higher-tiered contractor until it is paid. Rather, the payment is due from the owner. Nothing in the Prompt Payment Act allows a subcontractor to ignore the terms of its subcontract as to when payment is due. In fact, nothing in the language of the Prompt Payment Act alters the contracted-for time for payment at all. The premise of the Prompt Payment Act relates to a general contractor's "intent to withhold" payment from a subcontractor after payment has become "due" under the contract.

NRS 624.624(2) states in pertinent part:

---

247 *D.R. Horton, Inc. v. Eighth Judicial Dist. Court ex rel. County of Clark*, 123 Nev. 468, 168 P.3d 731, 738 (2007) ("The court reads legislative enactments as a whole in order to understand legislative intent. *No part of the statute may be rendered meaningless* and language should not be read to produce absurd or unreasonable results.") (emphasis added).

248 *Citizens for Cold Springs v. City of Reno*, 125 Nev. 625, 631, 218 P.3d 847, 851 (2009)(quoting *Allstate Insurance Co. v. Fackett*, 125 Nev.132, 206 P.3d 572, 576 (2009)).

249 The argument is often posed here that the statute requires a schedule of payments to contain a date certain, or else be deemed void and unenforceable. But a contrary argument exists. NRS 624.624(1) simply provides that when a written contract exists, the payment must be made as contemplated in the contract. Nothing in the terms "shall pay" creates any obligation beyond that which is contemplated in the parties' agreement as to the date of payment, including the vitiation of an applicable pay-if-paid clause.

If a higher-tiered contractor has complied with subsection 3, the higher-tiered contractor may:
(a) Withhold from any payment owed to the lower-tiered subcontractor ....

NRS 624.624(3) states:

If ... a higher-tiered contractor intends to withhold any amount from a payment to be made to a lower-tiered subcontractor, the higher-tiered contractor must give, on or before the date the payment is due, a written notice to the lower-tiered subcontractor of any amount that will be withheld.

Nothing in the referenced paragraphs speaks of the higher-tiered contractor's intent to withhold because of a lack of payment under a "pay-if-paid" clause. To do so would be a misnomer. When the higher-tiered contractor does not pay because he has not been paid, the higher-tiered contractor does not intend to withhold anything. Instead, he would pay the lower-tiered subcontractor, if he had the money to do so. But he cannot--there was no payment made to him to "withhold" from the subcontractor.[250]

According to dictionary.com,[251] "to withhold" means "to hold back, restrain or check; to deduct from an employee's salary or wages." Likewise, the term "deduct" means "to take away, as from a sum or amount." When a higher-tiered contractor has not been paid by the Owner, there simply is nothing given to him that he can withhold or take away from the subcontractor. The lower-tiered subcontractors, when entering into the "pay-if-paid" provision, did not expect that the higher-tiered contractor to pay them from its own pocket. Otherwise, they would not have accepted the pay-if-paid provision in the first place. It is paradoxical to think that a lower-tiered contractor can agree to a contract term, and then sue the contracting party for breach of contract when he enforces it. The PPA does not support that proposition. To the contrary, the PPA supports the opposition conclusion--the lower-tier subcontractor is *not* authorized to sue the higher-tiered contractor when lack of payment comes from asserting a contingency payment clause in their contract.

NRS 624.626(1) provides that:

If:

---

[250] There should be no need to state that if a person has not received something belonging to another person, the first person cannot be said to be "withholding" that thing from the second person to whom it belongs. That would, in fact, be impossible.

[251] Dictionary.com Unabridged, based on the Random House Dictionary; Random House, Inc. 2009.

(a) A higher-tiered contractor fails to pay the lower-tiered subcontractor within the time provided in subsection 1 or 4 of NRS 624.624;

(b) A higher-tiered contractor fails to pay the lower-tiered subcontractor within 45 days after the 25th day of the month in which the lower-tiered subcontractor submits a request for payment, ***even if the higher-tiered contractor has not been paid and the agreement contains a provision which requires the higher-tiered contractor to pay the lower-tiered subcontractor only if or when the higher-tiered contractor is paid;***

(c) A higher-tiered contractor fails to give the lower-tiered subcontractor written notice of any withholding in the time and manner required by subsection 3 or 4 of NRS 624.624;

(d) After receipt of a notice of withholding pursuant to subsection 3 or 4 of NRS 624.624, the lower-tiered subcontractor gives the higher-tiered contractor written notice pursuant to subsection 4 of NRS 624.624 and thereby disputes in good faith and for reasonable cause the amount withheld or the condition or reason for the withholding,

The lower-tiered subcontractor ***may stop work*** *under the agreement until payment is received ....*

(emphasis added). But, NRS 624.626(2) goes on to state:

> *If a lower-tiered subcontractor stops work pursuant to* ***paragraph (a), (c) or (d) of subsection 1****, the lower-tiered subcontractor* ***may terminate the agreement*** *with the higher-tiered contractor by giving written notice of the termination to the higher-tiered contractor after stopping work ....*

(emphasis added).

Conspicuously absent from the ability to *terminate* in NRS 624.626(2) is the provision of NRS 624.626(1)(b), which allows the subcontractor to stop work if he has not been paid under a "pay-if-paid" clause. That is, a subcontractor who is not paid simply because the general has not been paid, may stop work, but is *not* authorized to terminate his subcontract with the general contractor under the Prompt Payment Act, if he has a "pay-if-paid" clause in his subcontract. This is a critical factor because only when a subcontract is terminated under the Prompt Payment Act may a subcontractor sue the general contractor for payment there under.

NRS 624.626(6) provides:

> *If ... the lower-tiered subcontractor stops work in accordance with this section* ***and*** *the agreement is terminated pursuant to subsection 2 ..., the lower-tiered subcontractor is entitled to recover from the higher-tiered contractor with whom the lower-tiered subcontractor has entered into an agreement the amount found by a trier of fact to be due the lower-tiered subcontractor ...*

Under NRS 624.626(6), the subcontractor is only entitled to recover unpaid money from a general contractor under a terminated agreement under subsections (a), (c), or (d) of NRS 624.626(2). They may not terminate under the "pay-if-paid" provisions of NRS 624.626(1)(b). The attempt by the subcontractor to terminate simply for a lack of payment when a "pay-if-paid" clause exists would actually be a breach of that subcontract and a violation of the Prompt Payment Act by the subcontractor, not the general contractor.

Hence, as the Nevada Supreme Court has ruled in *Bovis II*, the PPA cannot be used to claim that a "pay-if-paid" clause is void, *ab initio*. A "pay-if-paid" provision is clearly recognized and is assumed to be enforceable by the different handling of the situations respecting the Owner's payment of the general contractor. Without more actions by a general contractor that would either invalidate the "pay-if-paid" provision on a factual basis, or that are inconsistent with the general contractor's obligations to deal with its subcontractors in good faith, the PPA simply does not articulate a legal basis to disregard the terms of the subcontract contingency payment provision.

Some may also argue that the inclusion of a contingency payment agreement is a violation of the PPA's prohibition on contract clauses waiving or modifying the rights and protections of the PPA.[252] This argument is, again, only effective if one ignores the divergent treatment of payment under contingency payment clauses and how a lower-tiered contractor must act when such a clause is in play. As shown above, there can be no arguing that the timeframes and the actions allowed to a lower-tiered contractor are different. The different treatment must be accounted for. It would be far simpler for the legislature to have said specifically that the contingency payment clauses are not enforceable, rather than concoct a different set of rules when such a clause exists, if Legislative intent was to eliminate their applicability. The Nevada Supreme Court has determined that they are enforceable. The only thing remaining to the Court is to decide when and under what circumstances they are so.

4:16 OTHER CONTRACT PROVISIONS AFFECTING PAYMENT

Construction contracts generally provide that the owner will make payments to the contractor in installments, as the work progresses (i.e., progress payments). The owner's failure to make a progress payment may entitle the contractor to suspend its work on the project until the payment is made. Furthermore, the owner's failure to make a progress payment may give the contractor the right to rescind the contract and abandon the job permanently.[253] In Nevada, such rights are protected by statutory

[252] NRS 624.628(3).

[253] *Integrated, Inc. v. Alec Fergusson Elec. Contractors*, 250 Cal. App. 2d 287, 58 Cal. Rptr. 503 (4th Dist. 1967).

pronouncement.[254] Of course, the contractor always has the option to continue with the work even though progress payments have been missed. Upon completion of the work, the contractor will be entitled to recover the unpaid balance of the contract price as well as interest on the unpaid progress payments.[255] Any and all contract provisions that govern payment must be drafted with the requirements of the Nevada Prompt Payment Act firmly in mind, as any clauses violating or modifying the rights of contractors under the PPA are void and unenforceable.[256]

4:17 RETENTION

In general, retention is withheld pending acceptable completion of the Project. Various types of retention can be negotiated, but retention requirements are limited to 5% of the contract balance.[257] Additional withholding will be limited by provisions of the Prompt Payment Act. The contract must allow for the withholding of retention, or no retention may be withheld from the contractor.[258]

The payment of retention will place a subcontractor in a precarious position. Most subcontracts will allow the general contractor to withhold retention until 45 days after the work is completed and accepted by the Owner. Theoretically, this allows the general contractor to withhold funds beyond the last date for a subcontractor to record a mechanics lien against the Project, after a notice of completion is recorded. Thus, the subcontractor must choose to either trust the general contractor that he will pay the subcontractor, and forego his mechanics lien rights, or protect himself by recording his mechanics lien and risk alienating the general contractor or owner. Business judgment should be applied, then, to retention as early as possible, which would necessarily include an evaluation of the contractor and the prospects for continued work with that contractor in the future.

4:18. DOCUMENTATION REQUIREMENTS AND PROCEDURES

It has been said that construction projects are built with as much paper and ink as they are with lumber and concrete. It is perhaps more accurate to say they are built with more paper and ink than lumber and concrete. But documentation of a construction

---

[254] NRS 624.606, *et seq. See also* Chapter 3, Private Works Prompt Payment Act.

[255] *See* NRS 624.620.

[256] *See* NRS 624.628(3).

[257] It should be noted that contracts entered into before January 1, 2016 were allowed to have retention withheld up to 10% of the amount of the payment. This amount was reduced to the current 5% amount by Senate Bill 254 in the 2015 legislative session.

[258] *See* Section 3:6, Progress Payment Retention.

project is a critical tool for evaluation of the construction progress, as well as for resolution of construction claims. In fact, it is only by review of the contemporaneous record of a construction project can a true picture of the work progression be understood at trial or in arbitration. If the documentation is missing or poorly prepared, legitimate and substantial claims or defenses can be lost as a result. It is therefore critical that the construction contract require project documentation and distribution thereof.

The most common form of project documentation which has not already been discussed in this Chapter is daily construction logs. Daily construction logs are critical for understanding the day-to-day operations of the construction project. The contractor and all project subcontractors should keep daily construction logs. Copies of the subcontractor daily logs should be provided to the contractor by subcontract provision. Likewise, the contractor should be obligated to provide the owner with copies of its daily logs and to make subcontractor daily log entries available upon request for inspection. Daily log entries should be kept by project managers and superintendents and should list any activity on the project which is occurring on a specific day. The weather should be noted, the manpower of all subcontractors noted and timed and the specific work being performed should be summarized for each trade. In addition, notes in the daily logs should indicate any disputes that have arisen, delays being suffered on the project and any directives given by the owner or higher-tiered contractors recorded.

Similar to daily job logs, project managers should keep and maintain a project journal or diary for each project, recording in detail the activities on a project, notes of discussions and negotiations with the owner, architect or other contractors and record the resolutions of such negotiations. Journals should be kept on a running basis, dated and numbered as the job progresses to set forth the activities on a construction project.

Meeting minutes should be taken of all job meetings, noting the attendees, the meeting agenda and subjects, the discussion points and who offered the same, as well as any resolution or action items for meeting attendees to handle and report back by the next meeting. Meeting minutes should be promptly prepared after the meeting was adjourned and circulated to all attendees of the meeting for review, comment and/or approval. Comments should be entered into the meeting minutes and a final version circulated. Disagreements with the contents of meeting minutes should be made in writing and retained in the job folder.

Photographs of construction projects are an invaluable tool if handled correctly. Key is to retain the photos or digital records along with all information about the photograph being taken. Specifically, the date, time, location and identification of the person taking the photo should be kept with the photo itself. If a digital camera is used, the date and calendar on the camera should be accurately saved and the location and identity of the photographer entered into the photograph metadata or with the photo printout.

Sufficient notes of the issue being depicted in the photo should be retained so that the issue can be recalled and recognized years later when the photo is presented in evidence.

Change order requests and request for information logs should be maintained. As change orders are requested, or requests for information generated, a log of each one should be kept tracking the item number, a description of the issue involved, the date the item was transmitted to the appropriate person and the date a response was received and what the response was to the item. If the item needs to be passed along to another party for response, those dates and times should be recorded as well. These logs should be constantly maintained and updated as items are added and responses are received. Follow up letters and requests should be sent as items transmitted are not promptly responded to by other parties. In general, it is a good practice to insert a default response due date in the contract provisions dealing with change order requests and requests for information in order to guide the responder on time frames. Drawing logs should be kept and updated with revised drawings, field sketches and delta revisions to architectural, structural, civil and other construction plans tracked.

As-built drawings should be maintained on an ongoing process, recording the actual progress of the work performed on the project. The as-built drawings should show any deviations from the original or final plan construction and demonstrate the construction issues encountered on the project. A final set of as-built construction drawings is usually required by the owner at the conclusion of the project and maintaining those as-built drawings as the work progresses allows for more accurate details of the work performed.

4:19 Dispute Resolution

Dispute and claim resolution should also be carefully reviewed and included in the construction contract documents. Many form agreements will require some form of negotiation, followed by one or more alternative dispute resolution techniques to resolve disputes between the parties. The construction practitioner, however, should not immediately assume that because a form agreement includes an arbitration provision, for example, that arbitration is the best form of dispute resolution for the project. Many other types of dispute resolution should be considered, including litigation when necessary.

In most construction contract dispute resolution processes, the initial indication that a claim exists is the provision of notice to the other party of the claim or dispute. While Nevada has indicated that the failure to provide timely notice of a claim under contract provisions is not necessarily detrimental to the claim,[259] the notification of the claim provisions should be included for no other purpose than requiring the claimant to provide some basic backup information supporting the claim to initiate the dispute resolution procedures. This will allow the other contracting party to evaluate the issue and prepare defenses and hopefully negotiate the issue to resolution long before more formal procedures are necessary. If negotiation fails, the first step of dispute resolution is some type of semi-formal resolution through a third party or parties to the actual dispute. This can occur in many forms, but the most popular are "partnering," use of a dispute resolution board or a project neutral to recommend resolution of the dispute.

In "partnering" the parties involve the next immediate supervisory or management personnel of each disputing party above those who cannot resolve the decision to meet and resolve the issue. The process repeats using the next highest management personnel until a full resolution is achieved or an impasse is declared. While this method of dispute resolution can be successful, often times it is hampered by the management personnel not being fully aware of the reasons the dispute exists or the implications of a less than satisfactory resolution to the construction project or the contractor. For the process to work correctly, it is generally understood that a fair amount of homework needs to be performed by the resolving "partners" to reach a reasonable and fair compromise on the issue.

The use of a dispute resolution board (DRB) can also be successful, however, the best situation is the compilation of a board consisting of a management level person from each contracting party and a project neutral who can break ties between the management personnel. The project neutral can be a voice of reason over the issue and generally should be a person familiar with construction law and the resolution process. Each party to the dispute presents their view on the issue to DRB along with the documentation evidence from which the dispute arises. The DRB make a decision on the issue, which can either be binding or can be a temporary resolution of the issue to keep the project moving, with a more formal resolution occurring upon the project completion through another method of resolving the matter.

A project neutral is a relatively new alternative dispute resolution procedure, where the parties actually agree at the contracting stage upon a person to resolve disputes between the parties during the construction process. The neutral is paid to stand ready to resolve disputes and to keep current with the project as it progresses through the construction phase. The disputing parties present summarized evidence to the neutral who rules summarily on an expedited basis. The decisions are usually final, though some

---

[259] *See Eagle's Nest Ltd. Partnership v. Brunzell,* 99 Nev. 710, 669 P.2d 714 (1983). *See also* NRS 624.628(3) and NRS 108.2453(2)(e) disallowing contract provisions that attempt to waive a contractor's right to payment under certain conditions.

contract provisions allow the neutral's decision to be challenged at a later time through arbitration or litigation of the cost of the dispute.

After the semi-formal resolution process fails, the parties move to a more formal resolution process or series of processes to finally resolve the dispute. These usually include mediation, arbitration or formal court based litigation to resolve the issues. Because of a perpetuated myth in legal circles by the proponents of alternative dispute resolution that alternative dispute resolution is faster, better and less expensive than litigation, binding arbitration has become the standard dispute resolution technique in construction and usually through a particular arbitration facilitator such as the American Arbitration Association or Judicial Arbitration and Mediation Services or any one of a number of other organizations. As arbitration has be implemented in practice, however, it has lost much of its allure towards a quicker and more cost effective resolution of the dispute. Further, the quality of arbitrators can be suspect in many cases and disputes are often resolved poorly or based on improper analysis, without the possibility of appeal or relief from the arbitration award. As such, careful consideration of different scenarios on how disputes may arise should be undertaken before a final dispute resolution technique is contractually agreed to between the parties.

Mediation is a formal resolution technique where an individual mediator intervenes between the disputing parties to achieve a settlement. In most cases, the mediator has no actual authority to order any party to take any action or to make a final decision about the case. The mediator can, however, use his expertise in dispute resolution to expose the weaknesses of each side's case and move the parties toward a mutual resolution of the claim. Mediation is sometimes best used when each of the parties has had the opportunity to review the claims of the other side of the dispute and to evaluate their own evidence in light of the disputing parties claims. If the disputing parties are emotionally entrenched in their positions, however, mediation will usually be unavailing and of little value to the dispute resolution process.

Binding arbitration is usually seen as just one step short of actual litigation. In fact, arbitration usually will be handled as a private trial, where the parties involved pay for the judge and the courtroom setting. Before choosing arbitration as the dispute resolution technique for your contract, the parties should consider the cost of using an arbitrator or arbitrators as the rules of any particular arbitration service provider require. Also, it should be considered that a binding arbitration award will not be overturned in most states (including Nevada) except for demonstrating that the arbitrator was biased or intentionally failed to follow the applicable law. For the most part, such a showing is manifestly difficult to demonstrate on appeal of the arbitrator's ruling. As such, the parties should draft methods for choosing the arbitrator and rules under which the arbitration will occur and how the arbitration will be paid for between the parties.

CHAPTER 5 CONSTRUCTION CLAIMS

5:1 INTRODUCTION

Many texts go into significant detail on asserting construction claims.[260] Like in other sections of this book we will not, but rather only generally discuss construction claims to support Nevada's legal take on the concepts discussed. This chapter will also discuss the presentation of construction claims and the responsibilities of practitioners in presenting construction claims.

5:2 DOCUMENTATION

We have discussed in Chapter 4 the use of project documentation and the need for contractual obligations for construction documentation and exchange.[261] In this section we will discuss the use of that documentation within the context of construction claim prosecution or defense.

It should be understood that in the presentation of any construction claim it is critical that the practitioner gather all facts and events leading to the dispute, so that a clear and precise presentation to the trier of fact can be made whether that is a mediator, arbitrator, judge or jury. While some arbitrators may have more understanding about construction than others, or even judges and juries will, the need to clearly explain the relevant history of the construction project will be of critical importance to your claim. The key component of the presentment of the project story is the contemporaneous project documentation that was created at the time the project was being constructed. The more detailed and accurate the contemporaneous documentation, the more likely the result of the claim presentation will be satisfactory to the claimant.

The most important elements of contemporaneous project documentation to support any claim are the daily reports and construction schedule updates. These documents tell the story of the project and will reveal the impact of the event that gives rise to the claim on the project. Ideally, these documents will complement each other, demonstrating both in the field work and the overall historical record of the construction progress that the event was damaging to the claimant.

If there are gaps in the record or these documents are not as accurate as need be, other documents can be used to fill in these issues. Regardless of whether there are gaps to fill, however, the practitioner will want to gather and review the additional documents to

---

[260] For a detailed discussion on construction claims, *see Bruner & O'Connor on Construction Law*, Volume 2.

[261] *See* Section 4:18, Documentation Requirements and Procedures.

use as either additional support or to disclose inconsistencies with the project record known. These records include inspection reports, plan revisions and comments from the jurisdictional authorities, project correspondence, schedule narratives, payment requests and records, change order requests and logs, requests for information and logs, project manager journals, subcontractor daily reports and time records.

In conjunction with the project documentation is the use of a construction expert to tell the project story using the contemporaneous record. Of course, the proper selection of an expert is critical to your claim, and of even more importance is the expert's ability to understand the method of construction as well as the means of construction in the particular area of their expertise.

5:3 Use of Expert Witnesses and Consultants

Selection of experts needs to be carefully undertaken and specifically tailored to your specific issues on which the construction claim is based. Construction claims related to failure of a contractor's performance or the impact on a contractor during performance can be referred to an expert in construction and scheduling. Damage issues related to the impact should be referred to an expert familiar with construction accounting and related damage calculation methods commonly used in construction claims. More specific design or function claims should be referred to consultants with expertise in the specific trades affected, such as electrical, structural steel, plumbing, heating, ventilation & air conditioning, fire / life safety systems, etc.

It is also preferable to retain an expert who has in the field experience to back up his/her theoretical knowledge. For instance, an expert in critical path method scheduling may know all the tricks available in the most current version of scheduling software. However, the ability of the expert to accurately analyze the schedule for constructability is vital to the case outcome. Simply knowing how software works and not knowing how construction actually occurs in the field does not make for a believable expert analysis. Also, if the expert must comment on the methods of construction or the likelihood of a certain string of events to occur when those events are to some degree influenced by the local authorities with jurisdiction over the project (such as building inspectors, plan checkers, etc.) it is often very helpful to ensure the retained expert has performed work in that jurisdiction. Nevada has many unique challenges that are not always to be found in a guideline or instruction package. Knowing where those challenges exist and having experience to navigate them is a valued asset for a consultant. As such, the expert's background should be vetted as much as possible and any information about her/his ability to report and testify should be obtained and reviewed.

Once the expert is retained, there becomes a large question of what s/he should be provided and how to use the expert to her/his best advantage. If possible, the expert should be provided as much information about the claim, negative and positive, as can be provided. In this way, the expert can be prepared in his/her report to recognize problematic issues and account for them in her/his analysis before his/her initial report is completed or he must provide her/his deposition. It is also important to provide him/her with all deposition testimony and other documents that s/he needs to be aware of before his/her deposition testimony is taken.

Accordingly, the expert should be provided a complete list of involved parties in the project who are likely to be referenced in the claim or otherwise called as witnesses, and complete lists of their correspondence and email transmissions should also be provided.

5:4 Design Issues

Issues with regard to design of the project can lead to significant claims for the contractor or the owner to deal with moving forward during the project. The initial design concern is passing plan check with the jurisdictional authority over the project and obtaining a permit. The designer must be responsive to the questions and comments of the jurisdictional authority or the project runs a severe risk of delay at the outset of project commencement, which can be a legitimate cause of contractor claims for failure to provide project access.

Permit delays will prevent the contractor from commencing construction on a project, as the contractors cannot lawfully commence construction until a permit is obtained.[262] As such, the contractor who is prevented by design issues from being able to pull permits begins to accrue damages as the time for construction moves forward without work commencing. Similarly, the Owner may also incur damages against the Designer while the plans fail to proceed through plan check towards the issuance of a building permit.

Owners and their designers, therefore, should proceed with design and plan check comment responses in an expedited fashion and should thoroughly respond to the plan check comments and requirements. Failure to do so can cause significant problems with the design approval process, which can plague a project throughout its construction phase. At all times, parties should do their best to address issues from jurisdictional authorities in a comprehensive and timely manner. While each jurisdictional authority will have a procedure for seeking modification or waiver of specific code requirements or to challenge the interpretation of a plan check requirement or inspector in the field, such challenges need to be handled with professionalism and substantial support for the modification in every case and regardless of the circumstances surrounding the event.

---

[262] NRS 624.3011(2) provides:

> *If a contractor performs construction without obtaining any necessary building permit, there is a rebuttable presumption that the contractor willfully and deliberately violated the building laws of this state or of its political subdivisions.*

Subsequent to permits being pulled, design issues can arise. Despite the design professional's best efforts, rarely if ever will a design be perfect or complete upon commencement of construction. Design errors are to a large degree expected, and are resolved through the process known as requests for information, or "RFI," in the field language of construction. A classic RFI is the request of a contractor for coordination of the design, as two aspects of construction are in conflict and cannot be built as shown on the plans. This can arise as a result of a number of reasons, but the important issue is that the contractor needs a design "fix" before the work can proceed. The contractor will fill out an RFI and will transmit it to the person with whom he has contracted--in most cases the Owner--who is then obligated to transmit the RFI to the design professional for response. Once the design professional has responded to the Owner, the Owner must transmit the response to the Contractor, who will implement the design professional's response in the field. This process can cause changes, delays, disruptions or other impacts, which may create claims / change order requests for the Contractor against the Owner.

Claims through the RFI process can arise for several reasons, but some of the more common reasons are delay in the transmittal or response process, the extent of the change required by the response, or the lack of actual effective response to the issue. It is common on the contracting process to specify a time period for RFI responses. When that time period is violated, a contractor can claim the delay is disrupting or otherwise impacting the construction progress and damages are resulting. To best track such claims, an RFI log is used to track the dates of the requests and response times to RFIs. When RFI responses are demonstrated historically to be late, and those late responses can be demonstrated to affect the critical path of the construction process, an impact claim is usually available to the Contractor. Whether the owner or, ultimately, the design professional is responsible for that impact will again depend on each party's contribution to the impact on the RFI process. If the owner keeps an RFI log and can demonstrate a quick turnaround for the RFI to be transmitted to the design professional and a corresponding quick turnaround to the contractor of the response, the owner can demonstrate that the design professional was the ultimate cause of the delays, and place the damage there. While this will not entirely protect the owner from the contractor claim, it will allow for indemnification claims to arise against the design professional. Conversely, if the design professional can demonstrate quick responsiveness to the RFI once received, but a delay in the owner's process for transmittal, the impact can be argued as the owner's responsibility.

While the timing of the transmittal process is important, the timing is not always the end of the story. The number and issues of the RFIs can also be a telling factor in the claims process. In general, a large number of RFIs on a construction project will indicate one of two problems with the design--either the plans are not of sufficient quality for the performance of the work or the contractor has no ability to review the plans properly and is therefore not qualified to perform the work. Regardless, a large number of RFIs on a project can lead to legitimate claims of additional work or impacts from the contractor and can in some cases lead to an argument that the owner has abandoned the contract entirely -- a legal concept known as the cardinal change.

The response to an RFI can also generate claims in the form of change orders to the work as well as extensions of time for performance. If the RFI response causes a significant issue that will impact the construction process in a number of ways, the contractor is entitled to recover the additional costs incurred as a result of the design revision and if that revision causes the work to be delayed or will take more time for the completion, the contractor may also be entitled to additional time to complete the work. There is often a tension in this circumstance between the design professional and the contractor, which needs to be reviewed as part of the claims analysis process. Occasionally, a contractor will use the RFI response to claim an impact on the work, which goes far beyond the actual impact of the change. Likewise, a contractor can claim that a change actually impacts a number of areas that have not actually commenced construction. When a change is requested as a result of an RFI, the owner and the design professional should review the alleged impact with the contractor in light of the actual work performed to date and how the RFI response has changed that work already performed. Claims for impacts to work which has not already been performed can be reviewed with some legitimate questions, although it is certainly possible that materials pre-ordered or otherwise anticipated may be impacted. Certainly if the impact requires work in place to be removed and replaced, those impacts are legitimately claimed as extras. Expert witnesses need to be employed to vet these questions if the impacts are not clear or if scheduling issues arise as part of the claim package.

It is also possible to have claims asserted because the design does not actually work in the field or cannot be actually constructed in a reasonable and viable construction method. While the means and method of construction are nearly always a contractor issue, if the design is not one that a reasonable contractor can actually erect, the design professional may have some responsibility for providing an erection schedule or sequence to allow the design to be performed in the field. In this case, the contractor may have a difficult time demonstrating the inability of construction technique and the response from the owner and design professional will usually be an assertion that the contractor is inexperienced or not qualified. Again, these questions will need to be resolved through the use of expert testimony to demonstrate the constructability of the design and the qualifications of a reasonable contractor to perform that work.

Once the work is performed, the design may still give rise to owner claims as well. While the terms of the design services contract may affect the owner's claims for indemnity from contractor claims, the owner also may have claims that the design does not perform as required or that the materials and equipment specified for the design may not properly meet the owner's requirements. In these cases, the performance of the completed work will have to verify the design. It should be expected in this situation that the design professional will likely point to installation issues as the cause of the lack of proper performance. Again, the determination and resolution of these matters will require expert witness review and analysis.

5:5 Access and Commencement of Construction

One of the owner's duties that can also give rise to construction claims is the delivery of access to the site by the contractor when notice to proceed with construction is delivered. The owner is obligated to provide the contractor with access to and control over the project site in order to perform the work. If the contractor Is not able to proceed for any reason that is not his fault, the owner will be responsible to the contractor for the damages he suffers as a result. Access can be denied for a number of reasons, including the failure to obtain the proper design approvals, the failure to obtain a reasonable mode of ingress and egress from the work site, or the failure to provide any pre-requisite services necessary to allow the work to commence.

“Commencement of Construction” is defined in NRS 108.22112:

> *"Commencement of construction" means the date on which: 1. Work performed; or 2. Materials or equipment furnished in connection with a work of improvement, is visible from a reasonable inspection of the site.*

This definition is set forth in the Nevada mechanics lien statutes and may not be fully applicable for claims based on a lack of access to the site. Nevertheless, it is often the case that access is denied by the owner based on the fact that financing is not completely procured or there is some delay in the recordation process for the construction financing liens on the Project. While financing can be a critical issue for a lender on a Nevada construction site, it is important to understand why limiting the contractor's access to the site before recordation is a critical issue for construction owners and lenders.

Determining when to commence construction of a project is not simply a matter of completing the construction contract negotiations with the general contractor. When to commence construction needs to be carefully considered along with all other elements of the construction project. If a construction project will need the assistance of outside lenders to achieve completion, commencement of construction before the financing closes can be a costly proposition for the project developer, and can even jeopardize the entire project.

Lenders base decisions to loan funds on the level of risk associated with the profit to be made on the loan. The higher the risk, the higher and more certain the profit must be to make the loan worthwhile. One of the most critical factors in assessing risk is the priority of the lender's interest in the project subject of the loan, if the borrower defaults. The lender wants to insure that it has a first position--that is, all other liens or encumbrances, including mechanics liens, against the property will be behind the lender's position. If the project goes bankrupt, this first position will secure the lender's loan. If the lender is not in first position, other liens can supplant the lender, making the lender's security in the project worthless. The lender requires the borrower to provide a policy of title insurance, guaranteeing that the lender's first position on title will not be compromised.

Title insurance companies, therefore, require that the title be clear before they will issue a title insurance policy; that is, no lien will materialize and supersede the lender's title that they have insured. If such a lien does materialize, the Title Insurer will either have to litigate the validity of the lien, or pay off the liens to provide their insured--the lender--clear title. Both of these options can cost many times more than the premium charged for the title insurance. So the title insurance company wants to be certain of the title it insures before it issues the policy. Nevada law, however, gives mechanics lien claims priority over lender claims, if work is commenced before the lender's lien is recorded. Therefore, commencing construction before the lender's priority is secured is the bane of title insurance.

Nevada law provides that all mechanics liens arising from a construction project relate back and attach to the property on the first date of visible construction on the project site, regardless of when the work was actually performed.[263] All of these mechanics liens are superior to any lien which attaches to the project title after the work of construction has commenced, including any lender who has records a deed of trust for construction financing.[264] As a result of these statutes, when a developer decides to commence construction before securing financing, the Lender's priority is destroyed. The title insurer can no longer guarantee title to your lender; and so they will make onerous demands on you to issue the title policy, if they will issue one at all. Title becomes practically, if not actually, uninsurable.

Restoring priority of title to the property in favor of the lender probably cannot be accomplished under current law--at least not easily--and not without substantial costs and delay to the project. Some states, such as Florida, actually allow for restoring priority by statutory procedure. While priority can probably be re-established, the steps

---

[263] NRS 108.225(1)(a); *See J.E. Dunn Northwest, Inc. v. Corus Construction Venture LLC,* 127 Nev Adv.Op. 5, 249 P.3d 501 (2011); *Byrd Underground LLC v. Angaur LLC,* 130 Nev Adv.Op. 62, 332 P.3d 273 (2014).

[264] NRS 108.225(2); *See In re Fontainebleau Las Vegas Holdings, LLC,* 128 Nev.Adv.Op. 53, 289 P.3d 1199 (2012).

necessary are onerous and still offer no specific guarantee that they will result in lender priority over the mechanics lien claims.

The easiest and most reliable method to re-establish priority would be to record a surety bond to release all liens on the project.[265] Unfortunately, the bond must be procured in the amount of 150% of the general construction contract; e.g., on a $2.5 billion hotel casino project, the bond must be in the amount of $3.75 billion. Assuming that any developer had such bonding capacity available to them, and assuming that any surety would issue such a bond, the premium for the bond is likely to approach $75 million. Not a welcome or reasonable alternative for any developer.

Regardless, once the bond is secured and recorded, it must be served on anyone who provides the owner with a preliminary notice under NRS 108.245. By undertaking this activity, all mechanics' liens, regardless of their recording date, are attached to the bond. The project title is no longer affected by them and clear title can be conveyed to the lender and can be insured as well.

The second possibility is more complex, though it may be somewhat less expensive, and carries more risk. Theoretically, a lender's title priority may be re-established by stopping work on the project, having it deemed complete for mechanics lien purposes. Once the project is deemed "complete," the lender's deed of trust may be recorded and a "new" project commenced.

First, the "first" project would have to be "completed." The definition of "Completion of the work of improvement" in NRS 108.22116, would require all work on the project to cease. The developer then either: 1) accepts the work already performed as finished, without recourse, or 2) waits 30 days and then recording a Notice of Completion under NRS 108.228. This procedure would start the time to record mechanics' liens to run. The project owner would next wait the expiration of the period for mechanics liens to be recorded. If the owner accepts the work as complete, the period would be 90 days from the actual acceptance, or last delivery of labor or materials whichever was longer. If the owner decides instead to cease construction and comply with the Notice of Completion procedures, the waiting period is reduced to 40 days from recording the Notice of Completion. Any mechanics liens that are recorded would have to be paid in full and released.

After the waiting period expires and all mechanics liens are paid in full, the owner would have to re-negotiate contracts for the work to complete the construction project originally contemplated. The work could not re-commence under the original contracts. Doing so would render the section "completion" project just a continuation of the first,

---

265 NRS 108.2415(2).

thereby destroying the very benefit being sought by the work stoppage in the first place. There is, of course, no guarantee that the contractors and subcontractors would be willing to negotiate a new contract under similar terms or pricing that they originally had entered into with the owner or general contractor. Likewise, the termination of the original contracts could result in termination fees or even lawsuits for breach of contract, if termination for convenience provisions were not originally negotiated.

In either case, the termination and re-negotiation is likely to take a significant toll on the construction budget and the time for completion of the work. And then, of course, there is no guarantee that the effect of this procedure would actually work to re-establish lender priority under Nevada law. If mechanics liens are ultimately recorded in the future, it is likely that the effectiveness of this procedure would be challenged. The uncertainty of this mechanism is not likely to provide much assurance to a title insurance company seeking to reduce its litigation risk.

5:6 Claims Arising from Construction Changes

As discussed in previous chapters, the changes on a construction project are the most prolific source of construction claims and disputes. Whether or not a particular directive from the owner arises to the level of a compensable change is a huge issue for any construction project. In fact, it is probably safe to assert that literally no construction project will be completed without at least a minor dispute arising over change orders--minimally, the owner or the architect will direct the contractor to perform some work which the contractor will assert is a change, but the owner and/or architect will dispute as such. The ease of the solution of such directive will challenge the best arbitrator or mediator over the issue.

Change orders come in various forms: Actual, Constructive and Cardinal. The contractor who is handed a document entitled "change order" should understand that the owner believes a change to the contract amount, and potentially the contract completion date, is appropriate. Since all parties agree that the work constitutes a change, any dispute will involved the reasonableness of the contractor's price for the change and any extension of time quotation requested to perform the changed work. Contract clauses affecting the pricing of change orders should be consulted to resolve such disputes. Certain actions by the owner or the owner's agent may affect the contractor's work in the same way as if a formal change order was issued. A constructive change may also be a formal directive that is not designated as a change because the party who issues the directive does not view it as such. Since constructive changes are not clearly identified, they are a more substantial source of dispute.

The types of situations that can give rise to a constructive change are virtually limitless. Because these changes will not be labeled as such by the owner or architect, it is important that the contractor maintain a constant review of his work schedule to determine when it has been affected by the acts or omissions of others. This will require keeping watch on the performance of trade contractors and remaining diligent in the review of the effect of actual changes, RFIs and other directives. Conversely, the owner and architect need to be diligent to monitor when alternatives to the work or directives given to the contractor may cause actual change to occur in the field. Likewise, the contractor needs to closely monitor the subcontracted scopes of work and the field directives of its superintendents to know when a subcontractor has been given a change order.

A cardinal change occurs when the owner requires changes, which by their nature or total quantity, make the project fundamentally different than the project upon which the contractor based its bid. For this reason, cardinal changes may release the contractor from the terms of its bid and allow the contractor to recover the reasonable value of the labor and materials provided in and about the project, plus reasonable markups for overhead and profit. If the courts determine that a cardinal change has occurred, the courts will convert the fixed price contract into a time and materials contract.[266] While this option is certainly available, it should be very carefully considered before asserted as a claim. The burden to established that changes have been so substantial that the original project concept has been abandoned is difficult to prove and expensive to litigate, because in most cases the conversion of a fixed price contract into a time and material contract will make a dramatic increase in the cost of the work to the owner. Substantial justification in evidence and buttressed with expert testimony should be present before this claim is asserted.

In Nevada, there is simply no practical reason to claim that an oral change has occurred. First, almost every construction contract will attempt to void oral change orders. Secondly, with the mandatory implementation of unsigned or un-rejected change order requests into the construction contract time and price under the provisions of the Nevada Prompt Payment Act,[267] there is no longer any justification for a contractor or subcontractor to perform work without submitting timely a change order request and having that request flushed out long before the work is completed. Regardless, if an oral directive is believed to be a change order, the contractor should fully document the activity and time provided to perform the work. The contractor should make every effort to get the directive to perform in writing. Performing an oral change order is not without its risks. Current Nevada case law will state that oral change orders are not part of the project contract until they are reduced to writing.[268] While the Nevada Legislature has

---

[266] *Paterson v. Condos*, 55 Nev. 134, 28 P.2d 499 (1934); *J.A. Jones Const. Co. v. Lehrer McGovern Bovis, Inc.*, 120 Nev. 277, 89 P.3d 1009 (2004).

[267] NRS 624.606, *et seq.*; *see* Chapter 3, Private Works Prompt Payment Act.

[268] *See California Commercial v. Amedeo Vegas I, Inc.*, 119 Nev. 143, 67 P.3d 328 (2003).

arguably voided this case law through the 2003 and 2005 amendments to its mechanics lien statutes,[269] the argument remains that oral change orders are not part of a construction contract. Therefore, again, a contractor should not perform oral change order work until the change order is reduced to writing, as performance carries a substantial risk of nonpayment and therefore an eventual claim.

5:7 Claims Arising from Changed Conditions

Most construction contracts will contain a "changed conditions" clause, which allows a contractor to request additional compensation when the contractor finds subsurface or latent physical conditions at the site differing materially from those indicated in the contract (known as a "Type 1 Differing Site Condition") or previously unknown physical conditions at the site, of an unusual nature, differing materially from those ordinarily encountered and generally recognized as inherent in work of the character provided for in the contract (known as a "Type 2 Differing Site Condition"). In the absence of a statute, contract provision, or other legal obligation to the contrary, a contractor is not required to investigate hidden differing site conditions to determine the conditions lying beneath the project site. Instead, the contractor may rely upon the owner's investigation of the site and disclosed existing conditions. Whether the contract discloses site conditions or not, relief may be available to the contractor if the conditions are more severe than represented by the contract or are unusual and materially different than the typical conditions.

In dealing with differing site conditions, the contractor must comply with the notice requirements set forth in the contract. Notice must be provided promptly and before the conditions are disturbed so that the owner can investigate the condition before it is disturbed. This is particularly important in the case of excavation work. The contractor who does give notice of the condition or who fails to maintain accurate records of the impact of the condition upon his work may be barred or precluded from prosecuting a changed conditions claim.

Another important factor regarding a changed condition claim is the pre-bid site investigation. Construction contracts often contain exculpatory language requiring the contractor to make a pre-bid investigation of the site to become familiar with the work, observe the physical conditions of the site. The owner will usually defend against a contractor's differing site condition claim on the basis that the contractor was required to investigate the site before bidding the project, arguing that if the contractor had performed the physical inspection of the site in accordance with the contract, the condition would have discovered it and adjusted his contract price to deal with the

---

[269] NRS 108.221 through 108.246, inclusive; *see* Chapter 8, Nevada Mechanic's Liens.

condition. However, if the contractor can demonstrate that a site investigation would not have revealed the condition, the contractor's claim may survive. Moreover, some Courts have held that such perfunctory clauses are not effective when such an inspection would not have put the contractor on notice of the condition.[270]

5:8 LIQUIDATED DAMAGES V. ACTUAL DAMAGES

No business demonstrates the old adage "Time is money" more than construction. Delays cause both the owner and the contractor to suffer damages. If the owner can establish that the delay in the completion of the project was caused by the contractor, or one or more of its subcontractors or suppliers, the owner may be able to recover damages from the contractor. Even a partial failure of performance by the contractor may give rise to a delay damage claim by the owner. If an owner is constructing the improvement for its own use, or in the case of public projects, damages for late completion may be difficult to quantify. For that reason, among others, many owners include a liquidated damage provision in their construction contracts. Liquidated damages provisions are almost always found in public works contracts.

Liquidated damages clauses contractually fix the amount of the owner's damages (or the contractor's potential liability) for delays. The typical clause provides for the payment of a set amount by the contractor to the owner for each day that the project completion is delayed beyond the date set forth in the contract. However, liquidated damages are a substitute for actual damages and the two are not compatible. If a contract calls for liquidated damages, the owner cannot recover actual damages instead. As a general rule, actual damages are nearly always more substantial than liquidated damages, and given a particular project, actual damages may not be as difficult to determine as they may seem.

Liquidated damage clauses are presumed to be valid and the courts will enforce the liquidated damage clause unless the party seeking to invalidate the clause is able to prove that the provision was unreasonable under the circumstances existing at the time the contract was made.[271] Liquidated damages clauses can serve as an important factor in motivating the contractor to complete the project in a timely manner. However, these clauses should be viewed with caution. For example, an owner with substantial financing costs and/or the possible loss of rental income due to delay may have actual damages substantially greater than the liquidated amount of a few hundred dollars a day. Additionally, the very existence of the provision may cause the contractor to be particularly aggressive in attempting to establish and document the owner's fault in delaying construction.

---

[270] *See Spearin v. United States*, 248 U.S. 132 (1918) .; *see also Halcrow, Inc. v. Dist. Ct.*, 129 Nev.Adv.Op. 42, 302 P.3d 1148 (2013).

[271] *Joseph F. Sanson Inv. Co. v. 268 Ltd.*, 106 Nev. 429, 795 P.2d 493 (1990).

5:9 DELAY CLAIMS

All construction contracts contain either an express or implied completion date. The completion date imposes a constraint on the contractor's performance. It may be expressed as a date certain or a specific number of days from the issuance of a notice to proceed. If the contract does not contain an express completion date the courts will imply a reasonable completion date.

On most projects, contractors will experience a variety of impacts threatening to delay completion of the project until after the completion date, or beyond a reasonable period of time for completion. Contracts and courts group delays into several broad categories. These categories include excusable or inexcusable delays, compensable or non-compensable delays and concurrent delays. As a general rule, parties to a private works contract may include in their contract any provision upon which they agree. In the case of dispute, the courts will initially refer to the parties' contract as containing their entire agreement and will attempt to enforce the agreement as the parties intended. Whether or not a delay in the performance of the work is excusable or inexcusable depends to a large extent upon whether or not the owner and the contractor agreed that certain delays were to be considered a risk of the owner or a risk of the contractor.

Excusable delays are usually defined by the contract and entitle the contractor to additional time (i.e., an extension of time) within which to complete the construction of the project, provided that the contractor complies with the notice requirements. Excusable delays do not necessarily entitle the contractor to any increased compensation because of increased cost resulting from the delay. Excusable delays are usually unforeseen and are not the fault of either party.

On the other hand, an inexcusable delay is usually the fault of one party or the other. As set forth above, if the contractor fails to complete the construction of the subject improvement within the time set forth in the contract due to the contractor's own fault or the fault of its subcontractors or material suppliers, the contractor will be liable to the owner for damages. Likewise, if the owner delays the contractor's performance on the project, the owner may be liable to the contractor for any increased cost resulting from the owner-caused delay. Any delay that is within the control of the contractor is deemed to be an inexcusable delay. Inexcusable delays include: failure to properly man the job, failure to properly schedule the work, and the failure to provide equipment or material to the project in a timely manner. Inexcusable delays do not entitle the contractor to a time extension or extra compensation. In fact, the contractor may be liable for damages to the owner for damages sustained as the result of an inexcusable delay.

In most instances, the circumstances entitle a contractor to an extension of time are specifically enumerated in the construction contract. Once again, the inclusion (or exclusion) of certain events as excusable delays is a method of risk allocation between the parties. The contractor must analyze this clause in the light of the types of events the contractor is likely to encounter on the project and the risks associated with the occurrence of such events. On the other hand, if the contract provides that the contractor is entitled to a time extension and an equitable adjustment in the contract sum if the work is delayed by certain specified events, the owner has assumed the risk of loss associated with the occurrence of such events. Some examples of excusable delays are Acts of God, labor unrest or strikes, unusually severe weather, or unexpected and unforeseeable material shortages or unavailability which render it impossible for the contractor to perform. When such unforeseen events occur, the courts will relieve a contractor of its duty to perform.[272]

An excusable delay may entitle the contractor to a time extension in order to complete the contract, provided the basis for the extension falls within the appropriate contract provision and the contractor complies with the notice provision. Generally, an excusable delay does not entitle the contractor to any damages or increased compensation as a result of the delay since neither party is at fault (i.e., an excusable/non-compensable delay). Instead, the contractor receives a time extension which enables the contractor to complete the contract without penalty. If the owner, or one of the owner's representatives, causes certain delays, the contractor is entitled to both a time extension and additional compensation. An owner-caused delay often is termed a "compensable delay". The most common examples of an owner-caused/compensable delay include failure to provide access to the site, the issuance of defective plans and specifications, delays in responding to Requests for Information ("RFI"), shop drawings or submittals and/or delays in providing owner furnished equipment. However, Nevada law has altered this landscape somewhat with revisions to NRS 108.2453 and now arguably any delay, whether owner caused or otherwise may be compensable for the contractor.

NRS 108.2453(2) provides in pertinent part:

> *A condition, stipulation or provision in a contract or other agreement for the improvement of property or for the construction, alteration or repair of a work of improvement in this State that attempts to do any of the following is contrary to public policy and is void and unenforceable ... (e) Require a prime contractor or subcontractor to waive, release or extinguish a claim or right that the prime contractor or subcontractor may otherwise possess or acquire for delay, acceleration, disruption or impact damages or an extension of time for delays incurred, for any delay, acceleration, disruption or impact event which was unreasonable under the circumstances, not within*

---

[272] *Colorado Environments, Inc. v. Valley Grading Corp.*, 105 Nev. 464, 779 P.2d 80 (1989).

the contemplation of the parties at the time the contract was entered into, or for which the prime contractor or subcontractor is not responsible.

This provision was primarily an attempt to overrule the attempt by an owner to limit or avoid responsibility for owner-caused delays with a "no damages for delay" clause. These types of clauses typically provide that the contractor will be entitled to an extension of time for delays caused by the owner, but will not be entitled to recover monetary damages. The ability of the owner to limit damages as a result of delay now must be reserved to impact claims which are not unreasonable under the circumstances, are within the contemplation of the contracting parties when they entered into the no damage for delay agreement, or when the contractor in question is responsible for the damage. Many of these issues may be handled by careful drafting of the clause, however, as a general rule, owners should view any impact claim in Nevada as potentially compensable for the contractor.

It should also be noted, however, that under Nevada law even if a person technically complies with the terms of a contract he can still be found liable for breach of the implied covenant of good faith and fair dealing therein. It has been well established in Nevada that every contract imposes a duty on the Parties to act in good faith and deal fairly with each other.[273] Breach of this duty gives rise to contractual damages, and of course the goal of contractual damages is to make one whole.[274] But it is also recognized that mere performance of the terms of a contract will not shield the performer from damages for bad faith actions. As the Nevada Supreme Court noted:

> *[W]here the terms of a contract are literally complied with but one party to the contract deliberately countervenes [sic] the intention and spirit of the contract, that party can incur liability for breach of the implied covenant of good faith and fair dealing.*[275]

In many instances, it is not easy to determine which party to a construction contract is responsible for delay. When both parties are at fault and it is difficult to isolate the portion of blame that should be assigned to each party or the various types of delay overlap, the delay often is described as "concurrent delay." If an excusable or compensable delay occurs concurrently with an inexcusable delay, the overlapping portion of the delays is inexcusable because the contractor is unable to work due to its concurrent, inexcusable delay. If an excusable delay occurs concurrently with a

---

273 *A.C. Shaw Const., Inc. v. Washoe County*, 105 Nev. 913, 914, 784 P.2d 9, 9-10 (1989).

274 *See Hilton Hotels Corp. v. Butch Lewis Productions, Inc.*, 109 Nev. 1043, 862 P.2d 1207 (1993).

275 *Hilton Hotels Corp. v. Butch Lewis Productions, Inc.*, 109 Nev. 1043, 1048, 862 P.2d 1207 (1993), quoting *Hilton Hotels Corp. v. Butch Lewis Productions, Inc.*, 107 Nev. 226, 232, 808 P.2d 919, 925 (1991).

compensable delay, the delay will be considered excusable, but non-compensable, because the contractor was unable to work notwithstanding the owner-caused delay. In certain instances, owners assert concurrent delays as a defense to contractors' claims for additional compensation based on owner-caused (compensable) delays. Specifically, owners attempt to establish that there was a concurrent, contractor-caused delay to avoid liability for delay damages. Inasmuch as both parties are responsible for some delay in the concurrent delay situation and the delay of one party is inextricably intertwined with the delay caused by the other party, many courts formerly refused to apportion damages and determined that neither party was entitled to recover delay damages. Now, however, courts will attempt to apportion the delays among the responsible parties, allowing the apportioned component of damage to offset the other side's damage and awarding the balance to the party with the leased decree of fault.

5:10 Disruption of the Contract Work

As a general rule, along with the right to determine the means and methods of the construction work, the contractor generally is recognized to have the right to perform the work in the most logical and cost effective sequence possible. When the contractor's as planned sequence of performance is changed as a result of the owner's actions or omissions, the contractor has a claim for the resulting additional costs. Disruption must be a material alteration of the performance conditions expected at bid time. In disruptive situations, the performance conditions actually encountered do not correspond to the conditions contemplated in the bid and increase the difficulty and cost of the contractor's performance. Due to the relationship between disruption and the contractor's anticipated (or planned) method of performance, disruption often is referred to as "interference" or "hindrance" or "out of sequence work."

In the context of the construction project, disruption refers to any situation impacting on the efficiency of the contractor's operations. If the contractor's operations are disrupted during the performance of the work, the contractor may suffer increased costs as the result of the disruption (i.e., change in sequence), but it does not necessarily follow that his performance will be extended beyond the contract time for completion. On the other hand, delay claims are the result of events which prolong the time necessary to complete the performance of the contract. The significance of the distinction between disruption and delay is the type of damages that are recoverable by the contractor. The damages a contractor is entitled to recover for disruption are not the same type of damages the contractor is entitled to recover for "pure delay." The damages associated with disruption are likely to be increased labor costs due to inefficiency, increased labor costs due to the activation-deactivation of work, etc. As mentioned in the preceding section, the damages associated with "pure delay," result from an extended performance period. However, regardless of how they are categorized in Nevada, NRS 108.2453(2)(e) may render them compensable.

Another important concept in the consideration of delay and disruption claims is what is known as the "ripple effect." Because of the interrelationship between all of the various construction activities on a given project, it is readily apparent that the disruption of any particular operation is likely to have an effect upon succeeding activities even though they may not be directly affected by the cause of the original disruption. Keeping in mind that the basis of disruption is a variance between the sequence of operations anticipated by the contractor at bid and the sequence that actually occurs during construction, it should be easy to see that once a single operation is disrupted, the succeeding operations also are likely to be affected, even though they are not directly disrupted.

5:11 Acceleration

Acceleration occurs when an owner directs a prime contractor (or a prime contractor directs a subcontractor) to complete all or a certain portion of the work prior to the date specified in the contract for completion, or prior to a properly adjusted completion date (i.e., the date that would have resulted if the contractor had received the time extensions to which the contractor was entitled under the contract). Acceleration may be actual or constructive.

Ordinarily, the party who is required to accelerate performance incurs increased costs resulting from extra manpower, overtime, increased equipment rental or inefficiencies associated with the presence of additional work forces on the jobsite. Actual acceleration occurs when the prime contractor (or subcontractor) receives a specific directive to complete all or a portion of the work prior to the actual completion date set forth in the contract or the completion date that would be required of the contractor if proper time extensions were granted. Inasmuch as one party to the contract has issued a directive to complete the work within a shorter time than the originally specified contract performance period, there should be no doubt that such a directive is an order to accelerate. Likewise, the contractor's right to additional compensation is also clear. In most instances, an owner who directs a contractor to accelerate its performance will agree, in advance, to compensate the contractor for the additional cost of the acceleration.

On the other hand, and similar to constructive change orders discussed previously, constructive acceleration is not as clear-cut as an explicit directive from the owner to accelerate performance. Constructive acceleration occurs when the owner fails or refuses to properly adjust the construction schedule and the prime contractor (or subcontractor) is forced to complete the project ahead of a properly adjusted schedule. For example, a contractor may encounter an excusable delay, but is not granted the proper time extension for the delay. Instead, the contractor is instructed to complete performance within the originally specified contract time. In effect, the contractor is being told to complete the work in a shorter period than contemplated by the contract. This creates a claim for the contractor against the owner, based on acceleration and the impacts that will be suffered on the project by the ripple effect of the accelerated schedule. Issues such as multiple trades working within the same area, inefficiencies due to worker fatigue, complications for coordinated delivery of materials or even ingress and egress to the project site can increase the costs of the work to the contractor when his work is accelerated.

5:12 TERMINATING THE CONTRACT

Construction contracts generally contain specific provisions itemizing events of default. If an event of default occurs, the owner may terminate the construction contract for cause.[276] Termination is a drastic remedy. It involves both practical and legal considerations. Owners and contractors must be extremely careful when making the determination to terminate a construction contract during the construction period and must carefully document the events of default is a material breach of the contract, that an opportunity to cure the breach has been provided, (iii) that the other party has failed to remedy the default, and (iv) that the performance which is lacking is not excused by virtue of any act or omission on the part of the other party.

In making the decision to terminate, the terminating party must consider the impact of termination on the project. In most cases, there will be a significant economic cost to changing to a new contractor during the course of construction. It is difficult for any replacement contractor to mobilize and commence performance in the middle of a project, negotiate arrangements with subcontractors and suppliers to complete the project, assume the risk of poor performance by the replaced contractor and reestablish proper coordination among the trades for the completion of the work. It is for these reasons that a replacement contractor is apt to exact a high price from the owner for taking over a problem job. All of these costs can be seen as damages to be paid for by the party found to have been wrongful in the termination. For these reasons, it may be better to complete the project and bring an action for breach of contract after completion.

Prior to terminating the contractor's performance on any project, the owner must make certain that a clear-cut unexcused breach exists. Further, the owner must determine that the contractor's breach is material. A material breach of a contract is not a minor or slight deviation from the terms of the contract. A material breach occurs when one party fails to perform a substantial part of the contract, or one or more of the essential terms of the contract. Stated simply, a material breach defeats the very purpose of the contract. Many construction contracts allow one party to terminate the other upon the occurrence of a stipulated default or other failure of performance. They attempt to define what is

---

[276] In some cases, a dispute over payment may be the cause of termination under Nevada law. *See* Chapter 3: Nevada Prompt Payment Act.

considered to be a material breach of the contract. If a contract is terminated pursuant to one of these provisions, the default or breach need not be material. The termination is predicated upon the terminated party's failure to adhere to the letter of the contract.

If the owner terminates the contractor's performance as the result of a material breach on the contractor's part, the contractor will be liable to the owner for the damages caused by its breach. The measure of damages will usually be the amount by which the total project cost to the owner exceeds the amount that the owner would have paid under the original contract, and the contractor bears the burden of establishing that the owner added work to the contract or proving that the cost of the completion was unreasonable. If it is determined that the owner was not justified in terminating the contractor's performance on the project, the owner will be precluded from recovering the excess project costs from the contractor and the contractor may be entitled to recover the value of the work in place, as well as lost profits, from the owner.[277]

To alleviate the inherent problems with termination of a contractor for cause, many construction contracts will attempt to allow the owner to terminate the construction contract for the convenience of the owner. In this case, the owner has the unfettered right to terminate the contractor at any time, however, the owner will be liable to the contractor for the costs incurred by the contractor and any profits that the contractor would have earned upon completion of the contract. If the owner does not want to be obligated to pay additional sums to the terminated contractor, this is a matter of contract negotiation and will be enforced as such by Nevada courts.[278]

5:13 Claim Preparation and Presentation

To finish off this chapter, a practical discussion about construction claims preparation and presentation to a neutral or trier of fact. It must be understood by every construction practitioner that construction claims can be difficult to understand and not interesting to people not involved in some aspect of the construction industry. As such, the practitioner preparing a claim for presentation to a project owner or contractor, and arbitrator or a judge or a jury must understand his audience and tailor the material to make it understandable. Difficult concepts in scheduling analysis or inefficiency calculations can be dry, so it is important that the presentation of such claims be handled efficiently and effectively.

It is critical that a claim be reduced to the basic and most important aspects of the dispute. Construction projects will generate hundreds of minor squabbles and disputes, but in the arbitration hearing room these can come across as irrelevant or petty.

---

[277] *Kirkpatrick v. Temme*, 98 Nev. 523, 654 P.2d 1011 (1982).

[278] *See* Chapter 4 Construction Contracts.

Therefore, the experienced practitioner will seek to find the significant issues that can tell a compelling story and reserve left over time to address the smaller, less significant disputes.

It is also critical that all the facts be presented in a truthful and straightforward manner that cannot be easily disputed. This is accomplished by reviewing all of the contemporaneous construction documentation as well as the memories of witnesses that is available from all potential sources. As such, the prosecution of a construction claim is not an inexpensive exercise. A significant investment of time, money and effort is necessary to properly prosecute or defend a construction claim. Moreover, it should be understood that it does not cost significantly more money to prosecute a large construction claim than it does a small one, nor does it cost significantly less money to prosecute a small construction claim verses a large one. Construction claim preparation and analysis must be performed by experts, who are not involved in the transaction giving rise to the project. While they may be percipient witnesses to the activity, the fact that they performed the actual schedule analysis opens them to attack and allegations of schedule manipulation. So, while you will always need the assistance of percipient witnesses, it is also necessary to have the actual performance on the project reviewed and vetted by an independent expert witness.

On a construction project it is rare that any one party is totally blameless and the victim of another. In most cases, the party making the claim will be in some degree at fault for the occurrence giving rise to the claim. This should not be ignored by the practitioner, but should be fully acknowledged with the approach that while there were issues they were not the ultimate cause of the damage suffered. Due allocation of fault appears to be more reasonable and truthful than one who completely blames all the misery suffered on the other party. Likewise, fully understanding all the factors in causing a problem can lead to a reasonable and more efficient resolution of the dispute through negotiation, mediation or other informal settlement technique.

It is vital that the party have a competent witness tell its story. It is vital to the successful claim that the story of the project can be explained in an intelligent and reasonable manner. Many contractors who have worked hard in the field cannot tell the story of a construction claim in a neutral and even manner, however, in presenting the claim to a third party it is important to have the underlying story told based on facts and without excessive compassion or errors. If the percipient witnesses cannot perform in this matter, an expert witness can be used to lay out the ground work on the case, as the percipient witnesses provide testimony to back up the story. While presenting a case expert first may not be the most desirable methodology, if there is no story teller in the group of percipient witnesses it is a reasonable alternative to set out the road forward and allow the percipient witnesses to build the structure as the case progresses.

As a practitioner, give your expert witnesses a specific issue on which to render an opinion and then all the relevant evidence, testimony and information to evaluate before they prepare their reports, get to trial or to deposition testimony. Do not make the mistake of only giving the expert "enough information" to make his report. It is critical that an expert witness be fully prepared for the testimony they will provide. If information cannot be useful in formulating the expert's opinion, the expert will determine that. However, if the information is never provided to the expert, the expert has no answer for why information that may be relevant to the Trier of fact played no part in the expert's analysis and report of the claim. As a result, the expert seems to not be prepared and not to have thoroughly examined all of the facts. Instead, by providing the expert a specific issue to render an opinion and then all of the known facts and information available, the expert can prepare his opinion and be prepared not only to acknowledge the existence of certain facts but be prepared to defend any decision to discard those facts as irrelevant or to minimize them in his analysis.

It should always be kept in mind that the construction claim is a story of impact on the construction project and how it was intended to be built. When the contractor establishes a game plan for the construction, that game plan must be sound. If the game plan is not reasonable, the alleged impact creating a claim will not be established on a firm basis. Therefore, the entire plan of the contractor in seeking to perform the work is relevant to the construction claim process. The competent construction expert will evaluate first the bid and the as planned schedule to determine if there is a viable construction plan. If one exists, the expert can then build on the claim by overlaying the historical progress information and watching the plan be altered by the various event impacts. As the longest sequence of activity (known as the "critical path" of construction sequencing) changes, delays, disruptions and accelerations come to life and can be visibly demonstrated through computer presentation software. While this presentation methodology needs to be explained, it is very effective communication on how the project was impacted by various events. Only by reviewing and inputting the historical data against the planned construction sequence can the actual impact of events be demonstrated to a third party, especially a person with little or no construction experience.

CHAPTER 6 PUBLIC WORKS CONSTRUCTION

6:1 INTRODUCTION TO NEVADA PUBLIC WORKS CONSTRUCTION

Nevada's public works statutes can be difficult to understand when first reviewed. The statutory scheme has alternative sections for use by local government agencies and municipalities that differ somewhat from those of state managed projects. Likewise, the Nevada Department of Transportation ("NDOT") has a number of provisions that are alternate from those governing projects run by the Nevada Department of Public Works. Each of the local governmental agencies has its own adopted criteria, as allowed under the main provisions of the public works statutes. While the details of each local governmental regulation are beyond the scope of this book, the reader is encouraged to review the local department regulations in conjunction with the state-wide materials discussed herein to get a full understanding of a local governmental or NDOT project requirements.

In any event, unless adoption of local regulation is authorized within the context of NRS Chapter 338, or a differing statute directly indicates, the specific provisions of NRS Chapter 338 will apply to the concept, design, bidding and delivery of public works project within the state of Nevada. As with most construction related issues, there is little case law interpreting the Nevada statutory scheme within the public works procurement process. That case law is fully discussed in the ensuing materials as applicable.

This chapter will focus primarily on the procurement of construction projects as a whole. We do not attempt to delve into the areas of material or services procurement, except as they are dealt within in the context of public construction. This chapter will focus primarily on the methods and procedures for selecting designers and contractors to construct state or local governmentally funded projects and the methods by which those projects are authorized to be delivered.

6:2 PUBLIC WORKS DELIVERY METHODS

Construction delivery methods in Nevada have undergone some fairly radical alterations over the last few years. Prior to the 1999 legislative session, the only method for constructing larger construction projects within the state was competitive bidding. In 1999, at the request of several local governmental agencies the legislature enacted a statutory scheme for construction via the design-build delivery method. Due to the number of concerns raised from the construction community, the use of design-build was severely limited by only authorizing its practice for projects that met a high dollar level and required unique design and / or building techniques. As a result, no construction projects were actually constructed with this technique until significant changes to the restrictions were enacted in 2003. The criteria have been steadily relaxed since with ever more successful results.

Construction disputes have also lead to significant changes within the public works delivery methods. Several large projects in Clark County were constructed under design criteria that were arguably insufficient. The project delivery statutes did not allow for any type of construction review before bidding and left the designers in relative charge of the bidding criteria. When these projects resulted in massive litigation and unworkable construction projects for their intended purposes, the movement to allow construction management as an authorized delivery method gained significant momentum in the legislature. As a result, in 2007 both construction management at risk and construction management as agent have now been authorized as acceptable public works delivery techniques. Again, because these systems diverge from the competitive bidding arena, there are stringent criteria which must be followed to use these methods.

Current Nevada law then allows for the use of traditional competitive bidding, as well as design-build and construction management techniques when the projects meet certain criteria. All of these methods will be discussed in ensuing sections of this text. The adoption of new construction manager at risk process for selection of subcontractors may also allow for integrated design techniques to be utilized.

Procurement of design, has also undergone some change. The design selection process will be used both for traditional competitive bidding as well as the construction management delivery methods.

6:3 Selecting the Designer

In choosing a design professional for a public works construction project, the governmental entity may not use the competitive bidding process and must be based upon competence and qualifications and not on the basis of competitive fees.[279] In fact, an architect is prohibited from submitting information to the public agency as part of a proposal for a public works project which would enable the public agency to evaluate

---

[279] *See* NRS 625.530(3), which provides:

> *"The selection of a professional engineer, professional land surveyor or registered architect to perform services pursuant to subsection 1 must be made on the basis of the competence and qualifications of the engineer, land surveyor or architect for the type of services to be performed and not on the basis of competitive fees. If, after selection of the engineer, land surveyor or architect, an agreement upon a fair and reasonable fee cannot be reached with him or her, the public agency may terminate negotiations and select another engineer, land surveyor or architect."*

See also Nevada Com'n on Ethics v. JMA/Lucchesi, 110 Nev. 1, 7, 866 P.2d 297, 301-302, (1994).

the proposal on any basis other than competent and qualifications of the architect.[280] The only exception to this prohibition of cost is made for Design / Build Projects under NRS 338.1711, *et seq.* and NRS 408.3875, *et seq.* In addition, a system to provide Nevada based design professionals a preference in selection for public works project design has been implemented.

For state wide projects administered by the Nevada State Public Works Board (SPWB), the SPWB must directly employ designers for the projects they produce, and are statutorily required to adopt criteria for pre-qualification of design professional applicants before they may submit proposals on specific projects. Such contracts, being for the provisions of professional services, are not properly adopted for the competitive bidding process.[281] As such, the SPWB must specifically authorize the employment of design professionals on contracts in excess of $100,000,[282] but may delegate its authority for such purpose to the Manager of the public works department.

In selecting the design professional the SPWB must emphasize that the design proposals and completed design meet the adopted standards of design and construction.[283] While these are the adopted "minimum standards for the design of state buildings," exceptions are allowed if alternative satisfies purpose of the standard and strict compliance with the standard is not practicable because of unique project circumstances.[284] The SPWB Manager must inform design professional who are engaged to perform design services on specific projects of the authorized construction budget and require the preparation of contract documents in manner that enables the receipt of acceptable bids within the budget provided.[285] Design professional must redesign work at no cost to state so that

---

[280] NAC 623.800 provides:

> *"An architect, interior designer or residential designer who holds a certificate of registration shall not submit any information to the State of Nevada or any of its political subdivisions as part of a proposal for a publicly funded project which would enable the public agency to evaluate the proposal on any basis other than the competence and qualifications of the registrant to perform the type of services required."*

[281] NRS 332.115(1)(b): "Contracts which by their nature are not adapted to award by competitive bidding, including contracts for: ... (b) Professional services."

[282] NAC 341.015(2)

[283] The minimum standards for state buildings are found in NAC 341.045, which are too voluminous for this text.

[284] NAC 341.060.

[285] NAC 341.081 provides:

> *The Administrator shall inform the architects and engineers who prepare contract documents of the budget available for the construction. The Administrator shall require*

such a bid may be obtained.[286] The design professional is required to assure compliance with specific project criteria and conformance with state agency and safety requirements, local building codes, and project site adaptation of standard plans and specifications. Duties of the design professional who designs the project will also include the assistance of the public body with the review and evaluation of bids and the awarding of the contract, the review and response to requests for information, change orders and other contract issues and contract administration. Care should be taken, as a public body is required to report a design professional who provides a public body with plans which are substantially incomplete or have been rejected by the public body at least three times on the same project.[287]

The 2011 legislative session saw the introduction of a preference system in favor of Nevada based design professionals. Senate Bill 268 enacted NRS 338.173 which requires the State Board of Architecture, Interior Design and Residential Design,[288] State Board of Landscape Architecture,[289] and the State Board of Professional Engineers and Land Surveyors[290] in turn to adopt regulations allowing for the issuance of a certificate of eligibility to receive a preference on Nevada state public works design projects. In each case, the appropriate agency is to review affidavits from a licensee / registrant's certified public accountant attesting to the fact that the design professional has paid excise taxes in the state of Nevada in the amount of $1,500 for each 12 month period for a continuous 36 months prior to the submission of the affidavit. Although it is unclear precisely how the public body awarding the design professional contract is to utilize the preference in its selection process, the holder of the certificate of eligibility should be provided an "edge" over design professionals that cannot provide such a certificate. The ability to qualify for such a preference, however, appears to be more difficult for smaller Nevada based design professional firms to achieve than expected. Excise taxes under the applicable reference provision of NRS 363B.110 are not as substantial as originally anticipated by the legislation's sponsors. Still, Nevada based design professionals should consult their accounting professionals for evaluation of their qualifications for this certificate.

> *them to prepare those documents so that an acceptable bid within the amount of the budget can be obtained or to redesign the work at no cost to the State so that such a bid can be obtained.*

[286] NAC 341.081.

[287] NRS 338.175 & NRS 338.176.

[288] NRS 338.173(1).

[289] NRS 338.173(2).

[290] NRS 338.173(3).

The Board may hire Design Professional or a Construction Manager for assistance in the administration of a public work of construction.[291] If the administrative contract will exceed $250,000, the Administrator of the SPWB must appoint a selection committee to meet, review criteria and make recommendations to the Administrator, who will thereafter make recommendations to the SPWB for approval and hiring.[292] If the contract is less than $250,000 the manager may conduct the interview and selection process herself.[293] However, the selection should be based upon the relative experience, specialized technical knowledge, holding of relevant copyrights to the project design, and other factors that the Board may determine is relevant to the health, safety or welfare of the public.[294]

A design professional who is not otherwise a part of a design-build team constructing a design-build project must have certain contract clauses in its professional services contract with the governing body, which govern payment and disputes about payment, insurance coverage and professional liability coverage issues and may require the design professional to indemnify, defend and hold the state harmless from the design professional's negligence or errors.[295] These statutory provisions can include a provision that the prevailing party in any dispute be awarded its attorney's fees and costs upon resolution.[296]

6:4 Competitive Bidding: Design-Bid-Build Construction

Competitive bidding is required on most public works projects. There are, however, numerous exceptions to competitive bidding, set forth in statutes, city charters, ordinance, federal grants, etc. The purpose of competitive bidding is to "secure competition, save public funds, and to guard against favoritism, improvidence and corruption."[297] As a consequence of this determination, the Nevada public works statutes "are deemed to be for the benefit of the taxpayers and not the bidders, and are to be construed for the public good."[298] With limited exceptions, contracts awarded

---

[291] NAC 341.136 and NAC 341.141.

[292] NAC 341.136.

[293] NAC 341.141.

[294] NAC 341.141.

[295] NRS 338.155.

[296] NRS 338.155(1)(d).

[297] *Gulf Oil Corp. v. Clark County*, 94 Nev. 116, 118, 575 P.2d 1332, 1333 (1978).

[298] *Richardson Const., Inc. v. Clark County School Dist.*, 123 Nev. 61, 66, 156 P.3d 21, 24, (2007).

without competitive bidding are void. Most competitive bidding requirements are found in NRS Title 27 (Public Property and Purchasing) and NRS Title 28 (Public Works and Planning). Based on type or size of contract, population and annual tax financed expenditures of county where project is located, a particular project may be exempt from competitive bidding requirements. Emergency contracts do not require competitive bidding. Professional service selection is exempt from competitive bidding.

6:5 PRE-QUALIFICATION OF BIDDERS

The SPWB must by regulation adopt criteria for pre-qualifying bidders for public works projects. Bids may not be accepted from or contracts awarded to, non-qualified bidders.[299] Local Governments do not have the option of adopting a different pre-qualification criteria than that mandated by Nevada statute,[300] but may determine a bidder to be qualified if that bidder has been qualified by the SPWB, another local governing body or the Nevada Department of Transportation.[301]

The SPWB criteria adopted for qualifying bidders must not allow determination of an applicant as "qualified" by only one person, and may only include the following issues as items for qualification:[302] 1) Whether the applicant is financially able to perform the contract; 2) A listing of the principal personnel of the applicant; 3) A determination whether the applicant has ever breached any contracts with a public agency or any other person; 4) Whether or not the person is disqualified from public work bidding for a number of reasons, including failure to abide by the requirements of the Nevada First Act;[303] 5) The performance history of the applicant on other recent, similar contracts, if any, and 6) The truthfulness and completeness of the application for pre-qualification.[304] Similarly, subcontractors must be pre-qualified to bid on SPWB projects, however, licensed subcontractors are presumed by the statute to be qualified unless specific information has been brought to the SPWB's attention that the particular subcontractor does not meet the SPWB's regulations for qualification.[305] In this case, the subcontract must submit an application to the SPWB for pre-qualification. From this application, the SPWB must determine if the subcontractor meets the qualification criteria and make a

---

299 NRS 338.1375.

300 NRS 338.1377.

301 NRS 338.1382.

302 NRS 338.1379(5).

303 *See* Section 6:11 Nevada First Act Compliance.

304 NRS 338.1375.

305 NRS 338.1376.

determination whether to disqualify the subcontractor or not.[306] The subcontractor involved may appeal any adverse decision by the SPWB as to his qualifications to perform on SPWB projects.[307]

If a local government wishes to use criteria other than that adopted by the SPWB, it must use only those indicia of qualification set forth in NRS 338.1377.[308] These pre-qualification mandates include whether the applicant: 1) Has the proper licensed issued by the Nevada State Contractor's Board ("NSCB"); 2) Has sufficient bonding capacity for the project; 3) Has successfully completed an appropriate number of similar projects, but not more than five (5), over the last five (5) years prior to the specific project being qualified; 4) Has sufficiently trained and experienced personnel for the project; 5) Has breached any contracts in the five (5) years prior to the application; 6) Has ever been disqualified from being awarded a public works project, including for violation of the Nevada First Act;[309] 7) Has been convicted of employment discrimination within two (2) years preceding the application; 8) Has sufficient insurance coverage; 9) Has an established a legally compliant safety program; 10) Has any disciplinary history from the NSCB; 11) Has filed for bankruptcy protection within the five (5) years preceding the application; 12) Has filed a truthful and complete application, and 13) Has failed in any manner to perform, caused delay of completion or failed to perform within budget on any previous contract as specified therein.[310] These same criteria apply to pre-qualification of subcontractors on local government projects.

6:6 APPLICATION PROCESSING AND HEARINGS FOR DESIGNATION AS A "QUALIFIED BIDDER"

Once an application for qualification is received by the SPWB or local government agency, the application must be investigated and action taken on the application within 45 days.[311] The SPWB or local government must then notify the applicant in writing of determination results, and if the application is denied, the reasons therefore must be specified and the denied applicant must also be notified further of its rights to a hearing on the application denial.[312] The determination of qualification may be for any one specific project or may be for any project over a specifically adopted period of time by

---

306 NRS 338.1376(3).

307 NRS 338.1376(4).

308 NRS 338.1379(6).

309 *See* Section 6:11 Nevada First Act Compliance.

310 NRS 338.1377.

311 NRS 338.1379(2).

312 NRS 338.1379(3).

the SPWB or local government.[313] These time periods are found within the governing regulations of the governing body for the project. Any financial data gathered as part of the application investigation must be kept private and not made available to the public or allowed for public inspection.[314]

Denials of applications to qualify as bidders, or any determination under by the SPWB that a subcontractor is disqualified must be heard by the SPWB and local governmental agencies. A denied applicant must file for a written request for hearing within 10 days of receipt of the disqualification or adverse determination.[315] The hearing date must be set within 20 days of the request and cannot be set later than 45 days after request for hearing is received, expect upon specific written stipulation between the applicant and the applicable governing body.[316] Written notice of the hearing must be served by personal delivery or certified mail on the applicant not less than 10 days before the hearing date.[317] The burden of proof at the hearing is upon the denied applicant to demonstrate by substantial evidence that it is qualified to bid on the public work.[318] This is a significant burden upon the applicant, as holding him to a standard of providing "substantial" evidence will necessarily exceed the civil court proceeding standards of a preponderance of the evidence. Nevada's history in public works with contractors who have not been sufficiently qualified is long and tortured. While the scope of such history is not within the purpose of this book, the denied applicant looking to overturn such a denial must be prepared to demonstrate that any basis on which the application for qualification was denied should be excused or was the result of circumstances beyond the control of the applicant.

The governing body conducting the hearing is endowed with the power to administer oaths, take testimony and issue subpoenas and commissions for the attendance of witnesses and the production of records, documents and tangible items.[319] As a result, the applicant should take advantage of those powers in preparing its testimony. Likewise, the governing board should not place impediments in the way of the applicant or its ability to use the power of the governing board to compel the attendance of witnesses without extraordinary reason. The hearing process afforded to the applicant

---

[313] NRS 338.1379(4).

[314] NRS 338.1379(7).

[315] NRS 338.1381(1).

[316] NRS 338.1381(1).

[317] NRS 338.1381(2).

[318] NRS 338.1381(3).

[319] NRS 338.1381(4).

and outcomes are subject to constitutional challenges of due process through judicial review and appeal to the Nevada Supreme Court. The governing body is also empowered to seek judicial intervention in compelling the appearance of witnesses,[320] and likewise through contempt of court requests for continued violations. The governing board must make a determination of the appeal *during* the hearing,[321] though reasonable recess of the proceeding for deliberation would be allowed. There is no statutory limitation on the duration of the hearing. The determination made by the governing body is final for judicial review.[322]

6:7 Bidding Requirements & Exemptions

A number of complex rules govern what types of public works projects must be bid competitively or that may be delivered through alternative methods. Generally, these rules breakdown by project amount and/or the type of project involved. Smaller projects which are below certain thresholds may simply be awarded or may be performed by the governing body's own maintenance staff without procedural competitive bidding requirements. Larger and more complex projects may be required to pass vigorous approval methods and hearings before a delivery method is even selected. The criteria for each of these examples are discussed in ensuing sections of this treatise. In summary, however, a public body must analyze the project program in comparison to the obligations of NRS Chapter 338 before undertaking substantial steps toward bid requests or construction.

There are a couple of basic issues that must be understood as fairly clear absolutes. First, a public body may not attempt to circumvent the obligations of competitive bidding by dividing the project up into component parts, thereby avoiding the obligations to advertise for bids or to comply with the self-performance criteria.[323] This means that a contract cannot be issued for parts of a larger project, where the larger project cannot operate without the entirety of the parts, and also means the contract is isolated and stand alone.[324] For example, a contract to replace public park lighting may be left to a licensed electrical contractor, even though installation of light poles may require some minor concrete work. So long as that concrete work was incidental to the electrical

[320] NRS 338.1381(5).

[321] NRS 338.1381(6).

[322] NRS 338.1381(6). It should also be noted that judicial review referred to in the statute does not create a private right of action for the disqualified bidder, nor may a public body be sued for damages resulting from a denial of pre-qualified status. *Richardson Const., Inc. v. Clark County School Dist.*, 123 Nev. 61, 156 P.3d 21, (2007).

[323] NRS 338.1385(1)(c).

[324] NRS 338.139(1).

work, or the electrical contractor hired a licensed concrete subcontractor to perform it, the public body would not be prevented from contracting solely for the electrical work. However, if the lighting work was in actuality the new installation of lighting within the overall construction of a new public park, the governing body's attempt to award the lighting work separately may be suspect of violating the competitive bidding law.

Secondly, the public body is only going to be able to issue the contract to a contractor holding a Nevada contractor's license.[325] It is not sufficient that the contractor is in the process of obtaining a license at the time of bid, or that the contractor holds the proper license classification but is seeking an increase in his license bid limitation to cover the contract at the time of bidding. A contractor must hold the proper license and the bid must be within his license bid limitation at the time of bidding or the bid and any contract awarded is void and must be rescinded.[326] Severe penalties attach to contractors submitting bids without having previously received their license or license bid increases prior to soliciting any information related to or in fact placing actual bids within the State of Nevada.[327] As such, contractors and public bodies must meet the license obligations for contract requirements as a first priority issue.

There are a number of exclusions from the system of competitive bidding process of the state of Nevada. These are generally listed in the exempting statutes, which enumerate the types of projects which are not subject to competitive bidding,[328] The project excluded from the competitive bidding process of NRS Chapter 338 include construction, maintenance and repair of highways performed by the Nevada Department of Transportation ("NDOT")[329] normal maintenance of any school district property,[330] various regional water districts,[331] and projects that are intended to be constructed by design-build or construction management delivery methods.[332] These particular types of projects are governed by other statutes that will be discussed as appropriate later in this treatise. Absent one of these exceptions, Nevada law mandates that a governmental

---

325 NRS 338.13895.

326 NRS 338.13895(3).

327 *See* Chapter 2 Contractor Licensing and Related Issues.

328 NRS 338.1385(9).

329 NRS 338.1385(9)(b).

330 NRS 338.1385(9)(c).

331 NRS 338.1385(9)(d).

332 NRS 338.1385(9)(e) to (g).

entity shall not construct a public work without complying with the obligations of NRS 338.1385 on competitive bidding.[333]

6:8 Bidding Requirements Less Than $100,000.00 in Scope

NRS 338.1385(1) provides in pertinent part:

> *Except as otherwise provided in subsection 9, the State or a governing body or its authorized representative that awards a contract for a public work in accordance with paragraph (a) of subsection 1 of NRS 338.1373 shall not: ... (b) Commence a public work for which the estimated cost is $100,000 or less unless it complies with the provisions of NRS 338.1386, 338.13862 and 338.13864.*

Once the public body determines to commence a construction project for less than $100,000 it has two basic options: 1) Award the project to a properly licensed contract through a modified bid advertisement procedure or 2) perform the public work through its own forces.[334] If the public body determines to commence the work with its own forces, Nevada law requires some level of accountability through attestation by those in charge of the public body if the cost of the work will exceed $25,000. Those projects which are less than $25,000 need no attestation and are merely regulated by quarterly public reporting of the construction projects and their costs.[335] The attestation for projects between $25,000 and $100,000 requires that the responsible managing public officer of the public body to execute a written attestation, confirming the estimated cost of the work, the reasons why the work was determined to be performed by the public body itself, and that the work will adhere to the same quality standards required if the work was performed by a licensed contractor.[336] This attestation remains a public record within the files of the public body's administrative offices.[337]

If the work is not to be performed by the public body's own forces, the public body must advertise the project for bid. Projects under $25,000 must seek a bid from at least one licensed contractor.[338] Those projects between $25,000 and $100,000 must seek bids from at least 3 properly licensed contractors.[339] Unlike larger projects, these bid

---

333 NRS 338.1385(1).

334 NRS 338.1386.

335 NRS 338.1385(2).

336 NRS 338.13864(2)(a).

337 NRS 338.13864(2)(b).

338 NRS 338.13862(1)(b).

339 NRS 338.13862(1)(a).

offerings may be direct solicitations from the public entity to qualified licensed contractors[340] and do not need to be published in general to the public. Any bids received by the public entity need to be reviewed and analyzed for compliance with the solicitations. Bids that are not conforming to the plans and specifications, or that are submitted by unresponsive or irresponsible bidders must be rejected.[341] The projects must be awarded to the lowest responsive and responsible bidder,[342] unless the public interest would be served by a rejection of that bid.[343] Projects within this cost applicable range must be reported quarterly by the awarding body, listing the awarded contractors name, contract amount, description of the project and names of all solicited bidders.[344]

6:9 Bidding Requirements Beyond $100,000 in Scope

Larger projects in excess of $100,000 must be advertised for bid through the public bidding process, [345] which may be through competitive bidding, construction management at risk or through design-build delivery methods.[346] In competitive bidding, minimal requirements for bid advertising are that the invitation for bids be published in a general circulation newspaper within the county where the public work is going to be constructed.[347] If there is no such newspaper, then the invitation to bid must be published in a newspaper published within the state, and circulated within the county in which the public work will be constructed.[348] The advertisements must be to prequalified contractors or those exempted,[349] specify the place, date and time when plans and specifications are available, as well as the date, place and time when bids are to be submitted.[350] With one notable exception, the governing body must award the project to the lowest responsive and responsible bidder,[351] however, the noted

[340] NRS 338.13862(5)(a).

[341] NRS 338.13862(2).

[342] NRS 338.13862(5)(b).

[343] NRS 338.13862(2)(c).

[344] NRS 338.13862(3).

[345] NRS 338.1711(1).

[346] NRS 338.1711.

[347] NRS 338.1385(1)(a).

[348] NRS 338.1385(1)(1a).

[349] NRS 338.1379 or NRS 338.1382.

[350] NRS 338.1385(4).

[351] NRS 338.1385(5).

exception actually requires the public body to award the contract to the bidder who submits the statutorily defined "best bid," which is not necessarily the lowest responsive bid from a responsible bidder. To the contrary, the "best bid" is determined after the bidders are reviewed for a certificate of eligibility to receive a preference in bidding on public works, under the provisions of NRS 338.1389(2).[352] It is possible, then, that the best bid actually will exceed the lowest responsive bid by five percent (5%).

The governing body is empowered to reject any bids that are non-responsive, from bidders who are not responsible or pre-qualified, that are of a conforming quality or which should be rejected in the best interests of the public.[353] If no bids are received in response to the invitation to bid, the governing body may then rebid the project[354] or let the contract without competitive bidding, however, it has certain rules to follow in doing so: The governing body must publish a notice that no bids were received and then must consider any bid received as a result of that published notice. So long as the governing body waits seven (7) days after it publishes the notice, it may award the contract to the bidder who submits the lowest responsive and responsible bid.[355] This means that the subsequent bidder need not be pre-qualified to bid on the project, so long as he holds the necessary licenses and can provide the appropriate bonding and insurance, as no other statutory guidance is provided.

The governing body may also reject all bids and perform the public work itself, if it can determine that the public interest would be served by doing so.[356] Before undertaking the project, the governing body must prepare a written statement for public inspection that lists: 1) All persons who will be assigned to the public work; 2) All equipment and the number of hours that equipment is to be used on the public work as well as the operational cost per hour; 3) Estimate of cost of administration and support for the persons assigned to the work; 4) Estimate of the total cost of the work and 5) an estimate of the amount of savings the governing body expects to save as a result of performing the work itself.[357] Obviously, the statute is not set up to encourage self-performance, as it will render open to the public information which will measure the efficiency and effectiveness of that decision.

---

352 NRS 338.1385(5).

353 NRS 338.1385(6).

354 *Bldg. and Constr. Trades Council of N. Nevada v. State ex rel. Public Works Bd.*, 108 Nev. 605, 836 P.2d 633, (1992).

355 NRS 338.1385(7).

356 NRS 338.1385(8).

357 NRS 338.1385(8).

6:10 CERTIFICATE OF ELIGIBILITY FOR BIDDING PREFERENCE

As noted previously, the Nevada public works statutory scheme recognizes a 5% bidder's preference to those construction companies who hold a certificate of eligibility to receive a preference in bidding on public works.[358] The Nevada legislature enacted this bidder's preference law, in order to address serious concerns over out-of-state contractors engaging in one project leaving, demonstrating a lack of permanence and continuing presence in the state, as well as complicating the ability of the governing body to obtain warranty service on the work.[359] As a result, the legislature approved a system which requires a general contractor who paid sales and use taxes and/or governmental services taxes of not less than $5,000 per consecutive 12-month period for the 60 months immediately preceding the application for certification of eligibility.[360] This certificate of eligibility is available to specialty contractors as well.[361]

The certificate of eligibility is acquired by application to the NSCB, which must be based upon the affidavit of a certified public accountant that the contractor paid the requisite taxes while operating as a licensed contractor in this state.[362] The certificate can also be acquired by the purchase of all the assets and liabilities of a viable and operating construction firm that already possesses a contractor's license and a certificate of eligibility;[363] however, rules for acquisition of a licensed contractor in Nevada are complex and depending on how the transaction is handled may result in the instantaneous revocation of the contractor's license in certain circumstances.[364] Taxes paid by affiliate or parent companies operating as a contractor within the state can be used to support an application for certification, as well as the percentage of taxes paid apportioned to a contractor's interest in any contracting joint venture in the state.[365] If the eligible contractor holds more than one contractor's license in the state, however, an application for each license must be submitted.[366] The certificates are only good for a

---

358 NRS 338.1389. It should be noted that public works projects which are funded by federal assistance may not be subject to the bidder's preference law, if some federal statute or regulation would reduce or eliminate that funding. *See* NRS 338.1389(10).

359 *City of Las Vegas v. Kitchell Contractors, Inc. of Arizona*, 768 F. Supp. 742 (D. Nev. 1991).

360 NRS 338.1389(3).

361 NRS 338.1389(4).

362 NRS 338.1389(3) and (4).

363 NRS 338.1389(3)(b) and 338.1389(4)(b).

364 *See* Chapter 2, Contractor Licensing and Related Issues.

365 NRS 338.1389(5).

366 NRS 338.1389(8).

limited period of time and cease to be valid after that expiration.[367] Therefore, the contractor should re-submit the applications regularly to maintain its eligibility. In addition to the certificate of eligibility, the 2011 legislative session brought the passage of the Nevada First Act, which added the mandate to employ Nevada construction workers, Nevada design professionals, purchase materials from Nevada suppliers and register construction vehicles in the State of Nevada to obtain and hold a preference.[368]

Within the bidding context, a person who believes a contractor has submitted a certificate of eligibility that is false, is otherwise wrongfully held, or who has failed to comply with the Nevada First Act may file a written objection to the governing body, challenging the validity of the certificate.[369] The written objection must contain the proof substantiating the objection and be submitted to the governing body within three (3) days of bid opening on the affected project.[370] A written objection without substantiating proof may be rejected out of hand, while a supported objection must be reviewed and determined by the governing body to be valid.[371] No hearing on the matter is necessary to take action on the written objection.

6:11 Nevada Jobs First Act Compliance

As discussed in Chapter 1, Introduction, Nevada has seen the worst of the Great Recession, losing over two-thirds of its construction workforce since 2007. As displaced construction workers began to see out-of-state contractors obtaining what little work was actually available in Nevada from the federal government stimulus programs, Nevada legislators looked for ways to drive more of that public work to Nevada based contractors, or at least contractors who employed Nevada residents. As a result, a number of measures to drive public construction towards local contractors were enacted. One of the first such measures to go into effect was the Nevada First Act, referenced as Assembly Bill 144 from the 2011 legislative session. In sum, AB144 in its original form sought to drive public works contracts towards Nevada based contractors by requiring any contractor seeking to obtain the five percent (5%) preference to execute an affidavit upon award of the public works contract, agreeing that it will ensure that:

---

367 NRS 338.1389(7).

368 *See* Section 6:11 Nevada First Act Compliance.

369 NRS 338.1389(13).

370 NRS 338.1389(13).

371 NRS 338.1389(14).

- 50% of its work force, as well as that of all subcontractors, will hold Nevada issued driver's licenses or identification cards;
- All vehicles used on the public work will be registered in Nevada, or registered and partially apportioned in Nevada (as applicable);
- At least 50% of the design professionals used on the public work will have Nevada issued driver's licenses or identification cards;
- At least 25% of the materials used on the public work will be purchased from suppliers located in Nevada, and
- It will maintain payroll and other records to prove such compliance during the Project duration.

The penalty for breach of these obligations was the imposition of a ten percent (10%) gross contract price liquidated damage assessment against the contractor, or the voiding of its bid, as well as the prohibition of bidding again on a public work for one (1) year and the prohibition of being issued a preference certificate for five (5) years. All contract documents must reflect these requirements and liquidated damage provisions as elements of the contractor's work scope and conditions of the contract.

Obviously, a contractor's affidavit making these assurances, with the penalty of 10% gross contract value loss, the loss of the ability to bid public works at all for a full year, and the loss of a preference for 5 years, would constitute a significant impact to a contractor. The ability of the contractor to achieve these stated requirements alone may be difficult enough, but to potentially suffer these penalties for the failure of its subcontractors or third party design professionals raised large legal issues. But the contractor's ability to shift liability for breach under AB144 also had its limitations. As local construction groups discovered the impacts of AB144, efforts were made to amend its more onerous provisions before the 2011 legislative session ended. As a result, Assembly Bill 574 passed the legislature in its final hours. Signed by the Governor shortly after the session ended, AB574 amends the provisions of AB144. The result is the composite Nevada First Act, found in NRS 338.0117. In 2013, this provision was further refined to make the requirements more implementable.

NRS 338.0117 adds to the requirements of holding a certificate of eligibility for obtaining a preference in bidding the requirement of executing an affidavit whereby the general contractor agrees that:

- 50% of its work force, as well as that of all subcontractors, will hold Nevada issued driver's licenses or identification cards;[372]
- All vehicles used primarily for the public work will be registered in Nevada, or registered and partially apportioned in Nevada (as applicable);[373]

[372] NRS 338.0117(1)(a).

[373] NRS 338.0117(1)(b).

- At least 50% of the "design professionals working on the public work, including without limitation, employees of the design-build team and any subcontractor or consultant engaged in the design of the public work," will have Nevada issued driver's licenses or identification cards;[374] and
- It will maintain payroll and other records to prove such compliance during the Project duration.[375]

These terms must be included in all contracts entered into on the public work, including those between the public body and the contractor, the contractor and the subcontractors, the subcontractors and any subcontractors and suppliers,[376] as well as terms specifying the penalty for breach of these requirements will be the assessment by the public body of liquidated damages against the breaching party in the amount of one percent (1%) of the largest contract to which the breaching entity is a party.[377]

Compliance with the Nevada First Act is checked through the certified payroll system already in place.[378] Contractors and their subcontractors are required to keep an accurate record of the name, position, wages and benefits paid to each worker on the Project.[379] These certified payroll records must also include records of the employee driver's license or identification card numbers and the jurisdiction that issued the driver's license or identification card.[380] These records must be maintained for inspection by the public body issuing the contract, and the contractor must ensure that a copy of her report and a report for each subcontractor is delivered to the public body no later than 15 days after the end of each month. While these records are to be open to the public, the driver's license / ID card information is not and needs to be kept confidential by the public body.[381]

It should also be noted that under NRS 338.1415, any contractor who breaches a contractor for the amount of $25,000,000 or more as a result of a violation of the Nevada First Act is forbidden to bid on a public work by the State or any local government entity

---

[374] NRS 338.0117(1)(c).

[375] NRS 338.0117(1)(e).

[376] NRS 338.0117(2).

[377] NRS 338.0117(5) & (6).

[378] NRS 338.070.

[379] NRS 338.070(5)(a).

[380] NRS 338.070(5)(b).

[381] NRS 338.070(6).

for a period of one year after that breach.[382] Moreover, if a public body recovers liquidated damages from a contractor for violation of the Nevada First Act, the public body is required to report such recovery to the Nevada State Contractors Board, who will in turn maintain this information on the contractor's record for 6 years.[383]

The legislative history of AB 144 suggests that legislators were concerned with the ability of the public bodies to use the Nevada First Act and the penalties thereunder as leverage against retention. For this reason, the liquidated damages and loss of bid penalties cannot be extracted unless a court determines that the contractor has breached the obligations of the Nevada First Act provisions. This is not true of the loss of preference penalty, however. There is also indication that a series of forms were created to assist the Department of Labor and the Public Bodies to streamline and unify the compliance reports and other mandates. These forms, however, did not make it into the final legislative language, and could be issued as administrative code regulations or as addenda to the public work bid specifications. There is no legislative history reported for AB574 which would aid in the interpretation of these requirements.

Of the biggest concerns created by this legislation is the impact on contractors. On its face, the amended legislation arguably places the burden of compliance (as well as the penalties for breach) upon the actual contractor causing the breach. As a practical matter, however, the breach of such obligations by a subcontractor would necessarily be a breach of the general contractor's obligations to the owner as well, and it will be nearly impossible for the contractor to control where a subcontractor buys materials, where a design professional under direct contract with the public body has its design work performed, where a sub-subcontractor hires its workers, or how any of these parties maintain their payroll and employment records. Yet under the plain language of NRS 338.0117(1) this burden is still placed solely on the contractor, making it the only party to execute the affidavit of compliance to obtain the certification of eligibility for the bidding preference. Court interpretation will be necessary to clarify any ambiguities created.

6:12 Requirements for Bid Specifications and Requests

The governing body cannot just set out a set of plans and ask for bids. Rather, it is required to meet certain objectives so that bidders will have a fair and level playing field on which to compete for the award of a public work. Nevada has two separate methods for issuing requests for bids and preparation of the specifications. Except in the cases of construction management and design-build contracts, the SPWB must use the methodology set forth in NRS 338.140, while local governmental agencies must use the

382 NRS 338.1415

383 NRS 338.0117(5).

alternative procedures outlined in NRS 338.143.[384] Both of these methods will be outlined in ensuing sections. In sum, however, the requirements for bid specifications are set up so as not to favor any one party or contractor, and are generally mandated to achieve the legislative goals of achieving public benefit of fair competition:

> *"The legislature finds and declares that it is the policy of this State to ensure that the public receives the full benefits of fair competition among contractors and subcontractors in public works and has therefore enacted NRS 338.140 to limit the practice of shopping for bids for the construction, alteration and repair of public improvements."*[385]

One may seriously question whether the public benefits from a lack of bid shopping, as the goal of bid shopping is to find the lowest possible price for which the work can be accomplished, which is also the legislative mandate. However, the full benefit of fair competition is arguably to eliminate favoritism and the hidden dangers of corruption that bid shopping can bring. Also, one may reasonably question the wisdom of accepting the lowest bid as achieving the best work product that the public can receive. Regardless of which side of the argument on agrees with on any given project, the intention of the legislature to allow for competition is clearly seen in the regulatory provisions of NRS 338.140 and NRS 338.143.

6:13 BID SPECIFICATIONS FOR STATE PROJECTS

The public work bid specifications have certain minimum requirements that must be met before a governing body can issue them for bidding. With state public projects and any other governmental body that chooses to perform work according to its provisions, NRS 338.140 outlines a number of negatives to which bid specifications may not adhere. These negatives are generally in the form of policy statements, which someone challenging the sufficiency of bid specifications must demonstrate that the bid specifications achieve.

Public works bid specifications may not be drafted to limit bidding to any one specific contractor or going concern, either directly or indirectly.[386] Likewise, a particular product may not be sole sourced, unless the specification is set forth to match a product already in use on the project. Each product specification must have at least two brands or trade names as alternatively acceptable products and be followed by the words "or equal" to allow bidders to provide alternative materials of an equal quality.[387] An

---

[384] NRS 338.1373(1).

[385] NRS 338.140, Reviser's Note; Ch. 514, Stats. 1993

[386] NRS 338.140(1)(a).

[387] NRS 338.140(1)(b).

exception to this rule is allowed when the particular product being installed is unique or novel, or where the governing body is only aware of one brand or trade name for a product required for the project. In that case, the governing body may list only the one brand,[388] however, the governing body should be prepared for any challenge to the bid specifications and should also be open to an alternative product that may be presented as an "or equal" product. Contractors are granted a minimum of seven (7) days after the award of a contract to submit an "or equal" product as an acceptable alternative[389] and seek a substitution approval. If a contractor desires to use an alternative and bases its bid on such use, it would be better practice for the contractor to seek approval of the "or equal" prior to the submission of the bid through the issuance of a request for information or substitution, according to the requirements of the bid specifications. In this fashion, the contractor does not bear the risk of having the "or equal" alternative rejected and then having a bust in his bid for which there is no easy legal escape of liability.

The bid specifications may also not be drafted so as to require the contractor to incur or be responsible for extra costs that are the result of errors or omissions of the governing body in the preparation of the contracting documents.[390] This raises certain questions over the use of guaranteed maximum price contracts within the context of construction management or design-build contracting. While these issues are addressed in the sections dealing with these delivery methods, it should be noted that there is at least a facial conflict between the provision of NRS 338.140(1)(c) and the concept of construction management and design-build contracting which are premised on GMP based contract provisions. While both of these delivery methods generally seek to eliminate design and other errors that may be created by the involvement of the governing body, there remains the possibility of such errors and specifications allowing for the contractor involved to be held responsible for such errors and omissions of the governing body.

Finally, the specifications may not require the contractor to submit its financial data used in preparing the bid, except for certain clarification uses.[391] The statute does allow

---

[388] NRS 338.140(3).

[389] NRS 338.140(4).

[390] NRS 338.140(1)(c).

[391] NRS 338.140(1)(d) provides:

> *Except as otherwise provided in subsection 2, in such a manner as to require a bidder to furnish to the public body, whether before or after the bid is submitted, documents generated in the preparation or determination of prices included in the bid, except when requested by the public body for:*
> *(1) A determination of the price of additional work performed pursuant to a change order;*

for the governing body to request the bid and supporting documentation be submitted electronically, however, that does not allow the governing body or any other party to access the documents.[392] The electronic storage of the information may only be accessed by the bidder. The proprietary nature of the documentation is reserved to the bidder, with the sole exception if the information is necessary for the determination of the price of additional work performed under a change order.[393] The only other exception to this rule is the listing of subcontractors, as discussed in Section 6:15 Listing of Subcontractors.

6:14 Local government bid specifications alternative 2

Within the statutory scheme of Nevada's public works statutes, there is a section that is entitled Alternative Procedures for Local Governments,[394] however, the several statutes that are included within this "alternative procedures" are remarkably identical to those applying to the SPWB previously discussed.[395] In point of fact, the only difference between the two alternative procedures are the local government body, electing to proceed under the alternate procedure, need not prequalify its bidders or subcontractors as the SPWB is required to do[396] and the local government must conduct a constructability review before advertising the project for bid in certain circumstances.[397]

As previously discussed in Section 6:5, Pre-qualification of bidders, while a local government need not prequalify a contractor before that contractor may place a bid on a project governed by the alternative procedures, the local governing body cannot require any other qualification factors than those set forth in NRS 338.1377.[398] As a result, the

---

(2) An evaluation of claims for costs incurred for the performance of additional work;
(3) Preparation for arbitration or litigation;
(4) A determination of the validity of the protest of a bid;
(5) A determination of the validity of an increase or decrease in the price of a contract in accordance with a provision in the contract which authorizes such an increase or decrease to correspond to changing market conditions; or
(6) Any combination thereof.

392 NRS 338.140(2).

393 NRS 338.140(2).

394 NRS 338.143 to NRS 338.148.

395 *See* Sections 6:7 to 6:12, herein.

396 NRS 338.1385(3).

397 NRS 338.1435.

398 *See* Section 6:5 Pre-qualification of bidders.

alternative procedures differ from the state procedures in that no prequalification is necessary, only that the bidder meet the criteria set forth in NRS 338.1377. The local government may not condition qualification for bid on its projects on any other criteria, in order to reduce the possibility of the local government creating a criteria that favors particular contractors or classes of contractors over others (such as a requirements that the contractor be based in a particular county, for instance). This eliminates the potential for corruption and favoritism, which would not be in keeping with the goals of competitive bidding.

The other significant difference in the alternative procedure is the requirement of a constructability review. The requirement for a constructability review, enacted in 2007 by the Nevada legislature, was a reaction to a number of high profile projects which suffered significant delay and cost overrun claims based in large part on claims of deficient design. While the merits of those claims were (and are) heavily debated, it was clear that had constructability reviews been performed prior to bidding the projects, many of the conditions that ultimately caused problems with the projects would have been identified before the projects went to bid. Likewise, the local governing body would have had a basis against which to review and process change order and other claims of deficient design. As a result of these issues, and in conjunction with legislation allowing the use of the Construction Management at Risk delivery method, the constructability review was enacted.

Before a local government may advertise for bid a construction project that is based on a design that is being used for the first time on a public work, or on a project that has an estimated cost in excess of $10,000,000, the local governing body must perform a review of the plans and specifications to ensure they are complete and that they contain all the information necessary to construct the project.[399] This "constructability review" may only be performed by an architect, professional engineer or contractor who hold the appropriate registration or license required by the State of Nevada for their trade,[400] and must specifically include:

> *1) "A determination of whether a competent contractor would be able to construct the public work based on the approved plans and specifications"*[401] *and 2) "A review of the approved plans and specifications for the public work for completeness, clarity and economic feasibility."*[402]

---

399 NRS 338.1435(1).

400 NRS 338.1435(2).

401 NRS 338.1435(2)(a).

402 NRS 338.1435(2)(b).

If the local government does not have in its employ a person that meets the statutory requirements to perform this review, the local governing body may retain a third party consultant who does meet the qualifying standards to perform the review, and that consulting contract does not need to be awarded by competitive bidding.[403]

Given the mandate of NRS 338.1435 to review and confirm the plans and specifications are sufficient to allow a competent contractor to construction the work, a logical question is whether anyone but a licensed contractor would want to bear the risk of such a consulting role. It is often the case that architects and engineering practitioners seek to avoid any guarantees that the design will be complete and fully coordinated within their design contracts, acknowledging in many cases that no design is ever as complete as a contractor may wish it to be. Nevertheless, architects and engineers are fully authorized to perform these constructability reviews. The full impact and effectiveness of the constructability review remains to be seen in action and in implementation.

6:15 Listing of Subcontractors

Competitive bidding under both NRS 338.1385 and NRS 338.143 require the listing of subcontractor bids for certain portions of the work.[404] The overriding mandate of the legislature to preserve the public good through fair and open competition requires that subcontractors and the amounts of their bids be listed as part of the bid submission in certain tiers. This arguably protects the public from favoritism and corruption found where bid shopping or bid chiseling are allowed to occur. For this reason, bid specifications may list portions of the work which its estimates will exceed three percent (3%) of the cost of the work; and in this case, each bidder must list the subcontractors used in the bid to achieve those portions of the work.[405] Alternatively (and in most cases) the bid specifications do not provide 3 percent estimates. In this situation, the bid must list the first tier subcontractors whose work will constitute five percent (5%) or more of the total bid price,[406] along with the price of their work and their contractor's license number.[407] After bid opening, the contractors who submitted the three (3) lowest bids must submit an additional list of subcontractors who are to provide any portion of the work that exceeds 1 percent (1%) of the total bid price or $50,000,

---

[403] NRS 338.1435(3).

[404] NRS 338.141(1).

[405] NRS 338.141(1)(a).

[406] NRS 338.141(1)(b).

[407] NRS 338.141(2).

whichever is greater.[408] The three lowest bidders must submit this 1 percent list within 2 hours of bid opening.[409] The contractor who seeks to self-perform any portion of the work must list himself under these subcontractor listings as well, as may be applicable.[410]

Should a contractor not provide the subcontractor lists when required, submits them incompletely or with errors, his bid will be deemed non-responsive.[411] If the bidder's subcontractor list includes a subcontractor who has been disqualified to work on a public project pursuant to NRS 338.1376,[412] the bidder may substitute an alternative subcontractor before the award.[413] In the case of a local governing body, the alternative subcontractor substitution, however, may not increase the cost of the work to the local governing body.[414]

6:16 SUBSTITUTION OF LISTED SUBCONTRACTORS

Once a contractor's bid is accepted, that contractor may not substitute a listed subcontractor except for very specific circumstances set forth in the statutes. In fact, the listed subcontractor has been determined to have legal rights to enter into the contract and perform the work, once listed.[415] The only authorized reasons to replace a listed subcontractor are: 1) The governing body objects to the subcontractor's use; 2) the governing body approves the substitution under certain circumstances, or 3) the governing body determines that the listed subcontractor is not qualified to perform the work and requests substitution.[416]

If the governing body objects to the subcontractor, the governing body must provide a written request to the general contractor for change in the subcontractor, and pay all additional costs associated with the change.[417] In this situation, it is doubtful that the

---

408 NRS 338.141(1)(b).

409 NRS 338.141(1)(b).

410 NRS 338.141(1)(b).

411 NRS 338.141(4).

412 *See* Section 5, Pre-qualification of bidders.

413 NRS 338.141(4), cf. NRS 338.13895(1)

414 NRS 338.13895(2).

415 *Clark Pacific v. Krump Constr., Inc.*, 942 F. Supp. 1324 (D. Nev. 1996).

416 NRS 338.141(5).

417 NRS 338.141(5)(a).

subcontractor has any claim against the general contractor, but may be able to challenge the reasoning for the request with the governing body. If the substitution is in some way wrongful, one case has suggested that the substituted subcontractor may seek injunctive relief preventing the substitution.[418]

If the general contractor seeks to substitute a subcontractor on the project, the governing body must approve that substitution.[419] The governing body *must* approve the substitution if the governing body determines that: 1) The listed subcontractor has failed or refuses to execute a subcontract with the same general terms as all other subcontractors on the project were offered; 2) The listed subcontractor is insolvent or filed for bankruptcy; 3) The listed subcontractor fails to refuses to timely perform its subcontracted for obligations or cannot provide a payment or performance bond, or 4) The listed subcontractor is not properly licensed.[420] "General Terms" is defined within the statute as:

> *the terms and conditions of a contract that set the basic requirements for a public work and apply without regard to the particular trade or specialty of a subcontractor, but does not include any provision that controls or relates to the specific portion of the public work that will be completed by a subcontractor, including, without limitation, the materials to be used by the subcontractor or other details of the work to be performed by the subcontractor.*[421]

As demonstrated by this provision, the subcontractor who refuses to execute general terms and conditions can be substituted, but the statutes are not trying to regulate disputes between listed subcontractors and the general contractor over scopes of the subcontractor's work. Such disputes, although legitimate, cannot be used by the general contractor to obtain the governing body's mandatory approval of the substitution. However, given the governing body's ability to approve a substitution for the subcontractor's refusal to perform its work, if the general contractor's position is strong enough to demonstrate the subcontractor is simply refusing to perform work that is undeniably within his contract, a substitution may be made.[422]

Failure to follow the procedures of NRS 338.141in the substitution of listed subcontractors results in substantial penalties to the prime contractor. NRS 338.141(6)

---

[418] *Clark Pacific v. Krump Const., Inc.*, 942 F. Supp. 1324 (D. Nev. 1996).

[419] NRS 338.141(5)(b).

[420] NRS 338.141(5)(b)

[421] NRS 338.141(7)(b).

[422] NRS 338.141(5)(b)(4).

mandates a one percent (1%) penalty of the amount of the prime contract payable to the public body in the vent of unauthorized substitution.

Finally, it should be noted that when a general contractor has listed himself as the contractor to perform certain work and thereafter determines that he would rather substitute a subcontractor for that same work, this cannot be accomplished without substantial penalty.[423] Under the provisions of NRS 338.141(7), anytime the general contractor seeks to substitute a subcontractor to perform work originally listed as self-performed, the contractor will be assessed a penalty of the lesser of either two and a half percent (2.5%) of the total amount of the contract, or 35% of the estimate of the value of the self-performed work, whichever is less, not including any change orders that had been issued on the project. Previous law allowing for such a change when doing so would be in the best interest of the public body has been deleted under 2011 legislative amendments.

6:17 BIDS, BID ERRORS AND CORRECTIONS

Most bidding disputes are determined on the context in which the bid is made. If the project is a private one, for a private owner, financed with privately held funds, bidding is open to all parties without any regard to particular governing rules--other than the basic law of contracts. In the Public arena, however, "competitive bidding" is used to "secure competition, save public funds, and to guard against favoritism, improvidence and corruption."[424] As a result, many more rules are applicable to bidding in Public construction projects, as opposed to private works of improvement.

In deciding whether or not to bid specific projects, the contractor should carefully consider a number of factors. These factors are a mixture of business issues and legal issues, and can dramatically affect the project and the bid. A contractor should fully understand the scope of work on which he is bidding. A thorough review of the plans and specifications and ascertain what is included and excluded from the work, and whether or not the work is within the contractors capabilities. Likewise, the contractor should review his current license status and correct any issues such as increases in contract bid limitations. These factors should be considered and resolved prior to providing a bid, as bidding without proper licensing issues will cause the bid to be revoked and potentially cause the bidder issues with the NSCB. A review of site information, project performance specifications, scheduling requirements, bonding requirements, ownership, management, permitting issues and other unique aspects of the project is likewise recommended.

---

[423] NRS 338.141(7).

[424] *Gulf Oil Corp. v. Clark County*, 94 Nev. 116, 118, 575 P.2d 1332 (1978).

Make sure that the requirements to submit a bid are completely understood and nothing is left out from your submission package. While some technical errors may be overlooked, a contractor's bid package should be complete in every respect, as errors can often lead to disqualification of the bid, as most public works bidders that are disqualified on a project are done so on a lack of bid responsiveness.

In general, however, once a bid is submitted it is firm and may not be withdrawn until the time for acceptance or rejection has passed, or until the bid expires of its own terms. As a result, bidders who make errors are liable for the errors, unless an exception applies. Thus, a bid error will usually work to the detriment of the bidder, as he will be found liable for his bid, and will suffer the consequences of all bid errors.[425] Only when the bid error falls within an exception can the bid be corrected. It should be noted, however, that errors in business judgment do not constitute a legitimate reason to correct or withdraw a bid.

Although public works contract are generally governed by specific statutes primarily intended to benefit the public rather than for the benefit of the bidders, "public works contracts are not exempt from fundamental contract analysis."[426] In evaluating mistakes and determining of whether such mistakes are waivable, those mistakes that are capable of correction by ascertaining the bidder's intent from the "four-corners of the bid documents submitted and available" may be minor irregularities that are subject to waiver.[427] Where a clarification requires an interpretation outside of the "four corners of

---

[425] In *Dynaelectric Co. of Nevada, Inc. v. Clark & Sullivan Constructors, Inc.*, 127 Nev.Adv. Op. 41 (2011), The Nevada Supreme Court held that a contractor who refuses to honor its bid on a Nevada public work will be held liable to the affected general contractor who uses that bid in being awarded a contract for a public work on promissory estoppel grounds. The measures of damage are expectation, reliance or restitutionary, as the facts will warrant.

[426] *E.H. Oftedal and Sons, Inc. v. State ex rel. Montana Transp. Com'n*, 2002 MT 1, 308 Mont. 50, 40 P.3d 349, 353 (2002)

[427] *George & Benjamin General Contractors v. Gov't of Virgin Islands Dept. of Property and Procurement*, 34 V.I. 117, 921 F. Supp. 304, 311 (D.V.I. 1996). In George, the Court determined that the bidder's mistake as to totals provided in the bid documents was a matter of form, not substance, and thus, a minor irregularity that could be waived without prejudice to other bidders. Contractors were instructed to submit proposals on a two-page preprinted form, with an attached addendum. The form included a section labeled "BASE PROPOSAL" where the bidder was to insert the sum for all work described in the specifications and shown on the plans, while the addendum provided space for a breakdown of items, including add alternates. The lowest bidder mistakenly entered the base bid ($1,095,500) and all of the add alternates ($1,720,600) as the "BASE PROPOSAL" price for a total of $2,816,100, forming the subject of the dispute. The government agency readily recognized the discrepancy and adding up the figures provided in the bid documents was able to ascertain the base bid of $1,095,500 by subtracting the add alternates from the $2,816,100 amount. The bidder also supplied a bid bond valued at 5% of the $2,816,100, providing the agency with additional support from the bid documents to determine the bidder's intent.

the bid," ambiguity is injected into the public bidding process, eroding the objective basis upon which contracts are awarded and thereby opening "Pandora's Box" to the favoritism and corruption that public bid laws were established to prevent.[428] Furthermore, where a mistake involves a bid that is comprised of component items, and the government could not know from the face of the bid whether the disparity lies in the component items or in the summation, that bidder has an unfair competitive advantage by being able to second guess its bid based upon the outcome of other competing bids.[429]

The Court engaged in a lengthy discussion of minor informalities or irregularities, as opposed to material and substantial mistakes, under the relevant statutory scheme. In comparing the various types of mistakes contemplated by the Virgin Islands Code, the Court noted that a "salient theme" running through the sections that permit waiver of certain mistakes "is the ability of the contracting officer to ascertain what the bidder intended ... from the four-corners of the bid documents submitted and available to Procurement." In *George*, the agency "immediately recognized the irregularity and just as quickly ascertained the obvious intent of Unlimited from within the four-corners of its bid by adding up the figures on the Addendum." The Court continued by stating that:

Mistakes, on the other hand, even apparent clerical mistakes ... require information outside of the bid documents before the contracting officer can determine what was intended. A decimal point may obviously be misplaced, but Procurement would have no way of knowing where the bidder intended to place it without talking to the bidder. In other words, although the mistake may be obvious, the bid actually intended may not be (emphasis added).

Unlike *George*, where the apparent clerical mistake could be corrected by the public agency without any additional elaboration or clarification by the bidder, the facts of this case create an ambiguity that cannot be corrected by looking to the "four-corners" of the bid documents. In *George*, the public agency had an addendum that contained a breakdown of the add alternates. Accordingly, the agency could easily determine that the amount provided in the "BASE PROPOSAL" actually equaled the total of the base bid and add alternates, thereby allowing the agency to adjust the amounts without affecting the intent of the bidder. Furthermore, the bid bond was based on the total amount, which made it evident to the agency that the "BASE PROPOSAL" was actually an amount smaller that that provided.

428 *Don M. Barron Contractor, Inc. v. City of Natchitoches*, 879 So. 2d 414 (La. Ct. App. 3d Cir. 2004), writ denied, 888 So. 2d 839 (La. 2004), citing *V. C. Nora, Jr. Bldg. & Remodeling, Inc. v. State Through Dept. of Transp. and Development,* 635 So. 2d 466 (La. Ct. App. 3d Cir. 1994) (abrogated by, *Colvin v. Louisiana Patient's Compensation Fund Oversight* Bd., 947 So. 2d 15 (La. 2007)).

429 *Armstrong & Armstrong, Inc. v. U. S. By and Through Morton*, 514 F.2d 402, 403 (9th Cir. 1975). In Armstrong, the bidders were required to provide estimates on 82 separate items as well as a total bid representing the sum of the 82 estimates. The second lowest bidder, Bovee & Crail ("B&C"), had made an arithmetic mistake--the 82 item estimates should have added up to $1,413,000 whereas the total given by B&C was $1,418,000. The plaintiff, Armstrong & Armstrong, bid $1,415,000. The government corrected the arithmetic error and informed B&C that it would be deemed the lowest bidder at $1,413,000. According to the Court of Appeals, which adopted the district court's reasoning:

> *[t]he government could not know* ***from the face of the bid whether the error lay in one of the component items or in the summation****. Bovee & Crail stated that the error was in the addition. If, however, it had appeared that Bovee & Crail was already the low bidder Bovee & Crail could have informed the government that the error was not in the addition*

The most common of bid mistakes is the clerical error. As long as the error appears on the face of the bid, the mistake can and should be corrected by the contracting manager or owner. In general, however, the clerical error must be obvious from a review of the bid--decimal in the wrong place, obvious incorrect discounts, etc. The owner should verify the bid by request of the bidder. In the event that the error is not found by the owner, the bidder should make a timely notification to the owner of the mistake.

Mistakes in bids that render them unresponsive cannot be corrected, unless the mistake is minor and of an immaterial nature. For example, a responsive bid requirement is that the bid requires signature in six (6) different places on the bid documents. A bidder signs in five of the places, but inadvertently misses one of the signature places. The bid can be corrected to allow the bidder to sign the 6th signature line, because her intent to properly authenticate the bid is demonstrated from the five (5) other signatures. The omission of the sixth signature is minor and immaterial. On the other hand, suppose the prospective bidder fails to sign the bid form at all--raising a doubt as to the intent of the bidder to authenticate the bid. Such a mistake could not be corrected, as the failure to sign the bid at all would be a material variance from the bid requirements--i.e., the bid was unresponsive to the bid requirements. In some cases, the owner may allow a contractor who submits a mistaken bid may be allowed to withdraw that bid, prior to bid opening. Such a request should be supported by documentation, affidavits or other evidence supporting the mistake. The evidence, however, must be clear and convincing as to the existence of the mistake. Again, errors in business judgment will not justify the withdrawal of a bid.

Errors discovered in a bid after the award has been awarded by the contracting agency are not as easy to correct. In substance, the bidder must show that the contracting agency had actual notice of the mistake, or had constructive notice of the mistake at the time of award, and failed to verify the bid prior thereto. If the bidder can make the requisite showing, the contract can either be reformed to correct the price or rescinded. Failure to show sufficient evidence to justify the correction will result in the bidder having to accept the contract or to be found in breach thereof.

If the error in the bid is only discovered after commencement of construction, a reformation of the bid will only be allowed if the mistake is mutual between the parties. The mistake must affect the "essence of the agreement"--in other words, there is no agreement at all on the basic terms. In this case, the contract may be rescinded. On the

---

but in one of the component items, and thus maintain the higher bid. This opportunity to second guess one's bid after the bids have been opened subverts the competitive process, and creates the potential for abuse that federal procurement regulations are designed to prevent (emphasis added). Armstrong stands as an admonishment against compromising the public works bidding system.

other hand, if the mistake is not mutual, the correction must be made through the changes clause process. If the mistake is the bidders, and not the result of any errors on the part of the owner, the bidder is most likely liable for the cost of the bid error.

6:18 Bid Disputes and Protests

In response to a rash of unsuccessful and questionable bid protests in the early 2000s, the Nevada legislature in 2003 saw fit to bring a statutory basis to bid protests from unsuccessful bidders by enacting NRS 338.142. Under this section, a bid protest can only be initiated by the protestor by filing a written notice of protest with the public body awarding the contract within 5 days after the date the public body announces an intention to award the public work contract.[430] This notice must include a written statement setting out the specific reason why the protest is bring raised and what applicable law is alleged to be violated by the award of the project to the apparent lowest bidder.[431]

Although it is not always enforced, the governing body involved in the protest may require that a bid protest bond or cash equivalent be posted by the protestor in the amount of 25% of the bid amount or $250,000, whichever is less, upon the filing of the bid protest.[432] This amount is held as security against the cost and expenses incurred by the governing body due to the unsuccessful protest.[433] If the protest is upheld, the bond or cash equivalent is returned to the successful protester.[434] This seems somewhat unfair. NRS 338.142(6) indicates that neither the public body nor its authorized representative are liable for costs, attorneys fees or other damages sustained by the person who makes a bid, regardless of whether they file a bid protest. Moreover, it has been held that no private right of action exists against the governing body for an alleged violation of the public works statutes.[435] Obviously, there is no attempt to incentivize bidders for bringing bid protests over public works construction. The filing of the complete bid protest stays the any action by the public body to award the contract until

[430] NRS 338.142(1).

[431] NRS 338.142(2).

[432] NRS 338.142(3).

[433] NRS 338.142(7).

[434] NRS 338.142(7).

[435] *Richardson Const., Inc. v. Clark County School Dist.*, 123 Nev. 61, 156 P.3d 21 (2007). This prohibition on private right of action, however, is not necessarily carried over to the subcontractor who claims a violation by the successful bidder in any attempt to remove the listed subcontractor. *Clark Pacific v. Krump Const., Inc.*, 942 F. Supp. 1324 (D. Nev. 1996).

the protest has been heard and determined.[436] A lawsuit may not be commenced until the public body makes a determination on the bid protest.[437]

Bid protests are difficult items to manage and seeking clarity in the law surrounding successful bid protests is difficult to find in Nevada. Essentially, the governing body will be able to overlook minor bid errors or other issues which can be easily and fairly corrected. More significant errors cannot be overlooked and are subject to protest. It is critical for the protester to file the protest with the public body on a timely basis. Some governing bodies operate on four day work weeks in Nevada, which will further complicate the dates by which protests must be filed. It is always a good practice tip to contact the governing body when a protest is being contemplated in order to let them know of that the protest will be filed and clarifying who to present with the protest and when. Given the five day limitations of NRS 338.142(1), the protest must be prepared quickly and effectively within short preparation durations.

Assuming that the protest will be unsuccessful at the administrative level, a judicial determination is available. However, the only relief available is injunctive,[438] and may be lost through delay or in action.[439] Therefore, the protester must focus its resources on moving the matter quickly to district court to seek an injunction preventing the award, if the protest is not sustained at the administrative level.

It should likewise be noted that a form of bid protest is available for any contractor who is accused of a violation of the Nevada First Act. NRS 338.0117(3) allows for any person or entity who believes a violation of the Nevada First Act has occurred to make a written complaint to the public body awarding the contract, along with evidence substantiating the complaint. Upon receipt of the complaint, the public body is required to determine if there is substantial evidence and, if so, investigate the complaint. Upon a finding that the complaint is valid, the public body may award the contract to another party or if the contract is already awarded seek the penalties allowed under NRS 338.0117(5).[440]

6:19 CONSTRUCTION MANAGEMENT

---

[436] NRS 338.142(4).

[437] NRS 338.142(5).

[438] NRS 338.142(6).

[439] *Building and Constr. Trades Council of N. Nevada v. State ex rel. Public Works Bd.*, 108 Nev. 605, 611, P.2d 633, 637, (1992).

[440] NRS 338.0117(4).

Construction Management has been a staple in many state public works departments for many years. In Nevada, the legislature authorized the use of construction management at risk ("CMAR") as a delivery method for public works construction projects in 2007.[441] As such, there have been relatively few projects completed using the construction management at risk delivery method, although a number of currently in the works. Construction management at risk as formulated in Nevada requires a form of public subcontract selection. The 2011 revisions to the subcontractor selection process will make the CMAR much more attractive as a delivery method.

Construction management is the use of a licensed contracting professional (mandatorily for a construction manager at risk, a licensed general contractor in Nevada)[442] during the design process to vet the design and specifications for the purpose of refining errors, clarifying ambiguity, value engineering, pricing and otherwise streamlining of problems that may arise while the project is being constructed.[443] After the design has been completed, the construction manager takes on a more fundamental role as the general contractor (in the context of a construction manager at risk contract) or owners representative (in the context of a construction manager as agent contract) to ensure that the construction project is completed as designed and contemplated.[444]

By engaging the contractor during the design of the project, the goals of reducing conflicts and design errors are achieved, which also leads to the project having a better chance of being completed on time and within budget, and with a minimum of disputes between the project owner, the designer and the contractor. Legislative changes in 2011 allow subcontractor selection for preconstruction services on a negotiated price basis and for the selection of subcontractors for construction services on a qualification and selection process controlled by the CMAR. These changes greatly increase the effectiveness of CMAR as a efficient and productive delivery method.

6:20 Construction Manager as Agent

Governing bodies within the state of Nevada have been able to retain construction managers as agents, and have done so for many years.[445] These contracts are let similarly to those for design professionals, and are not based on competitive bidding.

---

[441] NRS 338.169.

[442] NRS 624.020(4); *cf.* NRS 624.700(1). However, construction managers as agents can also be registered architects or licensed engineers. NRS 338.1718(1)(a).

[443] NRS 338.1718.

[444] NRS 338.1718(1)(b).

[445] NRS 338.1717.

Instead, these contracts are denominated as professional services and are governed by the relevant provisions of NRS Chapter 332.[446] While the use of a construction manager as the owner's agent is possible and does have its uses, the availability of a construction management at risk (CMAR) can reveal the construction management as agent function for its worst aspect--the addition of substantial cost without a corresponding increase in project delivery efficiency.

The construction manager as agent (CMAA) performs most of the same pre-construction services of the construction manager at risk (CMAR), however, the CMAA's approach is not to prepare the drawings and specifications for his own use, but rather to prepare them for use of the eventual general contractor for the project.[447] As such, the use of CMAA has an additional cost component that is sometimes not necessary or is not as efficient as CMAR. The involvement of the CMAA does not increase the knowledge base of the eventual contractor who builds the project. While his involvement may clarify design questions or errors before the package is advertised for bid, the CMAA still cannot dictate to the eventual low bidder the means and methods of construction, the scheduling of work or other task that the general contractor may encounter or be responsible to perform.

The CMAA will also be useful to the owner in the evaluation of bids for responsiveness to the bid specifications. Arguably, a CMAA will be able to identify where bidding contractors have made bid errors and will be able to point these out to the governing body awarding the contracts. During the project, the CMAA usually monitors the contractor's performance and assists the owner in managing payment requests, change order requests, requests for information and other processes that the project owner may not be familiar with or where the owner may find himself subject to claims or unfair treatment at the hands of an unfair contractor.[448] Again, while these tasks can assist an owner with little to no experience in construction many are traditionally performed by design professionals as additional services. Therefore, the CMAA can fall into the trap of duplication of effort and unnecessary increase of project cost, which are to be avoided if at all possible.

6:21 Construction Manager at Risk

The statutory process for project delivery by construction management at risk (CMAR) has been streamlined into a two-step process combining elements of the competitive bidding process, while allowing certain contracting techniques (such as negotiation for

---

[446] NRS 338.1718(3); *see also* Section 6:3, Selecting the Designer.

[447] NRS 338.1717.

[448] NRS 338.1718(1)(b).

the best price and the use of shared savings clauses) that are not usually contemplated within the competitive bidding environment. The process therefore is open to subjective interpretation and influence, but changes from the 2011 legislative process have narrowed these issues to a large degree.

Initially, the governing body wishing to utilize CMAR will enter into two contracts with the eventual CMAR: one for pre-construction services, and the other to construct the actual project.[449] Before this may be accomplished, however, the CMAR candidates must be qualified. For state public works projects performed for the SPWB, the CMAR candidates must be prequalified in a similar manner as competitive bidding candidates under NRS 338.1379.[450] In addition, NRS 338.1691 provides:

> *To qualify to enter into contracts with a local government or its authorized representative for preconstruction services and to construct a public work, a construction manager at risk must: 1. Not have been found liable for breach of contract with respect to a previous project, other than a breach for legitimate cause, during the 5 years immediately preceding the date of the advertisement for statements of qualifications pursuant to NRS 338.1692; 2. Not have been disqualified from being awarded a contract pursuant to NRS 338.017, 338.13895, 338.1475 or 408.333, and 3. Be licensed as a contractor pursuant to chapter 624 of NRS ....*

As to the first criteria, there is no legislative insight as to the meaning of "breach for legitimate cause" which would allow a jurist or construction attorney to determine whether a previous breach of contract would not exclude the contractor as a qualified CMAR candidate. In the current era of litigation, all contractors at one time or another will be accused of breach of contract. If such cases are not resolved before judgment is entered, such judgments would be relevant to this qualification. While the CMAR candidate will have an opportunity to disclose the reasoning behind any breach of contract judgment,[451] the lack of an objective standard opens the door to favoritism and undue influence.

The second criterion is a simple finding by a previous governing body that the CMAR candidate has been disqualified from being a bidder on other public works projects. These reasons can be anything from failing to pay prevailing wages,[452] to bidding on a public work beyond the limits of one's contractors' license.[453] In short, a contractor who

---

[449] NRS 338.169(2).

[450] *See* Sections 6:5 to 6:6.

[451] NRS 338.1692(3)(f).

[452] NRS 338.017.

[453] NRS 338.13895 and NRS 338.1475.

wishes to bid on public works projects in Nevada is wise to closely guard his contractor's license and to abide by any criteria that is mandated by the NSCB.

The governing body seeking to award the CMAR contract must advertise for proposals from CMAR candidates under rules similar to those for advertising for competitive bids. The governing body will advertise for qualification statements in a newspaper of general circulation published within the county where the project is located or in a newspaper printed in the state and circulated in the county.[454] The advertisement must include: 1) a description of the public work; 2) an estimate of the cost of construction; 3) a description of the work that the governing body expects the CMAR to perform; 4) the dates that both pre-construction and actual construction are anticipated to being and end; 5) the deadline for submission of proposals for the CMAR work; 6) the name and contact information for the governing body's agent, and 7) a list of the criteria and relative weight each criteria will be given in evaluating the qualifications of the CMAR proposals.[455] If the project is being awarded by the SPWB, the advertisement must also include a statement that CMAR candidates must be pre-qualified under NRS 338.1379 before submitting its statement of qualification.[456]

The responding CMAR candidates must submit proposals that include: 1) the experience of the candidate with similar projects in both the public and private sectors, including a statement of the experience of the applicant in assisting with design as well as a description of such experience on projects in the State of Nevada; 2) references for the candidate; 3) evidence that the candidate has the required bonding and insurance capacity for the project, and 4) a statement explaining whether the applicant has been found liable for a breach of a construction or construction management contract (other than a breach for legitimate cause) within the previous 5 years before the advertisement for proposals; 5) has not been disqualified on a previous public work project; 6) the professional qualifications and experience of the applicant including resumes of key employees; 7) safety programs of the applicant; 8) proof of appropriate licensure under NRS Chapter 624; 9) a proposed plan for managing the preconstruction and construction of the public work.[457] Obviously, the CMAR proposal should closely conform to the requirements of the advertisement and should be prepared relative to the evaluation criteria and weight of each factor.

---

454 NRS 338.1692(1).

455 NRS 338.1692(2).

456 NRS 338.1692(2)(f).

457 NRS 338.1692(3).

The governing body must appoint a panel of at least three of its members to evaluate and rank the proposals received, two of which must have experience in the construction trade.[458] Each proposal must be verified for its adherence to the requirements of NRS 338.1692(3), as well as the advertisement criteria as specified within the advertisement for proposals.[459] There must also be assigned a relative weight for the possession of a certificate of eligibility to receive a preference in bidding on public works and execution of the affidavit of compliance with the Nevada First Act.[460] Once evaluated, the panel must rank the CMAR candidates by their proposal evaluation scores to determine the order of interview for the CMAR position. The public body must receive and select at least two but not more than five CMAR proposals to interview for the project.[461] If the governing body did not receive at least two qualified statements, the governing body may not perform the project with a CMAR,[462] and instead must select another method of project delivery.

The governing body then must conduct interviews of the highest scoring proposal applicants. The public body may request a preliminary estimate of the compensation requested for the management of the preconstruction services and the construction of the public work, but such amount cannot represent more than 20 percent of the score for the final evaluation of proposals.[463] Upon receiving the rankings from the panel, the governing body must then enter into negotiations with the highest ranked CMAR candidate for the contract for pre-construction services,[464] to achieve a contract for a fair and reasonable cost and services scope. If an estimate of the management fee was requested as part of the interview process that must be the public body's opening offer.[465] If the governing body cannot negotiate such a contract, it must terminate those

---

[458] NRS 338.1693(1).

[459] NRS 338.1693(2).

[460] *See* Section 6:10, Certificate of eligibility for bidding preference, *and* Section 6:11 Nevada First Act Compliance. It should also be noted that this assessment shall not be used if any federal statute or regulation for bids such preferences if the granting of federal assistance is eliminated or the amount thereof is reduced as a result.

[461] NRS 338.1693(4).

[462] NRS 338.1693(5).

[463] NRS 338.1693(4). This percentage score, however, must be a calculated score, which divides the lowest estimated amount by the proposal amount multiplied by the total points to be awarded for this category score. For example, if an interviewee proposes to seek $1,750,000 for the management services, and the low estimate was $1,500,000 and 20 total points were possible to be awarded, the calculation would look like this: ($1,500,000 / $1,750,000) x 20 = 17.14 points.

[464] NRS 338.1695(2).

[465] NRS 338.1693(6).

negotiations and negotiate instead with the next most qualified candidate from the ranking.[466] The failure to enter into a fair and reasonable contract with any of the ranked qualified CMAR candidates leads to a determination by the governing body to reject all CMAR candidates.[467] The results of the evaluations and rankings are public records and must be made available as such.[468]

If the pre-construction services contract negotiations are successful, the governing body and selected CMAR enter into a contract and the preconstruction services are performed. As the design or portions thereof are completed, the governing body and the CMAR enter into additional negotiations to contract for the construction of the public work.[469] The contract can either be a cost plus a fee with a guaranteed maximum price, a lump sum or a cost plus a fixed fee contract.[470] The contract may also include a shared savings provision when the contract contains a guaranteed maximum price.[471] If the CMAR and the governing body cannot negotiate an acceptable contract, the governing body may terminate the negotiations,[472] and may then award the construction contract through competitive bidding.[473] The public body, however, must accept a bid from the CMAR with whom it had a preconstruction services contract.[474]

---

[466] NRS 338.1693(6).

[467] NRS 338.1693(6).

[468] NRS 338.1693(4)(a).

[469] NRS 338.1696.

[470] NRS 338.1696(1).

[471] NRS 338.1697.

[472] Here is the second area ripe for disputes. As often happens in construction, when a contractor and the owner get certain criteria established, they will often begin work on the project before the final contract price is agreed to or the final terms are negotiated. The temptation will be high within the public works CMAR scenario to do the same, however, if negotiations are not ultimately successful, it may be difficult for the governing body to stop negotiations and move forward with a competitively bid project, especially if work has commenced. The CMAR statutes do not contemplate this situation or what damages may be incurred in doing so. Arguably, the CMAR who begins performance will claim breach of contract on the part of the governing body and may even claim bad faith in the negotiations. Presumably injunctive relief may be available to the CMAR as well. The governing body may be in a poor negotiating position with the CMAR who may be able to assert a claim for higher costs than originally planned as a result of the CMAR pre-construction services process. Also, there is no statutory language authorizing the governing body to withdraw the contract. To the contrary, there is a mandatory obligation to begin negotiations with the CMAR. As such, litigation is bound to arise if the pre-construction services contract has not been workable during its term.

[473] NRS 338.1696(2)(b).

[474] NRS 338.1696(2)(b).

Once the CMAR contract is negotiated, there are certain clauses that must be contacted within the agreement. Initially, the contract must include the mandatory provisions that every Nevada public works contract must contain,[475] and must also include for basic but important conditions as well: 1) a specific date that the project must be completed; 2) terms by which the CMAR agrees to name the governing body as an additional insured under its construction insurance policies; 3) require that the CMAR "*assume overall responsibility for ensuring that the preconstruction or construction of the public work, as applicable, is completed in a satisfactory manner*"; and 4) additional provisions that the CMAR and governing body deem appropriate.[476] Once the construction contract is entered into, the CMAR must be responsible for the selection, contracting, performance and payment to all necessary subcontractors, suppliers and independent contractors.[477] Furthermore, depending on the type of work involved, the CMAR may be required to perform some of the actual work itself.[478]

In 2011, new selection process must be used for the selection of subcontractors for the CMAR project, which is not subject to competitive bidding.[479] Initially, a contractor who has entered into a contract with a public body as a CMAR for preconstruction services may also enter into a negotiated contract with a subcontractor to provide preconstruction services as well. Under NRS 338.16935, the CMAR may engage a subcontractor who is properly licensed to assist the CMAR with: 1) identifying and selecting materials and equipment to be provided by subcontractors on the project; 2) creating a schedule for the provision of labor, materials or equipment; 3) establishing a budget for the construction of the public work and 4) make recommendations as to the design of the project pertaining to the subcontractor's particular trade.[480] The only limitation is that the subcontractor may not provide assistance on part of the work which is outside his licensed trade.[481] This ability to provide preconstruction services will also allow the use of an integrated design or integrated project delivery model with the CMAR delivery system.

---

[475] *See* Section 6:26 Prompt Payment Requirements.

[476] NRS 338.1698.

[477] NRS 338.16985(1).

[478] NRS 338.16985(2) and NRS 338.16985(3).

[479] NRS 338.16995.

[480] NRS 338.16935(1).

[481] NRS 338.16935(2).

After the design of the public work or a part there of has reached a level of detail and completion to allow for a subcontractor to submit a meaningful and responsive proposal, the CMAR may seek to obtain proposals from qualified trade contractors. The initial step is to prequalify subcontractors in the specific trades. To obtain qualified subcontractors, the CMAR must advertise in a newspaper of general circulation in the county where the project is located for submission of applications by qualified subcontractors.[482] At a minimum to qualify, a subcontractor must be licensed in the particular trade needed under NRS Chapter 624, and to be qualified under the provisions of NRS 338.16991. The determination of qualification is made by the CMAR, subject to the review and appeal to the public body.[483]

As indicated above, "after the design and schedule of the public work is sufficiently detailed and complete to allow a subcontractor to apply to qualify to submit a meaningful and responsive proposal"[484] for the provision of work on the project, the CMAR may begin the advertisement process for qualified subcontracting applicants. The advertisement must be made not later than 21 days before the applications must be submitted to the CMAR,[485] however, in order to allow time to prepare the application. The criteria the CMAR must use to select the subcontractors who are qualified to provide a proposal must be limited to the following items:

- The holding of the proper classification license and the monetary limit placed thereon by the NSCB;
- The financial ability of the applicant to provide the labor, materials, or equipment required on the public work;
- The ability of the applicant to provide the necessary bonding for the work required by the public body;
- The safety program and safety record of the applicant;
- Whether the applicant as breached any contracts with a public body or "person in this State or any other state" during the 5 years preceding the application;
- Whether the applicant has been disciplined by the NSCB or another state or federal agency for conduct that relates to the ability to perform the work;
- The performance history of the applicant on other recent and similar public or private projects in the state of Nevada;
- The applicant's principal personnel;
- Previous disqualifications of the applicant under NRS Chapter 338, and

---

482 NRS 338.16991(3).

483 NRS 338.16991(2).

484 NRS 338.16991(3).

485 NRS 338.16991(3).

- The truthfulness and completeness of the application provided.[486]

These provisions allow the CMAR considerable practical leeway to find acceptable subcontractor candidates. While the CMAR has the obligation to review qualifications of applications under the supervision of the public body to ensure compliance with the above,[487] and there is the ability of a applicant determined to be unqualified to appeal to the public body for relief,[488] ultimately the CMAR will have absolute discretion to chose the subcontractors for the work that they believe are best to handle it.[489] Once the CMAR establishes the list of qualified applicants, the CMAR must inform the public body of those on the list, and also inform those who applied of the outcome of the application evaluation.[490]

Once the design and schedule has reached a level of detail and completeness which will allow a subcontractor to submit a meaningful and responsive proposal, the CMAR may request proposals from subcontractors on the qualified list. Only subcontracts which will reach 1 percent or more of the total cost of the public work need to be solicited by the provisions of NRS 338.16995 to the qualified list.[491] Again, the CMAR must make its request not less than 21 days before the proposals are due to be submitted. The CMAR must provide a notice to the qualified applicants that includes:[492]

- A description of the design for the public work and a statement where a copy of the design documents may be obtained;
- A description of the type and scope of labor, equipment and materials to be provided;
- The date, time and place at which a mandatory pre-proposal meeting will take place;
- The dates on which the public work construction and completion are anticipated to occur;
- The date, time and to whom the proposals must be submitted;
- The date, time and place at which the proposals will be opened;

---

[486] NRS 338.16991(4).

[487] NRS 338.16991(5).

[488] NRS 338.16991(7).

[489] NRS 338.16995(9).

[490] NRS 338.16991(6).

[491] NRS 338.16995(2).

[492] NRS 338.16995(4).

- A description of the bonding and insurance requirements for subcontractors on the public work;
- Any other information reasonably necessary for the subcontractor to submit a responsive proposal, and
- A notice must include a statement in the following form:
- NOTICE: For a proposal for a subcontract on the public work to be considered:
- The subcontractor must be licensed pursuant to chapter 624 of NRS;
- The proposal must be timely received;
- The subcontractor must attend the pre-proposal meeting; and
- The subcontractor may not modify the proposal after the date and time the proposal is received.

As indicated in the Notice provisions, the applicant subcontractor may not modify a proposal once it is submitted. For the proposal to be considered responsive to the request for proposals, it must be timely summited and "substantially and materially conform to the details and requirements included in the proposal instructions and for the finalized bid package or the public work, including without limitation, details and requirements affecting price and performance."[493] The CMAR must open the proposals in the presence of representatives of the public body and the architect of record,[494] and must compile and provide the public body a list of the applicants and amounts of the proposals provided.[495] That list is to be provided to the public upon request.

For some reason not explained in the legislation, the CMAR must wait at least 10 days after the proposals are opened to begin its evaluation and selection process. The selection must be made from those proposals which are responsive and were received from qualified applicants who attended the pre-proposal meeting and where on the qualified list.[496] The CMAR does not need to select the subcontractor based solely on the price of its proposal.[497] Once selected, the CMAR must inform the public body of the subcontractor's identity.[498] The final rankings of the subcontractors must be made available by the CMAR to the public upon request, and the specific reasons why a subcontractor was not selected to that subcontractor upon request.[499] Once selected the

---

[493] NRS 338.16995(6).

[494] NRS 338.16995(7).

[495] NRS 338.16995(8).

[496] NRS 338.16995(9).

[497] NRS 338.16995(11).

[498] NRS 338.16995(9)(c).

[499] NRS 338.16995(14).

CMAR may not substitute the subcontractor, except with approval by the public body and for specific reasons, including the subcontractor's insolvency, failure to execute a subcontract, failure to perform, or the inability to obtain necessary performance and payment bonds.[500] If the public work will be constructed in phases, the CMAR does not need to repeat this process to award the additional phases to a subcontractor who was selected through this process for any other phase.[501] There is no provision for a protest of the selection of a subcontractor by the CMAR in NRS 338.16995.

These changes to the subcontractor selection procedure take substantial risk out of the CMAR process for general contractors. By allowing the CMAR to obtain preconstruction services for the public work and to allow the CMAR the ultimate choice in who to select to perform the subcontract trades, the process of CMAR may work to its best advantage.

6:22 Integrated Project Delivery with CMAR

Since the Leadership in Energy and Environmental Design ("LEED") construction certifications have become a building standard within public and private works construction, Nevada has seen a significant number of LEED certified projects constructed. The key component of LEED certification is construction by use of the Integrated Project Delivery management model. Integrated Project Delivery ("IPD") has been defined as "a project delivery approach that integrates people, systems, business structures and practices into a process that collaboratively harnesses the talents and insights of all participants to reduce waste and optimize efficiency through all phases of design, fabrication and construction."[502] While the goals of IPD as stated in this definition are laudable, in order to properly function, a complete shift of the adversarial mindset that is built into the design-bid-build construction delivery model has to occur. While CMAR, Design-Build, and other alternative delivery methods seek to create a more conducive construction model that reduces delivery costs and time by reducing disputes between the owner, designer, and contractor, the system is still plagued by the idea of shifting liability to the other parties in the construction paradigm. As a result, there is still significant opportunity for waste, inefficiencies, and resulting cost increases and disputes to arise.

As discussed above, CMAR seeks to reduce these factors by early involvement of the contractor in preconstruction activities. It is also intended that key trade contractors will also be involved as design progresses, in order to achieve and maximize project cost

---

[500] NRS 338.16995(13).

[501] NRS 338.16995(15).

[502] IPD Definition Task Group, 2007, which is an interdisciplinary group sponsored by the American Institute of Architects California Council and McGraw-Hill Construction.

savings through value engineering and thoroughness of design constructability review. These concepts are perfectly within the parameters of an IPD delivery method. In fact, Nevada public entities routinely use AIA form contract documents for their projects and the AIA have formulated form contracts using the IPD project management strategies. As one author described the documents:

> *Unlike traditional AIA agreements, [the new IPD AIA Documents], B195 and A195 do not include a scope of services; instead, this is spelled out in A295 General Conditions, which also establish a collaboration process for the owner-architect-constructor team. ... [The] "A295 writes up a process for early involvement on the part of the contractor, working with the architect through design development, providing constructability reviews, and developing a guaranteed maximum price." This approach changes only a little from the traditional risk-and-reward model.*[503]

As is demonstrated by this quote, the model for IPD within the mentioned AIA form documents complements well the CMAR process outlined in NRS 338.169, et seq. What makes IPD the game changer is the use of Building Information Modeling ("BIM") and the concept of inter-discipline liability waiver.

IPD is premised on the use of BIM to construct the project digitally on a computer *before* the shovels are placed in the ground. As described by the National Institute of Building Sciences:

> *A [Building Information Model, or] BIM is a three-dimensional digital representation of the physical and functional characteristics of a building. It is a shared resource of knowledge about a facility that can be used to make decisions about the building throughout its life-cycle, from the initial idea, to design and construction, through daily operations and eventual demolition. ... Using BIMs effectively can resolve problems and reduce expense and frustration. For example, when designing a building, there are floor plans, plumbing plans and heating, ventilation and air conditioning (HVAC) plans, often prepared by different people. Without effective communication, the designers risk having pipes, vents and beams colliding in the same space. A BIM allows all of the plans to be stored in a digital format together, so problems can be caught before construction begins.*[504]

When viewed in this light, the value of BIM and IPD to a public construction project begins to take visible form. In field construction design conflicts, failed or lack of coordination issues, requests for information, change order requests and negotiation,

---

503 Novitski, *New AIA Agreements Support Integrated Project Delivery*, Architectural Record, The McGraw-Hill Companies, Inc., July 2008.

504 National Institute of Building Sciences, 2009 Annual Report to the President of the United States, pg. 28; www.nibs.org/client/assets/files/nibs/NIBS 2009AnnualReport.pdf.

and the attendant disputes can potentially be eliminated, as the actual computer driven BIM demonstrates the conflicts that give rise to these efficiency-robbing disputes. While the risks and rewards of BIM pose unique and knotty legal questions that must be vetted in detail, the potential liability eliminating concepts cannot be denied.[505] For this reason and the key involvement of all construction team players at the outset of project concept, the IPD agreement includes inter-construction team liability waivers for contractual breach, except for willful misconduct.

At present, nothing within the parameters of NRS 338 would appear to either expressly forbid or expressly authorize the use of IPD and BIM management tools within the constructs of the CMAR or other project delivery protocols authorized for Nevada public works construction. So long as the formal steps of CMAR selection are complied with, the use of IPD management techniques should not be disallowed, and in fact should be sought for the reduction of liability for all parties.

6:23 Design-build

In 1999, the Nevada legislature enacted a series of statues in Chapter 338 to permit the use of design-build as a project delivery method for certain projects. In response to a number of limitations the initial legislation imposed on public entities, subsequent legislatures have made various changes to the law to make the design-build delivery method more accessible to local governments, and for the NDOT. Governing bodies are able to contract with design-build teams for the construction of a public work, so long as that public work falls into specific categories. Initially, the public work must be a discrete project; that is, a stand alone project which is not part of another larger public work,[506] the cost of which will exceed $5,000,000.[507] There is no longer a need to make the determination to construct using a design-build team at any kind of public hearing. The project needs only to meet the criteria set forth in NRS 338.1711(2) in order for the governing body to use the design-build delivery method.

Having once determined to use design-build, the governing body must qualify design-build team ("DBT") applicants using specific criteria found within NRS 338.1721 to NRS 338.1727.[508] Initially, this begins with the qualification of the design-build teams. As the

---

[505] For a thorough analysis of the benefits and potential pitfalls of the use of BIM, including the concept of mutual waivers of liability among the owner-designer-constructor team except for willful misconduct, *see* Ashcraft, *Building Information Modeling: A Framework for Collaboration*, Construction Lawyer, Vol. 28, No. 3 (American Bar Assoc., Summer 2008); *see also* Ashcraft, *Negotiating an Integrated Project Delivery Agreement* (Hansen Bridgett LLP, 2010).

[506] NRS 338.1711(2).

[507] NRS 338.1711(2).

[508] NRS 338.1715.

design build delivery method contemplates both the design and construction of the public work, it is necessary to expand the qualifications beyond those necessary for competitive bidding or CMAR delivery. The DBT must not only be able to construct the work, it must be able to design the work to the standards of a public project. Accordingly, the DBT must be able to provide: 1) the ability to provide performance and payment bonds for the project as required under NRS 339.025[509] as well as general liability, professional liability and errors and omissions insurance coverage for the project.[510] Similar to the qualifications as a CMAR, the DBT must be able to demonstrate that it had not been found liable for breach of any contract with respect to a previous project within the past 5 years before the design-build project is bid.[511] This provision carries the same unexplained exception for a "breach for a legitimate cause" that was discussed in the section on CMAR.[512]

The DBT must also not have been disqualified from being awarded a public works contract previously.[513] This requirement will be leveled at any entity that comprises the DBT, such as a joint venture partner. All the entities making up the DBT will need to be able to demonstrate a lack of disqualification or contract breach to ensure the DBT is not tainted by that issue. Similarly, the DBT will need to show it does in fact hold the appropriate Nevada issued licenses to perform the necessary work on the design-build project,[514] and as with all public works, if the project is to be performed for the SPWB, the prime contractor for the DBT will need to be pre-qualified to bid on state public works projects under NRS 338.1379.[515]

The governing body seeking to let a design-build project must advertise for qualified DBTs to submit preliminary proposals for the design-build project. Like other delivery method projects, the advertisements must be placed in a newspaper published within the county where the design-build project will be located, or if there is no paper published in the county, in a newspaper published in the state of Nevada and circulated in the county where the project is located.[516] The advertisement must include without

509 NRS 338.1721(1); *see* Section 6:24, Payment and Performance Bond Claims.

510 NRS 338.1721(2).

511 NRS 338.1721(3).

512 NRS 338.1721(6); *see* Section 6:20 Construction Manager at Risk.

513 NRS 338.1721(4).

514 NRS 338.1721(5).

515 *See* Sections 6:5 to 6:6.

516 NRS 338.1723(1).

any limitations or to other inclusions, at least the following information: 1) a description of the public work; 2) an estimate of the cost to design and the cost to construct the public work; 3) the anticipated dates when both the design and construction phases will each begin; 4) the date that preliminary proposals need to be submitted to the governing body; 5) providing the requirement for pre-qualification (if the design-build project is issued by the SPWB); 6) a description of the extent to which the designs must be completed for both preliminary and final proposals that will be submitted as part of the design-build proposal process; 7) a list of the qualification requirements under NRS 338.1721 as discussed above; a list of the determining factors used in the selection of DBTs, and the relative weight assigned to each factor; a request for additional information that may be used by the governing body to evaluate the final proposals; and a statement as to whether the governing body will reimburse all or a part of the unsuccessful DBT bidders' costs in preparing and submitting final proposals.[517] Like the selection process with a CMAR, the preliminary proposal will be viewed to begin an investigation process which leads to the selection of a lower number of finalists, who are then asked to prepare final proposals for the design-build project. Since the DBT will assume overall responsibility for the design and construction of the project, a heightened investigation and review process is necessary in the design-build context.

Once the preliminary proposals are submitted, the governing body will select between two and four finalists from the DBTs.[518] If the governing body does not receive at least two preliminary proposals, the governing body will not be able to use the design-build delivery method for the project and must use another authorized method.[519] The governing body selects its finalists by verifying the background information provided in the preliminary proposals, and evaluating the criteria advertised to be used in making the proposals.[520] The governing body will also evaluate a number of qualifying factors, including the applicant's professional qualifications and work history, safety record and programs and the plan to manage the design-build team itself during the project duration.[521] The results of the preliminary evaluations and rankings of the preliminary proposals are public records that must be made available by the governing body.[522]

---

517 NRS 338.1723(2).

518 NRS 338.1725(1).

519 NRS 338.1725(1).

520 NRS 338.1725(2)(a).

521 NRS 338.1725(2)(b).

522 NRS 338.1725(3).

After ranking the finalists, the governing body will send a written request to the selected finalists to submit a final proposal. The request will simply include the factors and weight assigned to the final selection criteria and the date the final proposals are to be submitted.[523] The cost of the public work must be assigned a minimum weight of 30 percent (30%) of the selection factor, and another five percent (5%) must be given to the holding of a valid certificate of eligibility for preference in bidding a public work.[524] The final proposals must be "*prepared thoroughly and responsive to the criteria that the public body will use to select the design-build team to design and construct the public work.*"[525] Any DBT whose final proposal does not meet this standard will not be entitled to be awarded the project or reimbursed for the cost of preparing the proposal.[526] There is no requirement for the DBT to submit any listing of subcontractors selected for the project under NRS 338.141,[527] unlike the competitive bidding or CMAR delivery methods.

From the final proposals, the governing body will enter into negotiations with the most qualified finalist to reach a fair and reasonable contract. Failing that, the public entity may terminate negotiations and enter into negotiations with the next qualified finalist until a contract I reached or to reject all applicants.[528] It will also reimburse the other finalists for their proposal efforts.[529] The design-build contract will include those required construction terms as all public works construction project must include,[530] and also provide break outs of the maximum prices that both the design and construction phases of the work will cost the governing body.[531] The preliminary and final proposals are made public records and are to be made available for public inspection.[532]

---

[523] NRS 338.1727(1).

[524] NRS 338.1727(3); *see also* Section 6:10, Certificate of Eligibility for Bidding Preference.

[525] NRS 338.1727(4).

[526] NRS 338.1727(4).

[527] NRS 338.1727(5).

[528] NRS 338.1727(6).

[529] NRS 338.1727(6).

[530] *See* Section 6:24, Mandatory Construction Clauses.

[531] NRS 338.1727(8).

[532] NRS 338.1727(9).

6:24 MANDATORY CONSTRUCTION CLAUSES

Nevada mandates that all public works construction contracts contain certain provisions.[533] These provisions include a requirement to pay prevailing wages in the county where the work is performed,[534] and that the amount of those wages prevailing for each class of worker be posted on the job site at a visible location to all the workers.[535]

Additionally, public works contracts must provide for resolution of disputes via a method of alternative dispute resolution.[536] This alternative dispute resolution requirement is binding upon all governing bodies contracting for construction,[537] with the sole exception of the NDOT.[538]

Likewise, every public works contract must include a provision requiring the contractor, subcontractors and all other persons providing labor, materials, equipment or otherwise comply with all applicable state laws and regulations, including licensing and the payment of sales and use taxes as may be applicable.[539]

In 2011, the legislature also restricted the ability of the public works contract to require a contractor to waive, release or extinguish a claim or right for damages or extensions of time that the contractor may have as a result of unreasonable length of delay, fraud, misrepresentation, concealment or bad faith by the public body, active interference with the work, or that requires the contractor or public body to be responsible for consequential damages.[540] Such provisions are void as against public policy of the state,[541] however, such provisions do not make liquidated damage provisions void.[542]

---

[533] NRS 338.020 to NRS 338.090.

[534] NRS 338.020.

[535] NRS 338.020(1) and (2).

[536] NRS 338.150(1).

[537] *Harris Associates v. Clark County School Dist.*, 119 Nev. 638, 81 P.3d 532 (2003).

[538] NRS 338.150(2).

[539] NRS 338.153.

[540] NRS 338.485(2)(c).

[541] NRS 338.485(2)(d).

[542] NRS 338.485(3).

Change Orders on public works projects cannot be altered significantly without authorization of the SPWB or in some circumstances the legislature. The Manager of the SPWB may be authorized to handle changes by the Board, however, without such delegation, the SPWB must specifically authorize changes in excess of $200,000.[543] Moreover, if a change increases or decreases the square footage of a project authorized by the legislation by ten (10%) percent or more, such a modification must be presented to the legislature for approval.[544]

6:25 Payment and Performance Bond Claims

Under NRS 339.025(1), a contractor who undertakes a public work of improvement in excess of $100,000 is required to supply a payment bond in an amount of at least fifty percent of the contract price. As a matter of public policy, Mechanics liens are not permitted against public land,[545] and therefore the payment bond acts as a substitute for Mechanics lien rights.[546]

Subcontractors and material suppliers may make claims against the payment bond in order to obtain payment for their services, if the general contractor or subcontractors do not otherwise make payment. The protection of the payment bond is limited remedy, however, as only those who have a direct contract with the general contractor or one of its subcontractors may make a claim against the public work payment bond.

If a potential claimant on a public works project has no direct contract with the project's general contractor, but is employed by a subcontractor, the claimant must provide a preliminary notice within 30 days after first supplying labor or materials to the project.[547] The failure to provide the notice entirely will waive the claimant's right to make a claim upon the payment bond entirely,[548] and providing the notice later than 30 days after commencement of construction only serves to limit the amount of recovery that the bond claimant may obtain.[549] The 30 day notice should be served on the general

---

543 NAC 341.015(6).

544 NAC 341.017.

545 *Gill v. Paysee*, 48 Nev. 12, 226 P. 302 (1924). There are, however, some exceptions to this general rule. *See* discussion at Section 8:6, The Nevada Preliminary Notice.

546 Nevada law does not provide stop notice remedies as some states have enacted.

547 NRS 339.035(2)(a); *see* Form 6-1 in Appendix A.

548 *Garff v. J. R. Bradley Co.*, 84 Nev. 79, 436 P.2d 428 (1968); *Hartford Fire Ins. Co. v. Trustees of Constr. Indus.*, 125 Nev. 16, 208 P.3d 884 (2009).

contractor by certified mail, return receipt requested. The right to make a claim on a payment bond is limited to the third tier of claimants. Thus material suppliers to sub-subcontractors have no right of action against a Nevada public works payment bond.

A claimant without a direct contract with the general contractor must also serve the general contractor with a 90 day notice of payment bond claim, similar to that required on a federal project.[550] This 90 day notice must be served certified mail, return receipt requested, and must set forth the amount of the claim and the name of the subcontractor or debtor to whom the claimant supplied labor or materials. Failure to send the notice is fatal to the payment bond claim. The notice must be given within 90 days after a claimant has stopped furnishing work or materials to the project.

The governing body must provide a copy of the general contract and the performance and payment bonds issued by the general contractor if requested to do so. The application for a copy of these documents should be accompanied by an affidavit that the person requesting is an interested party.[551] Upon receipt of the application and affidavit, the governing body must provide a certified copy of the documents, which will be prima facie evidence of the contents execution and delivery of the bond for the public work.[552]

No claim may be made against the payment bond, unless the claimant has a direct contract with the general contractor or one of its subcontractors. Suit must be filed on a payment bond claim within one year of last supplying labor or materials to the project.[553] Suit may not be filed until 90 days after last supplying labor or materials.[554]

6:26. Performance Contracts for Cost-Saving Measures (Energy Retrofits)

A little known program was enacted in 2005 by the Nevada state legislature to let state performance contracts for operating cost-savings measures.[555] These programs are fairly unique public projects that are intended to pay for their own cost through

---

[549] The bond claimant may only recover for the labor, material, equipment, etc., provided 30 days prior to the service of the 30 day notice and that supplied thereafter. *Amfac Distribution Corp. v. Housing Authority of City of Las Vegas, Nev.*, 100 Nev. 573, 688 P.2d 318 (1984).

[550] NRS 339.035(2)(b); *see* Form 6-2 in Appendix A.

[551] *See* Form 6-3 in Appendix A.

[552] NRS 339.045.

[553] NRS 339.055.

[554] NRS 339.035(1).

[555] NRS 333A.010 to NRS 333A.150.

"operating cost savings."[556] realized by the governing body through "operating systems cost-savings measures."[557] They are contracted with specialized entities that have

---

[556] NRS 333A.030 provides:

> *"Operating cost savings" means any expenses that are eliminated or avoided on a long-term basis as a result of the installation or modification of equipment, or services performed by a qualified service company. The term does not include any savings that are realized solely because of a shift in the cost of personnel or other similar short-term cost savings.*

[557] NRS 333A.040 provides:

> *"Operating cost-savings measure" means any improvement, repair or alteration to a building, or any equipment, fixture or furnishing to be added or used in a building that is designed to reduce operating costs, including those costs related to electrical energy and demand, thermal energy, water consumption, waste disposal and contract-labor costs, and increase the operating efficiency of the building for the appointed functions that are cost-effective. The term includes, without limitation:*
> *1. Procurement of low-cost energy supplies, including electricity and natural gas.*
> *2. Procurement of cost savings as a result of outsourcing energy needs for electrical power, heating and cooling.*
> *3. Operational or maintenance labor savings resulting from reduced costs for maintenance contracts as provided through reduction of required maintenance or operating tasks, including, without limitation, replacement of filters and lighting products, and equipment failures.*
> *4. Investment in equipment, products and materials, and strategies for building operation, or any combination thereof, designed to reduce energy and other utility expenses, including, without limitation:*
> *(a) Costs for materials and labor required to replace old equipment with new, more efficient equipment.*
> *(b) Storm windows or doors, caulking or weather stripping, multiglazed windows or doors, heat-absorbing or heat-reflective glazed or coated windows or doors, reductions in glass area, and other modifications to windows and doors that will reduce energy consumption.*
> *(c) Automated or computerized energy control systems.*
> *(d) Replacement of, or modifications to, heating, ventilation or air-conditioning systems.*
> *(e) Replacement of, or modifications to, lighting fixtures.*
> *(f) Improvements to the indoor air quality of a building that conform to all requirements of an applicable building code.*
> *(g) Energy recovery systems.*
> *(h) Systems for combined cooling, heating and power that produce steam or other forms of energy, for use primarily within the building or a complex of buildings.*
> *(i) Installation of, or modifications to, existing systems for daylighting, including lighting control systems.*
> *(j) Installation of, or modification to, technologies that use renewable or alternative energy sources.*
> *(k) Programs relating to building operation that reduce operating costs, including, without limitation, computerized programs, training and other similar activities.*
> *(l) Programs for improvement of steam traps to reduce operating costs.*
> *(m) Devices that reduce water consumption in buildings, for lawns and for other irrigation applications.*

achieved certain certifications as "qualified service companies."[558] In sum, the governing body is required to enter into a performance contract with a qualified service company for the purchase and installation of an operating cost-saving measure to reduce operating costs related to energy, water or other operating costs.[559] The performance contract is not subject to any of the laws governing procurement of government contracts under NRS Chapter 333 or public contracting under NRS Chapter 333.[560] The qualified service companies are determined by the SPWB meeting a number of specific criteria. The SPWB is required to adopt qualifying criteria for the qualified service companies, and has done so in Nevada Revised Statutes Chapter 333A.[561] Once major concern of contractors was the lack of a statutory requirement that the qualified service companies be licensed as contractors with the State of Nevada, however, this issue has been established by the SPWB to be a minimum requirement.

Once the projects are completed, the governing body is required to perform service audits of the cost-savings measures to measure their success.[562] The governing bodies are authorized to retain third-party consultants to assist in the coordination of the work with the qualified service company selected for the project.

> *(n) Any additional improvements to building infrastructures that produce energy and operating cost savings, significantly reduce energy consumption or increase the operating efficiency of the buildings for their appointed functions, provided that such improvements comply with applicable building codes.*
> *(o) Trash compaction and waste minimization.*
> *5. Investment in educational programs relating to occupational behavior that are designed to reduce the consumption of energy or water, or both, and the generation of waste.*

558 NRS 333A.070 provides:

> *"Qualified service company" means a person with a record of established projects or a person with demonstrated technical, operational, financial and managerial capabilities to design and carry out operating cost-savings measures and other similar building improvements, and who has the ability to secure necessary financial measures to ensure related guarantees for operating cost savings.*

559 NRS 333A.075.

560 NRS 333A.075(1).

561 NRS 333A.120 provides:

> *Qualifications and application for placement on list. (NRS 333A.080, 341.070) Each applicant who desires to be placed on the qualified service company list must:*
> *1. Be licensed as a contractor pursuant to chapter 624 of NRS and qualified as a bidder pursuant to NRS 338.1379; and*
> *2. Submit an application to the Manager on a form prescribed by the Board.*

562 NRS 333A.082 and NRS 333A.084.

The project's financing is usually established through bonds or performance guarantee obligations of installation and purchase contracts or lease-purchase contracts with the suppliers of the materials or third parties. The governing body may not finance the contract through the qualified service company.[563] As a result, the performance contracts are not subject to competitive bidding requirements or any other restriction imposed upon the government for the purchase of goods or services.[564] However, the contractors performing the work must meet the prevailing wage obligations set forth in NRS 338.020 to NRS 338.090.[565]

6:27 PROMPT PAYMENT REQUIREMENTS

Similar to the provisions of NRS 624.606 to NRS 624.630, inclusive discussed in Chapter 3, Nevada has provided a prompt payment act that is applicable to public works of construction,[566] with the sole exception of NDOT projects.[567] Similar to the private works prompt payment act, a person involved on a public works project may not waive or modify any right obligation or liability imposed on him pursuant to the Nevada Public Works Prompt Payment Act. Likewise, any contract provision that attempts to so waive or modify the prompt payment act is void.[568] Likewise, any release or waive that must be provided by a contractor, subcontractor or supplier to receive a progress or retainage payment on a public work is always conditional and limited to the amount of the payment actually received.[569]

Payment requests may be submitted by a contractor to the governing body not less than on a monthly basis, unless the contract provides for a more frequent timeframe.[570] The public body must pay the contractor within 30 days after the contractor submits its invoicing.[571] There is a mandatory ten percent (10%) withholding on the payments made until the contract is 50% paid out, then the governing body has the option of not

---

563 NRS 333A.090.

564 NRS 333A.090(2)(b)(2).

565 NRS 333A.120.

566 NRS 338.400 to NRS 338.645.

567 NRS 338.480.

568 NRS 338.485.

569 NRS 338.490.

570 NRS 338.510.

571 NRS 338.515(1).

withholding additional retention amounts, so long as the governing body believes the work is properly progressing[572] for an ultimate five percent (5%) retention on the project. However, the governing body is not allowed to withhold retention on materials, supplies or equipment that are actually identified in the contract, have been delivered and stored in a location available for installation or use on the project, and are in short supply or were specially ordered for the project.[573]

The governing body may (but is not required to) withhold from the contractor's payment an amount it deems necessary to correct or repair work performed by the contractor which is not in conformance with the contract requirements.[574] In order to make that withholding, the governing body must submit a written notice to the contractor that it intends to withhold all or part of the progress payment. That notice must be given within 20 days of the contractor submitting the payment request to the governing body.[575] The written notice must include a specific and detailed explanation for the reason for withholding, including the amount to be withheld. The affected contractor may correct the condition giving rise to the withholding and then provide the governing body with a written notice of correction, which if accepted will require the governing body to pay the withheld money within 30 days following receipt of the next payment request.[576]

Unlike the private works prompt payment act, however, the contractor who has had its payment withheld cannot stop work on the public work. Instead, the affected contractor must be paid interest on the money wrongfully withheld.[577] The interest rate is the highest rates paid on a 90 day certificate of deposit as quoted by three separate financial institutions,[578] but only must be paid once a quarter when the interest rises to $500, annually if the interest never reaches the $500 level, or upon completion of the work and all money for the project becoming due, whichever occurs first.[579] All money withheld on a project becomes due and payable to the contractor upon the governing body occupying the project or the recording of a notice of completion for the project.[580] A

[572] NRS 338.515(1).

[573] NRS 338.515(2).

[574] NRS 338.525(1).

[575] NRS 338.525(2).

[576] NRS 338.525(3).

[577] NRS 338.530.

[578] NRS 338.515(6).

[579] NRS 338.515(6).

contractor may also file a petition with the district court for the issuance of a writ of mandamus to compel the governing body to either make payment due or to provide the appropriate written notice of the reason why payment was not made, though little direction to the district court is given as part of the statutory scheme.[581]

As for subcontractors and suppliers, a public works general contractor is required to pay to the subcontractor or supplier moneys intended by the governing body to be paid to that party. This payment amount is a "direct proportion" calculation to the amount of the contractor's billing that the subcontractor or supplier's billing totals.[582] The contractor must make the payment within 10 days of receipt from the governing body of the amount of payment made.[583] Retention amounts must correspond to that withheld from the contractor by the governing body under NRS 338.515.[584]

The contractor may also withhold payment made from the subcontractor, if within 10 days of receipt of payment from the governing body the contractor provides written notice of his intention to withhold to the subcontractor or supplier.[585] The written notice must provide the subcontractor or supplier the amount being withheld and a detailed explanation for the reasons for withholding. However, if the governing body pays the full amount of the subcontractor or supplier's request for payment to the contractor, the contractor may not withhold any money from the subcontractor.[586] If a contractor wrongfully withholds money from the subcontractor or supplier, the contractor will be required to pay interest on the money withheld.[587] Likewise, the aggrieved party may file a motion with the court for an order to show cause why the contractor should not pay the money withheld.[588] Once again, there is little direction provided to the district court in handling such a motion, however, it is fairly certain that the court is not required to make detailed findings of fact. The court is required to handle the motion on a summary basis, looking to submitted affidavits to make its decision.[589] As such, the

---

580 NRS 338.520.

581 NRS 338.630.

582 NRS 338.550(1).

583 NRS 338.550(2).

584 NRS 338.555.

585 NRS 338.560.

586 NRS 338.560(4)(b).

587 NRS 338.565.

588 NRS 338.635.

589 NRS 338.635(2).

application is not an "action" that commences a lawsuit and will not suffice to begin one. The court may issue an order compelling the contractor to pay wrongfully withheld amounts, or may issue an order confirming the amount is correctly withheld. The court is not empowered to enter a judgment, and presumably will enforce any order to pay withheld funds through contempt of court proceedings.[590]

[590] NRS 338.635(6).

CHAPTER 7 RESIDENTIAL CONSTRUCTION DEFECT CLAIMS

7:1 INTRODUCTION

Residential construction defect claims are governed in Nevada by a discrete set of statutes found in NRS 40.600 to NRS 40.770, inclusive. While ostensibly contained within the Nevada judicial system and operating within it, the construction defect claims are actually handled within a subsystem of the judicial branch with its own rules, procedures and operations seemingly unfazed by the other portions of the judicial functions. Construction defect cases are assigned to specific judges designated for the case type and are handled by their own local-local procedures handled down by the specific designated judges. Deemed complex simply by their nature, special masters are routinely appointed and mediators are immediately assigned to specific cases. Each year, usually in the fall, the designated trial court judges sit "en banc" to handout trial dates and set deadlines for the matters to proceed in a large, all cases and all participants hearing that last sometimes days, depending on the number of cases handled.

Because of the large volume of construction insurance defense tenders, there is a relatively small group of attorneys who frequently appear in the construction defect cases and over the years, separate and unwritten rules of procedure have been established which practitioners can only learn by attending the hearings, special master meetings and mediation sessions. On the whole, the process is not favored by anyone involved in the construction process--not developers, contractors, subcontractors or suppliers. In 2015, the Nevada legislature passed AB125[591] which in substantial ways gutted the provisions of Nevada's residential construction defect statutes. Yet, at least for the foreseeable future, construction defect lawsuits and the methodologies developed over the years most likely remain constant for worry that the ability to effectively manage and resolve these disputes will be lost. While this treatise again does not attempt to exhaust all the issues that can arise within construction defect lawsuits in general, instead we will focus on the Nevada issues that arise within those statutory provisions affectionately known as "Chapter 40" in Nevada judicial parlance.

At the time of printing, the Nevada Legislative Counsel Bureau had not released the updated statutes incorporating changes from the 2015 legislative session. Since the previous version of NRS Chapter 40 may remain in effect as cases filed previously work through the court system, reference will be made to note where and how the AB125 revisions affect Chapter 40's provisions. Of important note, AB125 had a staggered effective date for its various provisions.[592] Uniquely, the bill actually attempts to apply

---

591 AB125 bill text can be found here: http://leg.state.nv.us/Session/78th2015/Reports/history.cfm?ID=291

592 AB125 Section 21.

retroactively to alter certain provisions of potentially existing claims. Whether that attempt will withstand the inevitable legal challenges remains to be seen. Regardless, the staggered effective dates will be noted through the following information as applicable.

It is also fairly unknown how the trial courts will interpret the new statutes. Therefore, as the provisions of AB125 are discussed, commentary will be made from the approved legislative text or legislative intent garnered from the legislative committee minutes. How the new provisions will actually be put into practice will remain to be seen.[593]

7:2 Managing Customer Claims and Expectations

A construction book on Nevada construction law should provide some insight into the source of Nevada construction defect claims and make suggestions for how to avoid them in the first place. While the more cynical critics will assert that construction defect claims are mostly in the imagination of greedy construction defect plaintiff attorneys and their nefariously corrupt construction defect "experts," more accurate understanding of construction defect claims must begin with the service that developers and homebuilders provide to their customers who purchase single family homes, townhomes and condominiums. It is not a stretch to believe that most construction defect lawsuits are only asserted when numerous attempts to get needed repairs completed on a timely and professional basis are ignored. Once the homebuyer has

[593] Chapter 40 residential construction defect claims are a strongly political subject in Nevada. Until AB125 was enacted, construction industry interests and lobbyists had tried multiple times to get revisions made to the statutory provisions, without success. Only one change in 2003 was enacted, and thereafter the construction industry believed the revisions had numerous unintended consequences. The statutory scheme was the primary motivator for one of the largest FBI corruption investigations in Nevada history, leading to the conviction of more than 40 participants in the scheme, including lawyers, police officers, contractors, and various citizens. *See* http://www.reviewjournal.com/news/las-vegas/last-defendant-massive-hoa-scheme-sentenced-prison and related stories thereto. In 2015, it was mostly the unexpected change from Democratic majority to Republican majority in both the state Assembly and Senate that resulted in the passage of AB125. AB125 had been introduced on the first day of the legislative session and little more than a week later, a joint Assembly / Senate Judiciary Committee hearing was held to consider the bill. Testimony was largely one sided for those seeking reform and passage of the bill, with one lone lawyer speaking and one other supporter signed up against AB125's passage and 32 pages of listed attendees in support. *See Comments of Chairman Hansen, Minutes of the Assembly / Senate Joint Judiciary Committee hearing, February 11, 2015, pgs. 27 & 39.* The short time window between introduction and consideration of AB125 caused considerable partisan acrimony. *Id.*, at pages 28-38. With only 1 minor amendment, AB125 obtained final passage from the Assembly on February 13, 2015, and final passage from the Senate on February 18, 2015 on a largely partisan vote – just 15 days after it was introduced. It was signed into law on February 24, 2015 by Gov. Brian Sandoval as the first piece of legislation to become law from the 2015 legislative session. Certain provisions took effect immediately, including sections dealing with the applicable statute of limitation and statute of repose found in NRS 11.202 applying *"retroactively to actions in which the substantial completion of the improvement to the real property occurred before the effective date of this act."* AB125, Section 21(5). AB125's potential impact on the ability to assert a Nevada residential construction defect claim is enormous.

reached a level of dissatisfaction with the homebuilder that he feels without other alternative, the homebuilder turns to the construction defect attorney for assistance. By that time, the ability to resolve the dispute without invoking the reach of Chapter 40 is for all intents and purposes lost. And once that point is reached, the only losers in the situation is the homebuilder the subcontractors who constructed the home, and the homeowner. By fun, the winners are the attorneys and the experts.

For developers and general contractors, the best advice to avoid construction defect lawsuits is to set up comprehensive customer satisfaction and warranty programs that actually seek to fix repairs long before they become construction defect lawsuits. It is simple enough to hand a defect claim over to the developer's insurance company to resolve, but ultimately the cost of policy premiums, litigation expenses, self-insured retentions, policy cancellations, difficulty in finding replacement coverage and other financial elements, not to mention the substantial cost of customer dissatisfaction, disloyalty and complaints will outweigh the short term gains in failing to perform basic repairs. Further, the ability to resolve disputes with the homeowner without interference by attorneys is also lost once the homeowner retains counsel. Being proactive with customer and warranty service will stop the homeowner from seeking counsel to initiate a chapter 40 construction defect proceeding.

And perhaps more importantly, the acts of seeking repair solutions can establish credibility in the eyes of those who may ultimately sit on juries. In Nevada, there was only not one reported defense verdict in a Chapter 40 construction defect case since the construction defect statutes were first enacted in 1995. There have been, however, some insignificant judgment awards of late in cases where those accused of construction defects were able to demonstrate serious and good faith attempts to repair defects, even though some of those defects were questionable. When this has occurred, the jury awards have been under previous offers of judgment, which allowed for the recovery of attorneys fees and costs against the plaintiffs, thereby nullifying the effects of the verdicts. These cases prove that serious customer service will often times carry the day in the face of questionable defect claims.

The impact of AB125 on these claims has yet to be fully realized, but it will undoubtedly be substantial. In many ways, AB125's revisions allow homebuilders to return to poor customer service and denial of warranty claims with impunity. These effects will be explained in the following sections.

7:3 Applicability of Residential Defect Statutes

Of significant concern to Nevada construction industry members is the reach of the statutory scheme. Under previous Chapter 40, a construction defect was defined as:

[A] defect in the design, construction, manufacture, repair or landscaping of a new residence, of an alteration of or addition to an existing residence, or of an appurtenance and includes, without limitation, the design, construction, manufacture, repair or landscaping of a new residence, of an alteration of or addition to an existing residence, or of an appurtenance:

1. Which is done in violation of law, including, without limitation, in violation of local codes or ordinances;

2. Which proximately causes physical damage to the residence, an appurtenance or the real property to which the residence or appurtenance is affixed;

3. Which is not completed in a good and workmanlike manner in accordance with the generally accepted standard of care in the industry for that type of design, construction, manufacture, repair or landscaping; or

4. Which presents an unreasonable risk of injury to a person or property.[594]

Under this definition, the construction defect must be found in a "new residence" or in "an alteration or addition to an existing residence." A fair amount of litigation has arisen over the definition of "new residence" within the meaning of this statute, especially as apartment complexes started to become converted into condominiums and sold to new buyers. What happened when there were construction defects in the original construction, but that work was completed years previous when building codes were substantially different than when the units were converted for sale. Would Chapter 40 apply to those original defects that were never previously reported?

In *Westpark Owners' Ass'n v. Eighth Judicial Dist. Court ex rel. County of Clark,*[595] the Nevada Supreme Court reviewed a condominium conversion claim involving 108 apartment units which were converted and sold as condos seven years after they were originally constructed. The Developer (and the trial court) had determined that the units were neither "residences" (as defined by NRS 40.630), nor "new" (under NRS 40.615), and therefore the owners did not have any claims under Chapter 40 to assert against the Developer. On these points the Nevada Supreme Court reversed the trial court's ruling. First, the Court determined that the trial court was incorrect in declaring the conversions were not "residences" under NRS 40.630.[596] Under a plain reading of the statute, the conversions qualified as "residences" upon sale to the purchasers. Where the trial court was correct was in determining that the converted units were not "new."

---

[594] NRS 40.615.

[595] *Westpark Owners' Ass'n v. Eighth Judicial Dist. Court ex rel. County of Clark,* 123 Nev. 349, 167 P.3d 421 (2007).

[596] NRS 40.630 provides:

> *"Residence" means any dwelling in which title to the individual units is transferred to the owners.*

In seeking a definition of the term "new residence" the Court struggled with its equal obligations to construe Chapter 40 with the legislation's intent to protect homebuyers by providing a proves to hold contractors liable for defective original construction, while avoiding an interpretation of the law which would lead to an absurd result. Obviously, a dwelling lived in for several years could not be considered "new" if it was eventually sold. But allowing a developer to circumvent its responsibility through use of units as "model homes" or leasing them to "straw-men" until a certain time period expired could not be allowed either. Ultimately, to bridge the gap the Court created a new rule, concluding *"that a residence is 'new' when it is a product of original construction that has been unoccupied as a dwelling from the completion of its construction until the point of sale."* Because the 108 units had been occupied by renters for seven years after they were constructed, they could not be "new" under the Court's definition. Therefore, Chapter 40 claims were not available for any defects existing as part of the original construction of the units.

The Court did, however, reverse the trial court to allow the homebuyers to sue under Chapter 40 for any defects found to exist in any modification or alteration made during the conversion for sale. Likewise, the Court also allowed the case to proceed as to other claims the homebuyers might have had outside of the Chapter 40 matrix, such as for breach of any express warranty made during the sale.

The *Westpark* decision was hailed by the construction defect defense bar as potentially eliminating the application of Chapter 40 claims anytime a single family residence had been sold to someone other than its original purchaser. While a significant stretch, in a subsequent construction defect case the defense argued that under *Westpark*, any home that had previously been occupied as a dwelling before the subsequent owners obtained title to the homes and commenced a lawsuit for the alleged construction defects therein could not constitute a "new residence" under NRS 624.615.[597] The Nevada Supreme Court disagreed finding that such a ruling would:

> *undermine the Legislature's intent to provide an expansive remedy for homeowners and protection for developers and leads to disparate treatment among otherwise similarly situated homeowners. Instead, any home that is a product of original construction, unoccupied as a dwelling from the completion of its construction until the point of its original sale, constitutes a "new residence" for NRS Chapter 40 purposes. . . .*[598]

---

[597] *Anse, Inc. v. Eighth Judicial Dist. Court of State ex rel. County of Clark,* 124 Nev. 862, 864, 192 P.3d 738, 740 (2008).

[598] *Anse, Inc. v. Eighth Judicial Dist. Court of State ex rel. County of Clark,* 124, Nev. 862, 865, 192 P.3d 738, 740 (2008).

As such, NRS Chapter 40 will only apply to new construction which has been unoccupied until its primary sale. Again, in the context of a condominium conversion from an apartment building, NRS Chapter 40 would not apply to any defects arising from the original construction of the apartment units, but would apply to any construction performed during the conversion process to prepare the units for sale.[599]

Since Chapter 40 does not apply to any building that is not occupied as a residence, it is understandable that such statutes do not apply to any building which is not occupied as a residence. However, as Nevada has entered the building boom of mixed use developments, commercial elements connected to residential units may be found to be encompassed by the statutory scheme. NRS 40.615 applies to a residential unit and to "an appurtenance" to the residence. NRS 40.605(1) defines "appurtenance" as:

> *a structure, installation, facility, amenity or other improvement that is appurtenant to or benefits one or more residences, but is not a part of the dwelling unit. The term includes, without limitation, the parcel of real property, recreational facilities, golf courses, walls, sidewalks, driveways, landscaping, common elements and limited common elements other than those described in NRS 116.2102, and other structures, installations, facilities and amenities associated with or benefiting one or more residences.*

Definitively, commercial use developments which are part of the mixed use development containing the residential unit will be included in the definition of appurtenance to which Chapter 40 applies. As such, commercial contractors should be careful in obtaining insurance coverage for mixed use development construction to ensure that the coverage will not be affected by the combination of commercial appurtenances which arguably is associated with or benefiting any of the residential units.

AB125 amends NRS 40.615 substantially. It now reads:

> *[A] defect in the design, construction, manufacture, repair or landscaping of a new residence, of an alteration of or addition to an existing residence, or of an appurtenance and includes, without limitation, the design, construction, manufacture, repair or landscaping of a new residence, of an alteration of or addition to an existing residence, or of an appurtenance:*
>
> *1. Which presents an unreasonable risk of injury to a person or property; or*
>
> *2. Which is not completed in a good and workmanlike manner and proximately causes physical damage to the residence, an appurtenance or the real property to which the residence or appurtenance is affixed.*[600]

---

[599] *Westpark Owners' Ass'n v. Eighth Judicial Dist. Court ex rel. County of Clark*, 123 Nev. 349, 167 P.3d 421 (2007).

[600] AB125, Section 6.

While the definition still contains the limitation as applicable only to a "new residence" as discussed in *Westpark*, the actual condition must (1) actually be resulting from the contractor's failure to perform the work in a good and workmanlike manner *and* actually be the legal cause of physical damage to the improvement *or* (2) present an unreasonable risk of personal injury, in order to be considered "defective". This is a massive change. Previous law would consider any deviation from the minimum requirements of building code, no matter its actual impact on the construction's performance, as a defect. Under AB125 that same deviation from code only becomes a defect if it also actually causes physical damage. This alteration is obviously addressed to claims previously asserted that were minor building code infractions but had no provable or demonstrable impact on the performance of residence. For example, if building code minimum requires shear-wall plywood nail spacing to be no greater than 12 inches on center, measuring the actual nail spacing to be 12 1/8 inches would be a code violation. The engineering impact on the resistance to shearing forces from such a deviation is almost imperceptible. Under the previous definition, the deviation from the building code would have been considered a "constructional defect" and liability would most likely have been demonstrated merely from the deviation. Under the AB125 definition, the deviation can only result in liability if the complainer demonstrates the deviation also is causing physical damage to the residence. A seemingly much higher standard.

Arguably, there must be *some* physical damage from the minor deviation. Over the span of 10' x 16' shear wall, with studs 16" on center, there should be 11 nails per stud, for 10 studs (not counting king-studs) or 110 nails on the shear-wall. The deviation noted above would only add 1¼" of space per stud. What this deviation's impact on specific shear-wall load handling capability would be is a matter of expert analysis but, theoretically, it must have *some* impact. Whether or not that impact equates to physical damage is, again, an issue for expert testimony. While this alone may still allow for a constructional defect case to get to a jury, the other amendments from AB125 will further dis-incentivize litigation over such issues.

7:4 Contractors under Chapter 40

Homeowners might be surprised to learn that the definition of a contractor under Chapter 40 who may be liable for construction defects and the damages associated therewith include themselves, if they performed any work on the residence which is later determined to be defective construction. NRS 40.620 provides:

"Contractor" means a person who, with or without a license issued pursuant to chapter 624 of NRS, by himself or herself or through the person's agents, employees or subcontractors:

1. Develops, constructs, alters, repairs, improves or landscapes a residence, appurtenance or any part thereof;

2. Develops a site for a residence, appurtenance or any part thereof; or

3. Sells a residence or appurtenance, any part of which the person, by himself or herself or through the person's agents, employees or subcontractors, has developed, constructed, altered, repaired, improved or landscaped.

This definition clearly includes any homeowner who through contractors or others constructions alters or repairs any residence. As such, the individual homeowner who improves his property is liable for construction defects to subsequent purchasers of the dwelling. While in practical application individuals would rarely be pursued for construction defect claims in absence of a significant amount of applicable insurance coverage, the statutory scheme reaches to individuals as well as professional developers, homebuilders and contractors.

7:5 Notice requirements

Under the original law, before a constructional defect case is brought in Nevada, there are a number of notice requirements which need to be provided to place the statutory scheme in effect. Before a lawsuit may be commenced on construction defects or before any existing complaint may be amended to add claims of new or additional construction defects, the claimant must give the contractor notice of the defect and the opportunity to inspect and the election to repair the defective condition.[601] Likewise, if there is a home

---

[601] NRS 40.645 provides:

> *1. Except as otherwise provided in this section and NRS 40.670, before a claimant commences an action or amends a complaint to add a cause of action for a constructional defect against a contractor, subcontractor, supplier or design professional, the claimant:*
> *(a) Must give written notice by certified mail, return receipt requested, to the contractor, at the contractor's address listed in the records of the State Contractors' Board or in the records of the office of the county or city clerk or at the contractor's last known address if his address is not listed in those records; and*
> *(b) May give written notice by certified mail, return receipt requested, to any subcontractor, supplier or design professional known to the claimant who may be responsible for the constructional defect, if the claimant knows that the contractor is no longer licensed in this State or that the contractor no longer acts as a contractor in this State.*
> *2. The notice given pursuant to subsection 1 must:*
> *(a) Include a statement that the notice is being given to satisfy the requirements of this section;*
> *(b) Specify in reasonable detail the defects or any damages or injuries to each residence or appurtenance that is the subject of the claim; and*

repair warranty that covers the home, AB125 adds the additional restriction that a notice of constructional defect cannot be sent until the home repair warranty insurer formally rejects the claim under the home warranty policy.[602] The notice must be

---

(c) Describe in reasonable detail the cause of the defects if the cause is known, the nature and extent that is known of the damage or injury resulting from the defects and the location of each defect within each residence or appurtenance to the extent known.
3. Notice that includes an expert opinion concerning the cause of the constructional defects and the nature and extent of the damage or injury resulting from the defects which is based on a valid and reliable representative sample of the components of the residences or appurtenances may be used as notice of the common constructional defects within the residences or appurtenances to which the expert opinion applies.
4. Except as otherwise provided in subsection 5, one notice may be sent relating to all similarly situated owners of residences or appurtenances within a single development that allegedly have common constructional defects if:
(a) An expert opinion is obtained concerning the cause of the common constructional defects and the nature and extent of the damage or injury resulting from the common constructional defects;
(b) That expert opinion concludes that based on a valid and reliable representative sample of the components of the residences and appurtenances included in the notice, it is the opinion of the expert that those similarly situated residences and appurtenances may have such common constructional defects; and
(c) A copy of the expert opinion is included with the notice.
5. A representative of a homeowner's association may send notice pursuant to this section on behalf of an association that is responsible for a residence or appurtenance if the representative is acting within the scope of the representative's duties pursuant to chapter 116 or 117 of NRS.
6. Notice is not required pursuant to this section before commencing an action if:
(a) The contractor, subcontractor, supplier or design professional has filed an action against the claimant; or
(b) The claimant has filed a formal complaint with a law enforcement agency against the contractor, subcontractor, supplier or design professional for threatening to commit or committing an act of violence or a criminal offense against the claimant or the property of the claimant.

[602] AB125 Section 14 revises NRS 40.650(3) to provide:

(3) If a residence or appurtenance that is the subject of the claim is covered by a homeowner's warranty that is purchased by or on behalf of a claimant pursuant to NRS 690B.100 to 690B.180, inclusive:
(a) A claimant may not send a notice pursuant to NRS 40.645 or pursue a claim pursuant to NRS 40.600 to NRS 40.695, inclusive, and sections 2 and 3 of this act unless the claimant has first submitted a claim under the homeowner's warranty and the insurer has denied the claim.
(b) A claimant must include in a notice given pursuant to NRS 40.645 only claims for the constructional defects that were denied by the insurer.
(c) If coverage under a homeowner's warranty is denied by an insurer in bad faith, the homeowner and the contractor, subcontractor, supplier or design professional have a right of action for the sums that would have been paid if coverage had been provided, plus reasonable attorneys' fees and costs.

provided by certified mail, return receipt requested, and must specify that the notice is sent to satisfy the requirements of NRS Chapter 40, and specifically identify the defects, damages or injuries and describe "in reasonable detail" the cause, location of the defect and the nature and extent of the damage caused thereby. If the defect is claimed to be a common defect among multiple residences, the notice may include an expert report based on a "valid and reliable sample" of the residences. This notice is not required if the complaint alleging construction defects is in response to a lawsuit filed by the contractor, or if the claimant has filed a formal criminal complaint against the contractor for threatening to or actually committing an act of violence against the claimant or his property.[603]

A common complaint of construction defect defense counsel is that the claimant has not provided sufficient information about the defective condition or the location thereof to afford the contractor a legitimate opportunity to cure the defective condition. In 2003, the Nevada Legislature gave residential developers and contractors the right to repair alleged construction defects before the homeowner could commence litigation against them. In practice, however, the right to repair seemed realistically limited to defect claims involving only a couple of homes. Once the number of homes increased, the right to repair was essentially lost. Plaintiff construction defect attorneys would provide extrapolated defect lists, which in most cases did not adequately inform the affected contractors of any actual defects, nor their supposed locations within the residence. Without such information, the contractor had to guess where any actual defect may be discovered. The cost, time and futility of such exercises effectively deprived the contractors of their statutorily mandated right to repair.

To compound this issue, the extrapolated defect notices provided by plaintiffs rarely met statutory requirements. An extrapolated notice required the defect claims to be based on a "valid and reliable representative sample" of the homes involved in the defect claims. Only if the sample provided a statistically valid determination that the defects were common within the community could the notice be sufficient to put the contractor on notice. But defect experts rarely attempt to justify their allegations of common

---

> *(d) Statutes of limitation or repose applicable to a claim based on a constructional defect governed by NRS 40.600 to NRS 40.695, inclusive, and sections 2 and 3 of this act are tolled from the time notice of the claim under the homeowner's warranty is submitted to the insurer until 30 days after the insurer rejects the claim in who or in part, in writing.*

[603] This claim of construction defect has been used as a defense to contractors asserting legitimate payment claims against homeowners who refuse to pay for work performed. If the homeowner asserts construction defect claims under the previous Chapter 40 statutes, the contractor will often lose control of the claim and the mechanics lien or other request for payment can be lost in the maze of the construction defect machine. One significant unexpected consequence of the 2003 legislative reforms was the allowance of a counter-claim for construction defects without requiring the claimant to provide notice and the opportunity to cure.

constructional defect claims with statistically reliable examinations. It was not common for contractors to be provided with data to verify the claims of valid and reliable sampling, and there was little if any care taken to assure that the units sampled for testing were representative of the entire community. Most of the time, a contractor could not tell from the reports which units were tested, let alone what defects were found in those units. Plaintiff's attorneys would refuse to allow the contractors to question the homeowners to determine what was wrong. With these impediments, few multi-unit constructional defect claims ended up being repaired without years of litigation.

This issue was addressed by the Nevada Supreme Court in *D.R. Horton, Inc. v. Eighth Judicial Dist. Court ex rel. County of Clark,*[604] where the Nevada Supreme Court determined that an "adequate extrapolated pre-litigation notice must have a reasonable statistical basis to describe the alleged defects and their locations in reasonable detail sufficient to afford contractors a meaningful opportunity to repair the alleged defects," and established the Reasonable Threshold Test "to guide district courts in making written findings on whether a pre-litigation notice satisfies that threshold." If the extrapolated constructional defect notice meets the test, district courts have wide discretion to determine the adequacy of the notice, if challenged by the contractor.

The Court found that it was clear that the Legislature intended to preserve an opportunity for contractors to repair the homes they construct, and that contractors are entitled to reasonable notice of alleged defects in their homes so that they can verify and repair those defects before litigation begins. While contractors are responsible for the costs of making repairs if they choose to do so, the homeowner asserting defects exist have "a duty to provide reasonable notice of what defects exist and a reasonable approximation of the location of those defects."

Using an extrapolated defect notice was intended by the Legislature to allow homeowners to use expert opinion and extrapolation to give notice of common defects in multiple homes, so long as the notice satisfies the "reasonable detail" requirements of NRS 40.645(2). Extrapolation encompasses the statistical use by an expert witness of a valid and reliable representative sample to formulate an opinion that similarly situated residences may have common constructional defects. However, the Court determined that the scope of the extrapolated notice must be narrow. Homes must be divided into subsets. Homes included within the scope of an extrapolated notice typically will be similarly situated only if they are part of a subset of homes within the development that demonstrate the defect. They may be subset by a particular product or type of

---

[604] *D.R. Horton, Inc. v. Eighth Judicial Dist. Court ex rel. County of Clark*, 123 Nev. 468, 168 P.3d 731 (2007).

construction used. Regardless of the limited category, an extrapolated notice is valid only if it identifies the subset or characteristics of the subset to which it applies.

The district court should require the claimants' expert to test and verify the existence of the alleged defect in at least one of the homes in each subset of homes included within the scope of the extrapolated notice. The claimants must thereafter provide the address of each home tested and clearly identify the subset of homes to which the pre-litigation notice applies, and investigate further to narrow their notice to an identified subset of homes within the community that has the purported defect. Thereafter, the claimants should test and verify the defect in at least one home from each subset of homes in the community, and then extrapolate the percentage of homes within each subset that they believe are likely to contain the defect. The district courts must then employ their wide discretion in determining whether a valid and representative sample has been used for the size and make-up of each subset, and may determine that a notice is not reasonable unless a defect is confirmed in more than one home in each subset.

The Court indicated that these guidelines merely set the minimum threshold that an extrapolated pre-litigation notice must satisfy. Once the district court determines that a notice is reasonable, the contractor bears the burden of verifying and repairing the alleged defects in every home in the subset of homes identified in the extrapolated notice. In practice, however, the reasonable threshold test has not been given significant support at the trial court level. Still, it is incumbent upon construction defect defense counsel to raise the issue of sufficiency of defect notice, especially in large complex defect cases where common construction defects are alleged.

AB125 has again significantly impacted the Notice requirements of NRS 40.645,[605] to address many of the unfairness and unexpected consequence concerns raised by

---

605 Under AB125, Section 8, NRS 40.645 will now read as follows:

> *1. Except as otherwise provided in this section and NRS 40.670, before a claimant commences an action or amends a complaint to add a cause of action for a constructional defect against a contractor, subcontractor, supplier or design professional, the claimant:*
> *(a) Must give written notice by certified mail, return receipt requested, to the contractor, at the contractor's address listed in the records of the State Contractors' Board or in the records of the office of the county or city clerk or at the contractor's last known address if his address is not listed in those records; and*
> *(b) May give written notice by certified mail, return receipt requested, to any subcontractor, supplier or design professional known to the claimant who may be responsible for the constructional defect, if the claimant knows that the contractor is no longer licensed in this State or that the contractor no longer acts as a contractor in this State.*
> *2. The notice given pursuant to subsection 1 must:*
> *(a) Include a statement that the notice is being given to satisfy the requirements of this section;*

contractors and their counsel. These changes are again designed to address the concern that under the previous Chapter 40 cases, an expert report providing unclear or inaccurate construction defect descriptions would lead contractors seeking to actually repair alleged defects on a very expensive search for alleged defects that may not exist or cannot be precisely located. Now, when a notice of construction defect is sent, the notice itself must specifically identify the *exact* location and nature of the defect and damage it causes to the new residence involved. More importantly, the notice must now be signed by a person giving the notice, and if on behalf of others, must certify that description of the nature and location of the defect under the penalty of perjury.[606]

7:6 RESPONSE OF CONTRACTORS TO A CHAPTER 40 DEFECT NOTICE

Once the contractor receives the construction defect notice, the contractor must do several things to preserve both his right to repair the defect and to preserve his right to seek indemnity and contribution from the subcontractors who may have performed the work itself. NRS 40.6452[607] requires that the contractor within 60 days of receiving the

---

> *(b) Identify in specific detail each defect, damage and injury to each residence or appurtenance that is subject of the claim, including, without limitation, the exact location of each such defect, damage and injury;*
> *(c) Describe in reasonable detail the cause of the defects if the cause is known and the nature and extent that is known of the damage or injury resulting from the defects; and*
> *(d) Include a signed statement, by each named owner of a residence or appurtenance in the notice, that each such owner verifies that such defect, damage and injury specified in the notice exists in the residence or appurtenance owned by him or her. If such a notice is sent on behalf of a homeowner's association, the statement required by this paragraph must be signed under the penalty of perjury by a member of the executive board or an officer of the homeowners' association.*
> *3. A representative of a homeowner's association may send notice pursuant to this section on behalf of an association if the representative is acting within the scope of the representative's duties pursuant to chapter 116 or 117 of NRS.*
> *4. Notice is not required pursuant to this section before commencing an action if:*
> *(a) The contractor, subcontractor, supplier or design professional has filed an action against the claimant; or*
> *(b) The claimant has filed a formal complaint with a law enforcement agency against the contractor, subcontractor, supplier or design professional for threatening to commit or committing an act of violence or a criminal offense against the claimant or the property of the claimant.*

[606] *See* AB125 Section 8.

[607] NRS 40.6452 provides:

> *1. Except as otherwise provided in subsection 2, not later than 60 days after a contractor receives a notice pursuant to subsection 4 of NRS 40.645 which alleges common constructional defects to residences or appurtenances within a single development and which complies with the requirements of subsection 4 of NRS 40.645 for giving such notice,*

the contractor may respond to the named owners of the residences or appurtenances in the notice in the manner set forth in NRS 40.6472.

2. The contractor may provide a disclosure of the notice of the alleged common constructional defects to each unnamed owner of a residence or appurtenance within the development to whom the notice may apply in the manner set forth in this section. The disclosure must be sent by certified mail, return receipt requested, to the home address of each such owner. The disclosure must be mailed not later than 60 days after the contractor receives the notice of the alleged common constructional defects, except that if the common constructional defects may pose an imminent threat to health and safety, the disclosure must be mailed as soon as reasonably practicable, but not later than 20 days after the contractor receives the notice.

3. The disclosure of a notice of alleged common constructional defects provided by a contractor to the unnamed owners to whom the notice may apply pursuant to subsection 2 must include, without limitation:

(a) A description of the alleged common constructional defects identified in the notice that may exist in the residence or appurtenance;

(b) A statement that notice alleging common constructional defects has been given to the contractor which may apply to the owner;

(c) A statement advising the owner that the owner has 30 days within which to request the contractor to inspect the residence or appurtenance to determine whether the residence or appurtenance has the alleged common constructional defects;

(d) A form which the owner may use to request such an inspection or a description of the manner in which the owner may request such an inspection;

(e) A statement advising the owner that if the owner fails to request an inspection pursuant to this section, no notice shall be deemed to have been given by the owner for the alleged common constructional defects; and

(f) A statement that if the owner chooses not to request an inspection of the owner's residence or appurtenance, the owner is not precluded from sending a notice pursuant to NRS 40.645 individually or commencing an action or amending a complaint to add a cause of action for a constructional defect individually after complying with the requirements set forth in NRS 40.600 to 40.695, inclusive.

4. If an unnamed owner requests an inspection of the owner's residence or appurtenance in accordance with subsection 3, the contractor must provide the response required pursuant to NRS 40.6472 not later than 45 days after the date on which the contractor receives the request.

5. If a contractor who receives a notice pursuant to subsection 4 of NRS 40.645 does not provide a disclosure to unnamed owners as authorized pursuant to this section, the owners of the residences or appurtenances to whom the notice may apply may commence an action for the constructional defect without complying with any other provision set forth in NRS 40.600 to 40.695, inclusive. This subsection does not establish or prohibit the right to maintain a class action.

6. If a contractor fails to provide a disclosure to an unnamed owner to whom the notice of common constructional defects was intended to apply:

(a) The contractor shall be deemed to have waived the contractor's right to inspect and repair any common constructional defect that was identified in the notice with respect to that owner; and

(b) The owner is not required to comply with the provisions set forth in NRS 40.645 or 40.647 before commencing an action or amending a complaint to add a cause of action based on that common constructional defect.

notice of construction defect claim to respond to the notice by requesting of each named homeowner in the notice the right to inspect the project for alleged defects. Further, the Contractor can elect to request to inspect the homes of unnamed homeowners in the affected community. The unnamed homeowners may request an inspection of the residence, as well. However, if the unnamed homeowners do not request an inspection, they cannot commence a separate action until they provide their own notice of constructional defects to the contractor as required by NRS 40.645. If the contractor fails to provide the notice to the unnamed homeowners, the contractor waives his right to inspect and repair the alleged defects, as well as his right to receive notice of the defect from those unnamed homeowners.

Likewise, the contractor is obligated, in order to preserve any claims of warranty or indemnity, to provide all potentially liable subcontractors and suppliers notice of the claimed construction defects within 30 days of receipt of the Chapter 40 defect notice.[608]

---

[608] NRS 40.646 provides:

> *1. Except as otherwise provided in subsection 2, not later than 30 days after the date on which a contractor receives notice of a constructional defect pursuant to NRS 40.645, the contractor shall forward a copy of the notice by certified mail, return receipt requested, to the last known address of each subcontractor, supplier or design professional whom the contractor reasonably believes is responsible for a defect specified in the notice.*
> *2. If a contractor does not provide notice as required pursuant to subsection 1, the contractor may not commence an action against the subcontractor, supplier or design professional related to the constructional defect unless the contractor demonstrates that, after making a good faith effort, the contractor was unable to identify the subcontractor, supplier or design professional whom the contractor believes is responsible for the defect within the time provided pursuant to subsection 1.*
> *3. Except as otherwise provided in subsection 4, not later than 30 days after receiving notice from the contractor pursuant to this section, the subcontractor, supplier or design professional shall inspect the alleged constructional defect in accordance with subsection 1 of NRS 40.6462 and provide the contractor with a written statement indicating:*
> *(a) Whether the subcontractor, supplier or design professional has elected to repair the defect for which the contractor believes the subcontractor, supplier or design professional is responsible; and*
> *(b) If the subcontractor, supplier or design professional elects to repair the defect, an estimate of the length of time required for the repair, and at least two proposed dates on and times at which the subcontractor, supplier or design professional is able to begin making the repair.*
> *4. If the notice of a constructional defect forwarded by the contractor was given pursuant to subsection 4 of NRS 40.645 and the contractor provides a disclosure of the notice of the alleged common constructional defects to the unnamed owners to whom the notice may apply pursuant to NRS 40.6452:*
> *(a) The contractor shall, in addition to the notice provided pursuant to subsection 1, upon receipt of a request for an inspection, forward a copy of the request to or notify each subcontractor, supplier or design professional who may be responsible for the alleged defect of the request not later than 5 working days after receiving such a request; and*

AB125 has made this requirement stronger by eliminating options of contractors to provide subcontractors, material suppliers and design professionals notice of the claims.[609] The subcontractors, suppliers and design professionals likewise have the right to request an inspection of the alleged construction defects and to exercise a right to repair the defective condition before litigation is commenced.[610] Again, AB125

> *(b) Not later than 20 days after receiving notice from the contractor of such a request, the subcontractor, supplier or design professional shall inspect the alleged constructional defect in accordance with subsection 2 of NRS 40.6462 and provide the contractor with a written statement indicating:*
> *(1) Whether the subcontractor, supplier or design professional has elected to repair the defect for which the contractor believes the subcontractor, supplier or design professional is responsible; and*
> *(2) If the subcontractor, supplier or design professional elects to repair the defect, an estimate of the length of time required for the repair, and at least two proposed dates on and times at which the subcontractor, supplier or design professional is able to begin making the repair.*
> *5. If a subcontractor, supplier or design professional elects to repair the constructional defect, the contractor or claimant may hold the subcontractor liable for any repair which does not eliminate the defect.*

609 AB125 Section 9 revises NRS 40.646 to read:

> *1. Except as otherwise provided in subsection 2, not later than 30 days after the date on which a contractor receives notice of a constructional defect pursuant to NRS 40.645, the contractor shall forward a copy of the notice by certified mail, return receipt requested, to the last known address of each subcontractor, supplier or design professional whom the contractor reasonably believes is responsible for a defect specified in the notice.*
> *2. If a contractor does not provide notice as required pursuant to subsection 1, the contractor may not commence an action against the subcontractor, supplier or design professional related to the constructional defect unless the contractor demonstrates that, after making a good faith effort, the contractor was unable to identify the subcontractor, supplier or design professional whom the contractor believes is responsible for the defect within the time provided pursuant to subsection 1.*
> *3. Not later than 30 days after receiving notice from the contractor pursuant to this section, the subcontractor, supplier or design professional shall inspect the alleged constructional defect in accordance with NRS 40.6462 and provide the contractor with a written statement indicating:*
> *(a) Whether the subcontractor, supplier or design professional has elected to repair the defect for which the contractor believes the subcontractor, supplier or design professional is responsible; and*
> *(b) If the subcontractor, supplier or design professional elects to repair the defect, an estimate of the length of time required for the repair, and at least two proposed dates on and times at which the subcontractor, supplier or design professional is able to begin making the repair.*
> *4. If a subcontractor, supplier or design professional elects to repair the constructional defect, the contractor or claimant may hold the subcontractor liable for any repair which does not eliminate the defect.*

610 NRS 40.6462 provides:

substantially revises the rules for subcontractor, supplier and design professional inspections.[611] If the contractor fails to provide the notice of defect to the subcontractors and suppliers timely, the contractor cannot seek to recover from that subcontractor or supplier for the alleged defects or any indemnification. However, like the contractors, the subcontractors and suppliers are at a further disadvantage if the original notice of construction defects fails to properly or sufficiently identify the defect and its location in the affected property.

The claimants must provide the contractors, subcontractors and suppliers reasonable opportunity to inspect and repair the defects if requested to do so. Failure to provide that opportunity requires the Court to dismiss or stay any lawsuit filed as a result of the defect claim until the opportunity to inspect or repair is provided.[612] Once again, AB125

> *1. Except as otherwise provided in subsection 2, after notice of a constructional defect is given to a contractor pursuant to NRS 40.645, the claimant shall, upon reasonable notice, allow the contractor and each subcontractor, supplier or design professional who may be responsible for the alleged defect reasonable access to the residence or appurtenance that is the subject of the notice to determine the nature and extent of a constructional defect and the nature and extent of repairs that may be necessary. To the extent possible, the persons entitled to inspect shall coordinate and conduct the inspections in a manner which minimizes the inconvenience to the claimant.*
> *2. If notice is given to the contractor pursuant to subsection 4 of NRS 40.645, the contractor and each subcontractor, supplier or design professional who may be responsible for the defect do not have the right to inspect the residence or appurtenance of an owner who is not named in the notice unless the owner requests the inspection in the manner set forth in NRS 40.6452. If the owner does not request the inspection, the owner shall be deemed not to have provided notice pursuant to NRS 40.645.*

611 AB125 Section 10 revises NRS 40.6462 to read as follows:

> *After notice of a constructional defect is given to a contractor pursuant to NRS 40.645, the claimant shall, upon reasonable notice, allow the contractor and each subcontractor, supplier or design professional who may be responsible for the alleged defect reasonable access to the residence or appurtenance that is the subject of the notice to determine the nature and extent of a constructional defect and the nature and extent of repairs that may be necessary. To the extent possible, the persons entitled to inspect shall coordinate and conduct the inspections in a manner which minimizes the inconvenience to the claimant.*

612 NRS 40.647 provides:

> *1. Except as otherwise provided in NRS 40.6452, after notice of a constructional defect is given pursuant to NRS 40.645, before a claimant may commence an action or amend a complaint to add a cause of action for a constructional defect against a contractor, subcontractor, supplier or design professional, the claimant must:*
> *(a) Allow an inspection of the alleged constructional defect to be conducted pursuant to NRS 40.6462; and*
> *(b) Allow the contractor, subcontractor, supplier or design professional a reasonable opportunity to repair the constructional defect or cause the defect to be repaired if an election to repair is made pursuant to NRS 40.6472.*

places additional restrictions on claimants when the inspections occur, in order to preserve the defect claims.[613]

Once the inspection is made, the contractor (having received responses from the subcontractors and suppliers as well) is required to provide notice to the defect claimant of its intended action.[614] Under AB125, the ability of the contractor to make a response

---

> *2. If a claimant commences an action without complying with subsection 1 or NRS 40.645, the court shall:*
> *(a) Dismiss the action without prejudice and compel the claimant to comply with those provisions before filing another action; or*
> *(b) If dismissal of the action would prevent the claimant from filing another action because the action would be procedurally barred by the statute of limitations or statute of repose, the court shall stay the proceeding pending compliance with those provisions by the claimant.*

613 AB125 Section 11 revises NRS 40.647 to read as follows:

> *1. After notice of a constructional defect is given pursuant to NRS 40.645, before a claimant may commence an action or amend a complaint to add a cause of action for a constructional defect against a contractor, subcontractor, supplier or design professional, the claimant must:*
> *(a) Allow an inspection of the alleged constructional defect to be conducted pursuant to NRS 40.6462;*
> *(b) Be present at an inspection conducted pursuant to NRS 40.6462 and identify the exact location of each alleged constructional defect specified in the notice and, if the notice includes an expert opinion concerning the alleged constructional defect, the expert, or a representative of the expert who has knowledge of the alleged construction defect, must also be present at the inspection and identify the exact location of each alleged constructional defect for which the expert provided an opinion; and*
> *(c) Allow the contractor, subcontractor, supplier or design professional a reasonable opportunity to repair the constructional defect or cause the defect to be repaired if an election to repair is made pursuant to NRS 40.6472.*
> *2. If a claimant commences an action without complying with subsection 1 or NRS 40.645, the court shall:*
> *(a) Dismiss the action without prejudice and compel the claimant to comply with those provisions before filing another action; or*
> *(b) If dismissal of the action would prevent the claimant from filing another action because the action would be procedurally barred by the statute of limitations or statute of repose, the court shall stay the proceeding pending compliance with those provisions by the claimant.*

614 NRS 40.6472 provides:

> *1. Except as otherwise provided in NRS 40.670 and 40.672 and NRS 40.6452, a written response must be sent by certified mail, return receipt requested, to a claimant who gives notice of a constructional defect pursuant to NRS 40.645:*
> *(a) By the contractor not later than 90 days after the contractor receives the notice; and*

under NRS 40.6452 *without* the input and response of subcontractors, suppliers and design professionals is eliminated.[615] The completeness of the response has often been used by the claimants to assert that the right to repair has been waived. It is therefore suggested that a response of some form be provided for every category of response sought, including whether a repair can be made and any monetary compensation to be offered to the claimant. This response must be sent to the defect claimant within 90 days of the receipt of the notice of defective condition for single family homes. The failure of the contractor to offer to repair the defect authorizes the claimant to commence a lawsuit on the construction defect claim.

7:7 Warranty limitations and statute of limitations; Impacts Related to Condominium Hotels and other Mixed-Use Developments

In general, the limit of a developer's defect and warranty obligation to its purchaser is not an easy matter to ascertain with any level of assurance. Before 2016, Nevada construction defect law did not favor project developers; contractual disclaimers are not favored and have generally been of little legal effect. As a practical matter, contractual disclaimers should not be relied on to be completely effective in application under the current Nevada court system. The development of the Condominium Hotel in Southern

---

(b) If notice was sent to a subcontractor, supplier or design professional, by the subcontractor, supplier or design professional not later than 90 days after the date that the subcontractor, supplier or design professional receives the notice.

2. The written response sent pursuant to subsection 1 must respond to each constructional defect in the notice and:

(a) Must state whether the contractor, subcontractor, supplier or design professional has elected to repair the defect or cause the defect to be repaired. If an election to repair is included in the response and the repair will cause the claimant to move from the claimant's home during the repair, the election must also include monetary compensation in an amount reasonably necessary for temporary housing or for storage of household items, or for both, if necessary.

(b) May include a proposal for monetary compensation, which may include contribution from a subcontractor, supplier or design professional.

(c) May disclaim liability for the constructional defect and state the reasons for such a disclaimer.

3. If the claimant is a homeowners' association, the association shall send a copy of the response to each member of the association not later than 30 days after receiving the response.

4. If the contractor, subcontractor, supplier or design professional has elected not to repair the constructional defect, the claimant or contractor may bring a cause of action for the constructional defect or amend a complaint to add a cause of action for the constructional defect.

5. If the contractor, subcontractor, supplier or design professional has elected to repair the constructional defect, the claimant must provide the contractor, subcontractor, supplier or design professional with a reasonable opportunity to repair the constructional defect

.

615 *See* AB125 Section 12.

Nevada has raised some interesting issues with regard to the application of Nevada's Construction Defect statutes found in NRS 40.600, et seq. Many developers have attempted to limit those defect claims and warranties through the use of contractual waivers and warranty limitations. Legislation related to condominium hotels and Nevada Supreme Court decisions in the construction defect arena have established some new issues that developers of condominium and mixed-use facilities that include residences should be aware.

Nevada statutory law applicable to warranty claims may differ depending on whether the issue is one of failing to meet a warranty of quality or fails to meet a minimum standard of care or operation and thereby causes injury and damages. Nevada law applicable to injury and damages claims provides that an action may not be brought against the developer of property after a certain period of time has lapsed after a project is substantially complete (statute of repose) or after discovery of the defective condition (statute of limitations). The time limitations are triggered by the type of defect involved and the responsible party's level of intentional action. In general, the statutes of repose and limitation for latent and patent defects are 8 and 6 years, respectively, from the date of substantial completion.[616] Both of these terms are extended 2 additional years when the defects are discovered in the final year of the limitations period, for a outside total statute of limitations period of 10 and 8 years from substantial completion, respectively. For fraudulently concealed defects or defects caused by willful misconduct, there is no limitation period.[617] AB125 does not miss these statutes in their revisions either, which substantially reduces the statute of limitations and statute of repose times (restricting both to 6 years after substantial completion)[618] and some may argue eliminates the exception for fraud entirely.

---

[616] NRS 11.204 and NRS 11.205.

[617] NRS 11.202.

[618] AB125 Section 17 revises NRS 11.202 to read as follows:

> *1. No action may be commenced against the owner, occupier or any person performing or furnishing the design, planning, supervision or observation of construction, or the construction of an improvement to real property more than 6 years after the substantial completion of such an improvement, for the recovery of damages for:*
> *(a) Any deficiency in the design, planning, supervision or observation of construction or the construction of such an improvement;*
> *(b) Injury to real or personal property caused by any such deficiency; or*
> *(c) Injury to or the wrongful death of a person caused by any such deficiency.*
> *2. The provisions of this section do not apply:*
> *(a) To a claim for indemnity or contribution.*
> *(b) In an action brought against:*
> *(1) The owner or keeper of any hotel, inn, motel, motor court, boardinghouse or lodging house in this State on account of his or her liability as an innkeeper.*
> *(2) Any person on account of a defect in a product.*

Nevada's construction defect statutes[619] alter these timeframes under certain circumstances. In particular, the statutes of limitations and repose are tolled after a notice of defect is given under NRS 40.645, until 30 days after mediation of that dispute is completed.[620] AB125 changes these time frames for construction defect claims,[621] to the shorter of 30 days after the notice is given or 1 year after mediation is concluded or waived, unless the court finds that good cause exists to extend them further. They also obtain a tolling for the time that any applicable home warranty insurer is considering the claim before rejection.[622]

Under the old law, the outside statutory time limitations to bring an action to recover damages for defective construction is 8 years for patent defects and 10 years for latent defects from the date of substantial completion of the Unit's construction, unless a notice of construction defect is given, which will toll that limitation period. While some express and/or implied warranty claims may be excluded by contractual terms, NRS Chapter 40 construction defect claim waivers will only be effective if: 1) The defects waived are specifically known by all parties, and 2) They are specifically waived by the purchaser in writing. General defect waivers are not valid. In *Westpark Owners' Ass'n v. Eighth Judicial Dist. Court ex rel. County of Clark*,[623] the Nevada Supreme Court stated in footnote 36:

---

[619] NRS 40.600 to NRS 40.695, inclusive.

[620] NRS 40.695.

[621] AB125 Section 16 revises NRS 40.695 to read as follows:

> *1. Except as otherwise provided in subsections 2 and 3, statutes of limitation or repose applicable to a claim based on a constructional defect governed by NRS 40.600 to NRS 40.695, inclusive, and sections 2 and 3 of this act are tolled from the time notice of the claim is given until the earlier of:*
> *(a)One year after notice of the claim is given; or*
> *(b)Thirty days after mediation is concluded or waived in writing pursuant to NRS 40.680..*
> *2. Statutes of limitation and repose may be tolled under this section for a period longer than 1 year after notice of the claim is given only if, in an action for a construction defect brought by a claimant after the applicable statute of limitations or repose has expired, the claimant demonstrates to the satisfaction of the court that good cause exists to toll the statute of limitation and repose under this section for a longer period.*
> *3. Tolling under this section applies to a third party regardless of whether the party is required to appear in the proceeding.*

[622] AB125 Section 14.

[623] *Westpark Owners' Ass'n v. Eighth Judicial Dist. Court ex rel. County of Clark*, 123 Nev. 349, 167 P.3d 421 (2007).

[W]e conclude that the alleged contractual [Chapter 40] waivers are invalid. While NRS 40.640(5) allows a contractor and homebuyer to stipulate to a waiver of any potential claims under NRS Chapter 40, the 'waived' constructional defect must be disclosed to the buyer in clear language before the purchase of the residence. Here, the waivers did not disclose any constructional defects; they stated only that certain defects 'may' exist and listed a number of potential defects. This vague language was not sufficient to waive any claims pursuant to NRS Chapter 40.

As such, general waivers will not be sufficient to avoid defect claims under Chapter 40.

As for any express or implied warranty of quality that the unit will be: 1) free from defective materials and 2) constructed in accordance with applicable law, according to sound standards of engineering and construction and in a workmanlike manner, a 6 year statute of limitations applies from the buyer's acquisition of the unit.[624] To the extent of any applicable warranty of quality, the 6 year statute of limitations may be limited to not less than 2 years by separate agreement with the purchaser.[625] However, there is an additional limitation on waivers of implied warranties of quality.

As the "true" condominium projects are part of planned unit developments, implied warranties of quality may not be excluded by contractual language, but express warranties as to quality may be excluded by appropriate contract language.[626] For the condominium hotel units, however, the passage and implementation of the Condominium-Hotel Act changes this limitation on the condo-hotel unit sales. NRS 116B.780 does allow exclusion of implied warranties of quality by "as is" and "with all faults" contractual language. As such, there may be no authorized "express or implied warranty of quality" on condo-hotel units with the proper exclusionary language.

In summary, the old Nevada law will hold condominium developers to a 10 year statute of limitations for latent defects in construction that cause injury or damage. An 8 year statute of limitations applies to known defects or patent defects that cause such injury or damage. Express or implied warranties in planned unit development projects which are not excluded carry a 6 year statute of limitations, which may be reduced to not less than 2 years upon execution of a separate written agreement with the unit buyer. Condominium Hotel Units may exclude both express and implied warranties of quality by contractual language. If such language is not used, the same 6 year statute of limitation applies, which may be reduced by separate written agreement to 2 years. On claims that arise after AB125 takes effect, the statutes of limitation and reposed are

[624] NRS 116.4116.

[625] NRS 116.4116.

[626] NRS 116.4115.

reduced to 6 years from the date of substantial completion of the new residence. AB125 does not appear to impact on current statutory or case law relating to waiver of such claims.

7:8 RIGHT TO REPAIR ISSUES

If the contractor elects to repair the defective condition, the repairs must be completed according to the requirements of NRS 40.648.[627] Under the former law, if there are four

[627] NRS 40.648 provides:

> *1. If the response provided pursuant to NRS 40.6472 includes an election to repair the constructional defect:*
> *(a) The repairs may be performed by the contractor, subcontractor, supplier or design professional, if such person is properly licensed, bonded and insured to perform the repairs and, if such person is not, the repairs may be performed by another person who meets those qualifications.*
> *(b) The repairs must be performed:*
> *(1) On reasonable dates and at reasonable times agreed to in advance with the claimant;*
> *(2) In compliance with any applicable building code and in a good and workmanlike manner in accordance with the generally accepted standard of care in the industry for that type of repair; and*
> *(3) In a manner which will not increase the cost of maintaining the residence or appurtenance than otherwise would have been required if the residence or appurtenance had been constructed without the constructional defect, unless the contractor and the claimant agree in writing that the contractor will compensate the claimant for the increased cost incurred as a result of the repair.*
> *(c) Any part of the residence or appurtenance that is not defective but which must be removed to correct the constructional defect must be replaced.*
> *(d) The contractor, subcontractor, supplier or design professional shall prevent, remove and indemnify the claimant against any mechanics' liens and materialmen's liens.*
> *2. Unless the claimant and the contractor, subcontractor, supplier or design professional agree to extend the time for repairs, the repairs must be completed:*
> *(a) If the notice was sent pursuant to subsection 4 of NRS 40.645 and there are four or fewer owners named in the notice, for the named owners, not later than 105 days after the date on which the contractor received the notice.*
> *(b) If the notice was sent pursuant to subsection 4 of NRS 40.645 and there are five or more owners named in the notice, for the named owners, not later than 150 days after the date on which the contractor received the notice.*
> *(c) If the notice was sent pursuant to subsection 4 of NRS 40.645, not later than 105 days after the date on which the contractor provides a disclosure of the notice to the unnamed owners to whom the notice applies pursuant to NRS 40.6452.*
> *(d) If the notice was not sent pursuant to subsection 4 of NRS 40.645:*
> *(1) Not later than 105 days after the date on which the notice of the constructional defect was received by the contractor, subcontractor, supplier or design professional if the notice of a constructional defect was received from four or fewer owners; or*
> *(2) Not later than 150 days after the date on which the notice of the constructional defect was received by the contractor, subcontractor, supplier or design professional if the notice was received from five or more owners or from a representative of a homeowners' association.*

or fewer homeowners involved in the construction defect notice, the contractor must commence and complete the repairs within 105 days after the date the contractor received the notice of construction defect, and then must provide the claimant with a written notice of nature and extent of the repairs undertaken. This means that the contractor must follow the following guidelines in order to meet the statutory requirements for construction defect claims:

> 1. *Upon receipt of the notice, the contractor has the obligation to notify all subcontractors and suppliers within 30 days of the notice;*
> 2. *Within 60 days of receipt of the notice the Contractor must request inspections of the defective conditions.*
> 3. *Within 90 days of receipt of the notice, the Contractor must provide the claimant with a written notice of its response to the defect notice and any request to repair;*
> 4. *Within 105 days of receipt of the notice, the Contractor must complete the repairs of the defective conditions, and*
> 5. *Within 30 days after the repairs are complete, the Contractor must provide the claimant with a written report describing in detail the repairs performed on the residence.*

If the defective condition involves five or more defective homes, then the time for repair is actually extended to 150 days from the date that the notice of defect was given, and within that time frame all residences within the notice must be repaired. The statute also allows for a reasonable agreement between the claimants and the contractor to establish a time for repair if the repairs are so extensive that completion within the statutory timeframe cannot be met, or in the absence of agreement, the court may establish a reasonable time. However, under no circumstances may the repairs be conditioned on the claimant's waiver of any claim of liability against the contractor, subcontractors or suppliers. Likewise, the repair does not relieve the contractor or subcontractors of liability to complete the repairs properly. If the repairs do not accomplish the goal of rectifying the defect, or if the repair is performed in a defective manner, the claimant is free to assert additional construction defect claims against the contractor.[628]

> *3. If repairs reasonably cannot be completed within the time set forth in subsection 2, the claimant and the contractor, subcontractor, supplier or design professional shall agree to a reasonable time within which to complete the repair. If the claimant and contractor, subcontractor, supplier or design professional cannot agree on such a time, any of them may petition the court to establish a reasonable time for completing the repair.*
> *4. Any election to repair made pursuant to NRS 40.6472 may not be made conditional upon a release of liability.*
> *5. Not later than 30 days after the repairs are completed, the contractor, subcontractor, supplier or design professional who repaired or caused the repair of a constructional defect shall provide the claimant with a written statement describing the nature and extent of the repair, the method used to repair the constructional defect and the extent of any materials or parts that were replaced during the repair.*

[628] NRS 40.667 provides:

Under AB125, some of the complexities involved in this distinction of the type of notice provided based on the number of homes involved in the constructional defect claim is eliminated.[629] Now the repairs simply must be performed within 105 days or 150 days

---

1. Except as otherwise provided in subsection 2, a written waiver or settlement agreement executed by a claimant after a contractor has corrected or otherwise repaired a constructional defect does not bar a claim for the constructional defect if it is determined that the contractor failed to correct or repair the defect properly.
2. The provisions of subsection 1 do not apply to any written waiver or settlement agreement described in subsection 1, unless:
(a) The claimant has obtained the opinion of an expert concerning the constructional defect;
(b) The claimant has provided the contractor with a written notice of the defect pursuant to NRS 40.645 and a copy of the expert's opinion; and
(c) The claimant and the contractor have complied with the requirements for inspection and repair as provided in NRS 40.600 to 40.695, inclusive.
3. The provisions of this section do not apply to repairs which are made pursuant to an election to repair pursuant to NRS 40.6472.
4. If a claimant does not prevail in any action which is not barred pursuant to this section, the court may:
(a) Deny the claimant's attorney's fees, fees for an expert witness or costs; and
(b) Award attorney's fees and costs to the contractor.

629 AB125 Section 13 revises NRS 40.648 to provide:

1. If the response provided pursuant to NRS 40.6472 includes an election to repair the constructional defect:
(a) The repairs may be performed by the contractor, subcontractor, supplier or design professional, if such person is properly licensed, bonded and insured to perform the repairs and, if such person is not, the repairs may be performed by another person who meets those qualifications.
(b) The repairs must be performed:
(1) On reasonable dates and at reasonable times agreed to in advance with the claimant;
(2) In compliance with any applicable building code and in a good and workmanlike manner in accordance with the generally accepted standard of care in the industry for that type of repair; and
(3) In a manner which will not increase the cost of maintaining the residence or appurtenance than otherwise would have been required if the residence or appurtenance had been constructed without the constructional defect, unless the contractor and the claimant agree in writing that the contractor will compensate the claimant for the increased cost incurred as a result of the repair.
(c) Any part of the residence or appurtenance that is not defective but which must be removed to correct the constructional defect must be replaced.
(d) The contractor, subcontractor, supplier or design professional shall prevent, remove and indemnify the claimant against any mechanics' liens and materialmen's liens.
2. Unless the claimant and the contractor, subcontractor, supplier or design professional agree to extend the time for repairs, the repairs must be completed:
(a) Not later than 105 days after the date on which the notice of the constructional defect was received by the contractor, subcontractor, supplier or design professional if the notice of a constructional defect was received from four or fewer owners; or

after the notice of constructional defect is given for 4 or fewer, or 5 or more homes, respectively, unless the claimant and the involved contractor, subcontractors, suppliers and design professionals agree otherwise. There still cannot be any condition of repairs based on a release of liability.

7:9 Commencing Litigation

If the commencement of litigation is not otherwise authorized, that is, if the contractor proposes a resolution of the dispute or a repair but an agreement of the issue cannot be reached with the claimant, the parties must engage in mediation under NRS 40.680,[630]

> *(b) Not later than 150 days after the date on which the notice of the constructional defect was received by the contractor, subcontractor, supplier or design professional if the notice was received from five or more owners or from a representative of a homeowners' association.*
> *3. If repairs reasonably cannot be completed within the time set forth in subsection 2, the claimant and the contractor, subcontractor, supplier or design professional shall agree to a reasonable time within which to complete the repair. If the claimant and contractor, subcontractor, supplier or design professional cannot agree on such a time, any of them may petition the court to establish a reasonable time for completing the repair.*
> *4. Any election to repair made pursuant to NRS 40.6472 may not be made conditional upon a release of liability.*
> *5. Not later than 30 days after the repairs are completed, the contractor, subcontractor, supplier or design professional who repaired or caused the repair of a constructional defect shall provide the claimant with a written statement describing the nature and extent of the repair, the method used to repair the constructional defect and the extent of any materials or parts that were replaced during the repair.*

[630] NRS 40.680 provides:

> *1. Except as otherwise provided in this chapter, before a claimant commences an action or amends a complaint to add a cause of action for a constructional defect against a contractor, subcontractor, supplier or design professional, the matter must be submitted to mediation, unless mediation is waived in writing by the contractor, subcontractor, supplier or design professional and the claimant.*
> *2. The claimant and each party alleged to have caused the constructional defect must select a mediator by agreement. If the claimant and the other parties fail to agree upon a mediator within 20 days after a mediator is first selected by the claimant, any party may petition the American Arbitration Association, the Nevada Arbitration Association, Nevada Dispute Resolution Services or any other mediation service acceptable to the parties for the appointment of a mediator. A mediator so appointed may discover only those documents or records which are necessary to conduct the mediation. The mediator shall convene the mediation within 30 days after the matter is submitted to the mediator and shall complete the mediation within 45 days after the matter is submitted to the mediator, unless the parties agree to extend the time.*
> *3. Before the mediation begins:*
> *(a) The claimant shall deposit $50 with the mediation service; and*
> *(b) Each other party shall deposit with the mediation service, in equal shares, the remaining amount estimated by the mediation service as necessary to pay the fees and expenses of the*

before litigation may be filed. Pre-mediation discovery may be authorized in this situation as well.[631] However, mediation in a Nevada construction defect case is not the same type of mediation that is thought of in other types of construction litigation. As will be discussed in Section 7:11 Mediation Considerations, mediation in Nevada construction defect cases is not really mediation is any sense of the word, but is a series of informal meetings where little substantial progress is made until sufficient numbers of mediations sessions are held to achieve a consensus.

After the mediation is not successful, or at any other time authorized by the statutory scheme, the claimant can commence a lawsuit against the contractor who constructed the home or homes claimed to be defective. So long as the contractor has complied with

---

mediator for the first session of mediation and shall deposit additional amounts demanded by the mediation service as incurred for that purpose.
4. Unless otherwise agreed, the total fees for each day of mediation and the mediator must not exceed $750 per day.
5. If the parties do not reach an agreement concerning the matter during mediation or if any party who is alleged to have caused the constructional defect fails to pay the required fees and appear, the claimant may commence an action or amend a complaint to add a cause of action for the constructional defect in court and:
(a) The reasonable costs and fees of the mediation are recoverable by the prevailing party as costs of the action.
(b) Any party may petition the court in which the action is commenced for the appointment of a special master.
6. A special master appointed pursuant to subsection 5 may:
(a) Review all pleadings, papers or documents filed with the court concerning the action.
(b) Coordinate the discovery of any books, records, papers or other documents by the parties, including the disclosure of witnesses and the taking of the deposition of any party.
(c) Order any inspections on the site of the property by a party and any consultants or experts of a party.
(d) Order settlement conferences and attendance at those conferences by any representative of the insurer of a party.
(e) Require any attorney representing a party to provide statements of legal and factual issues concerning the action.
(f) Refer to the judge who appointed the special master or to the presiding judge of the court in which the action is commenced any matter requiring assistance from the court.
The special master shall not, unless otherwise agreed by the parties, personally conduct any settlement conferences or engage in any ex parte meetings regarding the action.
7. Upon application by a party to the court in which the action is commenced, any decision or other action taken by a special master appointed pursuant to this section may be appealed to the court for a decision.
8. A report issued by a mediator or special master that indicates that a party has failed to appear before the mediator or special master or to mediate in good faith is admissible in the action, but a statement or admission made by a party in the course of mediation is not admissible.

[631] NRS 40.681.

its obligations under NRS 40.646, the contractor can in turn file a third party complaint against any responsible subcontractors or suppliers. Often times design professionals are brought in to the defect lawsuits on the claim that their design contributes to the defective condition, however, it should be noted that as a condition of involving a design professional in the process, an affidavit of both an attorney and a licensed design professional expert must be submitted certifying that the claim against the design professional has been investigated and has concluded that the lawsuit for professional negligence has a reasonable basis in law and fact.[632] Failure to supply such affidavits will result in the dismissal of the lawsuit against the design professional.[633]

7:10 Case Management Orders and Special Masters

After the lawsuit is filed, the court will usually appoint a special master to manage the discovery process of the litigation and make interim orders for case management. The special master's fees will be split among the parties, with the parties usually being assigned percentages based on their position in the lawsuit. In most cases, the fee will be split among the major groups of participants: The Plaintiff, the developer or contractor, the subcontractors and the design professionals. Each of these four groups will split an equal share of the costs, and if there are multiple parties within one of the four groups, the parties will split their portion equally within the group.

The special master will make what are known as standard orders within the construction defect process. These will usually involve the provision of certain deadlines by which third parties must be named and served with third party complaints, the establishment of a document depository and provision for payment of the depository's fees, criteria for document production and protocols for electronic discovery and evidence preservation, the dates by which parties must respond to standardized discovery requests (usually involving the number, applicability and coverage limitations on all applicable primary, secondary and excess insurance policies, as well as corporate formalities of all parties), and the appointment of a mediator and dates for mediation. The special master will also establish preliminary case management schedules and set dates for other disclosures, discovery cut off, expert disclosure, deposition completion and a date that trial will not be set before. The parties are then expected to serve any additional parties with the case management order and otherwise comply with the deadlines as established.

Periodically, the Special Master will hold hearings to handle various case issues and inquire of the case status. These sessions are handled to maintain and /or adjust the schedule as necessary to keep the case moving forward on the management path.

[632] NRS 40.6884.

[633] NRS 40.6885.

Discovery disputes are usually handled by letters to the special master or if more formal filings are necessary, the Special Master will direct specific briefing.

The parties can also expect that discovery will not be allowed until certain steps in mediation are complete. Written discovery is usually reserved and authorized by permission of the special master alone, in order to prevent the defense from inundating the claimant with multiple discovery obligations. Except for documents and expert reports, there is little discovery that takes place before mediations are complete.

7:11 Mediation considerations

As mentioned previously, mediation in construction defect cases is not the same as mediation for other types of construction claims. In Nevada, construction defect mediation is really not much more than a title placed on informal meetings between counsel and occasionally insurance carriers to ensure that all the parties have properly complied with the case management orders for disclosure and document production. Initial mediation sessions will set up site inspections and destructive testing requests and begin to get the mediator familiar with the case as well as the parties involved. Serious mediation discussions usually will not take place until several months of the process and multiple mediation sessions have taken place. Therefore, it should not be found unusual for defense attorneys to request their insurance carrier representatives not attend the mediation sessions or that their clients be excused until a potential settlement is actually possible as the case nears its trial date.

The defense should also not expect to take any depositions before mediation sessions begin or they are declared a total failure and the case begins trial preparation in earnest. The entire goal of the Nevada construction defect scheme is to achieve a negotiated settlement before any significant discovery, other than expert reports, is commenced, let alone completed. Because of this unique structure, construction defect claims can be very frustrating for contractors and other practitioners who do not regularly participate in the residential construction defect claim process. Unfortunately, there is little incentive for change to the system as the system has been recognized by other state defect jurisdictions as a model for handling construction defect claims.

7:12 Arbitration clauses

To address the failures and perceived in fairness of the residential construction defect system in Nevada, many contractors have attempted to draft home sales contracts with arbitration clauses or other types of waivers on the construction defect process. While the Nevada Supreme Court has not totally voided any such attempts, it has established significant impediments to such activities by requiring substantial disclosure for the protection of the consumer.[634] the Nevada Supreme Court has ruled that arbitration

[634] *See D.R. Horton, Inc. v. Green*, 120 Nev. 549, 96 P.3d 1159 (2004).

provisions which in effect waive the rights provided to homeowners for construction defect claims are unconscionable, and therefore void.

In *Gonski v. District Court,*[635] homeowners sought to purchase a home during the construction boom. The homeowners were required to deposit $10,000 with the builder to join a "lottery" for the right to purchase a home. Upon being notified they were chosen the homebuilder gave the potential buyers 5 days to come into the sales office and complete the transaction. When they arrived, they found a crowded waiting room, and where handed a stack of 25 documents, comprising almost 500 pages, and told they needed to execute the documents then. When they objected to the time provided to review the documents, the builder's representatives allegedly told them that many other buyers were waiting to take their place, if they did not want to sign. After obtaining no explanation of any of the terms in the documents, including the existence and effect on two conflicting arbitration clauses, they decided to execute the documents anyway, initialing each page of the documents. The arbitration clause was not highlighted in a normal font, was not separately entitled, and placed on page 15 of 19 pages of the sales agreement. A separate and conflicting arbitration agreement was included in the limited warranty document, which was also executed.

After purchasing the home, the buyer asserted a construction defect claim under Chapter 40 (NRS 40.655) and the developer moved to compel arbitration. The buyer objected to the arbitration motion on the grounds that the arbitration clause was procedurally and substantively unconscionable and should be voided. In addition to the circumstances under which the arbitration clauses were executed, the buyer asserted that the clauses were obscure, confusingly written, conflicting in their terms and failed to inform the buyer of their waiver of explicit rights under Chapter 40, including the requirement that a prevailing claimant would be entitled to attorneys fees. In this case, the first arbitration clause said that the developer would pay the initial costs of arbitration, but the second arbitration clause required that they split the fees and the claimant pay the initial arbitration commencement fees. The district court disagreed and ordered the case to arbitration. The Homeowner appealed.

The Nevada Supreme Court reversed and ruled the arbitration clause was void as both procedurally and substantively unconscionable. The Court reaffirmed the notion that the procedural / substantive paradigm was a sliding scale the more of one that existed, the less of the other was needed to find the clause unconscionable. In this case, both existed.

In finding procedural unconscionability existed, the Court pointed to the circumstances of the transaction leading to execution of the arbitration provisions, but also noted that

---

[635] *Gonski v. Second Judicial Dist. Ct. of State ex rel. Washoe*, 126 Nev. 51, 245 P.3d 1164 (2010).

the fact the clause was not highlighted, was buried in the back of a dense document of various terms, and did not adequately explain in laymen terms the arbitration provision's effect upon homeowner rights and the substantial costs involved. Nothing in the clause itself put the homeowner on notice that they were agreeing to forego important rights under Nevada's construction defect law. While these problems were not large in and of themselves, the weight of the substantive unconscionability made this lower amount of procedural unconscionability sufficient.

Thereafter, the Court indicated that the arbitration clause's effect of impliedly waiving substantive rights of the homeowners under Chapter 40 violated the public policy established by the legislature with the enactment of Chapter 40. Specifically, the Court determined that the documents failed to mention the potentially high costs of arbitration. While this was not sufficient by itself to render the arbitration clause unconscionable, the fact that the forum of the arbitration would be selected by a 3rd party meant the homeowner could not determine what the costs would be before deciding to execute the provision. Given this, the arbitration clause mandating the sharing of arbitration costs, but requiring the homeowner to pay the initial costs of commencement, made the arbitration clause was one-sided.

Further, the clause actually misrepresented the rights of the homeowners under Chapter 40 and the implicit waiver thereof. Chapter 40 provides substantive rights to the homeowners, including the ability to recover attorneys' fees, costs and other consequential damages. Chapter for applies to "any" construction defect, and developers may not limit its applicability to some defects at the expense of others. Finally, the Court held that arbitration clauses cannot be used to expressly or impliedly avoid rights and liabilities imposed under statutes, including Chapter 40. Doing so would violate the public policy of the state, as established by the legislative process.

In a concurrence and dissent, Justice Pickering would have remanded the matter back to the District Court with directions to have the enforceability of the arbitration provision handled by the Arbitrator. In a footnote response, however, the majority indicates that such a determination would require that the arbitration provision clearly and unmistakably state that the decision over arbitrability is to be handled the arbitrator. In this case, the developer had not raised the issue and may have waived it, but in any case the clause itself did not clearly and unmistakably commit those questions to the arbitrator.

This case highlights the problems that occur by the practice of burying arbitration provisions in small type and laying them out in a stack of documents. A better practice may be to provide a separate agreement which explains in everyday language the effect and costs of an arbitration provision in the context of a construction defect case. Regardless, the Nevada Supreme Court appears to be requiring the district courts to take a very hard look at the circumstances of the execution, and demand that the arbitration agreement is entered into fairly and with adequate notice and time to review.

Moreover, drafters of arbitration provisions must be certain the effect of an arbitration clause is merely to shift the location of the forum for adjudication of the claim, rather than the diminishment of substantive rights. The Nevada Supreme Court has clearly articulated a policy which will not allow the substantive rights of homeowners to be avoided simply by moving to arbitration. While the provisions of Chapter 40 have not previously been held to prevent contractual alteration of the provisions (and in fact, some cases actually have allowed waiver by specific disclosure of existing defects and acceptance thereof), the *Gonski* case actually seems to equate the provision of NRS 40.635(2) that the statutory scheme *"prevail[s] over any conflicting law otherwise applicable to the claim or cause of action"* to be in effect a provision making contractual waiver void and unenforceable to the extent that doing so would defeat the purpose of the statute. With the Court's reference to the construction defect law applying to "any construction defect claims," even known and disclosed defects may come into question, if the disclosure does not specifically and plainly announce the existence of the defect and allow sufficient time for the potential buyer to investigate.

Such protective measures include requiring arbitration clauses, jury waivers and other clauses causing individuals to waive rights afforded under NRS Chapter 40 to be fully disclosed, the homeowners to have the option and in fact be advised to seek independent legal counsel and other steps to protect the consumer before such clauses will be enforced. While there is again no direct prohibition, there seems to be a strong policy among the Nevada Supreme Court to avoid such measures, if at all possible.

7:13 DAMAGES AVAILABLE IN CONSTRUCTION DEFECT CASES

Curiously, the damage provisions under the previous version of Chapter 40 seem to read as a limitation on the amount of damages that a defect claimant may receive. In practice, the list of damages is expansive and even includes non-economic losses which are ordinarily barred under the economic loss doctrine.[636] The list of recoverable damages is found at NRS 40.655, which provides:

> *1. Except as otherwise provided in NRS 40.650, in a claim governed by NRS 40.600 to 40.695, inclusive, the claimant may recover only the following damages to the extent proximately caused by a constructional defect:*
> *(a) Any reasonable attorney's fees;*
> *(b) The reasonable cost of any repairs already made that were necessary and of any repairs yet to be made that are necessary to cure any constructional defect that the*

---

[636] *See Calloway v. City of Reno*, 116 Nev. 250, 993 P.2d 1259 (2000); *Olson v. Richard*, 120 Nev. 240, 89 P.3d 31 (2004).

contractor failed to cure and the reasonable expenses of temporary housing reasonably necessary during the repair;
(c) The reduction in market value of the residence or accessory structure, if any, to the extent the reduction is because of structural failure;
(d) The loss of the use of all or any part of the residence;
(e) The reasonable value of any other property damaged by the constructional defect;
(f) Any additional costs reasonably incurred by the claimant, including, but not limited to, any costs and fees incurred for the retention of experts to:
(1) Ascertain the nature and extent of the constructional defects;
(2) Evaluate appropriate corrective measures to estimate the value of loss of use; and
(3) Estimate the value of loss of use, the cost of temporary housing and the reduction of market value of the residence; and
(g) Any interest provided by statute.
2. The amount of any attorney's fees awarded pursuant to this section must be approved by the court.
3. If a contractor complies with the provisions of NRS 40.600 to 40.695, inclusive, the claimant may not recover from the contractor, as a result of the constructional defect, anything other than that which is provided pursuant to NRS 40.600 to 40.695, inclusive.
4. This section must not be construed as impairing any contractual rights between a contractor and a subcontractor, supplier or design professional.
5. As used in this section, "structural failure" means physical damage to the load-bearing portion of a residence or appurtenance caused by a failure of the load-bearing portion of the residence or appurtenance.

As most construction practitioners will notice, the ability of the construction defect claimant to recover not only the cost of repairs, but the diminution in market value, value of the lost of use, costs of temporary housing, attorney's fees and expert fees makes for a substantial windfall for the defect claimant by asserting any plausible claim. Likewise, the ability of defect plaintiff attorneys to recover both for contingency and actual attorney fees incurred is further incentive to file defect lawsuits. This was also addressed by substantial revisions in AB125.[637] Probably the most significant revision

[637] AB125 Section 15 revises NRS 40.655 to read as follows:

1. Except as otherwise provided in NRS 40.650, in a claim governed by NRS 40.600 to 40.695, inclusive, the claimant may recover only the following damages to the extent proximately caused by a constructional defect:
(a) The reasonable cost of any repairs already made that were necessary and of any repairs yet to be made that are necessary to cure any constructional defect that the contractor failed to cure and the reasonable expenses of temporary housing reasonably necessary during the repair;
(b) The reduction in market value of the residence or accessory structure, if any, to the extent the reduction is because of structural failure;
(c) The loss of the use of all or any part of the residence;
(d) The reasonable value of any other property damaged by the constructional defect;

made to the entire statutory scheme was the elimination of recovery of attorneys' fees as an element of damages. By this deletion, AB125 has relegated attorney's fee recovery to a matter of contract within the sales agreement for the original purchase of the new residence. This eliminates the incentive for attorneys to accept cases on a contingency fee basis, as such fees are usually substantial.

Finally, there are options for the developer to settle defect claims in other methods than that discussed, including the ability to repurchase the home from the homeowner, if the home was purchased within two years of the offer to repurchase and the offer includes payment for the residence at current market value without a defect, value of any improvements made by the owner, attorney's fees and expert costs, as well as all moving costs, loan fees and points for a new loan on a replacement home.[638] Meeting these obligations will have the offer deemed reasonable and in good faith under the statute.

(e) Any additional costs reasonably incurred by the claimant for constructional defects proven by the claimant, including, but not limited to, any costs and fees incurred for the retention of experts to:
(1) Ascertain the nature and extent of the constructional defects;
(2) Evaluate appropriate corrective measures to estimate the value of loss of use; and
(3) Estimate the value of loss of use, the cost of temporary housing and the reduction of market value of the residence; and
(f) Any interest provided by statute.
2. If a contractor complies with the provisions of NRS 40.600 to 40.695, inclusive, and sections 2 and 3 of this act, the claimant may not recover from the contractor, as a result of the constructional defect, any damages other than damages authorized pursuant to NRS 40.600 to 40.695, inclusive, and sections 2 and 3 of this act.
3. This section must not be construed as impairing any contractual rights between a contractor and a subcontractor, supplier or design professional.
4. As used in this section, "structural failure" means physical damage to the load-bearing portion of a residence or appurtenance caused by a failure of the load-bearing portion of the residence or appurtenance.

638 NRS 40.665.

CHAPTER 8 NEVADA MECHANIC'S LIENS

8:1 INTRODUCTION TO NEVADA MECHANICS LIENS

Nevada's mechanics lien law is unique in the United States. The Nevada mechanics lien law is almost entirely derived by work of the Nevada state legislature; although in recent years there have been significant changes and some Nevada Supreme Court decisions which have impacted the mechanic's lien law. There is no constitutional mandate by the State requiring the provision of a mechanics lien "right" to the people. Despite recent activity, there is precious little case law and the statutes themselves can be confusing, contradictory and sometimes lead to nonsensical results. Moreover, in response to the Venetian Lien Litigation, the entire mechanics lien law was substantially revised by the legislature in 2003 and continues to be adjusted every two years. Because of this lack of constitutional mandate and the uncertainty resulting from both the lack of Supreme Court interpretations and an ever-changing legislative scheme, the statutory right to a mechanics lien at one time could have been significantly affected by the agreements and actions of the parties to a construction contract. Therefore, owners, contractors, subcontractors, material suppliers, design professionals, and all other potential users of the Nevada lien law had to be wary of and pay strict attention to the terms of their construction contracts. However, in 2005 the legislature sought to restrict the ability of the parties to contractually impair the mechanics lien law.

The 2003 legislative session was the first successful attempt to rewrite the scheme of Nevada's mechanic's lien law in more than 100 years. The previous law was best suited to simple construction projects, with simple issues dividing the parties. Unfortunately, the revisions have done little to streamline and modernize the legal process involved with mechanics lien cases. While there is much discussion that can be had over various intricate details of other state mechanics lien laws, Nevada must be viewed simply as a standalone state. Major construction projects with multiple prime contracts, run by sophisticated construction management techniques with unique project delivery systems may still not be well supported by the law. Sophisticated business owners can be confounded and perplexed by the almost sophomoric approach Nevada's mechanics lien law will apply to the complex legal issues raised by these modern systems. While some efforts have been made to limit the progressive deterioration of the law's technical requirements, the effectiveness of such limitations is in doubt considering recent case decisions. The actual application of what little historical case law exists may also be questioned, given the significant statutory revisions in 2003 and 2005. Once a lien is recorded, however, avoiding the lien on a technical defense may still be difficult.

With notable exceptions discussed in the following sections, Nevada's Supreme Court has historically sided with lien claimants on mechanics lien issues, consistently requiring the trial courts of the State to "liberally construe" the law in favor of the lien claimants--

ordering trial judges for over 100 years not to get "bogged down" in the minutia of the statutes' technical details. As early as 1892, the Nevada Supreme Court ordered that statutory construction of the mechanics lien statutes "should not be carried to such extremes as serve only to perplex and embarrass a remedy intended to be simple and summary without adding anything to the security of the parties having an interest in the property sought to be charged with the lien."[639] This predisposition in favor of contractors continues despite the statutory revisions.[640] This judicial preposition is not favorable to project owners and general contractors dealing with subcontractors and suppliers.[641]

But this pre-disposition is not sufficient to allow a Nevada Court to eliminate all manner of obligation to comply with the statutory law. As the 2003 amendments to the mechanics lien statute make clear: "*Except as otherwise provided in NRS 108.221 to 108.246, inclusive, a person may not waive or modify a right, obligation or liability set forth in the provisions of NRS 108.221 to 108.246, inclusive.*"[642] This notion that a mechanics lien claimant must comply with the statutory requirements cannot be merely brushed away as not in keeping with historical Nevada Supreme Court mandates.[643] Quite to the contrary, in 1883 the Nevada Supreme Court required a balance between compliance with the statute and an overly strict interpretation, but did not give away any object of obligation to comply with the statute:

> *We have repeatedly declared that the act relating to mechanics' liens should be liberally construed; that the spirit and purpose of the law is to do substantial justice to all parties who may be affected by its provisions; and that courts should "avoid unfriendly strictness and mere technicality." Skyrme v. Occidental M. & M. Co. 8 Nev. 221; Hunter v. Truckee Lodge, 14 Nev. 28; Lonkey v. Wells, 16 Nev. 274. This rule should always be followed when the objections urged serve only to perplex and embarrass a remedy*

[639] *Maynard v. Ivey*, 21 Nev. 241, 245, 29 P. 1090 (1892).

[640] *Hardy Companies, Inc. v. SNMARK, LLC*, 126 Nev. 528, 245 P.3d 1149 (2010); *Lehrer McGovern Bovis, Inc. v. Bullock Insulation, In*, 185 P.3d 1055 (Nev. 2008), opinion withdrawn and superseded on denial of reh'g, *Lehrer McGovern Bovis, Inc. v. Bullock Insulation, Inc.*, 124 Nev. 1102. 197 P.3d 1032 (2008).

[641] *But see J.D. Const., Inc. v. IBEX Intern. Group, LLC*, 126 Nev. 366, 240 P.3d 1033 (2010), recognizing an owner's "significant interest in having his or her property be free of encumbrances."

[642] NRS 108.2453(1); *but see Hardy Companies, Inc. v. SNMARK, LLC*, 126 Nev. 528, 240 P.3d 1149 (2010), holding NRS 108.2453(1) "voids conditions, stipulations, or provisions in a contract that require a lien claimant to waive lien rights." The Court, however, does not explain how this interpretation of subsection (1) makes it any different than the express provisions of subsection (2), which specifically use this same language.

[643] *See Hardy Companies, Inc. v. SNMARK, LLC*, 126 Nev. 528, 245 P.3d 1149 (2010), holding that "(f)ailure to either fully or substantially comply with the mechanics lien statute will render a mechanics lien invalid as a matter of law."

intended to be simple and summary, without adding anything to the security of the parties having an interest in the property sought to be affected. But in following this rule, courts should always be careful not to impair the force of the statute or fritter away its meaning by construction. It must always be borne in mind that a mechanic's lien is purely of statutory creation, and that it can only be maintained by a substantial observance of, and compliance with, the provisions of the statute. It is "a remedy given by law, which secures the preference provided for, but which does not exist, however equitable the claim may be, unless the party brings himself within the provisions of the statute, and shows a substantial compliance with all its essential requirements." Phil. Mech. Liens, §89. Whatever is made necessary to the existence of the lien must be performed, or the attempt to create it will be futile. A substantial adherence to the terms of the statute in the notice of lien is indispensable. The omissions, if any, in the notice and claim as recorded, cannot, in essential particulars, be aided by any averments in the complaint, or by extrinsic evidence.[644]

As such, Nevada mechanics lien law must give structure and support to a full compliance with the statutory requirements when notice and prejudice may be suffered and when an obligation is found in the statutory law. While minor errors may be corrected and frivolous issues should not be overly burdensome to defeat the purpose of the statute to secure payment to contractors, contractors should not be allowed complete freedom to ignore the statutory obligations and still claim their statutory remedy.[645]

8:2 THEORY OF MECHANICS LIEN LAW

In the world of mechanics' lien rights, it seems no one is interested in what mechanics liens are or how they function within the context of real estate law. Since their purpose is to secure payment for contractors who by the sweat of their brow improve the real property of another, trial courts and legal practitioners tend to gloss over their significant and intricate structure of legal origin. But mechanics' liens are unknown from English common law, as most of our American legal concepts are derived. In fact they are to a large extent antithetical to our American beliefs about property rights. The oft quoted maxim "*A man's home is his castle*" is actually better qualified to read: "*A man's home is his castle, except when he has had work done to it and has not paid for it; because then his castle is subject to the Court's ability to sell it out from under him to pay for the work.*"[646]

---

[644] *Malter v. Falcon Min. Co.*, 18 Nev. 209, 212-213, 2 P. 50, 50-51 (1883).

[645] *See Hardy Companies, Inc. v. SNMARK, LLC*, 126 Nev. 528, 245 P.3d 1149 (2010), finding that the ability to amend a claim of lien to correct minor errors found in NRS 108.229(3) does not apply to errors in a preliminary notice, provided under NRS 108.245.

[646] As the United States Supreme Court held in 1934:

That is, of course, the ultimate outcome of a mechanics' lien lawsuit taken to its final resolution--the judicially ordered sale of a person's real property to pay off the costs of construction. While in practice this final outcome is usually averted by the payment of funds or the owner's bankruptcy, or the foreclosure of other liens which have priority over the mechanics' lien, still it is widely unrealized, even by the legislators that enact the mechanics lien remedy, that they are preparing a law that can oust a retiree from her only home; that can close down a thriving business; that can set orphans, and widows, and families and animals into the streets. Such is the mechanics' lien threat, and so it accomplishes its goal--get the contractor paid, or punish the owner who doesn't by taking away his right of quiet and peaceful ownership.

The first mechanics' lien laws were enacted in 1791 by the state of Maryland to allow for the construction of houses and other structures in the new province of Washington D.C.[647] The granting of a lien to a contractor for the construction of a building allows the contractor to secure the large amount of capital necessary to complete the work, without necessarily the need to obtain third party loans for the purpose. As a result, mechanic's liens have a dynamic structure that exists in theory when work begins, and only is final upon its "perfection" with the preparation, recordation and service of necessary documents. Still, like Newton's law of gravity or Einstein's laws of motion, one must not make the mistake of doubting a mechanics' lien's existence just because the final paperwork is not prepared, recorded and served: they are there on every construction project in Nevada on which visible work has commenced. And they are not lost because work has theoretically "stopped." Any owner of real estate (and any lawyer charged with investigation of any real estate transaction) *must* assume they bind the real property in question until proven otherwise.

A potential Nevada mechanics lien exists, in an inchoate state, upon the performance of the very first work by a contractor, design professional or materialman. A potential lien exists when the project is first "planned" by those who eventually see it implemented.[648]

> *"The owner contracting with a builder or making payments under the contract may be required to give heed to the equities of a subcontractor or workman adding value to the land."*

Hartford Accident & Indemnity Co. v. N. O. Nelson Mfg. Co., 291 U.S. 352, 54 S.Ct. 392, 78 L.Ed. 840 (1934).

[647] Fowler, *Lien on me: An in-depth analysis of Tennessee's mechanics' lien statute with regard to real property*, 32 U.Mem.L.Rev. 967 (2002).

[648] NRS 108.22184 states:

> *'Work' means* ***the planning****, design, geotechnical and environmental investigations, surveying, labor and services provided by a lien claimant for the construction, alteration or*

Further, all mechanics' liens relate back in time to the date of the first work provided, and hold priority over every other non-mechanics' type of lien, encumbrance, mortgage, deed of trust, or even sale.[649] As such, mechanics' liens are potentially preferred and have priority over nearly every lender's deed of trust and over every property owner's interest. They exist the moment the contractor steps foot on the work site and cannot be lost without payment for that work.[650] And once work has commenced, there is no practical method to re-establish a subsequent lender's priority over the inchoate liens.[651] A lender or title insurer must remove the lien as efficiently as possible (which usually means pay it off quickly) so as to prevent the expenditure of substantial fees and costs in a fruitless effort to object to the technical propriety of the lien itself.

Such legal power given to a contractor can have devastating effects, and can certainly be used for illicit purposes and in an unfair manner. While there are potentially serious penalties for a contractor to misuse the mechanics' lien right,[652] in practical effect these are never pursued. A practitioner dealing with a questionable mechanics' lien must be prepared to delve into the only defenses he will have to thwart the lien, and otherwise, find indemnification obligations that may provide alternative sources of recovery. The table is tilted in Nevada for the mechanics' lien claimant.

> *repair of any improvement, property or work of improvement whether the work is completed or partially completed (emphasis added.).*

649 NRS 108.225 states:

> *1. The liens provided for in NRS 108.221 to 108.246, inclusive, are preferred to:*
> *(a) Any lien, mortgage or other encumbrance which may have attached to the property after the commencement of construction of a work of improvement.*
> *(b) Any lien, mortgage or other encumbrance of which the lien claimant had no notice and which was unrecorded against the property at the commencement of construction of a work of improvement.*
> *2. Every mortgage or encumbrance imposed upon, or conveyance made of, property affected by the liens provided for in NRS 108.221 to 108.246, inclusive, after the commencement of construction of a work of improvement are subordinate and subject to the liens provided for in NRS 108.221 to 108.246, inclusive, regardless of the date of recording the notices of liens.*

650 For a full discussion of priority issues involving Nevada mechanics lien matters, *see* Section 8:30

651 *See* Section 8:22.

652 See NRS 108.226(4):

> *It is unlawful for a person knowingly to make a false statement in or relating to the recording of a notice of lien pursuant to the provisions of this section. A person who violates this subsection is guilty of a gross misdemeanor and shall be punished by a fine of not less than $5,000 nor more than $10,000.; see also NRS 624.3016(3).*

8:3 NO WAIVER OF STATUTORY LIEN RIGHTS, OBLIGATIONS OR LIABILITIES

Prior to 2003, errors or omissions in preliminary notices, mechanics liens, etc., were often held to be of no consequence in Nevada courts, unless some injury or prejudice actually resulted from the error in statutory compliance--and having a lien placed on your project is not a sufficient injury. The 2003 and 2005 legislative changes attempt to deal with this issue of uncertainty by eliminating the ability of a person to waive or modify a right, obligation or liability under the mechanics lien law, unless specifically allowed within the provisions of the mechanics lien law. Legislation introduced in 2003 and continued in 2005, established a new section into the mechanics lien law which addresses contractual waivers and releases of all types. This bill introduced new sections to the Nevada mechanics lien law. NRS 108.2453 sets forth a number of new limitations on waivers and releases of obligations and rights[653] NRS 108.2457 sets out mandatory language on progress and final releases used to induce payment to contractors and suppliers.[654] While releases will be dealt with in detail later in this Chapter, limitations on waivers of fundamental obligations under the lien statutes is appropriately dealt with here.

---

[653] NRS 108.2453 states in pertinent part:

> *1. Except as otherwise provided [in the Nevada mechanics lien law], a person may not waive or modify a right, obligation or liability set forth in the provisions of [the Nevada mechanics lien law].*
> *2. A condition, stipulation or provision in a contract or other agreement for the improvement of property or for the construction, alteration or repair of a work of improvement in this state that attempts to do any of the following is contrary to public policy and is void and unenforceable: (a). Require a lien claimant to waive rights provided by law to lien claimants or to limit the rights provided to lien claimants other than as expressly provided [in the Nevada mechanics lien law]; (b). Relieve a person of an obligation or liability imposed by the [Nevada mechanics lien law].*

[654] NRS 108.2457 provides in pertinent part:

> *1. Any term of a contract that attempts to waive or impair the lien rights of a contractor, subcontractor or supplier is void. An owner, contractor or subcontractor by any term of a contract, or otherwise, may not obtain the waiver of, or impair the lien rights of, a contractor, subcontractor or supplier, except as provided in this section. Any written consent given by a lien claimant that waives or limits any lien rights is unenforceable unless the lien claimant: (a) Executes and delivers a waiver and release that is signed by the lien claimant or the lien claimant's authorized agent in the form set forth in this section; and (b) In the case of a conditional waiver and release, receives payment of the amount identified in the conditional waiver and release.*
> *2. An oral or written statement purporting to waive, release or otherwise adversely affect the rights of a lien claimant is not enforceable and does not create any estoppel or impairment of a lien unless: (a) There is a written waiver and release in the form set forth in this section; and (b) The lien claimant received payment for the lien and then only to the extent of the payment received.*

Nevada's mechanics lien law has always been subject to the doctrine of substantial compliance. While the history of that doctrine would take volumes to recount, it was adequately summarized in the 1990 Nevada Supreme Court case known as *Fondren v. K/L Complex Ltd.*[655]

Likewise, it is abundantly clear that Nevada will no longer accept a pre-construction contractual waiver of the mechanics lien right. Prior to 2003, give the lack of a constitutional right to mechanic's liens, it was held that pre-construction contractual mechanic's lien waivers would be enforceable.[656] In response to *Dayside* and the then pending Venetian Lien Litigation matter where this preconstruction waiver defense was being asserted, the Nevada legislature enacted NRS 108.2457(1), voiding any contractual provisions waiving mechanics lien rights as a matter of public policy. A number of years later, the Nevada Supreme Court overruled *Dayside*, holding that the Venetian Lien Litigation attempt to enforce a pre-construction lien waiver was against public policy but left open the possibility that a mechanics lien waiver could be upheld based on a case-by-case public policy analysis.[657] While the case-by-case analysis seems moot given the applicability of NRS 108.2457(1) to contracts entered into after October 1, 2003, there could be some confusion within the trial courts as a result of this ruling. Since then, the Nevada Supreme Court has issued several additional rulings that bring the stringent protection of the mechanics lien right from contractual waiver more clearly into focus.[658]

8:4. Definition of "Lien Claimant"

In general, anyone who supplies labor, materials, services or equipment, with the intention to improve the property has a potential mechanics lien on that property for the value of his work or unpaid balance of his contract. In some states the right to claim a

---

655 *Fondren v. K/L Complex Ltd.*, 106 Nev. 705, 800 P.2d 719 (1990).

656 *Dayside Inc. v. First Judicial Dist. Court of State of Nevada, in and for Carson City*, 119 Nev. 404, 75 P.3d 384 (2003) (overruled by, *Lehrer McGovern Bovis, Inc. v. Bullock Insulation, Inc.*, 197 P.3d 1032 (Nev. 2008)).

657 *Lehrer McGovern Bovis, Inc. v. Bullock Insulation, Inc.*, 185 P.3d 1055 (Nev. 2008), opinion withdrawn and superseded on denial of reh'g, 197 P.3d 1032 (Nev. 2008). "*[W]e now overrule Dayside and conclude that it is appropriate for the district court to engage in a public policy analysis particular to each lien waiver provision that the court is asked to enforce. In doing so, we emphasize that not every lien waiver provision violates public policy. The enforceability of each lien waiver clause must be resolved on a case-by-case basis by considering whether the form of the lien waiver clause violates Nevada's public policy to secure payment for contractors.*"

658 Much of Nevada law concerning waivers of mechanics liens arises in the context of subordination of liens to deeds of trust. *See* Section 8:31 Mechanics Lien Priority And Equitable Subrogation.

mechanics lien does not extend to a material man who sells supplies to another material man who in turn sells materials to a contractor who incorporates them into the project. In such states it is said that a material man to a material man does not have Mechanics lien rights.

The Mechanics lien law of Nevada does not appear to be settled on this issue, and the revisions seem to extend the lien law claim to very distant potential claimants. NRS 108.2214, provides in pertinent part:

> *'Lien Claimant' means any person who provides work, material or equipment with a value of $500 or more to be used in or for the construction, alteration or repair of any improvement, property or work of improvement. The term includes, without limitation, every artisan, builder, contractor, laborer, lessor or renter of equipment, materialman, miner, subcontractor or other person who provides work, material or equipment and any person who performs services as an architect, engineer, land surveyor, or geologist, in relation to the improvement, property or work of improvement.*

Under this statute arguably a manufacturer who supplies materials to a distributor may have lien rights, if the goods can be traced to the project and if the manufacturer can show the intention to supply the material "to be used in or for" the improvement of the specific project. Case law indicates, however, that materials or labor must be intended by the supplier to "enhance the value" of the specific project.[659] Similar reasoning has been used to deny mechanics lien remedies to an installer of "fixtures" which may or must be removed without damage to the property when a tenant vacates the premises, even if they are necessary for the tenant's business operation.[660] In 2007, the Nevada Legislature further muddied these waters by extending the definition of "laborer" in NRS 108.2214 to include a fringe benefit trust fund or other similar entity.[661] Now union benefit trust funds can obtain mechanics lien claims without providing preliminary notices under NRS 108.245 or otherwise complying with the obligations of an independent entity.[662]

---

[659] *Didier v. Webster Mines Corporation*, 49 Nev. 5, 234 P. 520 (1925). A cook's services in providing meals for a work crew at the remote location of a construction project were not "lienable" because they did not enhance the value of the work of improvement.

[660] *Reno Electrical Works v. Ward*, 51 Nev. 291, 274 P. 196, 62 A.L.R. 247 (1929); *cf. Fondren v. K/L Complex Ltd.*, 106 Nev. 705, 800 P.2d 719 (1990).

[661] NRS 108.2214(2):

> *"As used in this section, 'laborer' includes, without limitation, an express trust fund to which any portion of the total compensation of a laborer, including without limitation, any fringe benefit, must be paid pursuant to an agreement with that laborer or the collective bargaining agent of that laborer."*

[662] *See* NRS 108.245(3) and Section 8:5, General contractor's obligation to provide notice of lien law.

8:5 GENERAL CONTRACTOR'S OBLIGATION TO PROVIDE NOTICE OF LIEN LAW

The key to any state mechanics lien law is that the owner receive notice of the law and of those who can claim a lien based thereon.[663] This notice to the owner is, therefore, critical to maintain the due process rights of the owner and the benefit of the lien statutes to the lien claimant.

Under Nevada Contractor's law, a general contractor has a duty to provide certain documentation to a construction project owner, at the time it enters into a construction contract. Such notices are required to inform the owner of the existence of the Mechanics lien laws, and to the effect and purpose of preliminary notices when received. For all private construction projects, the general contractor is required to provide a Notice of Mechanics Lien Law, pursuant to NRS 108.246.[664] For single family residential construction, in addition, the general contractor must provide a more detailed "Notice to Owner" provided by the Nevada Contractors License Board, as outlined in NAC 624.693 and NRS 624.321.

General contractors should be aware that NRS 108.235(2) requires the general contractor to defend any action brought to foreclose a Mechanics lien at its own expense, so long as the contractor has been paid by the owner for the lien claimant's work, material or equipment. Moreover, if a foreclosure action is filed the owner may withhold from the general contractor the amount of any lien, and if judgment is issued on the lien, the owner is entitled to indemnity from the contractor. For these reasons, the contractor who receives a Nevada Preliminary Notice should take pains to ensure that all potential claims are resolved.

8:6. THE NEVADA PRELIMINARY NOTICE

Crucial to the propriety of the mechanics lien claim is the service by the lien claimant of the Notice of Right to Lien, or as known to many practitioners of construction law, the Preliminary Notice. The service of a preliminary notice was deemed critical to the California Supreme Court in finding that the California mechanics lien law statutes did not violate the prohibition on due process rights of the property owners both under the fifth and the fourteenth amendments of the United States Constitution.[665] But Nevada takes a permissive approach. Mechanics lien rights are to be liberally construed in favor

---

[663] *Great Southern Fire Proof Hotel Co. v. Jones*, 193 U.S. 532, 549, 24 S. Ct. 576, 581, 48 L. Ed. 778 (1904); *Connolly Development, Inc. v. Superior Court*, 17 Cal. 3d 803, 820, 132 Cal. Rptr. 477, 553 P.2d 637 (1976).

[664] *See* Form 8-1 in Appendix A.

[665] *Connolly Development, Inc. v. Superior Court*, 17 Cal. 3d 803, 820-822, 132 Cal. Rptr. 477, 553 P.2d 637 (1976).

of mechanics lien claimants even when a preliminary notice is involved.[666] This rule would seem to fly in the face of Nevada's legislative mandate that:

> *Except as otherwise provided in NRS 108.221 to 108.246, inclusive, a person may not waive or modify a right, obligation or liability set forth in the provisions of NRS 108.221 to 108.246, inclusive.*[667]

Accordingly, when the Nevada legislature then states that a Notice of Right to Lien "shall" be served, such a mandate should not be lightly dismissed simply because mechanics' lien laws are to be liberally construed in favor of mechanics lien claimants. Yet this is precisely what the Nevada Supreme Court has allowed. The preliminary notice is key to the *constitutionality* of any mechanics' lien law, and the Nevada legislature has recognized this in the statutory scheme. NRS 108.245 provides in pertinent part:

> *1. Except as otherwise provided in subsection 5, every lien claimant, other than one who performs only labor, who claims the benefit of NRS 108.221 to 108.246, inclusive, shall, at any time after the first delivery of material or performance of work or services under his contract, deliver in person or by certified mail to the owner of the property a notice of right to lien ...*
>
> *...*
>
> *3. No lien for materials or equipment furnished or for work or services performed, except labor, may be perfected or enforced pursuant to NRS 108.221 to 108.246, inclusive, unless the notice has been given.*
>
> *...*
>
> *5. A prime contractor or other person who contracts directly with an owner or sells materials directly to an owner is not required to give notice pursuant to this section.*

The legislative intent that notice of those who may claim a lien be provided to the owner is immediately seen in the statutory structure. *Every* lien claimant *shall* serve a preliminary notice, *unless* you provide your work or materials directly to the project owner (who therefore would know who you are). The only exception here is the person who provides only labor--that is a laborer who is a "lien claimant," as defined in NRS 108.2214. And the legislative penalty for failing to provide such notice is also clear: *No lien* may be perfected or enforced *unless* the notice is given. Yet the Nevada Supreme Court has added another exception--"actual notice."[668] Substantial compliance with the lien laws, at least with regards to those safeguards that protect an owner's right to due process, are not to be merely dismissed as inconveniences.

---

[666] *Hardy Companies, Inc. v. SNMARK, LLC*, 126 Nev. 528, 245 P.3d 1149 (2010).

[667] NRS 108.2453(1).

[668] *Hardy Companies, Inc. v. SNMARK, LLC*, 126 Nev. 528, 245 P.3d 1149 (2010). *See also* Section 8:7.

The service requirements and contents are set forth in NRS 108.245 as mandatory obligations of the lien claimant. Lien claimants are, therefore, well advised to use a pre-printed form which has been reviewed for compliance with statutory requirements by a licensed Nevada attorney.[669] The purpose of a preliminary notice is to provide the project owner with knowledge that the claimant may have the right to record a Mechanics lien against the project if it is not paid.[670] The owner then is able to take specific steps to assure payment is received by the potential lien claimant. The Nevada Notice of Right to Lien must contain the following information:[671]

a) Name and address of the owner or reputed owner;
b) A general description of the work, materials or equipment provided;
c) The property description or street address;
d) The name of the contractor or subcontractor with whom the Claimant contracted; and
e) The name and address of the Claimant.

The Notice of Right to Lien must also contain the following disclaimer:

> *This is not a notice that the undersigned has not or does not expect to be paid, but a notice required by law that the undersigned may, at a future date, record a notice of lien as provided by law against the property if the undersigned is not paid.*

The Notice of Right to Lien should be signed by the claimant, but does not need to be verified, sworn or acknowledged in order to be effective. It is recommended that the notice contain a demand that the owner serve upon the claimant a copy of any Notice of Completion for the project. Although the owner is required to serve a copy of a Notice of Completion upon every person who delivers a Notice of Right to Lien, upon receipt of such a demand therefore, the owner is required to mail a copy of any Notice of Completion to the requestor within ten days of its recordation. If the owner fails to provide the notice, compliance with certain statutory time limitations are excused as to that requestor. While it is somewhat redundant, the author believes it never is a bad business practice to provide more notice than is legally required.

The Notice of Right to Lien should be served on the owner and the general contractor.[672] NRS 108.22148 defines the term "owner" under the statute to include owners of record

---

[669] *See* Form 8-2 in Appendix A.

[670] *Hardy Companies, Inc. v. SNMARK, LLC*, 126 Nev. 528, 245 P.3d 1149 (2010).

[671] NRS 108.245(1).

[672] NRS 108.245(1) provides in pertinent part:

on a deed or other recorded conveyance, reputed owners, persons listed as owner on the county tax assessor roles covering the property, or persons named as owners on the improvement building permit.[673] According to the Nevada Supreme Court, the preliminary notice must be served on all owners of a property in order to be effective.[674] Likewise, a tenant will fall into the category of an owner.[675] Under Nevada law, an "owner" can also include the State or a political subdivision of the state (a town or city) that owns property to be used for a private or nongovernmental purpose, or privately owned land which is leased by the State or a political subdivision thereof. A claimant who is the general contractor or has otherwise entered into a contract directly with the property owner need not give a preliminary notice. A subcontractor or supplier to a

---

> *A subcontractor or equipment or material supplier who gives such a notice must also deliver in person or send by certified mail a copy of the notice to the prime contractor for information only.*

673 NRS 108.22148 provides:

> *1. "Owner" includes:*
> *(a) The record owner or owners of the property or an improvement to the property as evidenced by a conveyance or other instrument which transfers that interest to the record owner or owners and is recorded in the office of the county recorder in which the improvement or the property is located;*
> *(b) The reputed owner or owners of the property or an improvement to the property;*
> *(c) The owner or owners of the property or an improvement to the property, as shown on the records of the county assessor for the county where the property or improvement is located;*
> *(d) The person or persons whose name appears as owner of the property or an improvement to the property on the building permit;*
> *(e) A person who claims an interest in or possesses less than a fee simple estate in the property;*
> *(f) This State or a political subdivision of this State, including, without limitation, an incorporated city or town, that owns the property or an improvement to the property if the property or improvement is used for a private or nongovernmental use or purpose; or*
> *(g) A person described in paragraph (a), (b), (c), (d) or (e) who leases the property or an improvement to the property to this State or a political subdivision of this State, including, without limitation, an incorporated city or town, if the property or improvement is privately owned.*
> *2. The term does not include:*
> *(a) A mortgagee;*
> *(b) A trustee or beneficiary of a deed of trust;*
> *(c) The owner or holder of a lien encumbering the property or an improvement to the property; or*
> *(d) Except as otherwise provided in paragraph (f) of subsection 1, this State or a political subdivision of this State, including, without limitation, an incorporated city or town.*

674 *Hardy Companies, Inc. v. SNMARK, LLC*, 126 Nev. 528, 245 P.3d 1149 (2010).

675 *Hardy Companies, Inc. v. SNMARK, LLC*, 126 Nev. 528, 245 P.3d 1149 (2010).

subcontractor must also serve a copy of the notice on the general contractor for information purposes, but the failure to do so will not invalidate the notice provided to the owner.[676] Rather, a single failure to provide the general contractor with a copy of the preliminary notice will subject a subcontractor to discipline under the Nevada Contractor's License Law.[677]

Those who would be filing lien claims should set up a system, where upon acceptance of a contract, preliminary notices are sent to the owner and general contractor. In this way, the potential lien claimant complies with the license law requirements and is automatically protected if the need to record a Mechanics lien arises. However, there is one concern. On private projects the Preliminary Notice may be served at any time after first supplying labor or materials to the project, but the recovered amount is limited to the value of work performed 31 days prior to the preliminary notice being served and everything thereafter.[678] This time frame is different from that for the Public Works Preliminary Notice, which must be given within 30 days.[679] There is no obvious reason for this one day discrepancy, and this can become a trap for the unwary. A lien claimant who performs both public and private construction work should then set up the system to provide the notice on all projects within 30 days of the first provision of work on the project.

It should also be noted that the service of the preliminary notice affects the amount recoverable on the lien claim. As the preliminary notice is required to and does so provide a right to a lien for work, materials services or equipment, that right to recover is limited to the amount of services, work, material or equipment provided in the 31 days prior to the date the notice was given and thereafter.[680] The recoverable amount of

---

676 NRS 108.245(1) provides in pertinent part:

> *The failure by a subcontractor to deliver the notice to the prime contractor is a ground for disciplinary proceedings against the subcontractor under chapter 624 of NRS but does not invalidate the notice to the owner.*

But see Hardy Companies, Inc. v. SNMARK, LLC, 126 Nev. 528, 245 P.3d 1149 (2010):

> *"Where a claimant is seeking to place and enforce a lien, NRS 108.245 requires that the claimant serve all parties whose interest it is seeking to affect. [&p;] [The lien claimant] has an affirmative duty of due diligence to ascertain the identity of the owner whose interest it is seeking to affect."*

677 NRS 624.3016(4).

678 NRS 108.245(1) and (6).

679 NRS 339.035(2).

680 NRS 108.245(6) provides:

the lien claim therefore should be limited if the preliminary notice is sent late, or should be eliminated if the preliminary notice is not sent at all, as no services, work, material or equipment would in such a case be sent 31 days before the date the notice is given and thereafter.[681]

Finally, it should be noted that the Preliminary Notice may be served on the owner and general contractor either by personal delivery or by certified mail.[682] While return receipt requested is not mentioned in the statute as required (and it therefore is not requirement to impart notice), it is recommended that the additional charge for this service be incurred. The claimant should always be able to prove that the Notice was properly served. Since personal service is usually impractical, it is recommended that service be made by certified mail. A copy of the Notice with the certification receipt and "green" receipt card should be kept in the job file. If the owner or general contractor refuses to accept certified mail, the claimant should keep the returned certified envelope, unopened, in the job file to prove compliance with NRS 108.245.

8:7 The "Actual Notice" Exception

In late 2010, the Nevada Supreme Court added a new exception to those required to provide a preliminary notice to perfect a mechanics lien--any lien claimant of whom the owner has actual knowledge of its identity as working on the construction site.[683] As part of *Hardy Companies, Inc. v. SNMARK, LLC*,[684] the Supreme Court affirmed its decision in *Fondren*,[685] and expanded the exceptions to include third party lien claimants with which the Owner of the project had no direct contract. To perfect a lien, a lien claimant now has two choices: 1) conform to the requirements of NRS 108.245 and properly serve a written preliminary notice, or 2) prove in court that the owner had "actual notice" of his or her participation on the project.

> *A lien claimant who is required by this section to give a notice of right to lien to an owner and who gives such a notice has a right to lien for materials or equipment furnished or for work or services performed in the 31 days before the date the notice of right to lien is given and for the materials or equipment furnished or for work or services performed anytime thereafter until the completion of the work of improvement.*

681 As NRS 108.245(6) was part of the 2003 amendments to the mechanics lien statutes, it is difficult to determine how the statutes will be interpreted under the Nevada Supreme Court's decision in *Hardy Companies, Inc. v. SNMARK, LLC*, 126 Nev. 528, 245 P.3d 1149 (2010) and the "actual notice" exception articulated therein.

682 NRS 108.245(1).

683 *Hardy Companies, Inc. v. SNMARK, LLC*, 126 Nev. 528, 245 P.3d 1149 (2010).

684 *Hardy Companies, Inc. v. SNMARK, LLC*, 126 Nev. 528, 245 P.3d 1149 (2010).

685 *Fondren v. K/L Complex Ltd.*, 106 Nev. 705, 800 P.2d 719 (1990).

In *Hardy*, the landlord entered into a lease agreement with a large retail tenant, who was required to construct improvements using a landlord approved general contractor. A provision in the executed lease specifically named O'Neil as the approved general contractor. After execution of the lease, the landlord recorded a Notice of Non-Responsibility under NRS 108.234, but failed to serve the notice on O'Neil as required by statute. After entering into the contract, O'Neil performed its work and provided its invoices for payment to the tenant. For certain work however, the landlord's managing agent specifically directed O'Neil's work. He also inspected the job site numerous times, and reviewed and approved O'Neil's invoice payments. O'Neil, in turn, entered into a subcontract with the subcontractor, Hardy. Hardy served a Nevada preliminary notice under NRS 108.245 on the tenant and O'Neil, but failed to serve the landlord or its agent. There was no evidence presented that the landlord had actual knowledge of Hardy on the project, to have directed its work, nor reviewed any of Hardy's invoices. Ultimately, the tenant filed for Chapter 7 bankruptcy protection and was liquidated. Both O'Neil and Hardy liened the project under NRS 108.226. The landlord moved for summary judgment on both mechanics liens claiming that it was not served with a Nevada preliminary notice, as required under NRS 108.245. The trial court granted the motion. The landlord argued that under the provisions of NRS 108.2453(1), the doctrine of substantial compliance articulated in *Fondren* had been abrogated. O'Neil and Hardy appealed.

On appeal, the Nevada Supreme Court noted that by enacting NRS 108.2453(1), the legislature had not implicitly overturned the long recognized doctrine of substantial compliance, as it related to mechanics liens. Initially, the Court noted that legislative intent is the primary consideration in interpreting an ambiguous statute. To discern such intent, the Court would consider the entire subject matter and policy of the mechanics lien statutes as a whole, so that all provisions are considered together, reconciled and harmonized. No part of the statute should be rendered meaningless or lead to an absurd or unreasonable result.

The Court noted in *Hardy* that NRS 108.2453(1) provides: "Except as otherwise provided in [the mechanics lien statutes] a person may not waive or modify a right, obligation or liability set forth in the ... [mechanics lien statutes]." The Court then asserts this provision could be reconciled with *Fondren*,[686] by holding that it is interpreted as "voiding conditions, stipulations, or provisions of a contract that require a lien claimant to waive lien rights."[687] Relying on the "presumption against [legislative] abrogation and alteration of common law, ..." it declared NRS 108.2453(1) to be ambiguous, and reviewed the legislative history surrounding the 2003 and 2005 mechanics lien law

[686] *Fondren v. K/L Complex Ltd.*, 106 Nev. 705, 800 P.2d 719 (1990).

[687] *Hardy Companies, Inc. v. SNMARK, LLC*, 126 Nev. 528, 245 P.3d 1149 (2010).

revisions. Finding no explicit statement overturning *Fondren* in the legislative history, the Court held that the legislature did not do so by enacting NRS 108.2453(1).[688]

Regardless, having established that the doctrine of substantial compliance has not been overruled, the Court held that NRS 108.245 requires the lien claimant to serve a preliminary notice on the Owner. In a lease, the tenant who holds the ownership right to possession of the property is included in the definition of "owner" under NRS 108.22148. Citing *Fondren*,[689] the Court held that the purpose of the preliminary notice is to "provide the owner with knowledge that work and materials are being incorporated into the property." The Court also emphasized, however, that it has continuously held "that the mechanics lien statutes are remedial in character and should be liberally construed; that substantial compliance with the statutory requirements is sufficient to perfect the lien if the property owner is not prejudiced."

Explicitly deciding not to use the reasoning that *Fondren* merely reflects liens recorded by "prime contractors" holding direct contracts with the owner, and that they are thereby exempt from the obligation to provide a preliminary notice under NRS 1087.245(5), the Court instead creates a factually driven test to establish an "actual notice" exception to the preliminary notice requirement.[690] Instead of following the legislative mandate in NRS 108.245(1) that a lien claimant "shall" serve a preliminary notice, the Court instead asserts that a property owner who negotiates a lease requiring substantial improvements has actual knowledge of potential lien claims. If that owner fails to file a notice of non-responsibility under NRS 108.234 after knowledge of the construction commencement, the construction is deemed performed at the owner's specific request. A property owner will have actual knowledge of potential lien claims if the property owner or the property owner's agent regularly inspects the project construction. Actual knowledge by the property owner's agent would also be imputed to the property owner. Thus, no preliminary notice would be required of those lien claimants with direct owner contracts, because the landlord had actual notice of their existence. In this circumstance, the Court held the general contractor was entitled to put

[688] This line of reasoning, however, begs the question of what does NRS 108.2453(2) address when it provides "[a condition, stipulation or provision in a contract" that "[r equire a lien claimant to waive [mechanics lien rights " is "contrary to public policy and is void and unenforceable"? If the first subsection merely repeats by implication what the second says explicitly, the second is rendered meaningless as it is merely repetitive of the first.

[689] *Fondren v. K/L Complex Ltd.*, 106 Nev. 705, 800 P.2d 719 (1990).

[690] It should be noted that nothing in the legislature history appears to support the concept that an "actual notice" exception was intended to be authorized.

on evidence of the landlord's knowledge of it on the project, thereby exercising an "actual knowledge" exception to the NRS 108.245 preliminary notice requirement.[691]

Turning to the subcontractor, Hardy, the Court made several additional comments. First, the Court noted that if the landlord had actual knowledge of Hardy on the project, Hardy could also take advantage of the actual knowledge exception. Actual knowledge of Hardy, however, could not be demonstrated just by the fact that construction occurred on the property. Since the owner could not know what subcontractors were on site, the actual knowledge exception would require evidence that the owner knew the identity of the subcontractor before it would apply. Moreover, the subcontractor could not simply provide a preliminary notice under NRS 108.245 to the landlord's tenant. Rather, NRS 108.245 "requires that the notice be given to the right person or entity. A failure to serve the right person or entity cannot be cured by NSR 108.229(3) [allowing amendments to claims of lien up to and including trial]."[692] In this case, the actual owner needs to receive a preliminary notice to perfect a lien. Also, NRS 108.245 requires that the lien claimant serve all parties whose interest it is seeking to affect by the lien. As such, "the service of one owner is not adequate to give notice to other owners of the potential claim."[693] Giving notice to the tenant would give notice sufficient to cover its interest in the property; it was insufficient to give notice to the landlord. Finally, the Court noted that the actual knowledge exception requires more than mere knowledge of construction activity. Rather, the owner must be shown to have actual knowledge of the identity of the lien claimant with whom he has no direct contract. This is a question of fact that must be proven in court, by the presentation of such factors as the owner supervising work by the lien claimant, reviewing billing statements of the lien claimant, or any other evidence that would make the owner aware of the lien claimant's identity.

Notwithstanding the Court's stated purpose, the reasoning here does not seem to comport with the overall structure of the mechanic's lien statutes. The decision creates redundancy in NRS 108.2453(2), and seems to disregard the "shall" requirements in NRS 108.245(1). Further, the decision does not consider the actual knowledge exception's effect on other sections of the mechanic's lien law. For instance, the provisions of NRS 108.245(6), which limits the amount recoverable on a lien claim to the value of work or material provided "... in the 31 days before the date the [preliminary] notice ... is given and ... thereafter until the completion of the work ..." are not mentioned.

---

[691] In fact, the Court specifically chose not to address the effect of NRS 108.245(5). *See Hardy, supra,* 126 Nev. 528, 245 P.3d 1149, at fn 11. The "actual notice" exception does not seem to take this statute into account.

[692] *Hardy Companies, Inc. v. SNMARK, LLC,* 126 Nev. 528, 245 P.3d 1149 (2010).

[693] *Hardy Companies, Inc. v. SNMARK, LLC,* 126 Nev. 528, 245 P.3d 1149 (2010).

This statutory limitation has to be implicitly ignored to allow an "actual knowledge" exception to function as articulated by the decision.

The opinion also seems internally inconsistent. While a tenant's actual knowledge will be imputed to the landlord to satisfy the actual knowledge requirement for a direct contractor, the subcontractor's provision of a preliminary notice under NRS 108.245 to the tenant is insufficient to put the same landlord on notice of a subcontractor's work. Wouldn't actual knowledge of one owner be imputable to other owners under agency principals as well? The subcontractor is almost better off using actual knowledge by making sure the owner knows they are on site, or simply noting in its daily logs that it had contact with the owner's representative. The simplicity and certainty of mandatory service of a preliminary notice appears by *Hardy* to be disregarded in favor of an uncertain test to show "actual knowledge" at trial. For an owner at least (and perhaps the general contractor that may need to defend him or her), this may seem to be an absurd result. Still, *Hardy* remains the law of the land and owners need to be ready for its effects on their project risk analysis.

8:8 15-DAY NOTICE OF INTENT TO LIEN

During the construction boom of the 1990s and early 2000s, residential subdivision construction was at its peak in Nevada. As a result of increased use of the mechanics lien law, many residential housing sales were stopped with the discovery of a mechanics lien that had attached to the property. This caused the residential homebuilders to seek some kind of additional notification before a mechanics lien could be recorded. In response to this request, the 2003 legislature enacted NRS 108.226(6), which mandates the service of a notice of intent to lien on residential construction projects only, which include apartment buildings. NRS 108.226(6) provides:

> *Except as otherwise provided in subsection 7, if a work of improvement involves the construction, alteration or repair of multifamily or single-family residences, including, without limitation, apartment houses, a lien claimant, except laborers, must serve a 15-day notice of intent to lien incorporating substantially the same information required in a notice of lien upon both the owner and the reputed prime contractor before recording a notice of lien. Service of the notice of intent to lien must be by personal delivery or certified mail and will extend the time for recording the notice of lien described in subsection 1 by 15 days. A notice of lien for materials or equipment furnished or to be furnished for work or services performed or to be performed, except labor, for a work of improvement involving the construction, alteration or repair of multifamily or single-family residences may not be perfected or enforced pursuant to NRS 108.221 to 108.246, inclusive, unless the 15-day notice of intent to lien has been given to the owner.*

Before a lien claimant may record or foreclose a mechanics lien on a residential construction project, the lien claimant must send a notice of intent to lien to the project owner.[694] The notice must be sent to the owner 15 days before the recordation of the lien claimant's notice of lien, either by certified mail or by personal delivery.

Service of the notice of intent to lien will extend the time to record a claim of lien 15 days from the date the notice is sent to the owner. The service of this notice on residential projects is mandatory, however, this section does not apply to commercial or other types of projects which are not residential in nature. As such, the service of a notice of intent to lien on a non-residential project will not extend the time to record the claim of lien, and care should be taken to prevent misunderstanding here.

This of course, begs the question of what type of project is residential construction? While the statute clearly indicates that multifamily and single-family residences, including apartments, are subject to this additional pre-lien notice, what other types of projects are as well? Does any project with a residential component qualify as needing a 15-day notice of intent to lien? With the proliferation of multi-use projects in Nevada, most new construction projects contain some type of residential component. In an effort to clarify this issue, in 2005 the Nevada legislature enacted NRS 108.226(7), which provides:

> *The provisions of subsection 6 do not apply to the construction of any nonresidential construction project.*

While this is not the clearest of directives, a reasonable interpretation of this clause is that the legislature intended to limit the application on the 15-day notice of intent to lien to those projects which contain some type of residential component. This would seem to include multi-use projects and residential projects with a commercial intent, such as senior living facilities, and boarding houses. Hence, practitioners should counsel their clients to be most conservative in their use of the 15-day notice of intent to lien: that is to serve the notice in all questionable cases, but to be sure not to rely on the 15-day extension of time to record a notice of lien allowed under NRS 108.226(6).

8:9 THE CLAIM OF LIEN

Once the need to enforce a mechanics lien becomes clear to the lien claimant, the Notice of lien must be prepared, recorded and served on the record owner for the project. While the act of recording the lien is fairly straight forward, much has been disputed in Nevada over the calculation of the amount of the lien itself, and so a fair amount of this Chapter will be devoted to that calculation. The current state of Nevada mechanics lien law, however, strongly favors the mechanics lien claimant, which because a prime or general contractor will be obligated to defend the owner in many cases from the lien

[694] *See* Form 8-11 in Appendix A.

claim by statute[695] will usually be a subcontractor or supplier. As a result, lien claimants can exact heavy tolls on general contractors and owners through the use of the mechanics lien process. It is by far the better practice to resolve payment and change order issues as soon as possible to avoid the effects of the mechanics lien process, rather than having to bond around or otherwise suffer the cloud of the in many cases legislatively authorized excessive lien on the property owner's title.

Of critical importance to the lien claimant, however, is his compliance with the requirements to have a proper contractors' license to perform the work for which the notice of lien is secured. NRS 108.222(2) provides:

> *If a contractor or professional is required to be licensed pursuant to the provisions of NRS to perform the work, the contractor or professional will only have a lien pursuant to subsection 1 if the contractor or professional is licensed to perform the work.*

While the details of licensing are discussed in Chapter 2 of this treatise, care should be followed to determine that a lien claimant has the proper license for the work performed and which forms the basis of the claim of lien. Moreover, it should be also determined that the contract amount, including change orders, are within the license limitations of the lien claimant's contractor's license. If the lien claimant has a license limitation that is below the amount of the lien claim itself, there is a legitimate basis for the courts to strike down the claim of lien as invalid and frivolous under NRS 108.2275.

8:10 Calculation of the Amount of the Notice of Lien

Calculation of the amount of the mechanics lien can be one of the most hotly contested issues in a mechanics lien claim and there are number of practical reasons. The amount of the mechanics lien claim will dictate the amount necessary to bond around the lien, in order to prevent a default on construction loans or to clear title to the property for sale, as well as the price of such a bond and the amount of security needed for that bond claim. These can calculate into astronomical sums that can significantly hinder the construction project itself. Part of this dispute will be an attempt to classify the lien amount into categories which by legislative *fiat* cannot be part of a lien claim, such as "consequential damages." Damages which are within the nebulous "consequential" category cannot be recovered in a mechanics lien action.[696] Consequential damages are

---

[695] See NRS 108.235(2).

[696] NRS 108.239(7) provides:

> *The court shall enter judgment according to the right of the parties, and shall, by decree, proceed to hear and determine the claims in a summary way, or may, if it be the district court, refer the claims to a special master to ascertain and report upon the liens and the amount justly due thereon. No consequential damages may be recovered in an action*

poorly defined by judicial pronouncement, at least as they are applicable to mechanics lien claims.[697] But much beyond consequential damages, the Nevada Supreme Court case of *California Commercial v. Amedeo Vegas I, Inc.*[698] also removed disputed change orders from the mechanics lien, holding that only when change orders were approved did they become part of the contract price, and thereby could be included in a claim of lien. So again in 2003 and 2005, the legislature addressed the issue to make the amount of the lien to include disputed work.[699] NRS 108.222(1) now provides in pertinent part:

> *pursuant to this section. All liens not so exhibited shall be deemed to be waived in favor of those which are so exhibited.*

This section has been traditionally viewed as disallowing consequential damages in a lien claim, however, such an argument is not necessarily in keeping with the context of this provision. NRS 108.239 deals with the Court's summary declaration of the rights of various parties in the mechanics lien claim, separating the claims for consequential damages from the "summary" determination of the mechanics lien claims. It is unclear from this context that the "amount" of the claim of lien so elaborately outlined in NRS 108.222(1) should be modified by the direction to the court of summary adjudication of the mechanics liens and the rights of the parties themselves.

697 In *California Commercial v. Amedeo Vegas I, Inc.*, 119 Nev. 143, 146 n.5, 67 P.3d 328 (2003), the Nevada Supreme Court stated:

> *Commercial tries to characterize its delay costs as direct damages, rather than consequential damages, to avoid this statute [NRS 108.239(7)]. However, delay costs are a foreseeable consequence of construction delays, and are therefore properly characterized as consequential damages.*

Likewise, in *Clark County School Dist. v. Rolling Plains Const., Inc.*, 117 Nev. 101, 106, 16 P.3d 1079, 1082-1083, 150 Ed. Law Rep. 926 (2001) (disapproved of by, *Sandy Valley Associates v. Sky Ranch Estates Owners Ass'n*, 117 Nev. 948, 35 P.3d 964 (2001)), the Court explained:

> *"In order to award consequential damages, the damages claimed for the breach of contract must be foreseeable. [citations omitted]. [F]oreseeability requires that: (1) damages for loss must 'fairly and reasonably be considered [as] arising naturally ... from such breach of contract itself,' and (2) the loss must be 'such as may reasonably be supposed to have been in the contemplation of both parties, at the time they made the contract as the probable result of the breach of it.'"*

But these legally correct interpretations of consequential damages do not comport with the traditional understanding that costs and expenses incurred in the construction of a project are lienable. For instance, when a contractor is delayed through no fault of his own, he still must pay the wages of his workmen through the period of delay. If the owner is the cause of the delay, should not the owner's property rightly be charged with the additional labor cost incurred by the owner's actions?

698 *California Commercial v. Amedeo Vegas I, Inc.*, 119 Nev. 143, 67 P.3d 328 (2003)

699 However, the Nevada Supreme Court seems unwilling to allow for implicit repeal of its rulings without a specific legislative declaration of intent. *See Hardy Companies, Inc. v. SNMARK, LLC*, 126 Nev. 528, 245 P.3d 1149 (2010). The legislative history does not include any specific repeal of the *California Commercial* decision.

> *[A] lien claimant has a lien upon the property, any improvements for which the work, materials and equipment were furnished or to be furnished, and any construction disbursement account established pursuant to NRS 108.2403, for:*
> *(a) If the parties agreed, by contract or otherwise, upon a specific price or method for determining a specific price for some or all of the work, material and equipment furnished or to be furnished by or through the lien claimant, the unpaid balance of the price agreed upon for such work, material or equipment, as the case may be, whether performed, furnished or to be performed or furnished at the instance of the owner or the owner's agent; and*
> *(b) If the parties did not agree, by contract or otherwise, upon a specific price or method for determining a specific price for some or all of the work, material and equipment furnished or to be furnished by or through the lien claimant, including, without limitation, any additional or changed work, material or equipment, an amount equal to the fair market value of such work, material or equipment, as the case may be, including a reasonable allowance for overhead and a profit, whether performed, furnished or to be performed or furnished at the instance of the owner or at the instance of the owner's agent.*

NRS 108.222(1) provides two alternative or coinciding measures of the amount of a claim of lien, as the case may be: a) the unpaid contract price, assuming a price or method for determining price was agreed to, AND b) the fair market value of work, material or equipment, including in each case a reasonable allowance for overhead and profit. Determination of the amount turns on whether an agreement on the entire contract price exists.

The statute does not require any particular form of contract. Contracts, however, come in three basic forms -- written, oral, and implied in law. The fact that subsection 1(a) references "the agreed upon price" would seem to imply that written and oral contracts fall under subsection (a). Implied in law contracts, then, would fall under subsection (b). This argument is bolstered by the legal concept of unjust enrichment, which implies that a service performed will be compensated by a return of value equal to that rendered, even when the method for determining that price has not been agreed to between the parties. One may be concerned that in the absence of a contract with the owner, a claimant may not have lien rights. Nevada case law clearly supports the argument that a claim of lien may be had even though recovery would be found contractually under the concept of quantum meruit.[700] NRS 108.22104 provides, moreover, that every contractor, subcontractor, or other person having charge or control of the construction of the work of improvement is deemed to be the agent of the owner for purposes of the Mechanics lien statutes.

---

[700] *California Commercial v. Amedeo Vegas I, Inc.*, 119 Nev. 143, 67 P.3d 328 (2003); *Udevco, Inc. v. Wagner*, 100 Nev. 185, 678 P.2d 679 (1984); *Paterson v. Condos*, 55 Nev. 134, 28 P.2d 499 (1934).

In both cases, however, the 2005 legislative changes seem to overrule current case law and allow both disputed and undisputed change order work to be included in the lien claim. In a case where the lien claimant and his contract partner have not agreed on a price or validity of all change order work claimed by the lien claimant, NRS 108.222(1) as amended in 2005, allows the lien claimant to claim both the unpaid balance of the agreed to contract price, as well as the amount claimed for unsigned change order work, or even disputed change order work. This legislative change seems to, in effect, overrule part of *California Commercial v. Amedeo Vegas I, Inc.*[701] holding that a lien claimant's lien is limited to the amount of his contract without any allowance for disputed or unsigned change order requests. "Consequential damages" (i.e., damages suffered to the claimant's business as a consequence of the failure of the owner or upper tier contractor to pay the claimant), however, still are arguably not to be included in a Mechanics lien claim.[702] Items such as extended home office overhead resulting from delay or inefficiencies caused by acceleration cannot be included in a Mechanics lien claim. Such damages are consequential to the delay or acceleration, and therefore run afoul of the prohibition on collection of consequential damages through the lien process.[703]

The basic formula is to start with the contract price, add any legitimate extras, then deduct payments and legitimate back-charges. If there is no contract price, start with the fair market value including change orders, reasonable overhead and profit, and deduct payments and legitimate back-charges. If labor and materials have been supplied to

---

[701] *California Commercial v. Amedeo Vegas I, Inc.*, 119 Nev. 143, 67 P.3d 328 (2003). *But see Hardy Companies, Inc. v. SNMARK, LLC*, 126 Nev. 528, 245 P.3d 1149 (2010).

[702] NRS 108.239(7).

[703] But arguably, such damages may be part of the contract price or at least a clearly designated damage claim in the contract price. NRS 108.2453(2)(e) provides:

> *"A condition, stipulation or provision in a contract or other agreement for the improvement of property or for the construction, alteration or repair of a work of improvement in this State that attempts to do any of the following is contrary to public policy and is void and unenforceable: ... (e) Require a prime contractor or subcontractor to waive, release or extinguish a claim or right that the prime contractor or subcontractor may otherwise possess or acquire for delay, acceleration, disruption or impact damages or an extension of time for delays incurred, for any delay, acceleration, disruption or impact event which was unreasonable under the circumstances, not within the contemplation of the parties at the time the contract was entered into, or for which the prime contractor or subcontractor is not responsible."*

If the contract clause prohibiting such damages are unenforceable, could they be part of the contract and therefore recoverable as "contract damages" rather than as "consequential damages"? Obviously, such an argument would depend on the wording of the contract and the circumstances of the claim, but it is possible that drafting of contract language defining such claims as contractual rather than consequential could allow them to be recovered under Nevada's current mechanics lien scheme.

more than one parcel of property, the amount of claim should be identified to each particular parcel. It is important to not intentionally overstate the amount of a lien claim, since willful overstatement could result in a loss of all lien rights. Clearly, however, legitimate claims for reasonable overhead and profit are includable within one's mechanics lien claim.

This analysis, of course, begs the question of how to determine the "fair market value" of particular work, materials or equipment. In general, the fair market value may not be the price the lien claimant would ordinarily agree to accept, or that the project owner would agree to pay. While the legal definition of such a term would be within the purview of expert witnesses, the use of the variously available estimator's guides available to the contracting industry would prove a valuable resource.

NRS 108.229(2) provides that a "variance" between the lien and the "proof" shall not be fatal to the lien claim, unless the variance results from fraud or is made intentionally, or has misled the adverse party to his prejudice.[704] Excessive lien amounts are subject to a motion to reduce the lien and subjects the claimant to costs and attorneys fees.[705] Moreover, making a knowingly false statement in a claim of lien is a crime, punishable by a fine of not less than $5,000 and not more than $10,000.[706]

Nevada contractors should be certain that their contract documents incorporate any change orders made subsequent to the execution of the contract. Further, change orders should be fully negotiated in writing and executed by the project owner prior to the performance of any work required by the change order. However, the revisions to NRS 108.222(1) seem to allow for the inclusion of disputed change orders or even change orders for work "to be performed"[707] in the mechanics lien amount. This amount is not what the lien claimant may ultimately obtain a judgment for upon completion of the mechanics lien foreclosure action, but it must be kept in mind that the claim of lien is

---

[704] NRS 108.229(2) provides:

> *Upon the trial of any action or suit to foreclose a lien, a variance between the lien and the proof does not defeat the lien and shall not be deemed material unless the variance:*
> *(a) Results from fraud or is made intentionally; or*
> *(b) Misleads an adverse party to the party's prejudice, but then only with respect to the adverse party who was prejudiced.*
> *In all cases of immaterial variance the notice of lien may be amended, by amendment duly recorded, to conform to the proof.*

[705] NRS 108.2275.

[706] NRS 108.226(4).

[707] NRS 108.222(1).

security for the lien claimant,[708] which the legislature has determined has priority over the interests of the property owner.

8:11 Jurisdiction for the Lien Claim

It should also be noted by the lien claimant that the Nevada Supreme Court will require the filing of a lawsuit in a Court of proper jurisdiction. The jurisdiction of Nevada's Justice Court will be limited to $10,000.00, and thus the Justice Court will have jurisdiction over any mechanic's lien claim when the amount of the lien is less than $10,000.00.[709] While the lien claimant's individual lien may not exceed this limit, the Nevada courts will look to the aggregate lien claims on a property to determine jurisdictional limitations when multiple lien claims are asserted, which might then strip the Justice Court of its jurisdiction over the mechanics lien claims.[710] Furthermore, the mechanics lien law specifically contemplates consolidation of all mechanics lien foreclosures on one property to be determined in one action.[711] Therefore, lien claimants filing in Justice Court should be prepared to have the matters transferred to Nevada District Court, once the aggregate jurisdictional limitation of the Justice Court is exceeded.

8:12 Incorporation of Materials into the Work

At the same time, the question of incorporation of materials into the project exists in the Mechanics lien context; i.e., must a materialman plead and prove whether its materials were actually incorporated into a construction project, in order to maintain a Mechanics lien action? Uniquely, the answer in Nevada is No.[712] In Nevada, a lien claimant must only prove that he intended to improve the construction project and that the materials were delivered to the job site or are otherwise made available to the Project. Therefore, an intention to enhance the value of a particular project coupled with delivery of materials to the project is probably sufficient to enforce a mechanics lien.

NRS 108.222(1) provides in pertinent part:

---

[708] *Lehrer McGovern Bovis, Inc. v. Bullock Insulation, Inc.*, 185 P.3d 1055 (Nev. 2008), opinion withdrawn and superseded on denial of reh'g, 197 P.3d 1032 (Nev. 2008).

[709] NRS 4.370(1)(j).

[710] *Phillips v. Snowden Placer Co.*, 40 Nev. 66, 160 P. 786 (1916).

[711] *See generally* NRS 108.239, and specifically subparagraph 6 authorizing consolidation of all actions; *Phillips v. Snowden Placer Co.*, 40 Nev. 66, 77, 160 P. 786 (1916).

[712] *See Simmons Self-Storage Partners LLC v. Rib Roof, Inc.*, 130 Nev.Adv.Op. 57, 247 P.3d 1107 (2014).

A 'lien claimant' has a lien upon the property, any improvements for which the work, materials and equipment were furnished or to be furnished ....

Many courts in states other than Nevada who have similar statutes have ruled that "furnishes" means "delivers."[713] Therefore, so long as the materialman delivers its materials to the particular job site with the intention of improving that job site, they are arguably entitled to a lien, even if the materials are diverted by another party. It is "immaterial" whether the labor, goods or services actually benefit the project, so long as the intent to do so is demonstrated.[714] The basis of such decisions is that the owner is in the best position to determine what materials are used in their construction projects.[715] This is not always correct, however. In many cases, the owner has no control over the materials delivered to a project, nor does she have any clear proof that the specific materials were delivered.

Regardless, the wise materialman will take steps to ensure its materials are delivered to the construction site itself, not to their customer's office or warehouse. The savvy owner, likewise, will use joint checks and other defensive methods outlined in this book to ensure all materials are paid for by the contractors who install them.

8:13 PROPERTY TO WHICH THE LIEN ATTACHES

NRS 108.222 provides that the Mechanics lien attaches to "the property, and any improvements for which the work, material or equipment were furnished or to be furnished ...."[716] NRS 108.22172 defines "property" as:

the land, real property or mining claim of an owner for which a work of improvement was provided, including all buildings, improvements and fixtures thereon, and a convenience space on, around and about the same, or so much as may be required for the convenient use and occupation thereof.

---

[713] *See Halbert's Lumber, Inc. v. Lucky Stores, Inc.*, 6 Cal. App. 4th 1233, 1240-1244, 8 Cal. Rptr. 2d 298, 302-305 (4th Dist. 1992).

[714] *Richmond Machinery Co. v. Bennett*, 48 Nev. 286, 229 P. 1098 (1924); *see also Nichols v. Levy*, 55 Nev. 310, 318, 32 P.2d 120 (1934):

> *As the [mechanics lien] statute does not embrace a condition that the property on which labor is expended or for which materials are furnished must be enhanced in value by reason thereof before lien rights will attach, we may not supply it.*

[715] *Richmond Machinery Co. v. Bennett*, 48 Nev. 286, 229 P. 1098 (1924).

[716] NRS 108.222(1).

The lien attaches, therefore, to all the structures on a piece of property that was improved, as well as the improvement itself. Clearly this is an expansion of the scope of the lien, as it will encompass every structure on a given piece of property, regardless of whether than structure was improved by the work, materials or equipment, so long as the structure is required for the convenient use and occupation of the structure liened.

Likewise, NRS 108.222 also notes that a mechanics lien will attach to "any construction disbursement account established" pursuant to requirements for tenant improvement contracts.[717] Likewise, property that is owned by government agencies are now subject to mechanics lien claims if that property is leased to a privately owned tenant or is used for a non-governmental purpose.[718]

8:14 Time for Recording the Claim of Lien

A great deal of consideration needs to be given to the understanding of when a mechanics lien needs to be recorded in order for it to be effective. In general, a Nevada claim of lien must be recorded within the later of the following time limitations:

> *a) Within 90 days after completion of the project;*
> *b) Within 90 days after the last delivery of material or equipment, or the last performance of work by the lien claimant; or*
> *c) Within 40 days immediately after the recording of a valid Nevada Notice of Completion.*[719]

While these time limits may seem self-explanatory, some practitioners have nevertheless been of the opinion that a contractor must record his mechanics lien within these time limits based not on actual completion of the work but rather on the actual completion of the contractor's own work. This is simply a misreading of the statute and

---

[717] *See* NRS 108.2403 to NRS 108.2407.

[718] *See* Section 8:6, The Nevada Preliminary Notice, for a discussion of the definition of "owner" under Nevada's mechanics lien law.

[719] NRS 108.226(1) provides:

> *1. To perfect a lien, a lien claimant must record a notice of lien in the office of the county recorder of the county where the property or some part thereof is located in the form provided in subsection 5:*
> *(a) Within 90 days after the date on which the latest of the following occurs:*
> *(1) The completion of the work of improvement;*
> *(2) The last delivery of material or furnishing of equipment by the lien claimant for the work of improvement; or*
> *(3) The last performance of work by the lien claimant for the work of improvement; or*
> *(b) Within 40 days after the recording of a valid notice of completion, if the notice of completion is recorded and served in the manner required pursuant to NRS 108.228.*

incorrect. A notice of claim of lien must be recorded within 90 days of the actual completion (for mechanics lien purposes) of the work of improvement, or 90 days after the individual contractor's work was finished, whichever is later. When the actual completion of the work of improvement occurs is an issue of some debate,[720] however, it is clear that the individual contractor's work is merely an extender of the time to record for that contractor, not a limiting factor.

In general, time limits will be strictly construed and the failure to timely record a mechanics lien may be fatal to the claim. The lien claimant must be careful, however, to fully analyze the factual circumstances surrounding the making of the construction contract and the scope of work required there under. Construction contracts calling for the construction of multiple structures under one contract will often not be complete for mechanics lien recordation purposes until the last structure required under the contract is built.[721] Moreover, Nevada case law indicates that continuing contracts will extend the

---

[720] *See* Section 8:19, Definition of "completion", for a discussion on "Completion" for mechanics lien purposes under Nevada law.

[721] *See* NRS 108.22188, providing in pertinent part:

> *"Work of improvement" means the entire structure or scheme of improvement as a whole, including, without limitation, all work, materials and equipment to be used in or for the construction, alteration or repair of the property or any improvement thereon, whether under multiple prime contracts or a single prime contract except as follows:*
>
> *1. If a scheme of improvement consists of the construction of two or more separate buildings and each building is constructed upon a separate legal parcel of land and pursuant to a separate prime contract for only that building, then each building shall be deemed a separate work of improvement....*

Under this analysis, the construction of multiple structures under a single construction contract indicates that the entire number of structures is part of the one scheme of improvement. As such, the time for recording a claim of lien on a work of improvement consisting of multiple structures is 90 days after the last structure is completed under the contract for the entire work of improvement under NRS 108.226. This has caught a number of developers somewhat at a loss, as claims of liens for one structure would not have to be recorded until the last structure on a project was built, if the developer enters into single contracts for the entire development. Developers are therefore encouraged to enter into separate prime contracts when multiple structures are contemplated, thereby starting the time limits on claims of lien as each building in the development is complete. However, this holding enjoys long standing support from Nevada Courts, having first been determined as early as 1876.

In *Capron v. Strout*, 11 Nev. 304, 1876 WL 4564 (1876), a mining foreman entered into a verbal employment contract for work on a month to month basis, and commenced work. Thereafter, a mortgage was issued on the mine. The foreman continued on his month to month employment for several additional years, ultimately recording a mechanic's lien for the wages, and filing suit to foreclose. While the court indicated that the contract for employment was actually a series of contracts verbally renewed, the lien claim still was valid over the mortgage. The Court held that when work is continuous, even though done under different contracts, the lien is preserved by timely recording *after* the work was completed. While

time for recording until the final delivery of materials or performance of work is made. Therefore, the time for recording may be different than originally anticipated.

One area of exception is also worthy of note: Under certain circumstances improvements to the site of a project which are separate from any contract for the erection of a structure shall be deemed a separate work of improvement for Mechanics lien purposes. NRS 108.22188(2) provides in pertinent part:

> *If the improvement of the site is provided for in a prime contract that is separate from all prime contracts for the construction of one or more buildings on the property, and if the improvement of the site was contemplated by the contracts to be a separate work of improvement to be completed before the commencement of construction of the buildings, the improvement of the site shall be deemed a separate work of improvement from the construction of the buildings and the commencement of construction of the improvement of the site does not constitute the commencement of construction of the buildings. As used in this subsection, "improvement of the site" means the development or enhancement of the property, preparatory to the commencement of construction of a building, and includes:*
> *(a) The demolition or removal of improvements, trees or other vegetation;*
> *(b) The drilling of test holes;*
> *(c) Grading, grubbing, filling or excavating;*
> *(d) Constructing or installing sewers or other public utilities; or*
> *(e) Constructing a vault, cellar or room under sidewalks or making improvements to the sidewalks in front of or adjoining the property.*

"Improvement at the site" is defined to include demolition and removal of improvements, trees and vegetation, drilling of test holes, grading, filling or otherwise improving land, or the construction and installation of sewers, or public utilities, vaults or sidewalks, which is also known has the "horizontal work" and is separate from the "vertical work" of erecting the buildings. This dichotomy is allowed to bring some order to the priority of work in the construction of residential housing developments.

Mechanics liens take their priority from the commencement of construction. Mortgages and deeds of trust securing construction loans take their priority from the dates when they are recorded. Since the commencement of site work at a project does not constitute the commencement of the erection of buildings and structures on the site, a mortgage or a deed of trust recorded after the commencement of site work but before the commencement of work on the structures will have priority over Mechanics lien claims

---

under the modern mechanics' lien provisions continuous work can be statutorily determined, it is clear that a lien need not be recorded until the work of the contractor is completed, or the actual project is completed, whichever is later.

arising out of construction of the structures, but will be junior to Mechanics lien claims arising out of the performance of site work. By statutorily dividing the work into two separate works of improvement, one for the horizontal work and one for the vertical work, the mechanics lien claims will only effect that portion of the work which is built with the specific construction loan. These priorities are simpler to handle within the context of a single lot sale, rather than having the entire subdivision subject to the liens of a particular lot's contractor.

8:15 Place of Recording

The Nevada Mechanics lien must be recorded in the county in which the project "or some part thereof" is located.[722] Recording in another county will render the Mechanics lien ineffective. If a property is located in more than one county the safer procedure would be to record the claim of lien in both counties. This is because a claim of lien may not cut off the rights of bona fide purchasers of the property unless they are given record notice of the recording of the claim. Record notice is achieved by recording the claim in the office of the county recorder where the property is located. A person purchasing property located in one county would not be charged with notice of a claim of mechanics lien recorded in another county.

8:16 Contents of the Claim of Lien

In order for the claim of lien to be valid, the notice itself must include all the information set forth in NRS 108.226(2). While the actual form of the lien is not necessarily critical to its validity, the contents are necessary to be provided. Specifically, the claim of lien must include:

> *a) A statement of the amount due after deducting all just credits and offsets;*
> *b) The name of the owner or reputed owner;*
> *c) The name of the person by whom the claimant was employed, or to whom the claimant furnished materials;*
> *d) A brief statement of the terms of payment on the lien claimant's contract, and;*
> *e) A description of the property sufficient for identification.*

The claim of lien must verified under oath.[723] The statute is conflicting on whether the claim of lien must be notarized. NRS 108.226(3) states that the notice of claim of lien

---

[722] NRS 108.226(1):

> *To perfect a lien, a lien claimant must record a notice of lien in the office of the county recorder of the county where the property or some part thereof is located ....*

[723] *"[A] mechanics lien is a written instrument that is required to be recorded. The proof that entitles it to be recorded is the verification." Arrington v. Wittenberg,* 12 Nev. 99, 101, 1877 WL 4335 (1877).

need not be "acknowledged" to be recorded--which is a general form of notarization.[724] NRS 108.226(5) however requires that the notice of claim of lien be in "substantially" the form set forth in the statute.[725] That form includes a notary block for the verification signature. Until this conflict is resolved, the lien claimant should notarize the signatures when preparing a lien claim.

There is no requirement of a complete itemization of the claimant's account in the mechanics lien. What is required is a statement of the payment terms of the contract. For example: "Payment terms of the contract require payment within 30 days of invoice" or "2% 10, Net 30" are acceptable examples.

A street address is a sufficient description of the property to support the validity of the Mechanics lien claim, but it is better for the claimant to utilize a legal description if it is available. The Nevada law requires that county recorder's offices not record any document affecting title to real property (such as a mechanics lien) without an appropriate assessor's parcel number ("APN") at the top of the document. Therefore, the property description must include the APN for the property. Use of a proper legal description will help to insure that the county recorder records the claim of lien in such a manner that a prospective purchaser will be able to properly identify the property subject to the claim. Minor errors will not be fatal to the claim, if the description gives notice of its existence.[726] If the Property description is the same as that in a Notice of Completion, it will be sufficient even if incorrect.[727]

If the project includes more than one structure located on multiple land parcels that had been subdivided prior to commencement of construction, the lien claimant must make an allocation of the lien claim amount against each structure and attach that allocation to the claim of lien. The allocation can be made based on a good faith estimate or pro rata basis. If each structure is built under separate contract, each structure is considered a separate work of improvement, and a separate claim of lien must be recorded for each separate work of improvement.[728]

---

[724] It should be noted that as early as 1877, the verification of the mechanics lien for recordation was a critical component thereof. As such, the county recorders were authorized to administer oaths in verification of the mechanics lien before recordation. *Arrington v. Wittenberg*, 12 Nev. 99, 101, 1877 WL 4335 (1877).

[725] *See* Form 8-3 in Appendix A.

[726] *See Dickson v. Corbett*, 11 Nev. 277, 1876 WL 4558 (1876).

[727] NRS 108.229(4).

[728] NRS 108.231.

8:17 MISTAKES IN LIEN INFORMATION AND AMENDMENTS

There is usually a large question of what happens when information in a notice of claim of lien is incorrect. In general, so long as the error is the result of innocent mistake and not active fraud, or does not materially mislead a party to his prejudice, a mechanics lien claim can be amended at any time up to and during trial. NRS 108.229 provides:

> *1. At any time before or during the trial of any action to foreclose a lien, a lien claimant may record an amended notice of lien to correct or clarify the lien claimant's notice of lien. The lien claimant shall serve the owner of the property with an amended notice of lien in the same manner as required for serving a notice of lien pursuant to NRS 108.227 and within 30 days after recording the amended notice of lien. A variance between a notice of lien and an amended notice of lien does not defeat the lien and shall not be deemed material unless the variance:*
> *(a) Results from fraud or is made intentionally; or*
> *(b) Misleads an adverse party to the party's prejudice, but then only with respect to the adverse party who was prejudiced.*
> *2. Upon the trial of any action or suit to foreclose a lien, a variance between the lien and the proof does not defeat the lien and shall not be deemed material unless the variance:*
> *(a) Results from fraud or is made intentionally; or*
> *(b) Misleads the adverse party to the party's prejudice, but then only with respect to the adverse party who was prejudiced.*
> *→In all cases of immaterial variance the notice of lien may be amended, by amendment duly recorded, to conform to the proof.*

This does not, however, allow for any aspect of a failed compliance with the statutory requirements to be waived or amended.[729] It should always be kept in mind that the obligations under the mechanics lien statutes may not be waived.[730] As such, one should not rely on the ability to amend a lien claim to allow for the failure of the lien claimant to comply with its statutory obligations.

It should also be noted that the ability to amend a lien negates against the concept that once a lien is released, it may be re-recorded. When claims of lien are partially paid, the claim of lien should be properly amended to show the reduced amount, rather than released and then re-recorded. In this way, the argument that a lien once released is void can be avoided.[731]

---

729 *See Hardy Companies, Inc. v. SNMARK, LLC*, 126 Nev. 528, 245 P.3d 1149 (2010), holding NRS 108.229 cannot be used to amend defective preliminary notices under NRS 108.245.

730 NRS 108.2453(1).

731 NRS 108.2453(1).

8:18 SERVICE OF CLAIM OF LIEN

After the claim of lien is recorded, a copy of the recorded claim of lien must be timely served on specific persons. NRS 108.227 provides:

> *1. In addition to the requirements of NRS 108.226, a copy of the notice of lien must be served upon the owner of the property within 30 days after recording the notice of lien, in one of the following ways:*
> *(a) By personally delivering a copy of the notice of lien to the owner or registered agent of the owner;*
> *(b) By mailing a copy of the notice of lien by certified mail, return receipt requested, to the owner at the owner's place of residence or the owner's usual place of business or to the registered agent of the owner at the address of the registered agent; or*
> *(c) If the place of residence or business of the owner and the address of the registered agent of the owner, if applicable, cannot be determined, by:*
> *(1) Fixing a copy of the notice of lien in a conspicuous place on the property;*
> *(2) Delivering a copy of the notice of lien to a person there residing, if such a person can be found; and*
> *(3) Mailing a copy of the notice of lien addressed to the owner at:*
> *(I) The place where the property is located;*
> *(II) The address of the owner as identified in the deed;*
> *(III) The address identified in the records of the office of the county assessor; or*
> *(IV) The address identified in the records of the county recorder of the county in which the property is located.*
> *2. If there is more than one owner, failure to serve a copy of the notice of lien upon a particular owner does not invalidate a notice of lien if properly served upon another owner.*
> *3. Each subcontractor who participates in the construction, improvement, alteration or repair of a work of improvement shall deliver a copy of each notice of lien required by NRS 108.226 to the prime contractor. The failure of a subcontractor to deliver the notice to the prime contractor is a ground for disciplinary proceedings pursuant to chapter 624 of NRS.*

Of worth noting is the fact that the "record owner" or his agent for service of process must be served. This information is not always easy to obtain, and requires a search of public records for certainty. While that may seem daunting, most of the more populated counties in Nevada have fairly elaborate websites that may be utilized to obtain this information. Ownership information for a particular parcel of land may be accessed through the county tax assessor's office, and this will also allow the lien claimant to locate the Assessor's Parcel Number for the property in question. This number is necessary for the lien claimant to have his claim of lien recorded by the County recorder.

Likewise, the agent for service of process for owners who are other than individuals can be located by searching the records of the Nevada Secretary of State. Again, this information can be found online at the Nevada Secretary of State website:

http://sos.state.nv.us. A lien claimant may also review the building permit records or other documents from the applicable building department with jurisdiction to determine who the owner is for service purposes.

In addition, any subcontractor on the project who records a notice of claim of lien thereon must serve a copy of the claim of lien upon the project general contractor. The failure to do so will subject the subcontractor to discipline under the Nevada Contractors License Law (NRS Chapter 624). However, failing to serve the record owner with the claim of lien may be fatal to the lien claim, as at least one case has held that the failure to serve the owner with the claim of lien justified dismissal of the claim.[732] This concept of strict compliance is again in keeping with the dictates of NRS 108.2453(1), showing a public policy not to allow waiver or a lack of compliance with the statutory obligations to be overlooked. As such, care should be taken to fully comply with the statutory requirements of the mechanics lien claim.

8:19 Definition of "Completion"

NRS 108.22116 defines "completion of the work of improvement" as follows:

> *1. The occupation or use by the owner, an agent of the owner or a representative of the owner of the work of improvement, accompanied by the cessation of all work on the work of improvement;*
>
> *2. The acceptance by the owner, an agent of the owner or a representative of the owner of the work of improvement, accompanied by the cessation of all work on the work of improvement; or*
>
> *3. The cessation of all work on a work of improvement for 30 consecutive days, provided a notice of completion is timely recorded and served and the work is not resumed under the same contract.*

It should be noted immediately that "completion of the work of improvement" is not the same as a contractual definition of "substantial completion," which may trigger certain obligations of payment of retention, commencement of warranty work or otherwise signal the beginning of project closeout. Rather, the definition of completion for mechanics lien purposes in Nevada statutes means the actual completion of the work of improvement; to wit, the cessation of all additional labor once the project has been occupied or accepted by the owner as complete. The two are not synonymous. Which raises the issue of what exactly is "warranty work" and whether such work or additional work after completion continues the time of actual completion for mechanics lien purposes. This question has not been fully decided in Nevada.

---

[732] *See Fisher Bros., Inc. v. Harrah Realty Co.*, 92 Nev. 65, 545 P.2d 203 (1976), holding that failing to serve the owner with a copy of the claim of lien as required by statute made mechanics lien claim unenforceable and subject to summary judgment.

In the ancient case of *Lonkey v. Wells,*[733] the Nevada Supreme Court considered whether additional work of installing picture moldings in a home under a separate contract from the original house construction and installed thereafter was a question of fact, and if the same were true, then the time of completion for mechanics lien recordation purposes was after the completion of the picture moldings.

In another historical case, *Tonopah Lumber Co. v. Nevada Amusement Co.,*[734] a lumber company who supplied material on an open account and on a continuing basis for a construction project was held to have asserted a valid mechanics lien, even though the actual construction project had been abandoned and then resumed under the auspices of a different owner. The lumber company was not at fault for the cessation of labor or had any knowledge of the abandonment and re-commencement of the work, and should not have its lien extinguished as a result.

In 1912 the Nevada Supreme Court revisited this same issue, in the case of *Self & Sellman Mill & Bldg. Co. v. Savage.*[735] In this case, a house was substantially completed with the exception of "certain interior electric fittings and other small items of work," which were completed some 4 months later. The electrical subcontractor recorded his notice of claim of lien after his work on these left over items was complete, which was outside the time of "substantial completion" of the rest of the structure. In this case, the Court upheld the mechanics lien because the completion of the original contract had not occurred on the substantial completion date.

From these historical contexts, it seems clear that work continuing under the original contract would not be "warranty work" or work to repair an item that was not correctly performed. Rather, the continuation of the mechanics lien time requires performance under the original contract that remains. Work that has been performed, albeit not properly so, or work of maintenance or repair on malfunctioning components cannot be used to determine that the time for recording a lien will continue. Rather, the time begins to run when all work required under the original contract has been completed. Warranty work should not extend the time to record a mechanics lien.

Of additional note, we have already discussed in §8:14, Time for recording the claim of lien, the fact that NRS 108.22188 states that when a "work of improvement" consists of more than one separate building, and each building is built under a separate contract, each building is a separate work of improvement for mechanics lien purposes. The time to record a Mechanics lien runs from the completion of each separate building. On the

---

733 *Lonkey v. Wells,* 16 Nev. 271, 1881 WL 4102 (1881).

734 *Tonopah Lumber Co. v. Nevada Amusement Co.,* 30 Nev. 445, 457, 97 P. 636 (1908).

735 *Self & Sellman Mill & Bldg. Co. v. Savage,* 34 Nev. 332, 335, 123 P. 333 (1912).

other hand, if separate buildings are constructed under a single contract, then completion of the last building will begin the time running for recordation of the claim of lien. Hence, a consideration of the entire scope of the work under the contract is an important consideration when determining compliance with the completion statutes.

Finally, there is the concept of abandonment of the contract and the cessation of all labor under separate contracts. In short, the cessation of all labor on a project for 30 days or more may constitute completion for mechanics lien purposes, so long as the contracts for this work are cancelled and no work there under is recommenced at a later date. The recording of a Notice of Completion would be required to institute this provision.[736]

8:20 NOTICE OF COMPLETION

Under NRS 108.228,[737] the owner has the option to record a notice of completion, which will reduce the time for mechanics liens to be recorded to 40 days after the notice is recorded.[738] To be valid, the Notice of Completion must be recorded after completion of the work of improvement, as defined in NRS 108.22116. If the owner does record a

---

[736] *See* Form 8-4 in Appendix A.

[737] NRS 108.228 provides:

> *1. The owner may record a notice of completion after the completion of the work of improvement.*
> *2. The notice of completion must be recorded in the office of the county recorder of the county where the property is located and must set forth:*
> *(a) The date of completion of the work of improvement.*
> *(b) The owner's name or owners' names, as the case may be, the address of the owner or addresses of the owners, as the case may be, and the nature of the title, if any, of the person signing the notice.*
> *(c) A description of the property sufficient for identification.*
> *(d) The name of the prime contractor or names of the prime contractors, if any.*
> *3. The notice must be verified by the owner or by some other person on the owner's behalf. The notice need not be acknowledged to be recorded.*
> *4. Upon recording the notice pursuant to this section, the owner shall, within 10 days after the notice is recorded, deliver a copy of the notice by certified mail, to:*
> *(a) Each prime contractor with whom the owner contracted for all or part of the work of improvement.*
> *(b) Each potential lien claimant who, before the notice was recorded pursuant to this section, either submitted a request to the owner to receive the notice or delivered a preliminary notice of right to lien pursuant to NRS 108.245.*
> *5. The failure of the owner to deliver a copy of the notice of completion in the time and manner provided in this section renders the notice of completion ineffective with respect to each prime contractor and lien claimant to whom a copy was required to be delivered pursuant to subsection 4.*

[738] NRS 108.226(1)(b).

notice of completion, the owner must prepare the Notice in the proper form,[739] and record the same in the county where the project is located. In addition, the owner must serve copies of the recorded Notice within ten (10) days after it is recorded to: a) any general contractor on the project, b) any potential lien claimant serving a preliminary notice on the project, and c) any potential lien claimant who has properly requested a copy of the notice of completion.[740] The notice must contain: 1) the date of completion; 2) the owner's name and address and the nature of the title of the person signing the notice, 3) a property description sufficient to provide identification of the property, and 4) the name of any general or prime contractor on the project. The notice must be verified, but does not need to be notarized. The Notice must be served on all proper parties by certified mail, return receipt requested. The failure of the owner to provide a copy of the Notice of Completion to a requesting claimant will invalidate the effect of the Notice of Completion against that claimant.[741]

8:21 Duration of Lien

The recorded Mechanics lien effectively binds the property for only six months unless a lawsuit is commenced to foreclose the lien, or an extension of time to commence the suit is agreed to between the claimant and the owner. NRS 108.233(1) provides:

> *A lien provided for in NRS 108.221 to 108.246, inclusive, must not bind the property subject to the lien for a period longer than 6 months after the date on which the notice of lien was recorded, unless:*
>
> *(a) Proceedings are commenced in a proper court within that time to enforce the same; or*
>
> *(b) The time to commence the action is extended by a written instrument signed by the lien claimant and by a person or persons in interest in the property subject to the lien, in which event, and as to only that person or those persons in interest signing the agreement, the time is extended, but no extension is valid unless in writing and recorded in the county recorder's office in which the notice of lien is recorded and unless the extension agreement is recorded within the 6-month period. The extension agreement, to be recorded, must be acknowledged as required by law for the acknowledgment of deeds. An action may be commenced within the extended time only against the persons signing the extension agreement and only as to their interests in the property are affected, and upon the lapse of the time specified in the extension agreement, an action may not thereafter be commenced, nor may a second extension be given.*

---

739 *See* Form 8-4 in Appendix A.

740 NRS 108.228(4).

741 NRS 108.228(5).

A lawsuit being commenced to foreclose the lien will obviously qualify as "proceedings," as will the filing of a Statement of Facts constituting a lien claim.[742] Likewise, an extension of the lien statute of limitations is possible under certain circumstances found in this section. Such an extension must be signed, notarized, and recorded in the County Recorder's Office within the initial six month period. This extension will only binds the interests of owners who sign the extension,[743] so care must be taken to determine all the persons who claim an interest in the project. However, the extension is not a complete salve to the need for additional time. If the extension would delay or postpone the collection of other liens, however, the extension is ineffective. NRS 108.233(3) provides:

> *If there are other notices of lien outstanding against the property, an extension must not be given upon a notice of lien which will tend to delay or postpone the collection of other liens evidenced by a notice of lien or encumbrances against the property.*

Therefore, all lien claimants on the Project must agree to extend their claims, not just certain lien claimants. If one claimant refuses and commences an action, all extensions are effectively moot due to the fact that all claimants must join in the foreclosure action or be held to have waived their lien claims in favor of the claimant, or minimally lose their entitlement to equal priority of those other lien claims not so extended.

A final question becomes important here: How many liens may be recorded by a lien claimant for one project, i.e., can a lien claimant whose claim of lien has expired under NRS 108.233(1) record another lien after the expiration (assuming the time to do so under NRS 108.226 has not expired as well)? The answer is somewhat complex and has not yet been decided by any Nevada court.

By way of simple logic, there should be no impediment to re-recording a new claim of lien when the original has expired. Logically, no party would be prejudiced by this result and the result would be in keeping with the Nevada public policy to secure payment to contractors. However, the statutory analysis does not seem to allow for such simplicity. NRS 108.233(2) provides:

> *For all purposes, a notice of lien shall be deemed to have expired as a lien against the property after the lapse of the 6-month period provided in subsection 1, and the recording of a notice of lien does not provide actual or constructive notice after the lapse of the 6-month period and as a lien on the property referred to in the notice of lien, unless, before the lapse of the 6-month period an extension agreement has been recorded, in which event, the lien will only continue as a lien on the interests of those persons signing the extension for the period specified in the extension. An extension must*

---

[742] NRS 108.239(3); *see also* discussion at Section 8:21, Duration of lien.

[743] NRS 108.233(1)(b).

not be given for a period in excess of 1 year beyond the date on which the notice of lien is recorded.

In this subsection 2, the possibility of re-recording a lien seems dashed. It is clear that "for all purposes" the lien has expired after the 6 month period. The fact that an extension could have been given under subsection 1 mitigates against an additional recording without a corresponding extension being provided as well, and in no event can the lien bind the property (even under written extension agreements) for longer than 1 year's time. If a lien claimant could merely record a new lien as the time for his original lien to expire approaches, there would be no need for this language and it would be mere surplusage. As the Nevada Supreme Court has often ruled, "no part of a statute may be rendered meaningless and its language should not be read to produce absurd or unreasonable results."[744] Therefore, this section of the statute must be explained within the context of this time limitations. Given its obvious language, it can only mean that a claim of lien may not be re-recorded to extend the time:

> *and the recording of a notice of lien does not provide actual or constructive notice after the lapse of the 6-month period ... unless, before the lapse of the 6 month period an extension agreement has been recorded ....*[745]

Likewise, the ability to amend a claim of lien at any time before the trial thereof,[746] would likewise indicate that a lien claimant only gets one lien on a project. There is no need or cause to record a release of lien, if the lien amount may be amended to reflect payments or credits, or additional work which may have to be provided. A lien claimant should not rely on the ability to release a lien and keep working, expecting that his lien rights to the project have not expired.[747]

---

[744] *D.R. Horton, Inc. v. Eighth Judicial Dist. Court ex rel. County of Clark*, 123 Nev. 468, 168 P.3d 731, 738 (2007) [citations omitted. .

[745] NRS 108.233(2) (emphasis added).

[746] NRS 108.229.

[747] As a practical matter, a lien claimant who liens a project mid-stream, only to be paid and to continue work should not simply release its lien. At a minimum, the lien should be released "without prejudice to the recording of a future lien for additional work," and in most cases, a resolution agreement with the project owner should be entered into which expressly indicates that the release of lien in exchange for payment is acknowledged to be without prejudice to the lien claimant's ability to record liens in the future. While public policy may be to secure payment to a contractor, the statutory scheme as a whole seems to favor the concept of "one-lien-per-contract-per-construction-project." The equities may not always favor the lien claimant under any particular set of facts and a lien claimant who is too quick to haul an owner into court on successive lien claims may find a non-sympathetic judicial ear at some point.

8:22 FORECLOSING THE CLAIM OF LIEN

The Claim of Lien is foreclosed by commencing an action in any court of competent jurisdiction in the country were the property covered by the lien is located, or through intervening in such a lawsuit initiated by another lien claimant by the filing of a Statement of Lien.[748] As discussed in Section 8:21, Duration of lien, the lawsuit must be

---

[748] NRS 108.239 provides:

> *1. A notice of lien may be enforced by an action in any court of competent jurisdiction that is located within the county where the property upon which the work of improvement is located, on setting out in the complaint the particulars of the demand, with a description of the property to be charged with the lien.*
> *2. At the time of filing the complaint and issuing the summons, the lien claimant shall:*
> *(a) File a notice of pendency of the action in the manner provided in NRS 14.010; and*
> *(b) Cause a notice of foreclosure to be published at least once a week for 3 successive weeks, in one newspaper published in the county, and if there is no newspaper published in the county, then in such mode as the court may determine, notifying all persons holding or claiming a notice of lien pursuant to the provisions of NRS 108.221 to 108.246, inclusive, on the property to file with the clerk and serve on the lien claimant and also on the defendant, if the defendant is within the State or is represented by counsel, written statements of the facts constituting their liens, together with the dates and amounts thereof.*
> *3. All persons holding or claiming a notice of lien may join a lien claimant's action by filing a statement of facts within a reasonable time after publication of the notice of foreclosure or receiving notice of the foreclosure, whichever occurs later. Any number of persons claiming liens may join in the same action if they timely file a statement of facts in the lien claimant's action. The lien claimant and other parties adversely interested must be allowed 20 days to answer the statements.*
> *4. If it appears from the records of the county recorder that there are other notices of lien recorded against the same property at the time of the commencement of the action, the lien claimant shall, in addition to and after the initial publication of the notice of foreclosure as provided in paragraph (b) of subsection 2, mail to those other lien claimants, by registered or certified mail, or deliver in person a copy of the notice of foreclosure as published.*
> *5. At the time of any change in the venue of the action, the lien claimant shall file a notice of pendency of the action, in the manner provided in NRS 14.010, and include in the notice the court and county to which the action is changed.*
> *6. When separate actions are commenced by lien claimants to foreclose on their respective notices of lien, the court may consolidate all the actions. The consolidation does not affect or change the priority of lien claims.*
> *7. The court shall enter judgment according to the right of the parties, and shall, by decree, proceed to hear and determine the claims in a summary way, or may, if it be the district court, refer the claims to a special master to ascertain and report upon the liens and the amount justly due thereon. No consequential damages may be recovered in an action pursuant to this section. All liens not so exhibited shall be deemed to be waived in favor of those which are so exhibited.*
> *8. Upon petition by a lien claimant for a preferential trial setting:*
> *(a) The court shall give preference in setting a date for the trial of an action brought pursuant to this section; and*
> *(b) If a lien action is designated as complex by the court, the court may take into account the rights and claims of all lien claimants in setting a date for the preferential trial.*

filed within six months of recording the lien, or, if an extension of time is given, within 12 months.[749] The cause of action to enforce a claim of lien will provide notice of the basic elements of the lien claim:

> *1. An obligation to pay for work performed and a proper license to perform it, if necessary;*
> *2. The preparation and service of a Notice of Right to Lien under NRS 108.245, or an applicable exemption from this obligation;*[750]
> *3. The performance of work for which payment was obligated;*
> *4. The failure of payment being made for the work performed;*
> *5. The identification of the property and project and owner thereof;*
> *6. The service of a notice of intent to lien, if one is required;*[75]

> *9. If the lienable amount of a lien claimant's lien is the subject of binding arbitration:*
> *(a) The court may, at the request of a party to the arbitration, stay the lien claimant's action to foreclose the lien pending the outcome of the binding arbitration. If the foreclosure on the lien involves the rights of other lien claimants or persons whose claims are not the subject of the binding arbitration, the court may stay the lien claimant's foreclosure proceeding only upon terms which are just and which afford the lien claimant a fair opportunity to protect his or her lien rights and priorities with respect to other lien claimants and persons.*
> *(b) Upon the granting of an award by the arbitrator, any party to the arbitration may seek an order from the court in the action to foreclose on the lien confirming or adopting the award and determining the lienable amount of the lien claimant's lien in accordance with the order, if any. Upon determining the lienable amount, the court shall enter a judgment or decree for the lienable amount, plus all amounts that may be awarded by the court to the lien claimant pursuant to NRS 108.237, and the court may include as part of the lien all costs and attorney's fees awarded to the lien claimant by the arbitrator and all costs and attorney's fees incurred by the lien claimant pertaining to any application or motion to confirm, adopt, modify or correct the award of the arbitrator. A judgment or decree entered by the court pursuant to this subsection may be enforced against the property as provided in subsections 10, 11 and 12.*
> *10. On ascertaining the whole amount of the liens with which the property is justly chargeable, as provided in NRS 108.221 to 108.246, inclusive, the court shall cause the property to be sold in satisfaction of all liens and the costs of sale, including all amounts awarded to all lien claimants pursuant to NRS 108.237, and any party in whose favor judgment may be rendered may cause the property to be sold within the time and in the manner provided for sales on execution, issued out of any district court, for the sale of real property.*
> *11. If the proceeds of sale, after payment of the costs of sale, are not sufficient to satisfy all liens to be included in the decree of sale, including all amounts awarded to all lien claimants pursuant to NRS 108.237, the proceeds must be apportioned according to the right of the various lien claimants. If the proceeds of the sale amount to more than the sum of all liens and the cost of sale, the remainder must be paid over to the owner of the property.*

[749] NRS 108.233.

[750] *See* Section 8:6 The Nevada preliminary notice.

[751] *See* Section 8:8 15 day notice of intent to lien.

7. The recordation and service of the Notice of Claim of Lien;[752]
8. Prayer for relief of selling the property to satisfy the lien.

At the same time, the claimant should record a notice of pendency of action (notice of *lis pendens*) as specified in NRS 14.010.[753] Likewise, the lien claimant must prepare a notice of foreclosure, which must be published in a newspaper of general circulation in the county, as well as served upon all other lien claimants of record on the property by certified mail.[754] This notice must notify all potential claimants that they must file statements of lien claims with the court, and serve them on the plaintiff and the defendant.[755]

The Statement of facts constituting a lien is a simplified version of a complaint to foreclose a Mechanics lien. The effect of filing and serving a Statement of facts constituting a lien is to add an action to foreclose the claimant's Mechanics lien to an existing action against the same property filed by another claimant. Thus, all claims arising from a specific construction project are consolidated in the same litigation. The Statement of facts constituting a lien must be filed in the initial lawsuit within a reasonable time after the last date the Notice of Foreclosure was published, or after receiving a copy of the notice of foreclosure, whichever occurs later.[756] The failure to do so will invalidate the lien claimant's claim of lien.[757]

The filing of a lawsuit to foreclose a Mechanics lien does not eliminate the right of the claimant to proceed against its customer individually.[758] Such claims are usually handled in the action foreclosing the lien claim. A separate action may also be filed against any party who directly contracted for the work or materials.

---

[752] *See* Sections 8:9 to 8:18.

[753] It should be noted here that the exact provision of NRS 108.239(2) indicates that the notice of *lis pendens* must be filed. This is an obvious drafting error and should be understood by the mechanics lien practitioner as such. NRS 14.010 indicates that to be effective a *lis pendens* needs to be recorded, not filed. As such, the reference to "filing" the notice "in the manner provided in NRS 14.010" simply means recorded. The *filing* of the notice of pendency of action with the court serves no legitimate purpose, whereas the *recording* of the document with the county recorder places all would be purchasers on notice that the mechanics lien of record on the property has in fact been foreclosed and title to the property is in question. Therefore, the filing of such a document is not necessary to the foreclosure, but the recording of the document is necessary to preserve the lien claimant's rights.

[754] NRS 108.239(2).

[755] NRS 108.239(3).

[756] NRS 108.239(3).

[757] *Crestline Inv. Group, Inc. v. Lewis,* 119 Nev. 365, 75 P.3d 363 (2003).

[758] NRS 108.238.

Likewise any such claim may be submitted to arbitration,[759] however, a foreclosure lawsuit will still be necessary to enforce the lien. The proper procedure is to file the action foreclosing the claim of lien and immediately move the court for an order staying the action pending arbitration.[760] The court in this action, however, may only stay the action on terms which are fair to other lien claimants who may not have such obligations to arbitrate. Once the arbitration has been resolved, the determination of the arbitrator of the lien amount needs to be brought back to the Court for final entry along with all other lien claimant's interests.[761]

Once all lien claims are adjudicated, the court will then award attorneys fees, costs and interest on the lien claim amounts and order the property sold to satisfy the total amount of the lien claims.[762] The proceeds will then be distributed according to their priority,[763] as determined by the Court.[764] Any remaining balance after all lien claims are disbursed is returned to the property owner, while any deficit suffered results in a deficiency judgment against the lien claimant's debtor.[765]

A mechanics lien claim is also entitled to a preferential trial setting.[766] This preferential setting is also allowed if the mechanics lien claim has been bonded,[767] and an action on the release of lien bond commenced under NRS 108.2413, et seq.

---

[759] NRS 108.239(9).

[760] NRS 108.239(9)(a).

[761] NRS 108.239(9)(b).

[762] For purposes of a final judgment, the trial court must order the property foreclosed on to be sold. With out this order for sale, a judgment for foreclosure of a mechanics' lien claim is not final and appealable. *Simmons Self-Storage v. Rib Roof, Inc.*, 127 Nev.Adv.Op. 6, 247 P.3d 1107 (2011).

[763] NRS 108.236(1). Lien claims are segregated into classes to which the court must assign a rank. NRS 108.236. The ranks of lien claims are as follows: 1. Labor claims. 2. Claims of material suppliers. 3. Claims of subcontractors. Architects, land surveyors, geologists and engineers may be included here if their contracts are with the general contractor. 4. General contractors, architects, land surveyors, geologists and engineers, if their contracts are with the project owner.

The end of the foreclosure of a mechanics lien is the sale, by the sheriff, at public auction, of the property subject to the lien. The proceeds from the sale are distributed in order of rank, with each rank being paid in full before the next rank receives any distribution.

[764] NRS 108.239(11).

[765] NRS 108.239(12).

[766] NRS 108.239(8).

[767] NRS 108.2421(3).

8:23 ASSIGNMENT OF CLAIM OF LIEN

Mechanics Liens, being actual property interests, are readily assignable as are any other tangible asset. However, as mechanics liens are inchoate rights until they are recorded, there is a procedure to handle their assignment within the mechanics lien statutes. NRS 108.243 provides:

> *1. Any lien may be assigned in the same manner as any other chose in action after it has been perfected by recording.*
> *2. An assignment of a lien before recording will not be effective until written notice of the assignment has been given to the owner by the assignee. The notice will be sufficient if delivered in person or mailed by certified mail to the owner. After such notice, the assignee may perfect the lien in the assignee's own name.*
> *3. One or more lien claimants of any class may assign their notices of lien by written assignment, signed by each assignor, to any other person or lien claimant of any class, and the assignee may commence and prosecute the action upon all of the notices of lien in the assignee's own name or in the name of the original lien claimant.*
> *4. In the event that a claim for which a lien may be filed is assigned before it is perfected, such assignment does not discharge or defeat the right to perfect the lien, if the lien is reassigned to the lien claimant, and thereafter the lien is timely perfected.*

Once a Mechanics lien has been recorded, it may be assigned without notice to the owner. It may also be assigned prior to recordation, but only upon notice to the owner, delivered by personal service or my certified mail. After the notice is provided, the assignee may record the claim of lien.

In certain cases, the district courts have been faced with the situation where a certain class of lien claimant has settled with another class and taken assignment of that other lien claimant's lien, in order to jump its priority to the next level. While some question was raised about this practice, the statute was again amended by the additional of subsection 3, allowing for this very strategy.

Finally, the assignment of inchoate rights cannot be finalized until they are perfected by the recording of the notice of claim of lien. As subsection 4 allows, the claim of lien may be reassigned to the original holder, then perfected by recording and ultimately assigned back to the assignee. In general, these exercises have little practical effect and seem unnecessary. However, often there is less risk in following the required exorcise strictly than in challenging the process in court through a claim of substantial compliance.

8:24 RELEASE AND DISCHARGE OF CLAIM OF LIEN

Once the claim of lien has been satisfied by paying it off, the lien claimant has an obligation to release the lien from the property. Failing to so voluntarily release the lien can subject the lien claimant to several layers of liability,[768] including attorney's fees and costs for removal. NRS 108.2437 provides in pertinent part:

> *1. As soon as practicable, but not later than 10 days after a notice of lien upon the property pursuant to NRS 108.221 to 108.246, inclusive, is fully satisfied or discharged, the lien claimant shall cause to be recorded a discharge or release of the notice of lien[769]....*
> *2. If the lien claimant fails to comply with the provisions of subsection 1, the lien claimant is liable in a civil action to the owner of the property, his or her heirs or assigns for any actual damages caused by the lien claimant's failure to comply with those provisions or $100, whichever is greater, and for a reasonable attorney's fee and the costs of bringing the action.*

As such, the failure to remove a lien when payment has been made to discharge the same can subject the lien claimant not only to a claim for discharge, but a lawsuit for the tort of slander of title, entitling the owner to payment of actual damages. Therefore, discharge of the lien should be expeditiously handled upon payment.

8:25 Release by Bond

NRS 108.2413 to NRS 108.2425 sets forth a procedure for release by providing a mechanics lien release bond or "bonding around" the mechanics lien. This may be accomplished either before or after a claim of lien has been recorded. In both cases, the owner or other party may obtain a release bond, issued by a surety licensed in the State of Nevada and approved by the U.S. Government, as demonstrated by its inclusion in the U.S. Treasury Department's List of Approved Sureties. In the case of a release bond issued for the entire project, the bond must be in the penal sum of 1.5 times the amount of the prime contract. In the case of a mechanics lien release bond for one particular lien claim, the amount must be in the amount of 1.5 times the amount of the lien. Once the bond is procured, the principal records the bond with the county recorder where the lien was recorded. In the case of the early release bond, all liens recorded against the Project will attach directly to the bond and never to the Property. For the individual lien release bond, the lien is released upon recordation. The end result is to free the property from the claim of lien while substituting the liability of the surety on the bond for the security that was previously provided by the lien on the owner's property. A copy of the recorded bond must be served upon the lien claimant and its counsel if a lawsuit has commenced, in the same manner as service of process of a lawsuit.

---

[768] Including the finding of a violation of the contractor's license law and being subject to discipline. NRS 624.3012(3) allows the lien claimant 75 days after receiving payment to discharge the lien.

[769] *See* Form 8-5 in Appendix A.

In both cases, the bond surety's liability is limited to the penal sum of the bond provided. If the Court determines that a particular lien release bond is insufficient to cover all claims of the lien claimant, it may order the principal on the bond to obtain a new bond in a higher amount, or to order an additional bond or other security be added to the bond already provided.

Lien claimants have 5 days after service of the bond to file an objection with the State District Court to the sufficiency of the surety. If the District Court finds the surety unacceptable, the lien will remain on the property, or the court will order a new and sufficient surety be substituted.

In 2005, the statute of limitations on a mechanics lien release bond was specifically delineated to be 9 months after the lien claimant was served with a copy of the release bond. In the case of the project wide release bond, the lien claimants have 9 months after the completion of the project to bring an action on the bond.

8:26 RELEASE BY MOTION

NRS 108.2275[770] provides a remedy for owners to remove frivolous or excessive liens from their properties by motion. The legislation is aimed at claimants who file

---

[770] NRS 108.2275 provides:

> *1. The debtor of the lien claimant or a party in interest in the property subject to the notice of lien who believes the notice of lien is frivolous and was made without reasonable cause, or that the amount of the notice of lien is excessive, may apply by motion to the district court for the county where the property or some part thereof is located for an order directing the lien claimant to appear before the court to show cause why the relief requested should not be granted.*
> *2. The motion must:*
> *(a) Set forth in detail the legal and factual grounds upon which relief is requested; and*
> *(b) Be supported by:*
> *(1) A notarized affidavit signed by the applicant setting forth a concise statement of the facts upon which the motion is based; and*
> *(2) Documentary evidence in support of the affidavit, if any.*
> *3. If the court issues an order for a hearing, the applicant shall serve notice of the application and order of the court on the lien claimant within 3 days after the court issues the order. The court shall conduct the hearing within not less than 15 days or more than 30 days after the court issues the order for a hearing.*
> *4. The order for a hearing must include a statement that if the lien claimant fails to appear at the time and place noted, the notice of lien will be released with prejudice and the lien claimant will be ordered to pay the reasonable costs the applicant incurs in bringing the motion, including reasonable attorney's fees.*
> *5. If, at the time the application is filed, an action to foreclose the notice of lien has not been filed, the clerk of the court shall assign a number to the application and obtain from the applicant a filing fee of $85. If an action has been filed to foreclose the notice of lien before*

fraudulent liens, or overstate the lien amount in order to put pressure on the owner or general contractor. Nevertheless, in practice the motion is used to remove liens that are not valid for various reasons, including failure to provide preliminary notices, untimely recording, etc.

While a precise standard is not articulated in the statute, most practitioners have historically asserted that the courts should review the lien claim under a summary judgment standard as outlined in Nevada Rules of Civil Procedure, Rule 56, that is, there is no genuine issue of material fact in dispute that the lien is either frivolous and made without reasonable cause, or is excessive. This view has now been obviated by the Nevada Supreme Court's decision in *J.D. Const., Inc. v. IBEX Intern. Group, LLC.*[771]

In *J.D. Construction*, the Nevada Supreme Court determined that because the determination of whether a lien is frivolous or excessive requires the determination of material facts, the District Court should make appropriate factual findings at a NRS 108.2275 hearing. Further, in making a ruling on lien amount excessiveness, the district courts should use a preponderance of the evidence standard to adjudicate the issue. On the other hand, a determination that a lien is frivolous would require a finding that there was no reasonable cause to record the lien. In either case, the district court upon request of the parties may take live testimony and allow discovery for the purpose of the 108.2275 hearing, but these are not necessary to a determination so long as both parties

---

the application was filed pursuant to this section, the application must be made a part of the action to foreclose the notice of lien.

6. If, after a hearing on the matter, the court determines that:

(a) The notice of lien is frivolous and was made without reasonable cause, the court shall make an order releasing the lien and awarding costs and reasonable attorney's fees to the applicant for bringing the motion.

(b) The amount of the notice of lien is excessive, the court may make an order reducing the notice of lien to an amount deemed appropriate by the court and awarding costs and reasonable attorney's fees to the applicant for bringing the motion.

(c) The notice of lien is not frivolous and was made with reasonable cause or that the amount of the notice of lien is not excessive, the court shall make an order awarding costs and reasonable attorney's fees to the lien claimant for defending the motion.

7. Proceedings conducted pursuant to this section do not affect any other rights and remedies otherwise available to the parties.

8. An appeal may be taken from an order made pursuant to subsection 6. A stay may not be granted if the district court does not release the lien pursuant to subsection 6.

9. If an order releasing or reducing a notice of lien is entered by the court, and the order is not stayed, the applicant may, within 5 days after the order is entered, record a certified copy of the order in the office of the county recorder of the county where the property or some part thereof is located. The recording of a certified copy of the order releasing or reducing a notice of lien is notice to any interested party that the notice of lien has been released or reduced.

[771] *J.D. Const., Inc. v. IBEX Intern. Group, LLC*, 240 P.3d 1033, 126 Nev. Adv. Op. No. 36 (Nev. 2010).

are provided a sufficient opportunity to present their cases--affidavits are sufficient to meet the due process rights of the involved parties. Whether a District Court's refusal to have live testimony at a hearing upon the request of the parties was a denial of due process was a question for another case.

Thus, under NRS 108.2275, the Court uses the affidavit process to determine if an order to show cause is appropriate, and once determined, the Court is free to hold and weigh evidence tending to show that the lien is either frivolous or excessive. In sum, the motion under NRS 108.2275 becomes a trial-within-a-trial on shortened time, and the court has only three options in which to rule: 1) the lien is frivolous and made without reasonable cause; 2) the lien is excessive and must be reduced, or 3) the lien is not frivolous and is not excessive,[772] and cannot make any other ruling arising from that matter.[773] Once that ruling is made, the Court has an obligation to award attorney's fees and costs to the prevailing party on the motion, if the challenge is made based on the lien being frivolous,[774] and may make an award of fees to the challenging party if the lien is reduced.[775] Oddly, the court must also award attorneys fees to the lien claimant, if the court does not reduce the lien after it has been challenged as excessive.[776]

Some additional issues arise from the *J.D. Construction* case. In its holding, the Court indicated that mechanics' liens are not, in fact, an interest in property, but are a legislative "taking," in that the owner is deprived of a significant property interest that entitles the owner to state and federal due process.[777] This is not necessarily in keeping with the theory of a mechanics lien as they are historically viewed,[778] and is difficult to reconcile with the ability of the lien claimant to *assign* lien claims as any other property rights under NRS 108.243.[779]

The statute provides that the debtor to the lien claimant, or any party with an interest in the property may apply for an order directing the claimant to show cause why the lien should not be reduced or dismissed. The petition must be made upon affidavits and

---

[772] NRS 108.2275(6).

[773] *Crestline Inv. Group, Inc. v. Lewis*, 119 Nev. 365, 75 P.3d 363 (2003).

[774] NRS 108.2275(6)(a) and (c).

[775] NRS 108.2275(6)(b).

[776] NRS 108.2275(6)(c).

[777] *J.D. Const., Inc. v. IBEX Intern. Group, LLC*, 240 P.3d 1033, 1040, 126 Nev. Adv. Op. No. 36 (Nev. 2010).

[778] *See* Section 8:2.

[779] *See* Section 8:23.

evidence to support the petitioner's claim. If the court agrees that a hearing should be held, it must give 15 to 30 days notice of the hearing.[780] Many times the courts will not be aware of this strict mandate and will issue the order to show cause on a shorter time basis, often because the moving party has provided a request for a shortened time period on some pending transaction or date with which the lien is interfering. While the trial courts are often accommodating to that request, there is no basis under the mechanics lien statute for the expedited hearing. Moreover, since the motion is effectively a challenge to the validity of the lien with limited due process, the Courts should be slow to shorten the time for a motion to less than the statutory minimum of 15 days. It should be noted that while the hearing must commence within 15 to 30 days, it need not be completed in that time, so long as the owner's rights to a speeding resolution of the validity or excessiveness of the lien is made expeditiously.[781]

A ruling on a motion under NRS 108.2275 is a final order and is immediately appealable, however, a ruling that the lien claim is not frivolous or excessive does not allow a stay to be entered during the time of the appeal's pendency.[782] As such, the fact that a ruling is being appealed should not be taken by the lien claimant as tolling any statute of limitations on the claim of lien itself. The lien claimant still must file suit to foreclose the mechanics lien timely under NRS 108.233 and NRS 108.239.[783] A foreclosure suit cannot be filed as a counter-claim to a petition to expunge or reduce under NRS 108.2275, however. Since a petition is not a "complaint," it cannot commence an action under Nevada Rules of Civil Procedure (NRCP) Rule 4. Likewise, a "petition" is not a proper "pleading" under NRCP Rule 7(a), to which a counter-claim may be filed. Rather, it is a "motion" under NRCP Rule 7(b). As such, it is improper legal practice to file a counter-claim to a petition under NRS 108.2275. The proper procedure is to file a complaint for foreclosure and to move the petitioning court to consolidate the two matters.

If the lien is ordered expunged or reduced under NRS 108.2275, the party removing the lien needs merely to record a copy of the certified order reducing or expunging the lien claim to release the property from the lien or reducing the same for all purposes.[784]

---

780 NRS 108.2275(3).

781 *J.D. Const., Inc. v. IBEX Intern. Group, LLC*, 240 P.3d 1033, 126 Nev. Adv. Op. No. 36 (Nev. 2010).

782 NRS 108.2275(8).

783 *See* Section 8:22, Foreclosing the claim of lien.

784 NRS 108.2275(9).

8:27 USING JOINT CHECKS ON NEVADA PROJECTS

The best defense to a lien claim is payment. Coupled with the use of joint checks, Nevada's progress and final payment release forms offer the best protection against liens, thought they are by no means complete protection. The process works as follows:

1. *List and chart all subcontractors of every tier and material suppliers who provide Nevada preliminary notices.*
2. *Require subcontractors to submit Conditional Progress Releases from all suppliers and sub-subcontractors who have sent preliminary notices, along with their progress payment requests.*
3. *Prepare joint checks for each supplier/sub-subcontractor in the amount of the conditional progress releases provided.*
4. *Require subcontractors to provide unconditional progress payment releases for the previous progress payment with each subsequent progress payment request.*
5. *Obtain a conditional final release from all sub-subcontractors and suppliers on processing the last progress payment request.*
6. *Obtain unconditional final releases before releasing any retention funds.*

In 2001, the Nevada legislature passed the Private Work Prompt Payment Act ("PPA"), which made significant changes to the contractor's license law in Nevada.[785] It is therefore all the more necessary for a owner or general contractor to utilize joint checks in their payments and to take necessary steps to ensure payment reaches all levels of Contractor and suppliers. In fact, as current Nevada law regards payment releases merely as receipts for actual payment, the use of joint checks is the only viable means to ensure that payments are being received by all tiers of the construction project hierarchy.

As noted above, an owner should utilize joint checks in the payment to contractors and suppliers. Nevada adopted the "joint check rule" in 1998, which states that "the endorsement of a joint check by one of the joint payees is deemed to be a payment to that payee and constitutes a waiver of the right to commence a lien foreclosure action."[786] Thus, the use of joint checks will assist the owner in the ensure payment has been attributed to the parties intended. In 2003 and 2005, however, the Nevada legislature modified the joint check rule by enacting NRS 108.2457(3).[787] The joint check

---

[785] *See* Chapter 3 Private Works Prompt Payment Act for a full discussion of the PPA.

[786] *Henry Products Inc. v. Tarmu*, 114 Nev. 1017, 967 P.2d 444 (1998).

[787] NRS 108.2457(3) provides in pertinent part:

> *Payment in the form of a two-party joint check made payable to a lien claimant and another joint payee who are in privity with each other shall, upon endorsement by the lien claimant and the joint check clearing the bank upon which it is drawn, be deemed to be payment to the lien claimant for only:*

rule now only applies when a joint check is issued to not more than two (2) parties who are in the same line of contractual privity, and the parties have executed a mandatory waiver and release document in conjunction therewith. When the joint check is issued, it will be deemed payment in the amount of the joint check, the amount the maker intended the recipient to receive from it, or the total amount due to the recipient, whichever is less.

Care must be taken here by the maker of the joint check. As will be seen in subsequent sections, the conditional payment release forms do not specify who the maker of the check is that will satisfy the condition of payment. As a result, the argument can and has been made that a conditional release has not been satisfied despite the execution of a joint check. Essentially, when a joint check is issued, one party to the joint check will obtain a conditional release and satisfy the payment condition by executing and delivering his own personal check for the release. In turn, the other joint payee provides an endorsement of the joint check. When the personal check from the first joint payee bounces, the second joint payment then asserts that the release was not properly given, as it was conditioned on the clearing of the personal check from the second joint payee.[788] In this case, the maker of the check must prove that he issued the joint check in favor of the first joint payee based on that joint payee's conditional release, and must also about that the first joint payee's acceptance of the second joint payee's personal check instead is a bad business decision, for which the first joint payee is responsible. To avoid this situation, it is wise for the maker of checks to always make joint checks for each conditional payment release he receives, and in the exact amount of the release. In that way, the maker of the check can convincingly demonstrate that the payment was based on the conditional release.

8:28 Progress and Final Payment Releases

It is vitally important under Nevada mechanics lien law to understand what does and does not happen upon the execution and delivery of a statutory payment release form. While the statutory forms used in Nevada follow the naming conventions and even language in some respects to those of many other states, Nevada's forms actually do very little in terms of releasing a contractor's rights to assert a lien or to make claims. The statutory basis of such releases contain so many loopholes and exclusions that the forms

---

(a) The amount of the joint check;
(b) The amount the payor intended to pay the lien claimant out of the joint check; or
(c) The balance owed to the lien claimant for the work, materials or equipment covered by the joint check, whichever is less.

788 The "public policy to secure payment to contractors" recognized by the Nevada Supreme Court in *Lehrer McGovern Bovis, Inc. v. Bullock Insulation, Inc.*, 185 P.3d 1055 (Nev. 2008), opinion withdrawn and superseded on denial of reh'g, 197 P.3d 1032 (Nev. 2008), will merely serve to bolster this argument for the downstream subcontractor or supplier.

are literally reduced to mere receipts for the exchange of funds and do nothing to alter or diminish a contractor's right to payment.

As in most other states that have adopted uniform and standardized payment release forms, the Nevada payment releases forms are found in four versions, covering four basic payment scenarios: Conditional Waiver and Release on Progress Payment;[789] Unconditional Waiver and Release on Progress Payment;[790] Conditional Waiver and Release on Final Payment,[791] and Unconditional Waiver and Release on Final Payment.[792] These forms are set forth in specific detail in NRS 108.2457(5)(a) to NRS 108.2457(5)(d), and their language is mandatory.[793] Unfortunately, an owner, lender or general contractor cannot wholly rely on the forms to be assured of payment, because the forms, regardless of their language, are void if payment is not received in exchange for their issuance.

First, it must be understood that there is now a recognized public policy that a contractor's payment is to be secured.[794] Second, the statutory scheme indicates that regardless of the language used in a release form, without payment there can be no release of any lien claimant's rights. NRS 108.2457(2) provides:

> *An oral or written statement purporting to waive, release or otherwise adversely affect the rights of a lien claimant is not enforceable and does not create any estoppel or impairment of a lien unless:*
> *(a) There is a written waiver and release in the form set forth in this section; and*
> *(b) The lien claimant received payment for the lien and then only to the extent of the payment received.*

---

[789] *See* Form 8-7 in Appendix A.

[790] *See* Form 8-8 in Appendix A.

[791] *See* Form 8-9 in Appendix A.

[792] *See* Form 8-10 in Appendix A.

[793] NRS 108.2457(5) provides "*The waiver and release given by any lien claimant is unenforceable unless it is in the following forms in the following circumstances:....*" Hence, the alteration of the form language is forbidden, and useless--if the form language is altered, the release is unenforceable at all. Therefore, one looking to receive payment need not fear the language of any release form set in front of him to exchange for payment. If the form is not in the proper language of the statute, the form is invalid and will not release any right of the lien claimant whatsoever.

[794] *Lehrer McGovern Bovis, Inc. v. Bullock Insulation, Inc.*, 185 P.3d 1055 (Nev. 2008), opinion withdrawn and superseded on denial of reh'g, 197 P.3d 1032 (Nev. 2008). While the analysis of the Nevada Supreme Court with regard to pay-if-paid provisions in this case is highly suspect, there can be little doubt that a public policy to secure payment to contractors has been clearly established by the Court, and that the legislative enactments since 2001 are highly supportive of that concept.

By the inclusion of the conjunctive term "and" between subsections a and b, the statute clearly establishes that regardless of the type of release used, payment must be received by the lien claimant. This conclusion is even more strongly understood when reviewing of the provisions of NRS 108.2457(5)(e), which provides:

> *Notwithstanding any language in any waiver and release form set forth in this section, if the payment given in exchange for any waiver and release of lien is made by check, draft or other such negotiable instrument, and the same fails to clear the bank on which it is drawn for any reason, then the waiver and release shall be deemed null, void and of no legal effect whatsoever and all liens, lien rights, bond rights, contract rights or any other right to recover payment afforded to the lien claimant in law or equity will not be affected by the lien claimant's execution of the waiver and release.*

As can be easily seen, therefore, that Nevada's release forms are not to be relied upon in every case. Even if the owner or general contractor is provided an *un*conditional release, it is still subject to a *condition* of payment being received and a check or other negotiable instrument clearing the bank on which it is drawn.[795] It is therefore all the more strongly advised that a system of joint checks be used for payment.

8:29 Notice of Non-Responsibility

NRS 108.234 provides that an owner may record a Notice of Non-Responsibility within three days of first learning of construction, alteration, or repair of its rented property, in order to protect its property interest arising from the construction work.[796] In order to be effective, the property owner needs to fall within the definition of a "disinterested owner" under NRS 108.234(7):

> *As used in this section, "disinterested owner" means an owner who:*
> *(a) Does not record a notice of waiver as provided in NRS 108.2405; and*
> *(b) Does not personally or through an agent or representative, directly or indirectly, contract for or cause a work of improvement, or any portion thereof, to be constructed, altered or repaired upon the property or an improvement of the owner.*
> *The term does not include an owner who is a lessor if the lessee fails to satisfy the requirements set forth in NRS 108.2403 and 108.2407.*

It is hard to imagine in today's retail leasing environment how any landlord would ever qualify as a "disinterested owner" under this definition. In no event can a property owner be considered a "disinterested owner" if his tenant fails to issue a notice of posted

[795] It is important to note that the unpublished case of *Insulation Contracting & Supply, Inc. v. S3H, Inc.*, No. 62856, 2015 WL 5774180 (Nev. Sept 29, 2015) made this very holding. Since this case is unpublished, however, it cannot be cited for authority in any Nevada state court under Supreme Court Rule 123.

[796] *See* Form 8-6 in Appendix A.

security and either provide a payment bond or establish and fund a construction disbursement account.

If the owner is a "disinterested owner" and wishes his property interest to be protected from the construction of his tenant, that owner must record a notice of non-responsibility with the county recorder where the project is located within 3 days of learning of the construction commencement, the execution of the lease or the effective date of the lease, whichever occurs first.[797] The notice must include: (1) The names and addresses of the disinterested owner and the person causing the work to be performed; (2) The location, address and legal description of the property where the improvement is being performed; (3) The nature and extent of the disinterested owner's interest in the improvement; (4) the date on which the disinterested owner learned of the improvement, and (5) A statement of whether the disinterested owner has notified the lessee of in writing of the requirements for recording a notice of posted security.[798] and the actual posting of security for the improvement[799] Likewise, the disinterested owner

---

[797] NRS 108.234(2) provides:

> *The interest of a disinterested owner in any improvement and the property upon which an improvement is constructed, altered or repaired is not subject to a notice of lien if the disinterested owner, within 3 days after he or she first obtains knowledge of the construction, alteration or repair, or the intended construction, alteration or repair, gives notice that he or she will not be responsible for the improvement by recording a notice in writing to that effect with the county recorder of the county where the property is located and, in the instance of a disinterested owner who is:*
> *(a) A lessor, the notice of nonresponsibility shall be deemed timely recorded if the notice is recorded within 3 days immediately following the effective date of the lease or by the time of the execution of the lease by all parties, whichever occurs first; or*
> *(b) An optionor, the notice of nonresponsibility shall be deemed timely recorded if the notice is recorded within 3 days immediately following the date on which the option is exercised in writing.*

[798] *See* Form 8-12 in Appendix A.

[799] NRS 108.234(3) provides:

> *To be effective and valid, each notice of nonresponsibility recorded pursuant to this section must identify:*
> *(a) The names and addresses of the disinterested owner and the person who is causing the work of improvement to be constructed, altered or repaired;*
> *(b) The location of the improvement and the address and legal description of the property upon which the improvement is or will be constructed, altered or repaired;*
> *(c) The nature and extent of the disinterested owner's interest in the improvement and the property upon which the improvement is or will be constructed, altered or repaired;*
> *(d) The date on which the disinterested owner first learned of the construction, alteration or repair of the improvement that is the subject of the notice of nonresponsibility; and*
> *(e) Whether the disinterested owner has notified the lessee in writing that the lessee must comply with the requirements of NRS 108.2403.*

must serve a copy of the notice of non-responsibility on the lessee and upon the prime contractor.[800] If a prime contractor receives a notice of non-responsibility, the prime contractor must post the notice in a conspicuous place on the work of improvement within 3 days of receipt, and serve a copy of the notice on each person who serves the prime contractor with a notice of right to lien under NRS 108.245.[801]

If an owner fails to comply with these requirements, the notice of non-responsibility will not be effective and the owner will not be able to assert this notice as a defense.

8:30 TENANT IMPROVEMENT CONTRACTS, PAYMENT BONDS, AND CONSTRUCTION DISBURSEMENT ACCOUNTS

A major alteration to the Nevada mechanics lien law is the addition of certain statutes regarding tenant improvement contracts. Under NRS 108.2403, before a tenant improvement contract can be commenced by a lessee of property, the lessee must issue a "Notice of Posted Security" and record the same with the county recorder for the county in which the project is located.[802] In addition to the Notice of Posted Security, the lessee must either establish and fund a construction disbursement account or obtain and record a payment bond for the benefit of potential lien claimants on the Project.[803] If the

---

[800] NRS 108.234(4) provides:

> *To be effective and valid, each notice of nonresponsibility that is recorded by a lessor pursuant to this section must be served by personal delivery or by certified mail, return receipt requested:*
> *(a) Upon the lessee within 10 days after the date on which the notice of nonresponsibility is recorded pursuant to subsection 2; and*
> *(b) Upon the prime contractor for the work of improvement within 10 days after the date on which the lessee contracts with the prime contractor for the construction, alteration or repair of the work of improvement.*

[801] NRS 108.234(5) provides:

> *If the prime contractor for the work of improvement receives a notice of nonresponsibility pursuant to paragraph (b) of subsection 4, the prime contractor shall:*
> *(a) Post a copy of the notice of nonresponsibility in an open and conspicuous place on the property within 3 days after his receipt of the notice of nonresponsibility; and*
> *(b) Serve a copy of the notice of nonresponsibility by personal delivery, facsimile or by certified mail, return receipt requested, upon each lien claimant from whom a notice of right to lien was received, within 10 days after receipt of the notice of nonresponsibility or a notice of right to lien, whichever occurs later.*

[802] *See* Form 8-13 in Appendix A.

[803] NRS 108.2403(1) provides:

lessee chooses to establish the construction disbursement account, the account must be set up with a third party construction control, as licensed under NRS 627.010, et seq. The lessee must fund the account with an amount equal to the total cost of the work of improvement, but no event less than the prime contract. The lessee must notify each person who serves him with a notice of right to lien under NRS 108.245 within 10 days after receipt of the preliminary notice. If the lessee chooses to have a payment bond issued instead, the bond must be issued by a Nevada licensed surety, and be in compliance with the requirements of NRS 108.2415. The bond must be recorded before commencement of construction, and a notice of the recording must also be served on each person who serves a notice of right to lien under NRS 108.245. This bond must also be served within 10 days of receipt of the preliminary notice.

The only exceptions to this requirement are when the property owner and lessor waives his rights to record a notice of non-responsibility under NRS 108.234, or in a county whose population is more than 400,000, the project is on airport land and is deemed for a commercial purpose.

In the event that the lessee fails to obtain and record the bond, the prime contractor on the project may stop work. If the lessee does not provide the security within 25 days after the work stoppage, the prime contractor may invalidate the construction contract and sue the tenant for damages, including lost profits, consequential damages, attorneys' fees and costs for him and all of this subcontractors and suppliers.

8:31 Mechanics Lien Priority and Equitable Subrogation

A major issue is the priority of mechanics' liens vis-a-vis recorded deeds of trust. As a general proposition, mechanics liens in Nevada are preferred to any sale, mortgage or

---

Except as otherwise provided in NRS 108.2405, before a lessee may cause a work of improvement to be constructed, altered or repaired upon property that the lessee is leasing, the lessee shall:
(a) Record a notice of posted security with the county recorder of the county where the property is located upon which the improvement is or will be constructed, altered or repaired; and
(b) Either:
(1) Establish a construction disbursement account and:
(I) Fund the account in an amount equal to the total cost of the work of improvement, but in no event less than the total amount of the prime contract;
(II) Obtain the services of a construction control to administer the construction disbursement account; and
(III) Notify each person who gives the lessee a notice of right to lien of the establishment of the construction disbursement account as provided in paragraph (f) of subsection 2; or
(2) Record a surety bond for the prime contract that meets the requirements of subsection 2 of NRS 108.2415 and notify each person who gives the lessee a notice of right to lien of the recording of the surety bond as provided in paragraph (f) of subsection 2.

deed of trust that is recorded after the commencement of construction that gives rise to a mechanics lien.[804] Commencement of construction is generally defined as the date that visible work of construction is found on the construction project site.[805] As discussed in Section 8:2 above, under NRS 108.225, mechanics liens seem to exist on a project from the moment of physical work being performed, even though the paperwork evidencing them might not actually be recorded until much later. For this reason, mechanics liens can be described as inchoate: actual, but not yet fully developed by the recording of a document. These inchoate mechanics liens have priority over any other type of lien recorded after the inchoate lien was created by the performance of actual construction work. While this concept requires a bit of abstract thinking, it is a simple result of protecting the contractor's right to payment from the moment he begins work. Upon sale of the property, the mechanics liens must be paid off first, even though the physical paperwork for the liens may not have been recorded until a later date than any existing deed of trust. As such, a lender deed of trust recorded after the commencement of construction arguably has no priority over the mechanics liens. Conversely, if a deed of trust is recorded before the first date that construction is visible on the project, the deed of trust holder would have first right to any sale proceeds from the property.

As a practical matter, prior to the 2008 recession in Nevada, construction lenders would often want to see demonstrable equity and commitment by project owners to a project before providing construction loan funding. As historical evidence only demonstrated a rise in property values, construction lenders and title insurers had not focused on best practices to ensure title priority had not been broken with inchoate mechanics lien rights arising from a prior commencement of construction work upon recordation of the applicable deed of trust. As a consequence, it was not unusual for construction work to

---

[804] NRS 108.225 provides:

> *1. The liens provided for in NRS 108.221 to 108.246, inclusive, are preferred to:*
> *(a) Any lien, mortgage or other encumbrance which may have attached to the property after the commencement of construction of a work of improvement.*
> *(b) Any lien, mortgage or other encumbrance of which the lien claimant had no notice and which was unrecorded against the property at the commencement of construction of a work of improvement.*
> *2. Every mortgage or encumbrance imposed upon, or conveyance made of, property affected by the liens provided for in NRS 108.221 to 108.246, inclusive, after the commencement of construction of a work of improvement are subordinate and subject to the liens provided for in NRS 108.221 to 108.246, inclusive, regardless of the date of recording the notices of liens.*

[805] NRS 108.22112 provides:

> *"Commencement of construction" means the date on which:*
> *1. Work performed; or*
> *2. Materials or equipment furnished in connection with a work of improvement, is visible from a reasonable inspection of the site.*

have commenced, and often substantially progressed, when new construction loan commitments were issued based on title insurance policies issued without exception for mechanics lien claims. With the economic collapse hitting property values particularly hard however, the value of in progress construction projects dropped precipitously. As a necessary consequence, mechanics lien claimants became obligated to claim priority over construction deeds of trust in order to obtain the fullest possible recovery. Given the lack of best practices previously used, title insurance attorneys have begun seeking ways to avoid the penalty of NRS 108.225 and the most popular argument has been the assertion of equitable subrogation of the mechanics lien claim.

Essentially, the doctrine of equitable subrogation means that it would be fundamentally unfair for a court to allow one lien claim to have priority over another claim, and to assuage that unfairness the court should find that the second in time lien should take precedence over the first, even though the law would require it to do otherwise. As applied against the inchoate nature of mechanics liens, the lenders argue that existence of an original purchase money lender--a lender from whom a loan was obtained to acquire the constructed property in the first place--was always known to the mechanics lien claimants, and as such, when the second lender paid off that purchase money loan they should simply be placed in the same priority position of that lender--the mechanics lien claimants would be no worse off than if the second loan had never occurred. As a consequence, the second lenders should be able to foreclose their deeds of trust without paying anything to the mechanics lien claimants for their work, just as the original purchase money lender could have done. The provisions of NRS 108.225 should not apply. Advocates of the equitable subrogation doctrine point to one Nevada case holding that a judgment lien was subject to the doctrine.[806]

To counter this argument, the mechanics lien claimants point out that as a foundational matter, the Nevada Supreme Court has always refused to enforce equitable doctrines when a statute had been enacted by the legislature covering the specific issue, even on public policy grounds.[807] As such, the Court should not even discuss the equitable theory. Even if considered, Nevada public policy on the issue would favor the mechanics lien claimants, as Nevada recognizes a specific public policy that contractors should be paid for their work.[808] The provisions of NRS 108.225 were specifically enacted as part of the mechanics lien statutory scheme to support that public policy, which has been routinely held to favor contractors and is required to be interpreted liberally on their

---

806 *See Houston v. Bank of America Federal Savings Bank*, 119 Nev. 485, 490, 78 P.3d 71 (2003).

807 *See Mello v. Woodhouse*, 110 Nev. 366, 373, 872 P.2d 337 (1994); *Smith v. Smith*, 68 Nev. 10, 226 P.2d 279 (1951); *Pellegrini v. State*, 117 Nev. 860, 878, 34 P.3d 519, 531 (2001) and *Beazer Homes Nevada, Inc. v. Eighth Judicial Dist. Court ex rel. County of Clark*, 120 Nev. 575, 578, fn. 4, 97 P.3d 1132 (2004).

808 *Lehrer McGovern Bovis, Inc. v. Bullock Insulation, Inc.*, 197 P.3d 1032, 1041 (Nev. 2008).

behalf.[809] More importantly, because lenders are sophisticated business entities and have knowledge that construction was being performed on the property, they could and should have taken steps to protect themselves from mechanics lien claims they knew would arise. If they did not, they were chargeable with "culpable and inexcusable neglect."[810] Finally, the fact that the second lender would receive the benefit of all the contractor's labor without payment, if the doctrine of equitable subrogation was applied, would largely outweigh the unfairness to the second lender who could have resolved those risks by insisting the contractors get paid before calling their loans. Such a result would be manifest injustice.

In 2012, the Court dispensed with the use of equitable subrogation to provide a lender priority over mechanics liens in *In re Fontainebleau Las Vegas Holdings LLC.*[811] *Fontainebleau* likewise dispensed with the idea that a lien claimant could contractually waive its rights to record a mechanics lien before it even started work.[812] However, the Court also hinted that a contractual subordination agreement may be enforceable after construction had commenced by noting that "neither NRS 108.2453 nor NRS 108.2457 completely prohibit waiver of or impairment to the right to a mechanic's lien after it arises." Rather, "non-prospective subordination agreements may be enforced as long as they meet the statutory requirements of NRS 108.2457." *Id.* What exactly was needed in a contractual subordination agreement to meet the statutory requirements of NRS 108.2457 was left for another day.

In 2015, the Court considered the question of whether *Fontainebleau* invalidated a partial subordination agreement that essentially switched the position of deeds of trust, one with priority over mechanics lien claimants and the other without.[813] Noting a split between jurisdictions, the NSC sided with the majority which held that a general subordination agreement that has "no affect" on lien holders that are not parties to the subordination agreement, should be read as effecting a "partial subordination." Since the mechanics lien claimants were not a party to the subordination agreement, the court would not ascribe a purpose to the parties to enhance the priority of non-parties to the agreement.[814] On this basis, the Court could not find that NRS 108.225 precluded a

---

[809] *See Malter v. Falcon Min. Co.*, 18 Nev. 209, 212-213, 2 P. 50, 50-51 (1883); *Lehrer McGovern Bovis, Inc. v. Bullock Insulation, Inc.*, 197 P.3d 1032, 1041 (Nev. 2008).

[810] *See Lawyers Title Ins. Corp. v. Feldsher*, 42 Cal. App. 4th 41, 53, 49 Cal. Rptr. 2d 542 (2d Dist. 1996).

[811] *In Re Fontainebleau Las Vegas Holdings LLC*, 128 Nev. Adv. Op. 53, 289 P.3d 1199 (2012).

[812] *Id.*, 289 P.3d at 1214

[813] *In re: Manhattan West Mechanic's Lien Litigation*, 131 Nev.Adv.Op. 70 (2015).

[814] *Id.*, at pg. 12.

partial subordination agreement "between lienholders with priority over mechanic's liens and those with lesser priority in situations where the mechanics' liens will be left in exactly the same position as if the subordination agreement had never occurred," [815]and distinguished *Fontainebleau* by noting in that case the mechanics lien claimants were parties to the subordination agreement which attempted to subordinate the mechanics lien priority position despite the provisions of NRS 108.225.[816] This point was "crucial" to the NSC's decision:

> *Crucially, nothing about the subordination agreement alters the amount of debt that [the lien claimant] was junior to, and thus, the subordination agreement does not violate NRS 108.225.*[8 7]

While *Manhattan West* might seem like a bell-weather change in the Court's thinking on mechanics lien priority because it supports the idea that effect should be given to contractual agreements between parties that impact mechanics liens even in contravention of the Nevada Mechanics Lien Law's pronouncements otherwise, such an interpretation is undoubtedly a stretch too far. The key factor in the Court's opinion was the lack of a contractual agreement including the mechanics lien claimants, as well as a lack of impact of the agreement on the lien claimant's priority position. The actual language of *Manhattan West* would seem to indicate almost an outright ban of subordination agreements when mechanics lien claimants are parties to them, and/or when the effect of the subordination is to subject the mechanics lien claim to additional debt. Such an indication can be seen in the Court's interpretation of NRS 108.2457.

In the unpublished decision in *Insulation Contracting & Supply, Inc. v. S3H, Inc.*,[818] issued at almost the same time as *Manhattan West*, the Court made clear it considers waiver or impairment of mechanics lien claimant rights without full payment very difficult. In fact, the Court specifically states that under NRS 108.2457(2)(b) "lien waivers cannot be enforced unless the waiving party is paid in full."[819] NRS 108.2457(2) provides:

> *[a]n oral or written statement purporting to waive, release or otherwise adversely affect the rights of a lien claimant is not enforceable and does not create any estoppel or*

---

[815] *Id.*, at pg. 14.

[816] *Id.*, at fn. 7.

[817] *Manhattan West, supra*, 131 Nev.Adv.Op. 70, at pg. 14.

[818] *Insulation Contracting & Supply, Inc. v. S3H, Inc.*, No. 62856, 2015 WL 5774180 (Nev. Sept 29, 2015). While an unpublished opinion cannot currently be cited as authority under SCR 123, it should be noted that 1) the Court repealed the provisions of SCR 123 (*See* ADKT No. 506), and 2) a petition is currently pending under NRAP 36(f) for the *Insulation Contracting* decision to be reissued as a published decision.

[819] *Insulation Contracting, supra.*, at pg. 3.

> *impairment of a lien unless ... (b) The lien claimant received payment for the lien and then only to the extent of the payment received.*

Fontainebleau advises that a contractual subordination agreement seeking to subordinate an existing mechanics lien priority right may be enforceable *if* it complies with the provisions of NRS 108.2457. *Manhattan West* states that a partial subordination agreement is enforceable specifically and crucially *because it does not* at all affect the priority of existing mechanics lien claimants and NRS 108.2457 *requires* a lien claimant be *paid in full* to impair a mechanics lien right. It is therefore very difficult to expect that the Court will enforce a contractual subordination of mechanics liens which results in less than payment in full to the subordinating mechanics lien claimants.

CHAPTER 9 MISCELLANEOUS CONSTRUCTION ISSUES

9:1 WORKER'S COMPENSATION

Somewhat unique among worker's compensation schemes, Nevada's workers compensation Insurance is the exclusive remedy for an injured worker on a Nevada Construction Project. The injured worker, regardless of what subcontractor, contractor or supplier he works for is deemed in Nevada to be the employee of any general contractor and owner, as well as the co-employee of any subcontractor on a project. As such, the injured worker may not sue a co-employer for injuries suffered on the project or during the course of performing his job functions. The sole recourse for injured worker is the worker's compensation insurance benefits provided by the employer.

NRS 616A.020(1) provides in pertinent part:

> *The rights and remedies provided in [the Nevada Industrial Insurance Act] ... shall be exclusive ... of all other rights and remedies of the employee ... at common law ... on account of such injury.*

Further, NRS 616A.265(1) provides in pertinent part:

> *"Injury" ... means a sudden and tangible happening of a traumatic nature, producing an immediate or prompt result which is established by medical evidence, including injuries to prosthetic devices.*

Under Nevada law, the project owner and its general contractor are deemed the co-employers of the injured worker, and all subcontractors are deemed co-employees of the worker, making them immune from lawsuits for negligence or other injury by the injured worker or his estate. As the Nevada Supreme Court stated in *Meers v. Haughton Elevator, a Div. of Reliance Elec. Co.*:[820]

> *It is well established that employers, and persons in the same employ as a person injured in the course of employment, are immune from liability under the Nevada Industrial Insurance Act.*

Further, this protection extends to others involved in a "common enterprise" of the construction project, when there is a licensed general contractor involved. As the Nevada Supreme Court held in *Richards v. Republic Silver State Disposal, Inc.*:[821]

---

[820] *Meers v. Haughton Elevator, a Div. of Reliance Elec. Co.*, 101 Nev. 283, 285, 701 P.2d 1006, 1007 (1985).

[821] *Richards v. Republic Silver State Disposal, Inc.*, 122 Nev. 1213, 148 P.3d 684, 687 (2006).

The scope of this 'statutory employer' definition is broadened for principal contractors, ... which are usually deemed the statutory employers not only of their directly hired employees, but also of the employees of their subcontractors and independent contractors.

This broadened protection, however, does not extend to independent operators or third party tortfeasers who cause injury.[822] As stated by the Nevada Supreme Court in *GES, Inc. v. Corbitt*:[823]

Under the NIIA, workers' compensation is an employee's only remedy against his employer and co-employees for an industrial injury; however, the injured worker may pursue a common law tort action against any tortfeaser who is not his statutory employer or co-employee.

As such, a worker who is injured while working in the public street by a third party driving on the under construction road would be limited to his workers compensation benefits provided by his employer, but could maintain an independent action against the driver of the vehicle who caused his injuries.

Nevada has not determined that a co-employee has no right to seek from another co-employee damages through subrogation to the injured employee's rights, though it is possible that the Nevada Supreme Court would disallow such actions. When co-employers maintain substantial self-insured retentions or deductibles, those co-employers may want to recover the out of pocket costs paid to their injured workers, when that injury is actually caused by another subcontractor on the project. This ability to recover from the responsible subcontractor is known as subrogation. Normally, an insurer does not have the right to recover for paid benefits, because the insurer "stands in the shoes" of its injured.

When an employee receives an injury for which compensation is payable pursuant to [the NIIA] and which was caused under circumstances creating a legal liability in some person other than the employer or a person in the same employ ... to pay damages, ...the insurer ... has a right of action against the person so liable to pay damages and is subrogated to the rights of the injured employee . . . .[824]

While subcontractors and their employees of same principal contractor are considered co-employees with each other, NRS 616C.215(2)(b) does not seem to prohibit recovery of damages against co-employee in subrogation. Any such alleged prohibition arises

[822] *See* NRS 616B.603.

[823] *GES, Inc. v. Corbitt*, 117 Nev. 265, 268, 21 P.3d 11, 13 (2001).

[824] NRS 616C.215(2).

from a claim that it is implied in language "or a person in the same employ" and *not* the explicit language. But that is not the usual way the law is applied. In absence of a prohibition, common law rights will apply.

> *In the context of worker's compensation, absent a statutory subrogation right, the non-negligent employer who has been required to pay worker's compensation benefits to its employee for injuries caused by a third-party's negligence has a common law right of subrogation to the employee's claim against the third-party tortfeasor.*[825]

At best, the statutory language of NRS 616C.215(2)(b) creates subrogation for insurer when 3rd party tortfeasor is cause of injury. Moreover, "injury" definition does not include the damages suffered by the co-employee--that is, economic damages resulting from the injury--payment of self-insured retention, increased costs, and lost productivity. These damages are arguably independent of those suffered by the injured worker and accrue directly from action causing the injured to the worker's employer. These rights are potentially viable as independent causes of action.

9:2 Controlled Insurance Programs and Wrap Policies

Nevada authorizes the use of owner controlled insurance programs[826] on construction projects for comprehensive insurance purposes. If the owner intends to or contemplates the use of an OCIP for insurance purposes, the disclosure of that potential use must be made at the time of bid advertisement.[827]

---

[825] *AT&T Technologies, Inc. v. Reid*, 109 Nev. 592, 596, 855 P.2d 533, 535 (1993).

[826] NRS 616A.282 defines Owner Controlled Insurance Program as “"a consolidated insurance program that is established and administered by the owner of the construction project."

[827] NRS 616B.735 provides:

> *With respect to a construction project for which the owner intends to establish and administer an owner-controlled insurance program or the principal contractor intends to establish and administer a contractor-controlled insurance program, the owner or principal contractor, as appropriate, shall:*
> *1. In the notice or advertisement for bids for the construction of the project, state:*
> *(a) That the employees of contractors and subcontractors who are engaged in the construction of the project will be covered under a consolidated insurance program when such employees work at the site of the project; and*
> *(b) Whether such a program will be an owner-controlled insurance program or a contractor-controlled insurance program; and*
> *2. Hold a pre-bid conference at which it provides to potential contractors and subcontractors, without limitation, the following information:*
> *(a) A general explanation of the manner in which a consolidated insurance program operates;*
> *(b) An overview of the provisions of NRS 616B.710 to 616B.737, inclusive;*
> *(c) A general description of the safety procedures that will be required as part of the consolidated insurance program; and*

OCIP programs have been used in Nevada on a variety of projects, however, as residential projects become integrated with commercial or other non-residential projects and as condominium towers are built using more traditional commercial builders, care should be taken to select a program that is sufficient for the project, including any potential construction defect claims.[828] Many contractor's general commercial liability policies exclude residential work or work that involves residential units and also exclude any projects on which a OCIP or other "wrap" coverage policy exists. The difficulty, however, is ensuring there is sufficient coverage in the wrap program to meet the eventual needs of the project arising from construction defect claims, should they arise.

9:3 GENERAL CONTRACTOR'S LIABILITY TO DEFINED BENEFIT TRUST FUND CLAIMS

Another unique aspect to Nevada law is that a general contractor on a project which uses unionized labor is deemed the employer of all unionized workers for the payment of compensation and benefits owed to the union defined benefits trust fund. Prior to the 2015 legislative session, NRS 608.150 provided:

> *1. Every original contractor making or taking any contract in this State for the erection, construction, alteration or repair of any building or structure, or other work, shall assume and is liable for the indebtedness for labor incurred by any subcontractor or any contractors acting under, by or for the original contractor in performing any labor, construction or other work included in the subject of the original contract, for labor, and for the requirements imposed by chapters 616A to 617, inclusive, of NRS.*
>
> *2. It is unlawful for any contractor or any other person to fail to comply with the provisions of subsection 1, or to attempt to evade the responsibility imposed thereby, or to do any other act or thing tending to render nugatory the provisions of this section.*
>
> *3. The district attorney of any county wherein the defendant may reside or be found shall institute civil proceedings against any such original contractor failing to comply with the provisions of this section in a civil action for the amount of all wages and damage that may be owing or have accrued as a result of the failure of any subcontractor acting under the original contractor, and any property of the original contractor, not exempt by law, is subject to attachment and execution for the payment of any judgment that may be recovered in any action under the provisions of this section.*

(d) The procedures pursuant to which claims for industrial insurance will be administered.

[828] *See* Chapter 7 Residential Construction Defect Claims.

As a result of this statute, union defined benefit trust funds regularly assert claims against general contractors for the unpaid wages and/or benefits of subcontractors which the general contractor had previously used on a construction project. Moreover, the union benefit trust fund has a four (4) year statute of limitations on claims brought for unpaid benefits. It is often the case, therefore, that a general contractor will be sued to recover unpaid benefits for a subcontractor, years after the project has been completed and fully paid.

Likewise, the defined benefit trust has mechanics lien rights against a construction project as well. NRS 108.2214 provides:

> *1. "Lien claimant" means any person who provides work, material or equipment with a value of $500 or more to be used in or for the construction, alteration or repair of any improvement, property or work of improvement. The term includes, without limitation, every artisan, builder, contractor, laborer, lessor or renter of equipment, materialman, miner, subcontractor or other person who provides work, material or equipment, and any person who performs services as an architect, engineer, land surveyor or geologist, in relation to the improvement, property or work of improvement.*
>
> *2. As used in this section, "laborer" includes, without limitation, an express trust fund to which any portion of the total compensation of a laborer, including, without limitation, any fringe benefit, must be paid pursuant to an agreement with that laborer or the collective bargaining agent of that laborer.*

The union benefit trust, in practice, will not provide a definitive amount of money due from a signatory contractor until a complete audit of the signatory's books and records has been completed by the trust fund's auditors. As such, the trust fund will only record liens of approximate value, pending audits. Similarly, the trust fund will not provide final releases in exchange for payment of claims until the audit is performed. As such this can be a difficult problem for a general contractor attempting to close out a project or to close out the books on a subcontractor.

Ironically, this conception of a union benefit trust fund as a laborer does not assist the Union Trust Funds in the public works context. In *Hartford Fire Ins. Co. v. Trustees of Const. Industry*,[829] the Nevada Supreme Court faced this very confrontation between the protection statute of the Nevada public works statutes and the obligation of a general contractor to cover the wage claims of its subcontractors' employees under NRS 608.150. In a certified question directed to it from the United States Court of Appeals for the 9th Circuit, the Nevada Supreme Court examined a situation where a union signatory subcontractor failed to pay the labor benefits due its employees and filed for bankruptcy. As a result, the court required the general contractor to pay for the benefits under NRS

[829] *Hartford Fire Ins. Co. v. Trustees of Const. Industry*, 125 Nev. 16, 208 P.3d 884 (2009)

608.150. However, the labor union benefit trust fund was also seeking to make a claim against the public works payment bond issued by the Contractor,[830] but had not provided the general contractor with a 30 day preliminary notice or the 90 day notice from the date of last labor.[831]

The Court ruled that as the union trust fund represented the employees of a subcontractor, the obligations of the payment bond claim statutes would apply to the employees themselves, if they wanted to make claims upon the payment bond. As the representatives of the employees, the union trust fund could not make claims on the bond without also complying with the notice requirements; the fact that many other federal courts have held that union trust funds do not need to provide statutory required notices because of their unique role in protecting employee pensions and health benefits did not persuade the Nevada Supreme Court. Rather, the Court suggested the union trust fund needed to lobby the Nevada legislature for a change in the notice requirement. If the labor union trust fund wanted to make a claim upon the public works surety bond, the labor union would have to demonstrate that it have provided the required notices under NRS 339.035.

As additional complexity for the contractor, the Nevada State Contractor's Board currently maintains the position that the offset of funds due to a subcontractor for one project against funds owed by the same contractor to the general is actually a diversion of funds in violation of NRS 624.3012. The NSCB has been known to issue administrative citations to general contractors who attempt to offset such debts, even if the subcontractor's contracts specifically allow for setoff. As a practical matter, there is little for the general contractor faced with this situation to do but pay the benefit trust fund claim and seek reimbursement from the subcontractor involved.

In 2015, however, the Nevada legislature passed SB223 which substantially revises NRS 608.150 to eliminate much of the unfairness to original contractors or prime contractors.[832] SB223 revised NRS 608.150[833] to alter the ambiguity over the term

---

830 *See* Section 6:24.

831 NRS 339.035(2).

832 SB223 2015 Nevada Legislative session, became effective October 1, 2015. As of the date of publication, however, the revisions of SB223 to the Nevada Statutes had not been completed by the Nevada Legislative Counsel Bureau. Therefore, references to the legislative changes will be noted by reference to the bill and the applicable section number.

833 SB223 revises NRS 608.150 to read as follows:

> *1. Except as otherwise provided in subsections 2 and 3, every prime contractor making or taking any contract in the State for the erection, construction, alteration or repair of any building or structure, or other work of improvement, shall assume and is liable for the*

"original contractor", significantly restrict the amount of money recoverable from the prime contractor , and impose notice and time requirements on claims for unpaid wages and benefits under this statute. SB223 also required that union benefit trust funds serve Notices of Right to Lien under NRS 108.245 in order to perfect a mechanics lien for unpaid wages or benefits,[834] and shorted the statute of limitations to a maximum of 1 year from substantial completion of the project to bring a claim.[835] At the time of publication, there was a challenge to SB223 on the grounds that it was pre-empted under ERISA,[836] but no decision on that challenge had been issued by the US District Court handling the matter.

9:4 Bankruptcy Implications on Construction Claims

Bankruptcy of a party in a construction project can cause considerable issues for the owner or contractor attempting to deal with the situation. While the filing of bankruptcy may constitute a default under most construction contracts, the non-defaulting party

---

> *indebtedness for labor incurred by any subcontractor or any contractors acting under, by or for the prime contractor in performing any labor, and for the requirements imposed by chapters 616A to 617, inclusive of NRS.*
> *2. The provisions of subsection 1 do not require a prime contractor to assume or be liable for any liability of a subcontractor or other contractor for any penalty, including, without limitation, interest, liquidated damages, attorney's fees or costs for the failure of the subcontractor or other contractor to make any contributions or other payments under any other law or agreement, including, without limitation, to a health or welfare fund or any other plan for the benefit of employees in accordance with a collective bargaining agreement.*
> *3. The provisions of subsection 1 do not require a prime contractor to assume or be liable for any liability of a subcontractor or other contractor for any amount for which the prime contractor did not receive proper notice in accordance with section 5 of this act.*
> *4. It is unlawful for any prime contractor to fail to comply with the provisions of subsection 1, or to attempt to evade the responsibility imposed thereby, or to do any other act or thing tending to render nugatory the provisions of this section.*
> *5. The district attorney of any county wherein the defendant may reside or be found shall institute civil proceedings against any such prime contractor failing to comply with the provisions of this section in a civil action for the amount of all wages and benefits that may be owing or have accrued as a result of the failure of any subcontractor acting under the prime contractor, and any property of the prime contractor, not exempt by law, is subject to attachment and execution for the payment of any judgment that may be recovered in any action under the provisions of this section.*
> *6. As used in this section, "prime contractor" has the meaning ascribed to it in NRS 108.22164.*

[834] SB223 Sections 3 & 4.

[835] SB223 Section 2.

[836] *See The Board of Trustees of the Glazing Health and Welfare Trust, et al., v. Chambers*, No. 15-CV-01754-KJD-VCF, USDC Nev.).

must bear in mind that upon the filing of the bankruptcy an automatic stay of any action taken against the debtor is immediately issued.[837] As a result, the non-bankruptcy party cannot simply terminate the construction contract upon the bankruptcy filing and move forward. Care must be taken to ensure that a violation of the automatic stay is not occurring.

The initial question is whether the bankrupt intends to complete any incomplete contracts. This is primarily a question for a bankrupt in a reorganization plan. If the bankrupt affirms its intention to proceed and complete the contract, then the non-bankrupt party must honor that commitment, though the bankruptcy court can require certain conditions on the debtor to assure the other party that complete performance is possible. If the debtor does not intend to complete the work, the non-bankrupt party should seek to have the bankruptcy trustee or the debtor in possession abandon the contract formally. However, in some cases a bankrupt entity may disappear entirely and in these cases, the contractor does have the right to set off damages resulting from the bankrupt's default.

A creditor's right to set off survives confirmation of a Chapter 11 plan. In *In re De Laurentis Entertainment Group Inc.*,[838] the Ninth Circuit addressed the apparent conflict between Section 1141 and Section 553 of the Bankruptcy Code. Section 1141 provides that "the property dealt with by the plan is free and clear of all claims and interests of creditors," and that the plan "discharges the debtor from any debt that arose before the date of such confirmation." 11 U.S.C.A. §§1141(c) and (d)(1)(A). But "Section 553 protects the right to a set off from the operation of the remainder of the bankruptcy code." Specifically, Section 553 states that "this title does not affect any right of a creditor to offset a mutual debt." 11 U.S.C.A. §553(a). The Carolco court noted that "[t]hese two sections are in direct conflict," and concluded that "section 553 must take precedence over section 1141." The "primacy of setoff is essential to the equitable treatment of creditors. A setoff is allowed as a defense to a claim brought by the debtor a creditor ... Absent a setoff, a creditor ... is in the worst of both worlds: it must pay its debt to the debtor in full, but is only entitled to receive a tiny fraction of the money the debtor owes it." The contractor's right to assert set off against the bankrupt survives the confirmation of debtor's chapter 11 plan. If the debtor fails to complete the reorganization plan, the contractor has the right to offset.

In the case of a bankrupt project owner, an unpaid contractor still has the right to take any actions necessary to perfect his statutory mechanics lien rights.[839] In this case, the

[837] 11 U.S.C.A. §362.

[838] *In re De Laurentis Entertainment Group Inc.*, 963 F.2d 1269, 1274 (9th Cir. 1992).

[839] 11 U.S.C.A. §546(b).

mechanics lien claimant may record its claim of lien and file with the bankruptcy court a notice of intent to perfect its mechanics lien claim. This action replaces the state law requirement of filing a lawsuit against the bankrupt debtor, which would be a violation of the automatic stay. The mechanics lien claims are considered secured debts in the debtor's property, and will be dealt with as part of the estate on a priority basis. However, the fact that the United States Bankruptcy Code allows for the perfection of mechanics lien claims, the mechanics lien claimant still must make a proper showing under the applicable state law that the mechanics lien claim is valid.[840] The bankruptcy trustee will still have available to it all defenses against the lien claim and otherwise.

840 *See* Chapter 8 Nevada Mechanic's Liens.

APPENDIX A

Form 2-1

NEVADA STATE CONTRACTORS BOARD APPLICANT BACKGROUND DISCLOSURE STATEMENT AND AUTHORIZATION FOR RELEASE OF INFORMATION

BUSINESS NAME: ______________________________

NRS 624.263 and NRS 624.265 authorizes the Nevada State Contractors Board (NSCB) to conduct background investigations for all persons listed on the license application, and to request fingerprints for submission to the Nevada Highway Patrol (NHP) and the FBI for a determination of identity, fugitive status or prior criminal history.

Misrepresentation is a violation of NRS 624.3013(2) and NRS 624.306(7) and is cause for denial of your application.

A COPY OF A VALID STATE DRIVER'S LICENSE OR VALID GOVERNMENT ISSUED PHOTO I.D. MUST ACCOMPANY THIS FORM. A separate form must be completed by each principal, member, officer, director, partner, or associate.

FIRST NAME		MIDDLE NAME		LAST NAME		
TITLE		DATE OF BIRTH		PLACE OF BIRTH		SOCIAL SECURITY NUMBER
OTHER NAME USED, (IF APPLICABLE)	SEX	RACE	HEIGHT	WEIGHT	HAIR COLOR	EYE COLOR
RESIDENCE ADDRESS (AND MAILING ADDRESS IF DIFFERENT)			CITY		STATE	ZIP

1. Have you ever, as an individual or principal of a corporation or other business entity, been convicted of, or pled guilty or no contest to a felony crime?

   ❑ No ❑ Yes – Attach a detailed explanation for each instance, including copies of the original complaint, or indictment and final judgment or conviction.

2. Have you ever, as an individual or principal of a corporation or other business entity, been convicted of, or pled guilty or no contest to any misdemeanor crime? (You may limit your response to misdemeanor convictions within the last 10 years, **unless** the crime involved violence against another person, fraud or theft).

   ❑ No ❑ Yes – Attach a detailed explanation for each instance.

3. Are there currently criminal charges pending against you?

   ❑ No ❑ Yes – Attach a detailed explanation, including a copy of the complaint, and/or charging document.

4. Within the last 7 years, have you filed or been adjudicated Bankrupt under your individual name, a corporate name or any other business entity name?

   ❑ No ❑ Yes – Attach a copy of the discharge document. If discharged less than 3 years, include a schedule of creditors listed in the bankruptcy petition. If the bankruptcy has not been discharged, include your plan or reorganization and proof of compliance.

5. Have you, or any business entities of which you were a member, partner, officer, director, or associate received any notice of liens, suits, judgments, or claims (including tax claims) which remain unsatisfied?

   ❑ No ❑ Yes – Attach a detailed explanation.

6. Are there now any unpaid past due bills for materials, services rendered, or labor?

   ❑ No ❑ Yes – Attach a detailed explanation.

7. Have you, or any business entities of which you were a member, partner, officer, director, associate, or qualified employee had a contractor's license denied, suspended, revoked, or otherwise disciplined **BY NEVADA OR ANY OTHER STATE? Are there any disciplinary proceedings currently pending against you, or any license on which you have appeared IN NEVADA OR ANY OTHER STATE?**

   ❑ No ❑ Yes – attach a detailed explanation including the name of the state in which the license was held, license number, and business name.

8. Do you have a proprietary interest (i.e., ownership, stock, shares) in this applicant? (This question does not pertain to sole proprietors)

   ❑ No ❑ Yes – Percentage Owned ______________

9. Are you a citizen of the United States of America?

   ❑ No ❑ Yes – **If no, attach a copy of INS card and Social Security Card.**

Applicant Background Disclosure Statement

Form 2-2

BUSINESS FINANCIAL STATEMENT

If you need assistance in completing this form, you are encouraged to seek the advice of an accountant.

Applicant / Licensee Name:______________________________

Business financial statement of ______________________ (Name) __________ (State Organized)

Business Entity: ❑Sole Proprietorship ❑Corporation ❑Limited Liability Company ❑Limited Partnership ❑General Partnership

Street Address City State Zip Phone Number

As Of ______________ Month / Date / Year

CURRENT ASSETS	Dollars	CURRENT LIABILITIES	Dollars
Cash – on hand........		Accounts payable (schedule 3)........	
Cash – in banks (schedule 1)........		Taxes payable........	
Securities - stocks / bonds (schedule 2)........		Other current liabilities (schedule 5)........	
Accounts receivable (schedule 3)........		Current notes payable Due within one (1) year (schedule 9)........	
Current notes receivable (schedule 4)........			
Other current assets (schedule 5)........			
Total Current Assets		**Total Current Liabilities**	
FIXED ASSETS	**Dollars**	**LONG TERM LIABILITIES**	**Dollars**
Real estate (schedule 6)		Real estate debt (schedule 6)........	
Vehicles & equipment (schedule 7)........		Other long-term debt (schedule 8)........	
Long term notes receivable (schedule 4)........		Long term notes payable (schedule 9)........	
Other assets and investments (schedule 8)........			
Total Fixed Assets		**Total Long Term Liabilities**	
TOTAL ASSETS		**TOTAL LIABILITIES**	
		EQUITY	
		Net Sales:	
		Net Profit:	
		Contingent Liabilities:	

Equity is total assets minus total liabilities

Form 2-3

NEVADA STATE CONTRACTORS BOARD

2310 CORPORATE CIRCLE, SUITE 200, HENDERSON, NEVADA, 89074 (702) 486-1100 FAX (702) 486-1190, INVESTIGATIONS (702) 486-1110
9670 GATEWAY DRIVE, SUITE 100, RENO, NEVADA, 89521 (775) 688-1141 FAX (775) 688-1271, INVESTIGATIONS (775) 688-1150
Website: www.nscb.state.nv.us

IMPORTANT NOTICE

Dear Applicant:

Many applications are rejected because they are incomplete or do not include the required supporting documents.

An incomplete application can needlessly delay you receiving your license. Delays can last several weeks or even months and possibly result in the application being voided and application fee forfeited.

Spending a few extra minutes now may save you weeks or months later!

Before you submit your application:

✓ Carefully read the application package and follow the specific instruction contained throughout the form.

✓ Make sure the application is properly signed.

✓ Include the non refundable $300.00 application fee. **(A $600.00 biennial license fee will be required after your application is approved, before your license can be issued).**

✓ Fill out all applicable information.

✓ Attach required supporting documentation.

✓ Make sure the required Reference Certificates substantiate a minimum four years of experience in the classification for which you are applying.

Form 2-4

NEVADA STATE CONTRACTORS BOARD

9670 GATEWAY DRIVE, SUITE 100, RENO, NEVADA, 89521 (775) 688-1141 FAX (775) 688-1271, INVESTIGATIONS (775) 688-1150
2310 CORPORATE CIRCLE, SUITE 200, HENDERSON, NEVADA, 89074 (702) 486-1100 FAX (702) 486-1190, INVESTIGATIONS (702) 486-1110
www.nscb.state.nv.us

OUT - OF - STATE LICENSE VERIFICATION FORM
THIS FORM MUST BE COMPLETED WHEN APPLYING FOR EXAM WAIVER BASED ON RECIPROCITY WITH ARIZONA, CALIFORNIA, OR UTAH

Applicant Name______________________________
Company Name______________________________
Street Address______________________________
City______________________________
State________________ Zip ______________

INSTRUCTION TO APPLICANT

Insert your name and address and complete the top portion of this request. Give the form to the appropriate agency. The verifying agency will mail the completed verification to you at the address you have listed. Include the completed form with your application.

I am requesting licensure in the State of Nevada as a____.

I am/have been licensed in the State of ______________________ issued under the company name of

______________________________. My Social Security # is ______________________.

I authorize you to release, to the State of Nevada, all information pertaining to license number:______________.

______________________________ ______________________________
Print Name of Applicant Signature of Applicant

NOTE TO APPLICANT: COMPLETE A SEPARATE FORM FOR EACH LICENSE NUMBER

TO VERIFYING STATE: Please furnish the information requested. Sign and verify the document. Place the completed form in an envelope, seal the envelope, and provide it to the applicant either in person or by mail.

Company Name ____
Type of License (Classification) ____
Original Date of Issue__________________ License Number______________
Amount of Limit (If any) ______________ Amount of Bond (If any)__________________
Any record of suspensions, revocations, other disciplinary actions, or current Complaints?________. If yes, please provide a copy of the action.
Current Status of License:______________ If not Active, Reason: ____________________
Name of Qualifying Individual & Title ____
Licensed by: ☐ Waiver of Exam (Basis of Waiver):______________________________
☐ Successful Completion of Exam - Specify Type:______________________________
☐ Endorsement from the State of: ______________________________
Other Personnel Listed & Titles____

AGENCY SEAL **SIGNATURE**______________________ **TITLE** __________________

Form 2-5

NEVADA STATE CONTRACTORS BOARD

9670 GATEWAY DRIVE, SUITE 100, RENO, NEVADA, 89521 (775) 688-1141 FAX (775) 688-1271, INVESTIGATIONS (775) 688-1150
2310 CORPORATE CIRCLE, SUITE 200, HENDERSON, NEVADA, 89074 (702) 486-1100 FAX (702) 486-1190, INVESTIGATIONS (702) 486-1110
www.nscb.state.nv.us

BANK VERIFICATION FORM

Name of Licensee/Applicant: ______________________________

Date: ______________

Items 1 through 3 of the following report are to be completed by the applicant. Items 4 through 10 are to be completed by the verifying bank. If the answer to any item is "none," please indicate same in the appropriate space. After completion by you and your bank, submit this form with your application.

1. **Name and address of bank:** ______________________________

2. **Signatures of account holder(s):**

______________________ Signature ______________________ Print Name

______________________ Signature ______________________ Print Name

3. **Information to be verified:**

Type of Account	Account Name	Account Number

TO VERIFYING BANK: Please furnish the information requested below.

4. **Classification of Account:** ❑Individual ❑Corporation ❑Partnership ❑Limited Partnership ❑Limited Liability Company

5. **Deposit accounts of applicants:**

*Account Name	Type	*Account Number	*Current Balance	*Six (6) Month Average	*Date Opened

***Required Information**

6. **Verification of Lines of Credit:**

Line of Credit Account #	Type of Credit Line	Approved Amount	Current Balance	Available Amount	Payments Required	Secured by
					$ Per	
					$ Per	
					$ Per	

7. **Additional information that may be of assistance in determination of credit worthiness: (Please include information on loans paid in full.)**

____

8. **Affix Bank Stamp or Business Card of Bank Representative**

9. **Name and Title:** ______________

10: **Date:** ______________

(Rev 3/05)

Form 2-6

NEVADA STATE CONTRACTORS BOARD

9670 GATEWAY DRIVE, SUITE 100, RENO, NEVADA, 89521 (775) 688-1141 FAX (775) 688-1271, INVESTIGATIONS (775) 688-1150
2310 CORPORATE CIRCLE, SUITE 200, HENDERSON, NEVADA, 89074 (702) 486-1100 FAX (702) 486-1190, INVESTIGATIONS (702) 486-1110
www.nscb.state.nv.us

INDEMNIFICATION INSTRUCTIONS AND REQUIREMENTS

An indemnification agreement allows the board to consider the financial strength of an individual or entity in addition to the applicant. Indemnification is not required, however, it provides an option to an applicant who may not otherwise qualify for a state contractor's license, or increase in monetary limit for an existing license. The agreement must be on a form prescribed by the board, and accompanied by financial documents as set forth below.

PERSONAL INDEMNIFICATION: A personal indemnification agreement is for use when an individual(s) is indemnifying another individual or another entity, i.e., corporation, limited liability company, limited partnership. The following documents are required:

1. A completed Personal Indemnification Agreement signed by the indemnitor. If the individual is married, both husband and wife must sign the agreement. If single, please state same on the form.
2. Required Financial Information (See below)

CORPORATE INDEMNIFICATION: A corporate indemnification agreement is for use when a corporation is indemnifying an individual or another entity, i.e., corporation, limited liability company, limited partnership. The following documents are required:

1. A completed Corporate Indemnification Agreement signed by a corporate officer and notarized.
2. A corporate resolution executed by the indemnifying corporation authorizing the execution of this agreement.
3. Required Financial Information (See below)

LIMITED LIABILITY COMPANY (LLC) INDEMNIFICATION: An LLC indemnification agreement is for use when an LLC is indemnifying an individual or another entity, i.e., corporation, limited liability company, limited partnership. The following documents are required:

1. A completed Limited Liability Company Indemnification Agreement signed by a Member or Manager.
2. A resolution executed by the indemnifying LLC, or other documentation authorizing the execution of this agreement.
3. Required Financial Information (See below)

LIMITED PARTNERSHIP INDEMNIFICATION: An Limited Partnership indemnification agreement is for use when a Limited Partnership is indemnifying an individual or another entity. The following documents are required:

1. A completed Limited Partnership Indemnification Agreement signed by the General Partner(s).
2. An agreement executed by the indemnifying Limited Partnership, or other documentation authorizing the execution of this agreement.
3. Required Financial Information (See below)

REQUIRED FINANCIAL INFORMATION

You must submit a current financial statement (statement) that meets the following criteria.

- For License Monetary Limits below $1,000,000 you must provide one of the following:
  - a) A current financial statement prepared by an independent certified public accountant; or
  - b) A current financial statement submitted on a form prescribed by the Board (available on the Board's website www.nscb.state.nv.us, click on contractor forms); or,
  - c) A current financial statement prepared using accounting software in accordance with generally accepted accounting principles and accompanied by an affidavit that verifies the accuracy of the financial statement.
- Note: Self-prepared or compiled statements must be current to within six months from the date the statement is received. Reviewed or audited statements must be current within one (1) year from the date the statement is received.
- For License Monetary Limits $1,000,000 or more, you must provide a financial statement that is prepared and reviewed or audited by a certified public accountant.
- All statements must be in U.S. dollars.
- All statements must include full disclosures.
- Business statements must include a classified balance sheet.
- Personal statements must include a supplemental schedule disclosing working capital and net worth.
- A completed bank verification form.

Form 2-6

NEVADA STATE CONTRACTORS BOARD

9670 GATEWAY DRIVE, SUITE 100, RENO, NEVADA, 89521 (775) 688-1141 FAX (775) 688-1271, INVESTIGATIONS (775) 688-1150
2310 CORPORATE CIRCLE, SUITE 200, HENDERSON, NEVADA, 89074 (702) 486-1100 FAX (702) 486-1190, INVESTIGATIONS (702) 486-1110
www.nscb.state.nv.us

INDEMNIFICATION INSTRUCTIONS AND REQUIREMENTS

An indemnification agreement allows the board to consider the financial strength of an individual or entity in addition to the applicant. Indemnification is not required, however, it provides an option to an applicant who may not otherwise qualify for a state contractor's license, or increase in monetary limit for an existing license. The agreement must be on a form prescribed by the board, and accompanied by financial documents as set forth below.

PERSONAL INDEMNIFICATION: A personal indemnification agreement is for use when an individual(s) is indemnifying another individual or another entity, i.e., corporation, limited liability company, limited partnership. The following documents are required:

1. A completed Personal Indemnification Agreement signed by the indemnitor. If the individual is married, both husband and wife must sign the agreement. If single, please state same on the form.
2. Required Financial Information (See below)

CORPORATE INDEMNIFICATION: A corporate indemnification agreement is for use when a corporation is indemnifying an individual or another entity, i.e., corporation, limited liability company, limited partnership. The following documents are required:

1. A completed Corporate Indemnification Agreement signed by a corporate officer and notarized.
2. A corporate resolution executed by the indemnifying corporation authorizing the execution of this agreement.
3. Required Financial Information (See below)

LIMITED LIABILITY COMPANY (LLC) INDEMNIFICATION: An LLC indemnification agreement is for use when an LLC is indemnifying an individual or another entity, i.e., corporation, limited liability company, limited partnership. The following documents are required:

1. A completed Limited Liability Company Indemnification Agreement signed by a Member or Manager.
2. A resolution executed by the indemnifying LLC, or other documentation authorizing the execution of this agreement.
3. Required Financial Information (See below)

LIMITED PARTNERSHIP INDEMNIFICATION: An Limited Partnership indemnification agreement is for use when a Limited Partnership is indemnifying an individual or another entity. The following documents are required:

1. A completed Limited Partnership Indemnification Agreement signed by the General Partner(s).
2. An agreement executed by the indemnifying Limited Partnership, or other documentation authorizing the execution of this agreement.
3. Required Financial Information (See below)

REQUIRED FINANCIAL INFORMATION

You must submit a current financial statement (statement) that meets the following criteria.

- For License Monetary Limits below $1,000,000 you must provide one of the following:
  - a) A current financial statement prepared by an independent certified public accountant; or
  - b) A current financial statement submitted on a form prescribed by the Board (available on the Board's website www.nscb.state.nv.us, click on contractor forms); or,
  - c) A current financial statement prepared using accounting software in accordance with generally accepted accounting principles and accompanied by an affidavit that verifies the accuracy of the financial statement.
- Note: Self-prepared or compiled statements must be current to within six months from the date the statement is received. Reviewed or audited statements must be current within one (1) year from the date the statement is received.
- For License Monetary Limits $1,000,000 or more, you must provide a financial statement that is prepared and reviewed or audited by a certified public accountant.
- All statements must be in U.S. dollars.
- All statements must include full disclosures.
- Business statements must include a classified balance sheet.
- Personal statements must include a supplemental schedule disclosing working capital and net worth.
- A completed bank verification form.

Form 2-7

NEVADA STATE CONTRACTORS BOARD

9670 GATEWAY DRIVE, SUITE 100, RENO, NEVADA, 89521 (775) 688-1141 FAX (775) 688-1271, INVESTIGATIONS (775) 688-1150
2310 CORPORATE CIRCLE, SUITE 200, HENDERSON, NEVADA, 89074 (702) 486-1100 FAX (702) 486-1190, INVESTIGATIONS (702) 486-1110
www.nscb.state.nv.us

INDEMNIFICATION INSTRUCTIONS AND REQUIREMENTS

An indemnification agreement allows the board to consider the financial strength of an individual or entity in addition to the applicant. Indemnification is not required, however, it provides an option to an applicant who may not otherwise qualify for a state contractor's license, or increase in monetary limit for an existing license. The agreement must be on a form prescribed by the board, and accompanied by financial documents as set forth below.

PERSONAL INDEMNIFICATION: A personal indemnification agreement is for use when an individual(s) is indemnifying another individual or another entity, i.e., corporation, limited liability company, limited partnership. The following documents are required:

1. A completed Personal Indemnification Agreement signed by the indemnitor. If the individual is married, both husband and wife must sign the agreement. If single, please state same on the form.
2. Required Financial Information (See below)

CORPORATE INDEMNIFICATION: A corporate indemnification agreement is for use when a corporation is indemnifying an individual or another entity, i.e., corporation, limited liability company, limited partnership. The following documents are required:

1. A completed Corporate Indemnification Agreement signed by a corporate officer and notarized.
2. A corporate resolution executed by the indemnifying corporation authorizing the execution of this agreement.
3. Required Financial Information (See below)

LIMITED LIABILITY COMPANY (LLC) INDEMNIFICATION: An LLC indemnification agreement is for use when an LLC is indemnifying an individual or another entity, i.e., corporation, limited liability company, limited partnership. The following documents are required:

1. A completed Limited Liability Company Indemnification Agreement signed by a Member or Manager.
2. A resolution executed by the indemnifying LLC, or other documentation authorizing the execution of this agreement.
3. Required Financial Information (See below)

LIMITED PARTNERSHIP INDEMNIFICATION: An Limited Partnership indemnification agreement is for use when a Limited Partnership is indemnifying an individual or another entity. The following documents are required:

1. A completed Limited Partnership Indemnification Agreement signed by the General Partner(s).
2. An agreement executed by the indemnifying Limited Partnership, or other documentation authorizing the execution of this agreement.
3. Required Financial Information (See below)

REQUIRED FINANCIAL INFORMATION

You must submit a current financial statement (statement) that meets the following criteria.

- For License Monetary Limits below $1,000,000 you must provide one of the following:
  - a) A current financial statement prepared by an independent certified public accountant; or
  - b) A current financial statement submitted on a form prescribed by the Board (available on the Board's website www.nscb.state.nv.us, click on contractor forms); or,
  - c) A current financial statement prepared using accounting software in accordance with generally accepted accounting principles and accompanied by an affidavit that verifies the accuracy of the financial statement.
- Note: Self-prepared or compiled statements must be current to within six months from the date the statement is received. Reviewed or audited statements must be current within one (1) year from the date the statement is received.
- For License Monetary Limits $1,000,000 or more, you must provide a financial statement that is prepared and reviewed or audited by a certified public accountant.
- All statements must be in U.S. dollars.
- All statements must include full disclosures.
- Business statements must include a classified balance sheet.
- Personal statements must include a supplemental schedule disclosing working capital and net worth.
- A completed bank verification form.

Form 2-8

NEVADA STATE CONTRACTORS BOARD

9670 GATEWAY DRIVE, SUITE 100, RENO, NEVADA, 89521 (775) 688-1141 FAX (775) 688-1271, INVESTIGATIONS (775) 688-1150
2310 CORPORATE CIRCLE, SUITE 200, HENDERSON, NEVADA, 89074 (702) 486-1100 FAX (702) 486-1190, INVESTIGATIONS (702) 486-1110
www.nscb.state.nv.us

GENERAL PARTNERSHIP INDEMNIFICATION AGREEMENT

FOR VALUE RECEIVED, the undersigned general partnership, does hereby indemnify the creditors of ______________________________ (hereinafter referred to as Licensee),
(USE FULL LEGAL NAME OF APPLICANT/ LICENSEE)
as guarantors and as sureties, against any loss or damage the said creditors may suffer as a result of licensee's failure to promptly pay obligations incurred by it in the ordinary course of construction business within the State of Nevada.

It is further agreed that the undersigned general partnership as surety, is firmly bound unto Licensee for the benefit of the said creditors; and, it is further agreed that this Agreement as a guaranty is separate and absolute, and that the undersigned general partnership is obligated hereunder as guarantors in addition to their obligations as sureties. No election of remedies is intended and the obligations hereunder are cumulative, joint and several.

This Agreement is continuing and shall remain in force until ninety (90) days after the undersigned general partnership has delivered a written notice of revocation to the Nevada State Contractors Board. Such revocation shall not affect any of the undersigned's obligations hereunder with respect to indebtedness theretofore incurred before the effective date of termination. (No release of one undersigned from liability hereunder, by operation of law or otherwise, shall release any other undersigned.)

Acceptance by creditors is waived and no continuation, renewal, change, or alteration in the contractors license granted to Licensee shall in any way relieve the undersigned, its successors or assigns from any liability assumed hereunder.

The undersigned further agrees to be subject to the jurisdiction of the courts of the State of Nevada and the Federal Courts for the District of Nevada, and laws of the State of Nevada in connection with all of its obligations and liabilities in connection with this Agreement.

Words used in this Agreement which import the plural number shall be deemed to include the singular; words used herein which import the singular shall also be deemed to include the plural.

DATE: ____________________

____
Name of General Partnership (Print Name) Physical Address City State Zip

______________________________ ______________________________
Signatures of ALL Partners Print Name Signatures of ALL Partners Print Name

______________________________ ______________________________
Signatures of ALL Partners Print Name Signatures of ALL Partners Print Name

ALL SIGNATURES MUST BE NOTARIZED:

Subscribed and sworn to before me this _______ day of ____________, _______

______________________________, Notary Public in and for County of _________State of _______.

My Commission Expires: ________________

Certification of Resident Agent for Indemnitor (Required only if indemnitor is not a Nevada resident)

I hereby certify that I am the resident agent for this indemnitor for the purpose of accepting service of process in the State of Nevada in connection with any and all legal actions instituted in the State of Nevada pertaining to this indemnification agreement for the benefit of the Nevada contractors licensee stated above. I recognize my obligation to notify the State Contractors Board, in writing, of any change in address.

____
(Print Name) Signature Physical Address City State Zip

Form 2-9

NEVADA STATE CONTRACTORS BOARD

9670 GATEWAY DRIVE, SUITE 100, RENO, NEVADA, 89521 (775) 688-1141 FAX (775) 688-1271, INVESTIGATIONS (775) 688-1150
2310 CORPORATE CIRCLE, SUITE 200, HENDERSON, NEVADA, 89074 (702) 486-1100 FAX (702) 486-1190, INVESTIGATIONS (702) 486-1110
www.nscb.state.nv.us

INDEMNIFICATION INSTRUCTIONS AND REQUIREMENTS

An indemnification agreement allows the board to consider the financial strength of an individual or entity in addition to the applicant. Indemnification is not required, however, it provides an option to an applicant who may not otherwise qualify for a state contractor's license, or increase in monetary limit for an existing license. The agreement must be on a form prescribed by the board, and accompanied by financial documents as set forth below.

PERSONAL INDEMNIFICATION: A personal indemnification agreement is for use when an individual(s) is indemnifying another individual or another entity, i.e., corporation, limited liability company, limited partnership. The following documents are required:

1. A completed Personal Indemnification Agreement signed by the indemnitor. If the individual is married, both husband and wife must sign the agreement. If single, please state same on the form.
2. Required Financial Information (See below)

CORPORATE INDEMNIFICATION: A corporate indemnification agreement is for use when a corporation is indemnifying an individual or another entity, i.e., corporation, limited liability company, limited partnership. The following documents are required:

1. A completed Corporate Indemnification Agreement signed by a corporate officer and notarized.
2. A corporate resolution executed by the indemnifying corporation authorizing the execution of this agreement.
3. Required Financial Information (See below)

LIMITED LIABILITY COMPANY (LLC) INDEMNIFICATION: An LLC indemnification agreement is for use when an LLC is indemnifying an individual or another entity, i.e., corporation, limited liability company, limited partnership. The following documents are required:

1. A completed Limited Liability Company Indemnification Agreement signed by a Member or Manager.
2. A resolution executed by the indemnifying LLC, or other documentation authorizing the execution of this agreement.
3. Required Financial Information (See below)

LIMITED PARTNERSHIP INDEMNIFICATION: An Limited Partnership indemnification agreement is for use when a Limited Partnership is indemnifying an individual or another entity. The following documents are required:

1. A completed Limited Partnership Indemnification Agreement signed by the General Partner(s).
2. An agreement executed by the indemnifying Limited Partnership, or other documentation authorizing the execution of this agreement.
3. Required Financial Information (See below)

REQUIRED FINANCIAL INFORMATION

You must submit a current financial statement (statement) that meets the following criteria.

- For License Monetary Limits below $1,000,000 you must provide one of the following:
  - a) A current financial statement prepared by an independent certified public accountant; or
  - b) A current financial statement submitted on a form prescribed by the Board (available on the Board's website www.nscb.state.nv.us, click on contractor forms); or,
  - c) A current financial statement prepared using accounting software in accordance with generally accepted accounting principles and accompanied by an affidavit that verifies the accuracy of the financial statement.
- Note: Self-prepared or compiled statements must be current to within six months from the date the statement is received. Reviewed or audited statements must be current within one (1) year from the date the statement is received.
- For License Monetary Limits $1,000,000 or more, you must provide a financial statement that is prepared and reviewed or audited by a certified public accountant.
- All statements must be in U.S. dollars.
- All statements must include full disclosures.
- Business statements must include a classified balance sheet.
- Personal statements must include a supplemental schedule disclosing working capital and net worth.
- A completed bank verification form.

Form 2-10

NEVADA STATE CONTRACTORS BOARD

9870 GATEWAY DRIVE, SUITE 100, RENO, NEVADA, 89521 (775) 688-1141 FAX (775) 688-1271, INVESTIGATIONS (775) 688-1150
2310 CORPORATE CIRCLE, SUITE 200, HENDERSON, NEVADA, 89074 (702) 486-1100 FAX (702) 486-1180, INVESTIGATIONS (702) 486-1110
www.nscb.state.nv.us

INDEMNIFICATION INSTRUCTIONS AND REQUIREMENTS

An indemnification agreement allows the board to consider the financial strength of an individual or entity in addition to the applicant. Indemnification is not required, however, it provides an option to an applicant who may not otherwise qualify for a state contractor's license, or increase in monetary limit for an existing license. The agreement must be on a form prescribed by the board, and accompanied by financial documents as set forth below.

PERSONAL INDEMNIFICATION: A personal indemnification agreement is for use when an individual(s) is indemnifying another individual or another entity, i.e., corporation, limited liability company, limited partnership. The following documents are required:

1. A completed Personal Indemnification Agreement signed by the indemnitor. If the individual is married, both husband and wife must sign the agreement. If single, please state same on the form.
2. Required Financial Information (See below)

CORPORATE INDEMNIFICATION: A corporate indemnification agreement is for use when a corporation is indemnifying an individual or another entity, i.e., corporation, limited liability company, limited partnership. The following documents are required:

1. A completed Corporate Indemnification Agreement signed by a corporate officer and notarized.
2. A corporate resolution executed by the indemnifying corporation authorizing the execution of this agreement.
3. Required Financial Information (See below)

LIMITED LIABILITY COMPANY (LLC) INDEMNIFICATION: An LLC indemnification agreement is for use when an LLC is indemnifying an individual or another entity, i.e., corporation, limited liability company, limited partnership. The following documents are required:

1. A completed Limited Liability Company Indemnification Agreement signed by a Member or Manager.
2. A resolution executed by the indemnifying LLC, or other documentation authorizing the execution of this agreement.
3. Required Financial Information (See below)

LIMITED PARTNERSHIP INDEMNIFICATION: An Limited Partnership indemnification agreement is for use when a Limited Partnership is indemnifying an individual or another entity. The following documents are required:

1. A completed Limited Partnership Indemnification Agreement signed by the General Partner(s).
2. An agreement executed by the indemnifying Limited Partnership, or other documentation authorizing the execution of this agreement.
3. Required Financial Information (See below)

REQUIRED FINANCIAL INFORMATION

You must submit a current financial statement (statement) that meets the following criteria.

- For License Monetary Limits below $1,000,000 you must provide one of the following:
  a) A current financial statement prepared by an independent certified public accountant; or
  b) A current financial statement submitted on a form prescribed by the Board (available on the Board's website www.nscb.state.nv.us, click on contractor forms); or,
  c) A current financial statement prepared using accounting software in accordance with generally accepted accounting principles and accompanied by an affidavit that verifies the accuracy of the financial statement.
- Note: Self-prepared or compiled statements must be current to within six months from the date the statement is received. Reviewed or audited statements must be current within one (1) year from the date the statement is received.
- For License Monetary Limits $1,000,000 or more, you must provide a financial statement that is prepared and reviewed or audited by a certified public accountant.
- All statements must be in U.S. dollars.
- All statements must include full disclosures.
- Business statements must include a classified balance sheet.
- Personal statements must include a supplemental schedule disclosing working capital and net worth.
- A completed bank verification form.

Form 2-11

NEVADA STATE CONTRACTORS BOARD

9670 GATEWAY DRIVE, SUITE 100, RENO, NEVADA, 89521 (775) 688-1141 FAX (775) 688-1271, INVESTIGATIONS (775) 688-1150
2310 CORPORATE CIRCLE, SUITE 200, HENDERSON, NEVADA, 89074 (702) 486-1100 FAX (702) 486-1190, INVESTIGATIONS (702) 486-1110

TRUST INDEMNIFICATION

FOR VALUE RECEIVED, the undersigned trustees on behalf of trust do hereby indemnify the creditors of ______________________, as guarantor and as surety, against any loss or damage the said creditors may suffer as result of ______________________'s failure to promptly pay obligations incurred by it in the ordinary course of construction business within the State of Nevada.

It is further agreed that the undersigned trust as surety, is firmly bound unto ______________________ for the benefit of the said creditor; and, it is further agreed that this Agreement as a guaranty is separate and absolute, and that the undersigned trustees on behalf of trust are obligated hereunder as guarantors in addition to its obligations as surety. No election of remedies is intended and the obligations hereunder are cumulative, joint and several.

This Agreement is continuing and shall remain in force until ninety (90) days after the undersigned trustees have delivered a written notice of revocation to the Nevada State Contractors Board. Such revocation shall not affect any of the undersigned's obligations hereunder with respect to indebtedness theretofore incurred before the effective date of termination. (No release of one undersigned from liability hereunder, by operation of law or otherwise, shall release any other undersigned.)

Acceptance by creditors is waived and no continuation, renewal, change, or alteration in the contractor's license granted to ______________________ shall in any way relieve the undersigned, its successors or assigns from any liability assumed hereunder.

The undersigned further agrees to be subject to the jurisdiction of the courts of the State of Nevada and the Federal Courts for the District of Nevada, and the laws of the State of Nevada in connection with all of it obligations and liabilities in connection with this Agreement.

Words used in this Agreement which import the plural number shall be deemed to include the singular; words used herein which import the singular shall also be deemed to include the plural.

Date: ____________

______________________ ______________________
Trust (Print Name) Address

______________________ ______________________ ______________________
Trustee (Print Name) Signature Address

______________________ ______________________ ______________________
Trustee (Print Name) Signature Address

Designation of Resident Agent (Required only if indemnitor is not a Nevada resident)

The indemnitor hereby designates ______________________ as the resident agent in the State of Nevada for service of process in matters pertaining to this indemnification with the State of Nevada.

Certification of Resident Agent for Indemnitor

I, ________________, hereby certify that I am the resident agent for this indemnitor for the purpose of accepting service of process in the State of Nevada in connection with any and all legal actions instituted in the State of Nevada pertaining to this indemnification agreement for the benefit of the Nevada contractors licensee stated above. I recognize my obligation to notify the State Contractors Board, in writing, of any changes in address.

______________________ ______________________
Resident Agent Address

ALL SIGNATURES ON THIS FORM MUST BE NOTARIZED

Revised 3/93

Form 2-12

NEVADA STATE CONTRACTORS BOARD

9670 GATEWAY DRIVE, SUITE 100, RENO, NEVADA, 89521 (775) 688-1141 FAX (775) 688-1271, INVESTIGATIONS (775) 688-1150
2310 CORPORATE CIRCLE, SUITE 200, HENDERSON, NEVADA, 89074 (702) 486-1100 FAX (702) 486-1190, INVESTIGATIONS (702) 486-1110
www.nscb.state.nv.us

APPLICATION FOR BOND CANCELLATION

General Instructions

In accordance with NRS 624.270 (5) if this license has been active for a period of 5 years you may be eligible to be relieved of the bond requirement. **To avoid suspension of your license, you must keep your bond in effect until the Board has granted approval of this application.**

1. **Please type or print in ink when completing this form.**
2. **Make sure the application is properly signed.**
3. **Read all instructions carefully.** The Board desires to provide courteous and timely service to all applicants. **To maximize its efficiency and the level of service, the Board will process complete applications only.** A complete application includes all applicable supporting documents and fees. The Board will not act as your agent in gathering information or supporting documents necessary for the consideration of this application. Incomplete applications will be returned to you.
4. **Complete each section and answer all questions on this form.**

SECTION 1 – BUSINESS NAME; LICENSE NUMBER

Business Name: Use the legal business name as it appears on your license. If there has been a change in your legal business name, a separate change of name application is required.

License Number: This form can be used for more than one license only if the licenses are held by the same business entity, and both meet the 5 year eligibility requirement.

Legal Business Name:____
(Use Name as Set Forth on the License)

License Number: ____________________

Phone No.: (_____)_______________

Facsimile No.: (_____)________________

Email Address: ____________________________

Form 2-13

NEVADA STATE CONTRACTORS BOARD

9670 GATEWAY DRIVE, SUITE 100, RENO, NEVADA, 89521 (775) 688-1141 FAX (775) 688-1271, INVESTIGATIONS (775) 688-1150
2310 CORPORATE CIRCLE, SUITE 200, HENDERSON, NEVADA, 89074 (702) 486-1100 FAX (702) 486-1190, INVESTIGATIONS (702) 486-1110
www.nscb.state.nv.us

RESIDENTIAL POOL AND SPA LICENSE BOND FOR THE PROTECTION OF CONSUMERS

License Bond No.: ______________________

KNOW ALL MEN BY THESE PRESENTS:

That ______________________________________, having a principal place of business in the city of _______________ in the State of________, as principal (hereinafter "Principal"), and ____, a corporation licensed to execute surety bonds under the provisions of the Nevada Insurance Code, and whose long-term obligations are rated "A" or better by a nationally recognized rating agency, as surety (hereinafter "Surety"), are held and firmly bound to the State of Nevada in the full and just sum of ______________________________ Dollars ($________________) for which payment well and truly to be made, the Principal and Surety bind themselves, their respective heirs, executors, administrators, successors, and assigns, jointly and severally, firmly by these presents.

THE CONDITIONS OF THIS OBLIGATION ARE SUCH THAT:
Whereas, the principal has applied for or holds a contractor's license with the Nevada State Contractors Board pursuant to Chapter 624 of Nevada Revised Statutes to perform work concerning residential pools and spas.

NOW, THEREFORE, this bond is made in favor of the State of Nevada solely for the benefit of a consumer who entered into a contract with a contractor to perform work concerning a residential pool or spa and :

(a) Is damaged by the failure of the contractor to perform the contract or to remove liens filed against the property; or
(b) Is injured by any unlawful act or omission of the contractor in the performance of a contract.

If an action is commenced on this bond, the Surety shall notify the Board of the action within thirty (30) days after; (a) being served with a complaint and summons; or (b) the action is commenced, whichever occurs first. The total aggregate liability of the Surety for all claims shall be limited to the face amount of the bond, irrespective of the number of years the bond is in force or the number of claims filed. The Surety shall have the right to terminate its suretyship under this obligation by serving written notice of its election so to do upon the State Contractors Board, at its office in Reno, Nevada, by certified mail at least sixty (60) days prior to the date of termination of suretyship. Thereafter, the Surety shall be discharged from liability hereunder for any default of the Principal occurring after the date of termination. The liability of the Surety shall be confined to acts, omissions, or defaults of the Principal occurring subsequent to the effective date hereof.

NO ACTION MAY BE COMMENCED on this bond after the expiration of two (2) years following the commission of the act upon which the action is based.

IN THE EVENT the Surety shall make any payments hereunder, without awaiting Court action, the bond amount shall be reduced to the extent of any payment made by the Surety in good faith under the bond, provided the Surety shall notify the Board, in writing, within ten (10) days of any payments made hereunder.

IN WITNESS WHEREOF, the Principal and said Surety have executed this instrument on the ________ day of____________, ______, to be effective on the ________ day of ____________________, ________.

By: ______________________________
(SIGNATURE OF NEVADA AGENT)

By: ______________________________
(SIGNATURE OF PRINCIPAL)

Agent License No.: ______________

Surety: ______________________________

Address: ______________________________

____

____
(SIGNATURE OF ATTORNEY-IN-FACT)

POWER OF ATTORNEY MUST BE ATTACHED

Form 2-14

NEVADA STATE CONTRACTORS BOARD
9670 GATEWAY DRIVE, SUITE 100, RENO, NEVADA, 89521 (775) 688-1141 FAX (775) 688-1271, INVESTIGATIONS (775) 688-1150
2310 CORPORATE CIRCLE, SUITE 200, HENDERSON, NEVADA, 89074, (702) 486-1100 FAX (702) 486-1190, INVESTIGATIONS (702) 486-1110
www.nscb.state.nv.us

BIENNIAL LICENSE RENEWAL APPLICATION
RESIDENTIAL RECOVERY FUND ASSESSMENT

Residential Recovery Fund: Chapter 624 of NRS was amended by the Nevada State Legislature in 1999 by enacting a residential recovery fund. Effective October 1, 1999, each residential contractor is required to pay an assessment to the Fund at time renewal. Under the Act, if the owner / occupier of a single family residence is damaged financially by a project performed on their residence pursuant to a contract, including construction, remodeling, repair or other improvements, and the damage resulted from certain specific violations of Nevada law by a licensed Nevada contractor, the homeowner may apply for payment from the recovery fund.

This Fund is created from assessments of contractors who participate in the construction, remodeling, repair or improvement to residential housing.

Who Must Register With The Fund: Each licensee who will be providing "qualified services" must register with the Fund by submitting the required assessment as part of the license renewal application. "Qualified services" are defined below. Each licensee must either register with the Fund or certify that he is exempt from registration.

Residential Contractor: NRS 624.450 defines a residential contractor as a contractor who is licensed pursuant to this chapter (NRS 624) and who contracts with the owner of a single family residence to perform qualified services.

Qualified Services: NRS 624.440 defines qualified services as any construction, remodeling, repair or improvement performed by a residential contractor on a single family residence occupied by the owner of the residence.

Biennial Assessment: The assessment on each license is based on the monetary license limit.

1. If your license limit is $1,000,000 or less you are required to pay a biennial assessment of $200.
2. If your license limit is more than $1,000,000 but not unlimited you are required to pay a biennial assessment of $500.
3. If your license limit is "Unlimited" you are required to pay a biennial assessment of $1,000.

You must include the residential recovery fund assessment fee with your application for renewal, unless otherwise exempt.

The State Contractors Board desires to provide courteous and timely service to all licensees applying for or renewing a contractor's license. To maximize its efficiency and the level of service, the Board will process complete applications only. **Incomplete renewal applications will be returned to you. To ensure acceptance of your renewal application, make sure you include the residential recovery fund amount assessed, or the completed Certificate of Exemption.**

CERTIFICATE OF EXEMPTION FROM RESIDENTIAL RECOVERY FUND
AFFIDAVIT OF NON-RESIDENTIAL CONTRACTOR

Licensee: ______________________________ **License #:** __________
(Business name set forth on the license)

I being first duly sworn declare under penalty of perjury as follows:

- I am authorized to sign this Certificate of Exemption from Registration on behalf of the above named licensee.
- I hereby certify that the above named licensee will NOT be providing qualified services, as defined in NRS 624.440, and is not required to register with the Residential Recovery Fund as set forth in the provisions of NRS 624.
- I acknowledge that false certification of exemption from registration and the Fund may result in the loss of the above named licensee's license and possible criminal prosecution.

This Affidavit Must Be Notarized.
Subscribed and sworn to before me

Dated: ____________________

This ________ day of __________, 20 ___

____
(Signature of Principal or Owner)

____
Notary Public in and for:

____
(Print Name)

County of ________ State of ________

Form 2-15

NEVADA STATE CONTRACTORS BOARD

9670 GATEWAY DRIVE, SUITE 100, RENO, NEVADA, 89521 (775) 688-1141 FAX (775) 688-1271, INVESTIGATIONS (775) 688-1150
2310 CORPORATE CIRCLE, SUITE 200, HENDERSON, NEVADA, 89074 (702) 486-1100 FAX (702) 486-1190, INVESTIGATIONS (702) 486-1110
www.nscb.state.nv.us

CONSUMER INFORMATION CONCERNING MECHANICS' AND MATERIALMEN'S LIEN LAW

Under the Nevada Mechanics' and Materialmen's Lien Law, NRS Chapter 108, any contractor, subcontractor, laborer, supplier, or other person or entity who performs work or furnishes materials of $500.00 or more to improve the value of your property but is not paid for his or her work or supplies, has a right to place a lien on your home, land, or property where the work was performed and to sue you in court to obtain payment.

This means that after a court hearing, your home, land, and property could be sold by a court officer and the proceeds of the sale used to satisfy what you owe. This can happen even if you have paid your contractor in full but did not ask for and receive lien releases from the contractor's subcontractors, laborers, or suppliers.

To preserve their rights to file a claim or lien against your property, certain claimants such as subcontractors or material suppliers are each required to provide you with a document called a "Preliminary or Pre-lien Notice." A preliminary or pre-lien notice is not a lien against your property. Its purpose is to notify you of persons or entities who may have a right to file a lien against your property if they are not paid. In order to perfect their lien rights, contractors, subcontractors, suppliers, or laborers must file mechanics' liens with the county recorder, which then become recorded liens against your property. Generally, the maximum time allowed for filing a mechanics' lien against your property is 90 days after substantial completion of your project.

To insure extra protection for yourself and your property, you may wish to take one or more of the following steps:

1. Request that your contractor supply you with a payment and performance bond (not a license/surety bond), which guarantees completion of the project and payment of the subcontractors, materialmen, and laborers. A payment and performance bond provides that the contractor either complete the project or the bonding company will pay damages up to the amount of the bond. This payment and performance bond as well as a copy of the construction contract should be filed with the county recorder for your further protection. There is a fee for a payment and performance bond. The cost is usually from 1 to 6 percent of the contract amount, depending on the contractor's bonding ability.
2. Require that payments be made directly to subcontractors and material suppliers through a construction control. Funding services may be available, for a fee, in your area, which will establish voucher or other means of payment to your contractor. These services may also provide you with lien waivers and other forms of protection.
3. Issue joint checks for payment, made out to both your contractor and subcontractors or material suppliers involved in the project. The joint checks should be made payable to the persons or entities which send preliminary notices to you. These persons or entities have indicated that they may have lien rights on your property, therefore you need to protect yourself. This will help to insure that all persons due payment are actually paid.
4. Upon making payment on any completed phase of the project, and before making any further payments, require your contractor to provide you with unconditional "Waiver and Release" (lien release) forms signed by each material supplier, subcontractor, and laborer involved in that portion of the work for which payment was made.

Some stationary stores will sell the "Waiver and Release" forms if your contractor does not have them. The material suppliers, subcontractors, and laborers that you obtain releases from are those persons or entities who have filed preliminary notices with you. If you are not certain of the material suppliers, subcontractors, and laborers working on your project, you may obtain a list from your contractor. On projects involving improvements to a single-family residence or a duplex owned by individuals, the persons signing these releases lose the right to file a mechanics' lien claim against your property. In other types of construction, this protection may still be important, but may not be as complete. To protect yourself under this option, you must be certain that all material suppliers, subcontractors, and laborers have signed the "Waiver and Release" or "Lien Release" form. If a mechanics' lien has been filed against your property, it can only be voluntarily released by a recorded "Release of Mechanics' Lien" signed by the person or entity that filed the mechanics'

Form 2-16

NEVADA STATE CONTRACTORS BOARD

9670 GATEWAY DRIVE, SUITE 100, RENO, NEVADA, 89521 (775) 688-1141 FAX (775) 688-1271, INVESTIGATIONS (775) 688-1150
2310 CORPORATE CIRCLE, SUITE 200, HENDERSON, NEVADA, 89074 (702) 486-1100 FAX (702) 486-1190, INVESTIGATIONS (702) 486-1110
www.nscb.state.nv.us

RESIDENTIAL RECOVERY FUND CLAIM

In accordance with Nevada Revised Statutes (NRS) 624.400-624.550 and Nevada Administrative Code (NAC) 624.730 to 624.770 inclusive, a homeowner may file a claim with the Nevada State Contractors Board (NSCB) Residential Recovery Fund for recovery of damages incurred by the failure of a residential contractor to perform Qualified Services adequately. Qualified Services means any construction, remodeling, repair or improvement performed by a residential contractor on a single-family residence occupied by the owner of the residence.

FOR NSCB USE ONLY:
RECOVERY FUND CLAIM NUMBER: ______________ **NSCB COMPLAINT FILE NUMBER:** ______________

INSTRUCTIONS

1. Forms must be typed or printed in ink.
2. Attach the original completed, and signed Residential Recovery Fund Claim.
3. Attach the original completed, signed and notarized verification form.
4. Include a copy of your original construction contract plus any addendums or change orders.
5. Include documents that verify payment(s) made on the contact (i.e., checks; receipts; close of escrow settlement; executed lien release waivers; bank records of payments).

CLAIM FILED AGAINST:

Contractor's Company Name____

License Number __________ Business Phone: ( ) __________ Home Phone: ( ) __________

Contractor's Address: ____
Street Address City State Zip

CLAIM FILED BY:

Claimant's Name ____

Mailing Address: ____
Street Address City State Zip

Telephone No(s): ( ) ______________________

Address/Location where work was performed: ______________________________

Date Work Began ____________ New Construction Project? Yes ____ No ____ Remodel Project? Yes ____ No ____

Contract Date ______________ (Attach written contract) Do you own and occupy the Residence? Yes ____ No ____

Contract Amount: $______ Paid in full? Yes ____ No ____ Balance Due: $______ Amount of loss you are claiming $______

Date contractor last performed work on the defective item(s) claimed: ________ Date contractor abandoned project ________

Statement of facts relating to your claim about the Contractor's inadequate performance of qualified services: (use separate sheet(s) if necessary):
Specify in detail the nature of this claim ____
____
____
____
____

Form 2-17

NEVADA STATE CONTRACTORS BOARD

9670 GATEWAY DRIVE, SUITE 100, RENO, NEVADA, 89521 (775) 688-1141 FAX (775) 688-1271, INVESTIGATIONS (775) 688-1150
2310 CORPORATE CIRCLE, SUITE 200 HENDERSON, NEVADA, 89074, (702) 486-1100 FAX (702) 486-1190, INVESTIGATIONS (702) 486-1110

APPLICATION FOR CERTIFICATE OF ELIGIBILITY TO RECEIVE PREFERENCE IN BIDDING ON PUBLIC WORKS

In accordance with Nevada Revised Statutes (NRS) 338.147 and NRS 338.1389, a **general contractor as defined in Nevada Revised Statutes (NRS) 624.215 (2), (3)** or a **specialty contractor as defined in NRS 624.215(4) and authorized to bid on a public works project (See NRS 338)** may apply to the Nevada State Contractors' Board (NSCB) for a certificate of eligibility to receive preference in bidding on public works projects in the State of Nevada. The applicant must hold an active contractor's license in the State of Nevada, and submit executed affidavits (attached) as proof of eligibility. Inquiries concerning eligibility to receive a preference in bidding should be directed to your legal counsel.

If granted, the certificate of eligibility will expire on the annual license renewal date. A renewal application pursuant to NRS 338 and NAC 624 will be required.

INSTRUCTIONS

1. **Forms must be typed or printed in ink.**
2. **Make sure this application is signed by a principal of the licensee and properly notarized.**
3. **Attach the original completed, signed, and notarized Affidavit of Certified Public Accountant form.**
4. **Attach the original completed, signed, and notarized Affidavit of Contractor form.**
5. **Include the required fee of $500.00.**
6. **A separate application and fee must be submitted for each license classification for which a certificate of eligibility is requested.**

Licensee Name: ____
(Use name as set forth on the license)

Physical Address: ____
Street Address City State Zip

Mailing Address: ____
Street Address City State Zip

License No.: _________ License Issue Date: _________ Classification ___________ Nevada Tax ID No. _________

Phone No.: _______________ Facsimile No.: _________________

Name and address of Resident Agent in the State of Nevada for service of process:

____
(Print Name)

____
(Street Address)

____
(City) (State) (Zip)

I certify under penalty of perjury that the Licensee listed above is qualified to receive a certificate of eligibility pursuant to NRS 338.147 and NRS 338.1389, and have attached the required affidavits as proof of eligibility.

By: ______________________________ Title: ______________________________
(Signature) (Must be a principal of licensee and appear on license)

______________________________ Date: ______________________________
(Print Name)

The signature of each individual to this application must be subscribed and sworn to before a Notary Public.

Subscribed and sworn to before me

This __________day of ____________________, _____

____
Notary Public in and for said County and State

Form 2-18

NEVADA STATE CONTRACTORS BOARD

9670 GATEWAY DRIVE, SUITE 100, RENO, NEVADA, 89521 (775) 688-1141 FAX (775) 688-1271, INVESTIGATIONS (775) 688-1150
2310 CORPORATE CIRCLE, SUITE 200, HENDERSON, NEVADA, 89074, (702) 486-1100 FAX (702) 486-1190, INVESTIGATIONS (702) 486-1110

RENEWAL OF CERTIFICATE OF ELIGIBILITY TO RECEIVE PREFERENCE IN BIDDING ON PUBLIC WORKS

RENEWAL FEE: $300.00

Bidders Preference Certificate No: ____________________ **License No.:**____________________
License Classification: ____________________ **Nevada State Tax ID No.:**____________________

Name of Licensee: ____
(Use name as set forth on license)

Phone No.: (____)____________ Facsimile No.: (____)____________ Email Address: ____________________

Name and Signature of Principal of Licensee: ____
(Print Name) (Signature)

AFFIDAVIT OF CERTIFIED PUBLIC ACCOUNTANT SUBMITTED AS PROOF OF CONTRACTOR'S COMPLIANCE WITH THE PROVISIONS OF NRS 338.147 AND NRS 338.1389 TO RENEW CERTIFICATE OF ELIGIBILITY

I, ______________________________ ("Affiant"), is a duly licensed Certified Public Accountant in the State of ____________. License Number__________.

That on ______________________________, Affiant reviewed all necessary records of the above-named
(date must be within 30 days of submittal)
contractor (in accordance with generally accepted auditing standards) relating to tax payments made for business conducted under Nevada contractors license number ________.

The Affiant certifies, *under penalty of perjury*, as true and correct that the general contractor referenced above has, during the immediately preceding 12 months, paid the taxes required pursuant to NRS 338.147 and NRS 338.1389 to maintain his eligibility to hold such a certificate.

Dated this ______ day of ____________, ______.

____
Certified Public Accountant (Signature)

____
(Print Name)

____
(Street Address)

____
(City) (State) (Zip)

____
(Phone Number)

Subscribed and sworn to before me
This _____ day of ________________,______.

____
Notary Public in and for said County and State

A contractor who fails to submit an affidavit to the board to renew his Bidders Preference Certificate prior to the expiration date of his current certificate ceases to be eligible to receive a preference in bidding on public works unless he reapplies for and receives a certificate of eligibility pursuant to the provisions of NRS 338.1389 and NRS 338.147.

Form 2-19

NEVADA STATE CONTRACTORS BOARD

9670 GATEWAY DRIVE, SUITE 100, RENO, NEVADA 89521 (775) 688-1141 FAX (775) 688-1271, INVESTIGATIONS (775) 688-1150
2310 CORPORATE CIRCLE, SUITE 200, HENDERSON NEVADA, 89074 (702)486-1100 FAX (702) 486-1190 INVESTIGATIONS (702) 486-1110
Website: www.nscb.state.nv.us

APPLICATION FOR PERMANENT RAISE IN LIMIT

General Instructions

1. **Please type or print in ink when completing this form.**
2. **Make sure the application is properly signed.**
3. **Read all instructions carefully.** The Board desires to provide courteous and timely service to all applicants. To maximize its efficiency and the level of service, the Board will process complete applications only. **A complete application includes all applicable supporting documents and fees. The Board will not act as your agent in gathering information or supporting documents necessary for the consideration of this application. Incomplete applications will be returned to you.**
4. **Complete each section, answer all questions on this form, and attach any required supporting documentation.**
6. **Include required fee of $250.00**

SECTION 1 – BUSINESS NAME; LICENSE NUMBER

Business Name: Use the legal business name as it appears on your license. If there has been a change in your legal business name, a separate change of name application is required.

License Number: This form can be used for more than one license only if the licenses are held by the same business entity.

Legal Business Name: ____
(Use Name as Set Forth on the License)

License Number (s): ________________

Phone No.: (____)______________ **Facsimile No.:** (____)______________

SECTION 2 – MONETARY LIMIT REQUESTED

Monetary Limit: The monetary limit is the maximum contract a licensed contractor may undertake on one or more construction contracts on a single construction site or subdivision site for a single client. It is a violation of Nevada law to bid or contract in excess of the limit placed on the license by the Board.

The monetary limit is determined by consideration of the factors set forth in NRS 624.260, 624.263, and 624.265. (Copies of these statutes are available from our web site).

State the monetary limit desired: ______________________

FOR OFFICE USE ONLY – DO NOT WRITE IN THIS SPACE

Date Received: ________ Amount: ________ Receipt #: ________ File No.: ____________

Withdrawn Date: ____________ Reason: __________ Application No.:________

Approved: ________ Denied: ____________

Transaction Closed: Date: ______________ Entered by: __________

Form 2-20

NEVADA STATE CONTRACTORS BOARD

9670 GATEWAY DRIVE, SUITE 100, RENO, NEVADA, 89521 (775) 688-1141 FAX (775) 688-1271, INVESTIGATIONS (775) 688-1150
2310 CORPORATE CIRCLE, SUITE 200, HENDERSON, NEVADA, 89074 (702) 486-1100 FAX (702) 486-1190, INVESTIGATIONS (702) 486-1110
www.nscb.state.nv.us

APPLICATION FOR SINGLE PROJECT LIMIT INCREASE

IMPORTANT INFORMATION

In accordance with NAC 624.670, a licensee may apply to increase the established monetary limit for a single project only. **This application must be received by the Nevada State Contractors Board at least 2 working days before the date of the bid, not including the bid date.**

If the application is made in a timely manner, you may submit your bid before the Board acts on the application. **You must submit with the bid a statement that the bid is contingent upon the approval of this application by the Board.**

The Board has the authority to establish conditions for the approval of the application, such as requiring a payment and performance bond, or any other condition the Board finds necessary to protect the public interest. These contingencies must be met in order for the limit increase to be valid.

If approved, the approval will be valid for 60 days. If the bid date is delayed, or project re-bids after this time, it will be necessary to submit a new one-time raise in limit application.

General Instructions

1. **Please type, or print in ink when completing this form.**
2. **Make sure the application is properly signed.**
3. **Complete all portions of the application and attach all required supplemental information.**
4. **Attach all required financial information.**
5. **Include required fee of $75.00**

License No: ____________________

Business Name: ____
(Use Name as Set Forth on the License)

Phone No.: (____)____________ Facsimile No.: (____)____________

Email Address: ____

FOR OFFICE USE ONLY – DO NOT WRITE IN THIS SPACE

Date Received: ________ Amount Paid: ________ Receipt: ________ File No.: ____________

Withdrawn Date: ________ Reason: ____________ Application No.: ____________

Approved: ________ Denied: ____________

Checklist Approval Updated: ______________

Transaction Closed: Date: ____________ Entered By: ____________

Form 2-21

NEVADA STATE CONTRACTORS BOARD

9670 GATEWAY DRIVE, SUITE 100, RENO, NEVADA, 89521 (775) 688-1141 FAX (775) 688-1271, INVESTIGATIONS (775) 688-1150
2310 CORPORATE CIRCLE, SUITE 200, HENDERSON, NEVADA, 89074 (702) 486-1100 FAX (702) 486-1190, INVESTIGATIONS (702) 486-1110
www.nscb.state.nv.us

Instructions for Completion of the Consumer Information Form

1. Before filing a complaint, we strongly urge you to contact your contractor and advise him of your problems. Talk about the problems together; try to reach an agreement. We have found that many complaints can be resolved by simply opening the lines of communication. If talking does not work, make a list of your complaints, and provide a copy to the contractor, suggesting a reasonable time for response.

2. To obtain our assistance in resolving your problem, you will need to complete a consumer information form and return it to us. Please pay careful attention when completing the form. We can assist you more efficiently if your form is completed correctly.

3. The Nevada State Contractors Board may be able to help you in situations where: the contractor has not done what was agreed upon, has done it incorrectly, or if something has failed because of improper work. If the contractor was not licensed, our actions are limited. The Board cannot require an unlicensed person to make repairs or restitution. Unlicensed contracting activity is pursued through the justice court system following completion of an investigation.

4. For additional information, please read "How to File a Complaint Against a Contractor." The information sheets will explain how the Nevada State Contractors Board may be able to help you resolve your problem. The information will enable you to better determine if your complaint is within the jurisdiction of the Nevada State Contractors Board.

5. You will notice that the information form is divided into groups. The groups contain several areas for you to include information required for us to process your complaint. Only one contractor can be listed per information form. If you have questions about filling out the form, please call the nearest office of the Nevada State Contractors Board. **In Northern Nevada, call (775) 688-1150 or in Southern Nevada call (702) 486-1110.**

   Include in your complaint, everything you want to have considered by the Nevada State Contractors Board. Mail or take the completed information form(s) to the Nevada State Contractors Board office. You will need to show:

   - You had an agreement or contract with the contractor, involving construction related work at a job-site in Nevada.

   - Specific complaint items, such as listing of defective, substandard, or improper work, failure to make timely payments, causing a lien to be filed, abandonment, or other breach of the contract or agreement.

6. Please complete all boxes in all sections on the information form. Print or type all entries.

7. If your contract was an oral agreement, you must provide documentation to verify your complaint, such as legible reproducible copies of canceled checks, statements, or billings.

8. If your contract was a written agreement, provide a legible, reproducible copy of the entire contract or earnest money agreement bearing both the contractor's signature and your signature.

9. List the actual problems and the reason for your complaint. Additional pages may be attached if needed or you may write on the back of the form. Please return signed information forms and all copies of supporting documents to the Nevada State Contractors Board. If the complaint is filed on behalf of a company, the owner, a partner, or an officer must sign it. The information form may be returned to you if not signed.

Information contained in this document is meant to be instructional. The information is believed to be accurate at the time of its production. Questions regarding civil law and the civil court system should be addressed by an attorney. *Form 102*

NEVADA STATE CONTRACTORS' BOARD

9670 GATEWAY DRIVE, SUITE 100, RENO, NEVADA, 89521 (775) 688-1141 FAX (775) 688-1271, INVESTIGATIONS (775) 688-1150
2310 CORPORATE CIRCLE, SUITE 200, HENDERSON, NEVADA, 89074 (702) 486-1100 FAX (702) 486-1190, INVESTIGATIONS (702) 486-1110
www.nscb.state.nv.us

NRS 624.031 Applicability of chapter: Exemptions. The provisions of this chapter do not apply to:

4. An owner of property who is **building or improving a residential structure on the property for his own occupancy and not intended for sale or lease**. The sale or lease, or the offering for sale or lease, of the newly built structure within 1 year after its completion creates a rebuttable presumption for the purposes of this section that the building of the structure was performed with the intent to sell or lease that structure. *An owner of property who requests an exemption pursuant to this subsection must apply to the board for the exemption. The board shall adopt regulations setting forth the requirements for granting the exemption.*

If you are seeking an exemption from licensure pursuant to NRS 624.031(4) you must complete the following affidavit, obtain the required signatures, and submit the original to the building department with your application for a building permit.

OWNER BUILDER AFFIDAVIT OF EXEMPTION

I hereby certify that I am the owner of the property listed below, and that I am building or improving a residential structure on this property for my own occupancy and do not intend to sell or lease the property.

Parcel Number: ________________ Description of Work: ________________________________ Type of Permit ____________

I further acknowledge the following obligations and duties:

- If I sell or lease, or offer to sell or lease the newly built structure within 1 year after completion, it may be presumed that I have violated the provisions of this exemption and Chapter 624 of NRS.
- I may not hire an unlicensed person to act as my contractor, agent, or construction manager.
- I must directly supervise the construction.
- Any subcontractor(s) working on this project must be properly licensed by the Nevada State Contractors Board.
- **Any person working on my project who is not a licensed contractor must work under my direct supervision and must be employed by me. I must comply with all State and Federal laws as an employer in the State of Nevada, including payroll deductions (FICA and income tax withholding), provide industrial insurance coverage, and pay the required unemployment compensation for that employee.**
- If my project requires the repair, restoration, improvement or construction of a pool or spa, I acknowledge my obligation and duty to comply with the provisions of NRS 597.715
- I acknowledge that I have received copies of NRS 597.715 and NRS 278.573

I have read the above owner builder affidavit of exemption and certify that the information provided is true and correct to the best of my knowledge.

Dated this _____ day of ____________, _______

____
Legal Owner of Residential Property (Signature)

____
(Print Name)

____
Location of Single Family Residence

____
City State Zip

Witness: ______________________________

Owner/Builder Affidavit Revised 02/03

[Date]

[Prime Contractor / Lower-Tiered Contractor Name]
[Address]
[City], [State] [Zip Code]

Re: ***Notice of Intention to Withhold Payment***
NRS 624.609(3) / 624.624(3)
[Name of Project]

Dear ______:

Please be advised that *[Name of Owner or Higher-Tiered Contractor]* intends to withhold *[S________from your]* payment for payment request number ______ for the following reasons:

____ The amount of $ ________ is being withheld for retention, as allowed under *[insert specific section of contract allowing for withholding of retention]* of your construction contract dated _________.

____ The amount of $ ________ is being withheld on the basis that such labor, equipment and/or material billed for has not been performed or furnished to the project. Specifically *[describe in detail the work or items billed for that have not been performed and/or any calculation of percentage of work billed for but not performed]*.

____ The amount of $ ________ is being withheld for work that has been deficiently performed but has been included in your billing. This amount is calculated based on a reasonable estimate of the necessary cost to repair of $ _________, less a credit of 50% of the retention amount withheld as specified above. This withholding is authorized pursuant to *[insert citation to law or contract provision authorizing withholding]*, and is based on the following specifically deficient work: *[insert description of the deficient work to be repaired]*.

____ The amount of $ _______ is being withheld pursuant to an official notice from a state agency or defined benefit trust fund, a copy of which is enclosed for your review.

____ You have failed to provide one or more conditional waiver and release form with your payment application, which complies with the provisions of NRS 108.2457(5)(a) or (c), as applicable. No payment will be made until all originally executed forms have been submitted.

Respectfully,

____
[Signature of Authorized Agent]
[Name of Prime Contractor / Lower-Tiered Subcontractor]

cc: Owner
Higher-Tiered Contractors

[Date]

[Owner / Higher-Tiered Contractor Name]
[Address]
[City], [State] [Zip Code]

Re: ***Notice of Good Faith Dispute / Correction***
NRS 624.609(4) / 624.624(4)
[Name of Project]

Dear _______:

In response to your Notice of Intention to Withhold Payment dated ________, please be advised that *[insert name of prime contractor or lower-tiered subcontractor]* disputes the basis for withholding in good faith for the following reasons: *[describe basis of dispute and reasons why withholding is not proper]*. It is therefore requested that the Notice of Intention to Withhold on payment request number _______ be rescinded and payment made forthwith.

-or-

In response to your Notice of Withholding Payment dated ________, *[insert name of prime contractor or lower-tiered subcontractor]* made the following corrections to the work which you indicated was deficient: *[describe the scope and manner of the correction in reasonable detail]*. We believe this corrects any deficiency which was the basis for withholding and request that payment of the withheld amount be made as soon as possible, but no later than the next progress payment due date of _______.

Respectfully,

____
[Signature of Authorized Agent]
[Name of Prime Contractor / Lower-Tiered Subcontractor]

cc: Owner
Higher-Tiered Contractors
Sub-Subcontractors and Suppliers

[Date]

[Prime Contractor / Lower-Tiered Contractor Name]
[Address]
[City], [State] [Zip Code]

Re: ***Notice of Objection to Correction Notice***
NRS 624.609(4) / 624.624(4)
[Name of Project]

Dear ______:

[Name of owner or higher-tiered contractor] objects to the notice of correction for the following reasons:

____ The amount of $ ________ continues to be withheld on the basis that such labor, equipment and/or material billed for has not been performed or furnished to the project. Specifically *[describe in detail the work or items billed for that have not been performed and/or any calculation of percentage of work billed for but not performed]*.

____ The amount of $ ________ continues to be withheld for work that has been deficiently performed but has been included in your billing *[, however, this amount has been re-calculated based on the repairs that have been performed to a reasonable estimate of the necessary cost to repair of $ ________, less a credit of 50% of the retention amount withheld as previously advised]*. This withholding is authorized pursuant to *[insert citation to law or contract provision authorizing withholding]*, and is based on the following specifically work that remains deficient: *[insert description of the deficient work to be repaired]*.

____ The amount of $ _______ continues to be withheld pursuant to an official notice from a state agency or defined benefit trust fund, which has not been released by official notice from the notifying agency or benefit trust fund.

____ You have failed to provide one or more conditional waiver and release form with your payment application, which complies with the provisions of NRS 108.2457(5)(a) or (c), as applicable. No payment will be made until all originally executed forms have been submitted.

Respectfully,

____
[Signature of Authorized Agent]
[Name of Prime Contractor / Lower-Tiered Subcontractor]

cc: Owner
Higher-Tiered Contractors

[Date]

[Prime Contractor / Lower-Tiered Contractor Name]
[Address]
[City], [State] [Zip Code]

Re: ***Owner Response to Change Order Request***
NRS 624.610(1)
[Name of Project]

Dear _______:

Please be advised that *[Name of Owner or Higher-Tiered Contractor]* responds to your change order request number ______, received on __________, as follows:

____ The change order is accepted and a formal change order form will be prepared and presented to your office for execution shortly.

____ The Change Order Request is rejected as unreasonable for the following reasons: *[describe the reasons for the rejection of the change order request in reasonable detail]*. You are not authorized to bill against or otherwise treat this as a legitimate change order to your contract.

____ The Change Order Request cannot be processed in 30 days as set forth. The owner will require additional time and/or information to process the change order as follows: *[describe the additional time or information necessary to process the change order]*. Upon receipt the additional information, the owner will process your change order as soon as possible.

Respectfully,

____
[Signature of Authorized Agent]
[Name of Prime Contractor / Lower-Tiered Subcontractor]

[Date]

[Lower-Tiered Contractor Name]
[Address]
[City], [State] [Zip Code]

Re: ***Response to Change Order Request***
NRS 624.610(1)
[Name of Project]

Dear _______:

Please be advised that *[Name of Higher-Tiered Contractor]* responds to your change order request number ______, received on __________, as follows:

____ The change order is accepted and a formal change order form will be prepared and presented to your office for execution shortly.

____ The Change Order Request is rejected as unreasonable for the following reasons: *[describe the reasons for the rejection of the change order request in reasonable detail]*. You are not authorized to bill against or otherwise treat this as a legitimate change order to your contract.

Respectfully,

____
[Signature of Authorized Agent]
[Name of Higher-Tiered Contractor]

cc: Owner
Higher-Tiered Contractors

[Date]

[Owner / Higher-Tiered Contractor Name]
[Address]
[City], [State] [Zip Code]

Re: ***Notice of Intention to Stop Work***
NRS 624.610(1) / 624.626(1)
[Name of Project]

Dear ______:

Based on the failure of your company to make the payment due on ____________, and the lack of any timely served notice of intention to withhold payment as required under NRS 624.609, on [Date to Stop Work] -10 days after the date of this Notice - [Name of Prime Contractor or Lower-Tiered Subcontractor] will stop all work on the Project and will demobilize until payment is made.

-or-

Based on the failure of your company to execute or provide written notice of any reason to reject our Change Order Request No. ____ within 30 days of our delivery of the same pursuant to NRS 624.610(1)(d), on [Date to Stop Work] -10 days after the date of this Notice - [Name of Prime Contractor or Lower-Tiered Subcontractor] will stop all work on the Project and will demobilize until payment is made.

-or-

It has been ___ days since we have submitted our invoice # _____ to you for payment. While we understand that you have not made payment on that invoice because the owner [or higher-tiered contractor] has not made payment to you, NRS 624.610(1)(b) allows [name of lower-tiered subcontractor] to stop work even in this circumstance. Therefore, be advised that on [Date to Stop Work] -10 days after the date of this Notice - [Name of Prime Contractor or Lower-Tiered Subcontractor] will stop all work on the Project and will demobilize until payment is made.

Respectfully,

____
[Name of Authorized Agent]
[Name of Prime Contractor / Lower-Tiered Subcontractor]

cc: Owner
Higher-Tiered Contractors
Sub-Subcontractors and Suppliers

[Date]

[Owner / Higher-Tiered Contractor Name]
[Address]
[City], [State] [Zip Code]

Re: ***Notice of Intention to Terminate Contract***
NRS 624.610(2) / 624.626(4)
[Name of Project]

Dear ______:

Based on the failure of your company to make the payment due on ____________ after you were provided our notice of intent to stop work on __________, please be advised that pursuant to the provisions of NRS 624.610(2) *[or NRS 624.626(2), [name of prime contractor or lower-tiered subcontractor]* will consider the contract dated ________ for this project terminated. No further services will be performed under the terminated contract.

-or-

Based on the stoppage of the project for more than 15 days, and the failure of your company to allow the project to continue within 10 days after the date of this Notice, [Name of Prime Contractor or Lower-Tiered Subcontractor] will consider this contract terminated pursuant to the provisions of NRS 624.610(4) *[or NRS 624.626(4]* and will demobilize from the project. No further services will be performed under the terminated contract.

Respectfully,

____
[Name of Authorized Agent]
[Name of Prime Contractor / Lower-Tiered Subcontractor]

cc: Owner
Higher-Tiered Contractors
Sub-Subcontractors and Suppliers

[Date]

[Owner Name]
[Address]
[City], [State] [Zip Code]

Re: ***Notice of Availability of Project for Owner's Use or Occupancy***
NRS 624.620(1)
[Name of Project]

Dear _______:

Pursuant to NRS 624.620 you are hereby notified that the aforementioned project is available for the owner's use or occupancy as of __________. Pursuant to the provisions of NRS 624.620(1) final payment in the amount of $ __________ is due 30 days from this date of availability. A copy of the certificate of occupancy, if applicable, is included with this notice for your information.

-or-

Pursuant to the provisions of NRS 624.620, you are hereby notified that on __________ a portion of the aforementioned project has become available for the owner's use or occupancy. The percentage of the project so available is calculated at _____ percent. Pursuant to NRS 624.620(5), partial final payment is due to be paid in direct proportion of the value of the part of the building so available. The amount of the final payment due is $_________. This payment must be made within 30 days of the date the project became partially available for your use.

Respectfully,

____
[Name of Authorized Agent]
[Name of Prime Contractor]

[Date]

[Prime Contractor Name]
[Address]
[City], [State] [Zip Code]

Re: ***Notice of Intention to Withhold Payment***
NRS 624.620(3)
[Name of Project]

Dear _______:

Please be advised that *[Name of Owner or Higher-Tiered Contractor]* intends to withhold $________ from your *[partial]* final payment request for the following reasons:

____ The amount of $ ________ is being withheld for retention, as allowed under *[insert specific section of contract allowing for withholding of retention]* of your construction contract dated _________.

____ The amount of $ ________ is being withheld on the basis that such labor, equipment and/or material billed for has not been performed or furnished to the project. Specifically *[describe in detail the work or items billed for that have not been performed and/or any calculation of percentage of work billed for but not performed]*.

____ The amount of $ ________ is being withheld for work that has been deficiently performed but has been included in your billing. This amount is calculated based on a reasonable estimate of the necessary cost to repair of $ _________, less a credit of 50% of the retention amount withheld as specified above. This withholding is authorized pursuant to *[insert citation to law or contract provision authorizing withholding]*, and is based on the following specifically deficient work: *[insert description of the deficient work to be repaired]*.

____ The amount of $ _______ is being withheld pursuant to an official notice from a state agency or defined benefit trust fund, a copy of which is enclosed for your review.

____ You have failed to provide one or more conditional waiver and release form with your payment application, which complies with the provisions of NRS 108.2457(5)(a) or (c), as applicable. No payment will be made until all originally executed forms have been submitted.

Respectfully,

____
[Signature of Authorized Agent]
[Name of Prime Contractor / Lower-Tiered Subcontractor]

cc: Owner
Higher-Tiered Contractors

State of ________)
)
County of ________)

I, ____________________, being duly sworn, affirm that I did deliver a *[insert name of notice being delivered]* dated ___________, addressed as follows:

Insert address information and facsimile information]

___ by delivering the aforementioned document to the addressee at the address provided on ___________, at approximately _____ am / pm, and describing the document as noted above.

___ by sending the aforementioned document to the addressee via facsimile transfer to the facsimile telephone number provided above on ___________, at approximately _____ am/pm. A true and correct copy of the proof of successful transmission is attached hereto.

Further, Affiant saith not.

____
[Name of Affiant]

Subscribed and sworn before me,
This _____ day of ______, 20___

____
Notary Public
My Commission Expires ________

NOTICE OF RIGHT TO PAYMENT BOND CLAIM

(N.R.S. 339.015)

To: ______________________________

____

____

(General Contractor's Name and Address)

The undersigned hereby notifies you that it will supply materials or performed work or services as follows:

____

____

____

(General Description of Materials, Work or Services)

for the improvement of property identified as:

____

____

____

(Property Description or Street Address)

under contract with ______________________________.

(Name of Subcontractor)

THIS IS NOT A NOTICE THAT THE UNDERSIGNED HAS NOT BEEN OR DOES NOT EXPECT TO BE PAID, BUT A NOTICE REQUIRED BY LAW THAT THE UNDERSIGNED MAY, AT A FUTURE DATE, MAKE A CLAIM UPON ANY PAYMENT BOND YOU ISSUE AS PROVIDED BY LAW AGAINST THE PROJECT IF THE UNDERSIGNED IS NOT PAID.

By: ______________________________

____

____

____

(Claimant's Name, Address and Signature)

90 DAY NOTICE TO GENERAL CONTRACTOR OF CLAIM ON PAYMENT BOND

(N.R.S. 339.035)

To: ______________________________

____

____

(General Contractor's Name and Address)

The undersigned hereby notifies you that it has supplied materials or performed work or services within the last 90 days as follows:

____

____

____

(General Description of Materials, Work or Services)

the total value of which is $ ______________.

The above referenced materials are to be supplied (or work or services are to be performed) on and for the improvement of real property identified as:

____

____

____

(Property Description or Street Address)

and under contract with ______________________________.

(Subcontractor)

CLAIMANT HEREBY NOTIFIES YOU THAT UNLESS PAYMENT IS MADE PROMPTLY HEREAFTER FOR THE MATERIALS AND/OR LABOR SUPPLIED BY CLAIMANT, CLAIMANT INTENDS TO SEEK PAYMENT FROM YOU AND THE PAYMENT AND PERFORMANCE BOND PROVIDED BY YOU ON THE PROJECT PURSUANT TO N.R.S. 339.035

By: ______________________________

____

____

(Claimant's Name, Address and Signature)

APPLICATION FOR CERTIFIED COPY OF CONTRACT AND PAYMENT BOND AND AFFIDAVIT OF CLAIMANT

(N.R.S. 339.045)

TO:

Claimant _______________ hereby applies for a certified copy of the original construction contract and the payment bond (Bond No. _____________), issued on behalf of _____________ (General Contractor) for the (the "Project").

This application is made pursuant to Nevada Revised Statutes 339.045, and is based upon the attached affidavit of, the _______________ of Claimant _________________. The appropriate fee for the copy is enclosed. The copy of the payment bond and contract should be mailed to Claimant at the following address:____
____

Dated: ___________

By: _______________________________________

____

____

AFFIDAVIT

I ____, Being duly sworn, hereby declare and affirm:

I am the _____________ of Claimant _____________. Claimant is a subcontractor to ____, the general contractor for the project, located at ____
____.

Claimant has supplied labor and materials for the above referenced project and has not been paid in full therefore. The outstanding undisputed balance of $ ____________ is due and payable to Claimant from the general contractor. Claimant has made numerous demands for payment, but the general contractor has refused to make that payment now due. Therefore, Claimant seeks to make a claim on the Payment Bond provided by the general contractor for the project, as authorized under N.R.S. 339.035. Therefore, Claimant now requests a certified copy of the construction contract and payment bond pursuant to N.R.S. 339.045.

Further affiant sayeth not.

Dated: ___________________ ____

(Signature of Affiant)

Subscribed and sworn before me,

this ________ day of ______________ , ___________ .

By: ______________________

Notary Public

My Commission Expires: ______________________

NOTICE TO OWNER OF MECHANICS LIEN LAW

(N.R.S. 108.246)

To: ______________________________

____

____

(Owner's Name and Address)

The provisions of NRS 108.245, a part of the Mechanics' and materialmen's lien law of the State of Nevada, require, for your information and protection from hidden liens, that each person or other legal entity who supplies materials to or performs work on a construction project, other than one who performs only labor, deliver to the owner a notice of the materials or equipment supplied or the work performed. You may receive these notices in connection with the construction project which you propose to undertake.

By: ______________________________

____

____

(General Contractor's Name, Address and Signature)

NOTICE OF RIGHT TO LIEN

(N.R.S. 108.245)

To: ______________________________

____

____

(Owner's or General Contractor's Name and Address)

The undersigned hereby notifies you that it will supply materials or performed work or services as follows:

____

____

____

(General Description of Materials, Work or Services)

for the improvement of property identified as:

____

____

____

(Property Description or Street Address)

under contract with ______________________________________.

(General Contractor or Subcontractor)

THIS IS NOT A NOTICE THAT THE UNDERSIGNED HAS NOT BEEN OR DOES NOT EXPECT TO BE PAID, BUT A NOTICE REQUIRED BY LAW THAT THE UNDERSIGNED MAY, AT A FUTURE DATE, RECORD A NOTICE OF LIEN AS PROVIDED BY LAW AGAINST THE PROPERTY IF THE UNDERSIGNED IS NOT PAID.

By: ______________________________

____

____

____

(Claimant's Name, Address and Signature)

REQUEST FOR NOTICE OF COMPLETION:

The Owner is hereby requested, pursuant to N.R.S. 108.226, to provide the above claimant with a copy of any Notice of Completion recorded on this construction project.

NOTICE AND CLAIM OF LIEN

NOTICE OF LIEN

The undersigned claims a lien upon the property described in this notice for work, or equipment furnished or to be furnished for the improvement of the property:

1. The amount of the original contract is: $____

2. The total amount of all additional or changed work, materials and equipment, if any, is: $______

3. The total amount of all payments received to date is: $_______________________________

4. The amount of the lien, after deducting all just credits and offsets, is: $___________________

5. The name of the owner, if known, of the property is:_______________________________

6. The name of the person by whom the lien claimant was employed or to when the lien claimant furnished or agreed to furnish work, materials or equipment is: ____________________________

7. A brief statement of the terms of payment of the lien claimant's contract is:______________

8. A description of the property to be charged with the lien is:__________________________

____
(Print Name of Lien Claimant)
By:_____________________________
(Authorized Signature)

State of______________)
) ss.
County of_____________)

_________________________ (print name), being first duly sworn on oath according to law, deposes and says:

I have read the foregoing Notice of Lien, know the contents thereof and state that the same is true of my own personal knowledge, except those matters stated upon information and belief, and, as to those matters, I believe them to be true.

____
(Authorized Signature of Lien Claimant)

Subscribed and sworn to before me this
_____ day of the month of_______ of the year _______

____
(Notary Public in and for the County and State)

NOTICE OF COMPLETION

NOTICE IS HEREBY GIVEN that the certain construction project, located in the County of __________ , ________________ , State of Nevada, and more accurately described as:

____

____

____

(Street Address and Legal Description of Property)

____________ has been completed as of _________________. ______ has ceased work and all labor has stopped as of ____________________ and has been continuously stopped for _______ days.

The name(s) and address(es) of the owner(s) of the Property at the time the work was performed is/are:____

____.

The name of the General Contractor for the Project was:___________________________

____.

Dated: ___________ By: ____

____

____

____

(Enter Name and Nature of Title to Property of Signor)

VERIFICATION

I, _______________, am the ___________________ of ________________, Lien Claimant in the above Notice of Completion. I have read the Notice of Completion and know the contents thereof to be true of my own personal knowledge, except as to those matters stated upon information and belief, as to which matters I believe them to be true. I further state that the Notice of Completion contains correct and accurate information as to the completion of the project and/or cessation of labor thereon.

Dated: _______________ ______________________________

DISCHARGE OR RELEASE OF NOTICE OF LIEN

(N.R.S. 108.2437)

NOTICE IS HEREBY GIVEN THAT:

The undersigned did, on the ______ day of _________, 20___, record in Book _________________, as Document No. ____________________, in the office of the County Recorder of ________________ County, Nevada, its Claim and Notice of Lien, or has otherwise given notice of his intention to hold and claim a lien upon the following described property or improvements owned or purportedly owned by ___________________________________, located in the County of ______________, State of Nevada, to Wit:

NOW, THEREFORE, for valuable consideration the undersigned does release, satisfy and discharge his notice of lien on the property or improvements described above by reason of this Notice of Lien.

By: ____

____

____

____

(Claimant's Name, Address and Signature)

NOTICE OF NON-RESPONSIBILITY

NOTICE IS HEREBY GIVEN that:

1. The Undersigned is the disinterested owner of certain real property situated in the County of ________________________, State of Nevada, holding and claiming ____ interest in certain property located at:

   ____

   ____

   ____

   (Street Address of Property)

   and more accurately described as: ______________________________________

   ____

   (Legal Description of the property)

2. The Undersigned has discovered that ____

   ____

   (Name and Address of Tenant)

   is altering and improving the above described property.

3. The Undersigned first learned of the improvement on __________________. Three (3) days have not elapsed since the Undersigned has obtained this knowledge, signed or the effective date of a lease with ____.

   (Name of Tenant)

4. The Undersigned has provided written notice to the Tenant of its obligations to provide notice and security for this improvement under the Nevada mechanics lien law (NRS 108.2403, et seq.) and will not be responsible for the alterations, repairs, or improvements, or the materials or labor used or to be used on said building or land upon which it is situated.

Dated: ____________ By: ____

____

____

(Name, Address and Signature of Disinterested Owner)

STATE OF NEVADA }

COUNTY OF }

On the ______ day of __________________, 20____, personally appeared before me, a notary public, ____, personally known or proved to me to be the person whose name is subscribed to the above instrument who acknowledged that s/he executed the above instrument.

____

Notary Public

CONDITIONAL WAIVER AND RELEASE UPON PROGRESS PAYMENT

Property Name:
Property Location:
Undersigned's Customer:
Invoice/Payment Application Number:
Payment Amount:

Upon receipt by the undersigned of a check in the above referenced Payment Amount payable to the undersigned, and when the check has been properly endorsed and has been paid by the bank on which it is drawn, this document becomes effective to release and the undersigned shall be deemed to waive any notice of lien, any private bond right, any claim for payment and any rights under any similar ordinance, rule or statute related to payment rights that the undersigned has on the above described Property to the following extent:

This release covers a progress payment for the work, materials or equipment furnished by the undersigned to the Property or to the Undersigned's Customer, which are the subject of the Invoice or Payment Application, but only to the extent of the Payment Amount or such portion of the Payment Amount as the undersigned is actually paid, and does not cover any retention withheld, any items, modifications of changes pending approval, disputed items and claims, or items furnished that are not paid. Before any recipient of this document relies on it, he should verify evidence of payment to the undersigned. The undersigned warrants that he either has already paid or will use the money he received from this progress payment promptly to pay in full all his laborers, subcontractors, materialmen and suppliers for all work, materials or equipment that are the subject of this waiver and release.

DATED:___________________ ______________________________

Company Name

By:______________________________

Its:______________________________

UNCONDITIONAL WAIVER AND RELEASE UPON PROGRESS PAYMENT

Property Name:
Property Location:
Undersigned's Customer:
Invoice/Payment Application Number:
Payment Amount:

The undersigned has been paid and has received a progress payment in the above referenced Payment Amount for all work, materials and equipment the undersigned furnished to his Customer for the above described Property and does hereby waive and release any notice of lien, any private bond right, any claim for payment and any rights under any similar ordinance, rule or statute related to payment rights that the undersigned has on the above described Property to the following extent:

This release covers a progress payment for the work, materials and equipment furnished by the undersigned to the Property or to the Undersigned's Customer, which are the subject of the Invoice or Payment Application, but only to the extent of the Payment Amount or such portion of the Payment Amount as the undersigned is actually paid, and does not cover any retention withheld, any items, modifications of changes pending approval, disputed items and claims, or items furnished that are not paid. The undersigned warrants that he either has already paid or will use the money he received from this progress payment promptly to pay in full all his laborers, subcontractors, materialmen and suppliers for all work, materials or equipment that are the subject of this waiver and release.

DATED:________________ ____________________________
Company Name

By:____________________________

Its::____________________________

NOTICE: THIS DOCUMENT WAIVES RIGHTS UNCONDITIONALLY AND STATES THAT YOU HAVE BEEN PAID FOR GIVING UP THOSE RIGHTS. THIS DOCUMENT IS ENFORCEABLE AGAINST YOU IF YOU SIGN IT TO THE EXTENT OF THE PAYMENT AMOUNT OR THE AMOUNT RECEIVED. IF YOU HAVE NOT BEEN PAID, USE A CONDITIONAL RELEASE FORM.

CONDITIONAL WAIVER AND RELEASE UPON FINAL PAYMENT

Property Name:
Property Location:
Undersigned's Customer:
Invoice/Payment Application Number:
Payment Period:
Payment Amount:
Amount of Disputed Claims:

Upon receipt by the undersigned of a check in the above referenced Payment Amount payable to the undersigned, and when the check has been properly endorsed and has been paid by the bank on which it is drawn, this document becomes effective to the release and the undersigned shall be deemed to waive any notice of lien, any private bond right, any claim for payment and any rights under any similar ordinance, rule or statute related to payment rights that the undersigned has on the above described Property to the following extent:

This release covers the final payment to the undersigned for all work, materials or equipment furnished by the undersigned to the Property or to the Undersigned's Customer and does not cover payment for Disputed Claims, if any. Before any recipient of this document relies on it, he should verify evidence of payment to the undersigned. The undersigned warrants that he either has already paid or will use the money he receives from the final payment promptly to pay in full all his laborers, subcontractors, materialmen and suppliers for all work, materials or equipment that are the subject of this waiver and release.

DATED:____________________ ________________________________

Company Name

By: ______________________________

Its: ______________________________

UNCONDITIONAL WAIVER AND RELEASE UPON FINAL PAYMENT

Property Name:
Property Location:
Undersigned's Customer:
Invoice/Payment Application Number:
Payment Amount:
Amount of Disputed Claims:

The undersigned has been paid in full for all work, materials and equipment furnished to his Customer for the above described Property and does hereby waive and release any notice of lien, any private bond right, any claim for payment and any rights under any similar ordinance, rule or statute related to payment rights that the undersigned has on the above described Property, except for the payment of Disputed Claims, if any, noted above. The undersigned warrants that he either has already paid or will use the money he received from this final payment promptly to pay in full all his laborers, subcontractors, materialmen and suppliers for all work, materials and equipment that are the subject of this waiver and release.

DATED:__________________

____
Company Name

By:___________________________

Its::__________________________

NOTICE: THIS DOCUMENT WAIVES RIGHTS UNCONDITIONALLY AND STATES THAT YOU HAVE BEEN PAID FOR GIVING UP THOSE RIGHTS. THIS DOCUMENT IS ENFORCEABLE AGAINST YOU IF YOU SIGN IT, EVEN IF YOU HAVE NOT BEEN PAID. IF YOU HAVE NOT BEEN PAID, USE A CONDITIONAL RELEASE FORM.

NOTICE OF INTENT TO LIEN

To: ________________________________
____
____

PLEASE TAKE NOTICE that the undersigned has provided work, materials and/or equipment described as ______________________________________ to the residential project located at __________________________________ for the improvement thereof.

The undersigned has not been paid by______________________________________ ____________________________________ for such work, materials and/or equipment pursuant to its contract.

1. The Amount of the Original Contract is: $ _________
2. The total amount of all changes and additions is: $ _________
3. The total amount of all payments received to date is: $ _________
4. The amount due and owing to the undersigned is: $ _________

BE ADVISED THAT SHOULD THE AMOUNT DUE AND OWING TO THE UNDERSIGNED NOT BE PAID WITHIN 15 DAYS OF THE DATE OF THIS NOTICE OF INTENT TO LIEN, THE UNDERSIGNED SHALL CAUSE A CLAIM OF LIEN TO BE RECORDED AGAINST THE RESIDENTIAL PROJECT IN THE AMOUNT OF $ __________.

Dated: ____________________ ____________________________
____
____

Undersigned

NOTICE OF OBLIGATION TO POST SECURITY

TO: ______________________________
____
____
(Tenant)

Nevada Mechanics Lien Law (NRS 108.2403, et seq.) states that before you commence construction of your tenant improvement you must record a notice of posted security and either: 1) Provide and record a surety bond in the amount of 1.5 times the amount of your construction contract, or 2) Establish and fund a construction disbursement account with a licensed third party construction control service. You must also provide each prime contractor, subcontractor, supplier or other person who provides you with a Notice of Right to Lien under NRS 108.245 with a copy of the recorded notice of posted security or surety bond.

Failure to follow the obligations of the Nevada Mechanics Lien Law may subject you to claims from mechanics lien claimants, the stopping work on your project by your contractor(s) and may also be a violation of your lease obligation. You are urged to contact an attorney to assist with meeting your obligations under the Nevada Mechanics Lien Law as they relate to tenant improvement contracts.

____
____
____
(Landlord)

When Recorded Return To:	(For Recorder's Use Only)

APN: ________________

NOTICE OF POSTED SECURITY FOR TENANT IMPROVEMENT

NOTICE IS HEREBY GIVEN that ____ (Lessee) will be constructing a work of improvement located at: ____ and more accurately and legally described as:

The Lessee holds an interest in the property and work of improvement described as: ____.

As Security for this Tenant Improvement, Lessee has:

____ Established a construction disbursement account with: ______________________________ as Construction Control, Account # ________________, for this account on __________, and funded said account in the amount of $______________.

____ Obtained a surety bond from ______________________________ (Surety), Surety Bond # ________________, and recorded the Surety Bond with the County Recorder of _____ County on ______________, in Book No. ________________ as Instrument No. ___________ (A copy of said Surety Bond is attached hereto).

____
____
____
(Lessee)

Form 8-14

APN: ____________________

When recorded return to:

Name:
Address:
City: State: Zip:

NOTICE OF WAIVER OF RIGHT
TO RECORD A NOTICE OF NON-RESPONSIBILITY
[NRS 108.2405(1)(b)]

Owner:
Address:
City: State: Zip:
Property Name:
APN:
Property Description:

Tenant Improvement:
Tenant:
Address:
City: State: Zip:
Tenant Space Description:

Contract :
Anticipated
Completion Date:

NOTICE IS HEREBY GIVEN that the Owner of the above referenced Property pursuant to the provisions of NRS 108.2405(1)(b) hereby waives its rights under NRS 108.234 to record a Notice of Non-Responsibility for the above described Tenant Improvement only, and only to the extent of the parcel on which the Tenant Improvement is constructed. This waiver is limited to the above referenced Tenant Improvement of Tenant only and shall not apply to any tenant improvement commenced after the Anticipated Completion Date referenced above that is not a part of those performed under the above referenced Contract, including but not limited to any additional improvements made by the Tenant to the Tenant Improvement which are not part of the referenced Contract scope or made part thereof by change order.

Owner retains all rights under NRS 108.234 to record a notice of non-responsibility on any other tenant improvement being constructed on the Property being constructed at any time before, during or after the completion of the Tenant Improvement and this waiver shall not apply thereto.

Owner

By:____________________________

Title: __________________________

State of___________)
County of_________)
Subscribed and sworn before me
this_____ day of______, 20__

____
Notary Public

TABLE OF AUTHORITIES

CONSTITUTIONAL PROVISIONS

FEDERAL CASES

NEVADA STATE CASES

OTHER STATE CASES

FEDERAL STATUTES

STATE STATUTES

OTHER STATE STATUTES

NEVADA STATE REGULATIONS

NEVADA STATE RULES

OTHER AUTHORITIES

www.ingramcontent.com/pod-product-compliance
Lightning Source LLC
LaVergne TN
LVHW080014210926
848481LV00011B/3022
* 9 7 8 0 9 8 9 1 9 3 0 1 6 *